NORMANDIEFRONT

KATHOLISCHES

feldgefangbuch

Verlag E. S. Mittler & Sohn · Berlin SW 68

NORMANDIEFRONT

D-Day to Saint-Lô Through German Eyes

Vince Milano & Bruce Conner

I can still see those faces silently asking me 'What should we do now?' I was angry, mad at myself for not being sure what to tell them. I looked out the view slit. The Amis were gaining ground and from the sounds of the fighting some were up in the village behind us ... We would use the firepower of the MG42 to get us out of here ... I fired the last belt in short bursts to keep the Amis at a distance ... The final count was 64 rounds, a number I never forgot ... Rummaging through the mess Helmuth found two grenades. The plan would go, we hoped, like this. The two of them would throw out the grenades, one left, and one right. Then I would go out with the MG and make for the trench that was not too far away. From here I would cover them while they ran across. Willi could run, but Helmuth would be hampered by his wound. Instead of a rifle I gave him my pistol. For now, Willi carried two rifles. We all crouched in the entranceway. I took a deep breath and nodded to them. Both grenades flew out at the same time, explosions followed. I sprang through the doorway. Fearing the worst, I tensed up as I emerged into the open...

Obergrenadier Karl Wegner

Frontispiece: Obergrenadier Karl Wegner's Catholic prayer book.

First published 2011
This paperback edition published 2012
by Spellmount, an imprint of
The History Press
The Mill, Brimscombe Port
Stroud, Gloucestershire, GL5 2QG
www.thehistorypress.co.uk

British Library Cataloguing in Publication Data.
A catalogue record for this book is available from the British Library.

ISBN 978 0 7524 7145 7

Typesetting and origination by The History Press
Manufacturing managed by Jellyfish Print Solutions Ltd
Printed in India

CONTENTS

ACKNOWLEDGEMENTS

WE would like to thank our families and many friends who supported us in this endeavour. The first would be our wives, Elizabeth Milano and Susan Conner. Then would be the many good friends who gave assistance and encouragement: Paul Botting; John Botting; Phil Burkhart; Tara Burkhart; Jon Byron; Valerie Byron; Stephen Cheng; Jade Cheng; James Foote; Jeremy Foote; Christian Fuehr; Martin Galle; John Laramie; Kurt Milano; John Pagan; Joshua Pagan; James Rumrill; and Ronny Schindler.

All of the good people listed have helped us in many ways and all their contributions are very much appreciated. Amongst their ranks is one person who deserves to be 'Mentioned in Dispatches'. Without his tireless efforts and devotion, this work would have languished in a desk drawer. So we simply say: Paul Botting – well done and a heartfelt thank you.

Vince Milano & Bruce Conner

About the Authors

VINCE MILANO served in the US Army and the National Guard. He has amassed interviews, diaries, photographs and documents on the D-Day invasion over many years, and has written numerous articles for magazines such as *Combat, Defence, Die Neue Feldpost* and *Living History*. He is the author of *Germany Army Order of Battle 1918: A Collector's Guide*.

BRUCE CONNER served in the Massachusetts Military Reserve and is a military historian with a particular interest in the Second World War, prompted by his father's service as a doctor and officer in the US Army Medical Corps in Europe. He gives living history displays across the US with his co-author Vince Milano.

FOREWORD

WE hope that this book gives the reader a better understanding of the German side of the D-Day landings – and shows that not all German soldiers were highly motivated Nazis. For most of the soldiers, their motivation to fight to the end was born of their wish to return home to their loved ones.

My Grandfather never revisited Normandy because of his memories of the fighting and his bitter feelings about being left alone at the front by his superiors. Being in charge of men that could defend themselves only with small arms and exemplary devotion against an enemy with ever-increasing supplies of tanks, artillery and aircraft, he felt responsible for every soldier that died under his command.

Fighting and dying for the wrong cause, the soldiers of 352. Infanterie-Division nevertheless deserve respect for what they accomplished in Normandy until the unit was destroyed at St Lô.

Martin-Robert Galle, grandson of Oberst Ernst Goth,
Commanding Officer, Grenadier Regiment 916, 352. Infanterie-Division

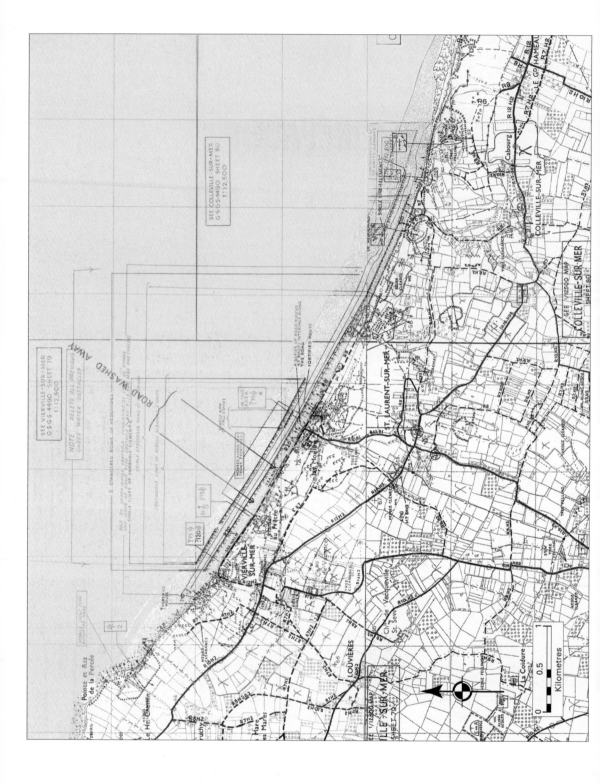

PREFACE

6 JUNE 1944 saw the greatest seaborne invasion in history. Millions of men were involved. Through the years, numerous books have been written on this subject, all tackling different aspects or providing different interpretations of the fighting. This book concentrates on one German division, 352. Infanterie-Division, and its involvement in Normandy. Often, the actions of this unit have been overlooked by historians who centre on more elite or famous divisions when writing about the German side. However, the 352nd played one of the most important roles in the campaign, nearly changing the outcome of the invasion.

This work is on occasion unspecific when discussing Allied units and their actions. This is done in attempt to give the reader the same perspective the German commanders had and upon which they based their tactical decisions. The accounts of the surviving veterans, both American and German, have been of inestimable value in giving a view of the invasion from the 'foxhole'. Some of these men have done historians a great service by recording their individual accounts during or just after the war. But most have set down their memories during interviews and in correspondences decades later. Painstaking efforts to verify and place these men's experiences have been made by the authors.

Why was this book written? It is not an attempt to glorify the German Army or the Third Reich in any way. The reasons go back to my youth. I lived with my family in a housing development which was solely for veterans of the US Military and their families. My father had been a US Marine and my mother served in the Women's Army Corps. All of my friends had at least one parent who served and at that time the vast majority had seen combat in the Second World War. I spent much of my time talking to these veterans while cutting lawns, delivering papers and shovelling snow for them. Throughout this time I learned of both World Wars through their memories. They talked vividly of their experiences, laughing at the funny incidents and welling up when relating the loss of close buddies. This was the war as they saw it, felt it and knew it. Time passed and these men faded away one by one. I grew older reading more books regarding the history of the campaigns I had heard so much about but few books ever equalled those vivid accounts. These veterans may have had a fact or two wrong regarding the overall campaign but their experiences rang true. In the end their stories, for the most part, were never recorded and are now lost to us for ever. Later in life, while serving as an infantryman my interest in the Normandy Invasion was sparked by the conversations I had with my uncle who landed with the US 4th Division on Utah Beach. My attention was drawn more to the events that occurred on Omaha Beach by a chance meeting I had with a German veteran of the campaign. His recollections brought me back to the veterans of my youth. I began to question what really happened on that beach and in the hedgerows, since many of the accounts I read were repetitive – the same versions reworked into different books. With very few exceptions, they were from the Allied point of view. As time passed, I found more German veterans who had been there. Their numbers were small. Smaller still was the number who would talk about their experiences. Then one German veteran – Werner Stahnke – who served in Russia and the Battle of the Bulge, commented to me that it was very sad that when they were all gone no one would really have a record of the war as they saw it. In the end I felt that the history of this campaign should be heard from both sides of the front line. We all must hold in high esteem the Allied soldiers who stormed the beaches, jumped into the darkness and slugged it out in the hedgerows to liberate Europe and save the world. However, this sacrifice and honour should not erase the experiences of the other side. In the end, regardless of uniform, the ordinary soldier is the same worldwide. This book is an effort to add these men's recollections to the overall story of the greatest air and seaborne invasion ever undertaken. Most of these men have passed on and it seemed wrong to let their memories fade from the pages of history. This is their war.

Vince Milano
Epping, New Hampshire, USA

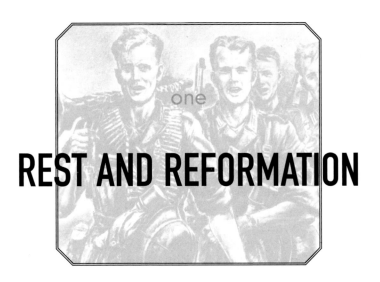

one

REST AND REFORMATION

THE late autumn morning of 5 December 1943 began grey and dreary. A military car in the same drab colour approached the ancient city of St Lô. The ranking occupant was Oberstleutnant Fritz Ziegelmann. He was the former Chief Quartermaster of the 7. Armee now on his way to his new assignment as the IA, Chief of Staff of a newly forming infantry division. Today was the first meeting of all the officers in the staff and those representing the assigned infantry and support units. Ziegelmann knew that his new posting was inevitable, since the tremendous losses incurred on the Eastern Front the previous summer. But he was still surprised to draw a combat assignment, especially since he was a member of the General Staff. This was signified by the crimson stripes running down the sides of his breeches. Even so, he would be the second-in-command of this new unit.

The car lurched to a halt in front of a weathered chateau. A guard opened the car door, standing rigidly at attention. Perhaps he thought Ziegelmann was a general, since they too wore crimson stripes down their trouser legs. The Oberstleutnant gave the guard a quick salute and headed straight into the building.

Inside, the formalities were brisk in order that the main business could be attended to. The first order of the day was to review the units and men that would form the base of the new division. These men would come from three different units, all of which had much combat experience. The smallest contingent would come from the Grenadier Regiment 546, which had lost most of its men at Stalingrad. These men now being assigned were those that had been wounded and flown out of the city early enough in the encirclement. The other two units were the 268th and 321. Infanterie-Divisions, the latter making up the bulk of the men. Both divisions had served in Russia, the 268th since 1941 and the 321st arrived there in December 1942. Both units had suffered large numbers of casualties during the Kursk Offensive during the summer of 1943; so many, that the General Staff decided to use them in forming new units instead of refitting them.

Other men who had seen fighting in Italy and North Africa, would come from hospitals and rest camps as they recovered from their wounds. To all these veterans would be added

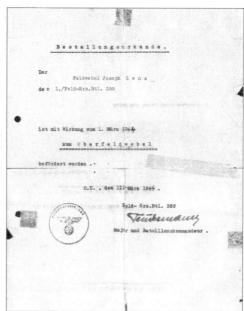

Left Feldwebel Josef Zens. One of the battle-hardened Eastern Front veterans used to train inexperienced young Grenadiers in 352. Infanterie-Division. (Ronny Schindler)

Right Promotion certificate advancing Feldwebel Josef Zens to Oberfeldwebel whilst serving in Feld-Ersatz-Bataillon 352 just prior to the invasion. (Ronny Schindler)

Left Grenadier Georg Seidl – Schlann, Germany, 1943.

Right Grenadier Eduard Schötz, November 1943, Schlann, Germany (now Slany, Czech Republic), dressed in the old training uniform during basic training.

German recruits take the oath of allegiance on the regimental colours.

several thousand new recruits, most from the army training camp at Schlann, Germany (now Slany, Czech Republic). Replacement Ersatz units would be assigned in Germany proper when the formation of the division was complete.

All of the officers in attendance had frontline experience, a fact that Ziegelmann recognised would accelerate the establishment of an effective fighting force. The main topic of discussion was the final field commitment of this new division, 352. Infanterie-Division. This issue was very important since it would dictate the type of training the 352nd would get. It was obvious to all present that with the conditions prevailing on the Eastern Front, it was the most likely place for their future field operations. So the 352nd would train to fight the Red Army, which meant learning to conduct successful operations while out-gunned, outnumbered and surrounded most of the time – all valuable lessons learned during the past two-and-a-half years of fighting.

Ziegelmann and his new staff were under orders to complete the organisation of the 352nd by the end of January 1944. He knew only too well that this was an unrealistic order, predominantly because of the supply problems that existed at that time. Orders are given to be obeyed, so the officers set about their monumental tasks.

While the mountains of paperwork piled up upon the desks of clerks, a long troop train screeched to a stop in St Lô's main rail yard. The dirty, brown cattle cars were packed to overflowing with the recruits assigned to the 352nd. Most were 17-year-old lads fresh from a hurried three-week training course in Slany.

Among the young soldiers peering out of the boxcar windows were Grenadiers Georg Seidl, Martin Eichenseer, Eduard Schötz and Karl Wegner. Like most of those with them, they were away from home for the first time in their lives.

In large masses they detrained; NCOs and officers who were set apart from the sea of helmeted youth by their peaked caps, soon had them in some sort of a loose formation. Then with a clattering of hobnailed boots and shouted names, men were divided and assigned to units. While most in this trainload had been assigned to Grenadier Regiment 916, Karl Wegner and his new friend, Willi Schuster, had been assigned to Grenadier Regiment 914. The other infantry regiment of the 352nd, the 915th, did not draw any new men that day. All three of these regiments had their quarters outside St Lô, which resulted in a march of several kilometres for the replacements. Transportation was only available for the officers and some of the more senior NCOs. Led by their new sergeants the columns headed north out of the city. Grenadier Wegner compared St Lô to his home in Hanover. On first impressions he did not like what he saw. He preferred his home city.

With the arrival of this first troop allocation the process of building a new division began in earnest. Before it had only been a 'clerk's war'. Except for the replacements, all other areas of procurement were frustratingly slow. Oberstleutnant Ziegelmann pulled every string he could, even calling in some favours owed to him by senior members of the local Quartermaster Corps. The results were negligible, they could not be given what the Allied air forces were destroying, and most of what was left went to Russia. He did succeed in getting leftover stockpiles of uniforms and equipment manufactured for the North Africa Campaign. This meant equipment with webbed canvas instead of the normal leather and uniforms in olive brown instead of field grey. The mix of web and leather equipment was already commonplace and not much of a problem. The uniforms, it was decided, would be issued to those troops who had not already been issued a summer HBT cotton uniform and to those that had worn out the ones they already possessed. The only alteration would be in the removal of the tropical-style insignia, to be replaced with the standard European issue.

The arrival of the New Year also brought the arrival of the new divisional commander. He was Generalleutnant Dietrich Kraiss, a 55-year-old Knight's Cross recipient. The first report he received from Ziegelmann was basically a complete list of the problems and shortcomings of the German supply system. For example, the artillery could not train replacements because they had no sights for their guns, nor could they move them since the harnesses for their horses had not yet arrived. Deliveries of both items were slated for some time in February 1944. As to the training of the infantry, the 352nd had only had three live-fire exercises, one per regiment, owing to lack of ammunition.

Since petrol was a rarity the transport units could not train replacement drivers and could only make priority deliveries by truck. All others were by horse-drawn wagon. The mounting pages of these types of problems exasperated Generalleutnant Kraiss. He made formal complaints to his superiors about these shortcomings but they could do nothing about it. As a result he decided to put all his energies into working with what he did have plenty of – men.

The majority of the troops were 17- and 18-year-old recruits, which meant that they did most of their teenage growing during the years of wartime rationing. The result was a lack of dairy and meat products, which meant underdeveloped muscles and bones. So training had to be curtailed until these men could be, quite literally, brought up to strength.

Obergefreiter Josef Brass, a veteran of 321. Infanterie-Division. who had served on the Eastern Front, stated that in his new unit, Pionier-Bataillon 352, the majority of the younger men could not finish the forced marches even with the prodding and threats of the sergeants. He believed that if sent to Russia the men would not survive.

Oberstleutnant Ziegelmann petitioned his superiors at 7. Armee for a dairy ration. This would consist primarily of milk and butter. The request was immediately denied. Upon

Left Iron Cross 2nd Class document, signed by Generalleutnant Kraiss while he was commander of a division in Russia.

Right Generalleutnant Dietrich Kraiss, commander of 352. Infanterie-Division.

Left Newly promoted Gefreiter Josef Brass relaxing during his time off in France, 1942.

Right Grenadier Franz Gockel in September 1943, aged seventeen. He is wearing a pre-war Model 29 tunic with wartime insignia. The buckle is the Weimar pattern without the swastika.

Obergefreiter Josef Brass and his comrades embark for Russia, December 1942. He is sitting in the doorway, his hands are on the shoulders of Obergefreiter Heinrich Lindemann who was his assistant gunner on the MG and was killed at his side during the Kursk offensive in August 1943. 2nd left, standing in the doorway is Pioneer Paul Hundiers who would survive the horrors of the Eastern Front only to perish outside the destroyed city of St Lô.

hearing of this decision Generalleutnant Kraiss authorised his Chief of Staff to procure, by purchase or barter, milk, butter and fresh meat from local farms. In his after-action report on the campaign, Ziegelmann noted that this was instrumental in bringing the young men up to strength prior to the invasion.

Another problem with the troops was communication, though not in the technical but human sense, with the 352nd's several 'Ostbatallions' (East Battalions). These were units comprised of volunteers from various ethnic groups in the Soviet Union. Though led by Germans, they were often of questionable fighting quality. These units were deliberately kept apart from all German units and regulated to low priority assignments or construction. Since the regaining of the Polish Corridor provinces and Alsace-Lorraine, men of military age living there who were born either of German parents or born when these areas had been part of Imperial Germany were required to serve. These men were collectively termed *Volksdeutsche* (Germanic Peoples). Although legally regarded as German citizens they spoke little or no German. Even with the Army's attempts to teach them through a series of picture word association manuals, communication problems arose, ranging from the comical to the life-threatening. Two incidents related by Grenadier Franz Gockel, serving in Nr 3 Kompanie, I Bataillon/Grenadier Regiment 726, illustrate both ends of this spectrum:

One day while building a bunker Unteroffizier E. called to two men to bring him a hammer while he held up a support beam that had come loose. He yelled repeatedly, while they both stood there and stared at him dumbfounded. Then one caught on to his intentions and ran off quickly. He came back with a big smile holding the hammer up and saying to it, 'Morteck, you are a hammer.' Morteck is the Polish word for hammer.

The other incident involved an Alsatian:

After coming back from a patrol we were turning in our weapons to the Armourer. A new man from Alsace handed over a loaded flare pistol. The Armourer told him to unload it but the Alsatian misunderstood him and pulled the trigger. The flare shot out, hitting the Armourer in the chest. It was a serious wound but the man survived.

Gockel notes that this soldier was given two weeks arrest and confinement. This was actually more of a reward than punishment since he was allowed to lounge around the bunker all day while the rest of the company was on fatigue duties and patrols. The language barriers would never be totally overcome.

There existed other shortfalls amongst the personnel. The cadre of NCOs was only at 70 per cent. One plus point was that the vast majority of these men were combat veterans. This would help greatly during training.

Despite these and many other shortcomings the 352nd had a strength of 12,000 by 1 March 1944. On that date the General Staff in Berlin declared the 352nd fully formed and at their disposal for deployment. Both Kraiss and Ziegelmann were surprised by this premature declaration by OKW (*Oberkommando der Werhrmacht*). They both felt that this

Japanese officers (extreme right next to officer wearing helmet) inspect heavy coastal artillery guns in Normandy 1943. The Germans hoped to gain from Japanese experience at repelling invasions.

Members of GR 914 on a rest break during anti-tank training, May 1944. The 'panzer' is constructed of wood, cardboard and sheet metal, to resemble a British tank. Next to the right hand Grenadier who is holding a rifle is a Teller mine, a multi-purpose explosive mine that could be buried, thrown at or planted inside armoured vehicles and bunkers. (Karl Wegner)

Coastal artillerymen with their truck on anti-invasion exercises in Normandy 1943. The headlight covers are French and British helmets.

was a political decision rather than a military one, since it would be important for OKW to declare as many new units formed and ready for the next summer of fighting as possible. It seemed to be of no consequence whether or not these units were properly equipped or trained for any missions that would be assigned to them. Kraiss questioned OKW about this and was informed that it was up to the divisions themselves to ensure that all their needs were fulfilled to be ready for deployment.

Piled on to the 352nd's mountain of problems was the first mission assigned to them on the day they were declared operational. Since January 1944 the division had had orders to ready a battlegroup for immediate deployment consisting of one grenadier regiment; one artillery battalion; and one pionier abteilung; one signal and supply abteilung. This unit was to be deployed anywhere in France, Belgium or Holland in time of emergency within 12 hours of receiving notice. This was one-third of the division's strength and the order had put a strain on the training schedules. The 1 March order extended this status to cover the entire 352nd and the ready battlegroup must still be maintained as it now had been earmarked as the corps reserve for the LXXXIV Armeekorps, to which the 352nd had been assigned. The only option that was open to Generalleutnant Kraiss was to rotate the units within the battlegroup in order that all units could partake in the divisional training exercises. This also meant that the division would be training to conduct operations at under-strength levels prior to the invasion of 6 June. This would in fact aid them greatly in the upcoming fighting but for now it was just a great inconvenience.

While the 352nd was juggling units to train and equip the men, the new commander of Army Group B was on a tour of his new area. Feldmarschall Erwin Rommel, the Desert Fox, was singularly unimpressed by what was shown to him. His inspection tour of the much-vaunted Atlantik Wall revealed to him that it was a myth generated by Goebbels' propaganda machine.

Troops guarding the coasts were under-strength, poorly trained and lacking in essential equipment. Most of the invasion defences were in and around major city harbours, as if the Allies would be disembarking from the *Queen Mary*. Defences in rural areas where probable landing beaches existed, provided there were any at all, showed a lack of tactical understanding of seaborne landings.

After in-depth tactical studies, Rommel felt the invasion would be in rural sectors because defences were light and the troops manning them were dispersed over larger areas. He also reasoned that the Normandy sector was the most probable target of any invasion because of its similarity to the bay at Salerno. Thus he decided to reinforce the sector between Caen and Brevands, then occupied only by 716. Infanterie-Division. Stationed there for two years, it was a low-calibre, static coastal defence unit of older men with a smattering of undertrained recruits.

The first order Kraiss received from Rommel was to dispatch his artillery regiment, Artillerie Regiment 352, into the 716th's sector to bolster the firepower available against any Allied landing. The regiment would still be under the 352nd's command and control, in other words the 716th would need Kraiss' permission to commit it to combat.

This action did not satisfy the Feldmarschall and as a result he ordered the entire 352. Grenadier-Division to take over the coastal sector now assigned to the 716th, effective 15 March 1944. The 716th would be given a much smaller part of the coast to defend in and around Caen, where it was felt they would have a much better chance of fending off

One of the many defensive positions on the Atlantik Wall.

any landing. However, the 716th was ordered to leave behind for absorption by the 352nd I and III Bataillons of Grenadier Regiment 726 under the command of Major Korfes, now the Commander of I/GR 726. These units would remain in their current positions north of Colleville sur Mer. In addition, the 716th would leave behind some Ostbatallions; more of a burden than a blessing. When this divisional move was completed, entire regiments would now defend sectors once manned by single battalions. The change tripled the strength along this coast. Even while the 352nd was in the process of moving Generalleutnant Kraiss received additional orders from Rommel:

1 The 352nd was to improve the beach defences along their part of the coast.
2 The 352nd would also be responsible for building and maintaining defensive positions from the coast inland all the way down to St Lô, and be responsible for security in this area.
3 The division was to maintain its current training schedule.

This overburdening of missions displeased all within the staff of the 352nd. They had only just begun their move and were now responsible for an area 30 kilometres long and 25 kilometres deep. This prompted Kraiss to request a meeting with General Marcks, the commander of LXXXIV Armeekorps.

   The discussion centred on the placement of the 352nd's forces taking into consideration all of the specific missions now assigned. Marcks informed Kraiss that Rommel and he had discussed probable Allied landing areas and objectives at a meeting several days before, summarising that the Allies could isolate the Cotentin Peninsula, taking the major ports there to build up for a major drive to Paris and beyond. Therefore it was most important for the 352nd to have the bulk of its troops along the coast, in a position to mount quick counterstrikes if a landing was successful. Kraiss would have to put the bulk of his men on his left flank, the Carentan Canal, since it was sparsely defended, and the 716th would be on his right. His reserves would be in this sector affording them good cover with the ability to reach any part of the division's area in a short time. This created a problem. Kraiss' reserves were also those assigned to General Marcks. This battlegroup, then Grenadier Regiment 916 and Pionier-Bataillon 352 but soon to change to Grenadier Regiment 915 and Fusilier-Bataillon 352, caused a heated argument between the two Generals – especially since Marcks required them to be much farther away from the coast. In the end Kraiss made a direct appeal to Rommel, who was an old friend. He pointed out the unreliability of the 716th, along with the distance between the 352nd and other reserves, chiefly the 21. Panzer-Division. Rommel agreed, and Kraiss was allowed to keep his division intact.

   The move was in full swing and the Grenadiers of the 352nd got their first views of the English Channel during the first week of April 1944. Oberst Goth, commander of the 916th, made an inspection of the two battalions of GR 726 now assigned to him. His report alarmed both Ziegelmann and Kraiss. At its current level of effectiveness, the Allies could land and overwhelm the 726th with little effort, establishing a beachhead in under an hour. Generalleutnant Kraiss ordered Ziegelmann to conduct an investigation to discover the reason for this disgraceful situation.

In his report, Ziegelmann outlined the reasons for the low fighting ability of GR 726. First, the regiment was constantly having its most able and experienced men transferred to combat duty on the Eastern Front. The remaining officers and NCOs lacked any clear initiative in training the unit to peak combat effectiveness. In the Oberstleutnant's opinion, several of the NCOs purposely kept the level low in order not to be sent to Russia. Secondly, the familiar supply and logistics problems hampered what training was being done. Kraiss ordered that this unit would now adhere to all the training schedules and efficiency ratings as the rest of the 352nd. He was determined to see to it that 726th would be able to hold their own in a pitched battle.

It was not very long after the 352nd's arrival when Rommel appeared to inspect the division's coastal deployment. Kraiss was away at a meeting with General Marcks at LXXXIV headquarters in St Lô, so the burden fell on Ziegelmann. He first pointed out to the Feldmarschall that they had not actually started work on the coastal zone yet. Rommel assured the Oberstleutnant that he was aware of this and was only there to check the actual placement of the 352nd's infantry units. With this understanding the two officers set out on their tour.

Rommel did not like what he found, reprimanding Ziegelmann on the spot. The reason for his anger was the placement of the regimental reserves within each individual unit's sector. These reserves, approximately a reinforced rifle company, were not close enough to the shore to fire upon enemy troops disembarking from landing craft. Rommel wanted every available weapon to have fields of fire on the beaches. In his defence, Ziegelmann stated that the width of the 352nd's front, 53 kilometres, combined

Mixed group of senior and battle-experienced NCOs from various combat branches meet during the early formation of 352. Infanterie-Division to coordinate training. Most have seen combat service on the Eastern Front as indicated by their awards. Left centre front row stands the *Hauptfeldwebel*, commonly referred to as 'Der Spiess'. His rank is indicated by the lace rings on his cuffs. (Martin Eichenseer)

with the unreliability of the divisions on both flanks required that these reserves be where they were in order to deal with any threat on the flanks or rear. Rommel was adamant; the reserves must be moved forward.

On his return, his much rebuked Chief of Staff informed Generalleutnant Kraiss of this order. Since it was he who had placed the reserves, Kraiss backed the stand that Ziegelmann had made against Rommel. However, orders from a Feldmarschall were to be obeyed. Kraiss decided to call Rommel and asked to discuss the issue in person. The following day they met and a compromise was found. The solution was to place the reserve companies on an angled line so that one, possibly two depending on terrain, could fire onto the beach while leaving the rest of the company far enough inland to deal with any of the threats that might arise along the flanks.

Inevitably, with one problem solved, another would take its place. Again, it was a tactical order, this time from Hitler himself. The infamous *Führerbefehl* decreed that each position be held to the last round and last man, forbidding any retreat. To Generalleutnant Kraiss this order made no military sense whatsoever. He had no other choice but to request a second meeting with Rommel.

At the second meeting Kraiss outlined some of the tactical questions regarding the enforcement of the Führerbefehl. Kraiss asked that if men from one strongpoint left their position to come to the aid of another, would they be in violation of the order? Or if a gun's position became indefensible and the crew moved it to another one, was this a violation as well? Rommel agreed that this was a foolish order but had no solution to it at the end of the meeting. After consideration and staff meetings about this problem the Feldmarschall issued his own order a few days later. The 'Rommel Befehl' declared that within divisional areas the tactical movement of subordinate units would be at the discretion of field commanders. The movement of the entire division would also require Rommel's permission and not Hitler's. With the issue settled, the 352nd finished the tactical move into the coastal sector. Kraiss reorganised his defences to fit the Rommel Befehl more effectively.

Two main battle lines were to be established. The first line, naturally, would be the coastal front. The second line was, depending on the terrain, 10 to 15 kilometres behind the coast. On these two lines, for a distance of 53 kilometres, Kraiss would place the bulk of his troops. This would enable him to move any part of his division during combat and enjoy the benefit of a second line of resistance if forced to withdraw from the coast. A further advantage of this placement would be much more manoeuvrability if there were large-scale air drops of troops within the 352nd's divisional sector.

The move to the coast, however, meant the supply situation became worse since the divisional supply units were now much farther away from the LXXXIV Armeekorps' depots. This, coupled with the 352nd being on standing alert to move anywhere in Europe for emergencies, meant constant delays in getting supplies since the supply units could only keep on hand what they could transport if the division was ordered to move. This amounted to only one or two days of rations of most items, including munitions, resulting in constant trips to the Corps supply depots for replenishment; a waste of time, manpower and petrol.

It was not just the higher levels of command who were displeased with the lack of preparation of the 716th; junior officers and enlisted men were also critical. Leutnant Hans Heinze, a Stalingrad survivor, was one of the first men from the 352nd to inspect the beach defences:

Two gunners pose gazing out into an empty English Channel. Smiles upon their faces indicate no knowledge of the Allied armada that will greet them on a cold, dreary morning several days hence.

Leutnant Heinze, newly commissioned, still wearing the insignia of the Jägers, in which he served as an enlisted man.

Leutnant Heinz Fuehr pictured as an
Unteroffizier, 14 July 1941 in Russia having
just been awarded the Iron Cross 2nd Class
and Infantry Assault Badge. In December 1941
he was wounded at the battle for Riga.

Added to the Grenadiers' daily duties was the
arduous task of felling trees and transporting
the lumber to the beaches for strengthening
coastal defences. (Martin Eichenseer)

My commander, Hauptmann Grimme and I decided to take a ride to the beach to look over our new area before we assigned any of the troops here. We reached the coast but could not find the Atlantik Wall. We finally did come to some bunkers surrounded by barbed wire and decided to get out and look around. We went right over the wire without even tearing our trousers. Then we met a Landser from the unit occupying the area. He had been there since 1940 and we asked him about the defences. He just said 'If the Tommies decide to invade and disturb our Holy peace we will roll out our gun and teach them how to be scared.' We found no cheer or solace in this remark. It was clear that much work was ahead of us.

Another newly promoted officer in the division found himself posted on the Channel coast. Leutnant Heinz Fuehr had seen five years of service so far, starting as a private in a machine-gun company, rising through the ranks while seeing active combat in the 1940 French Campaign and on the Eastern Front. As a leutnant (lieutenant), he was now posted to his first combat command:

At the end of 1943, I reported with three other officers to the 'Führer Reserve' in Berlin. The thought was in our mind that we would surely be sent back to Russia and it was with great joy that we learned of our being assigned to the Normandy area of France. Because of an Allied air raid on Hamburg, I reached my new unit a day too late. The Commander, Oberst Goth, was not pleased and gave me several days confinement as a punishment. I was assigned as a platoon leader in the 8th Kompanie Grenadier Regiment 916. The company commander was an Oberleutnant [Leutnant Berty?]. Sadly I don't remember his name. At first, as officers, we were allowed to be billeted in the homes of local farmers but later on we were required to be stationed in the fortifications with the troops. Most of the time soldiers constructed trenches and bunkers in combination with regular training. At the end of every day I had to report the progress of the work to the battalion commander [Hauptmann Grimme]. I was there when Feldmarschall Rommel visited our position in 1944. My platoon's position directly overhung the beach and we could fire clearly up and down it. There were no obstructions or bunkers of concrete, the few dug-outs were made of wood and the few houses that were there were torn down.

Generalleutnant Kraiss made the beach defences the 352nd's top priority. The first item to be tackled was the improvement and positioning of coastal obstacles. The anti-tank/landing-craft obstacles of criss-crossed steel girders were simple to construct and easy to put in place. Properly laid barbed wire was even less difficult to set up. The *Tschechen* were a different matter. These were long stakes made from tree trunks topped with mines or explosives that would detonate when struck by the bottom of a landing craft. They proved difficult to make and place, despite their simple composition.

The small trees needed for their construction had to be cut by hand and brought up from the Forêt de Cerisy by horse-drawn wagon, over 30 kilometres away. The process of driving them into the sand proved more difficult than realised. As it transpired, help came from a very unlikely source. Grenadier Franz Gockel:

The construction of the Tschechen was done with the help of the Bayeux Fire Brigade. One day they showed up with their equipment and with an amazingly simple method we sunk the tree trunks into the sand. The trunks were supported by a tripod and sunk in to the required

August 1941, Lille, France. 1st Kompanie, 321 Pionier Bataillon. Finals for the Armeekorps Master Soldier competition. Events included 100m rifle shoot and 25 kilometres speed march in full gear, Josef Brass stated that this Kompanie won the competition by completing the speed march in 3 hours and 40 seconds. Josef Brass is standing centre, hands on pouches. Tallest man in photo on right is Pionier Fritz Klipp, one of the few Eastern Front survivors from this Kompanie. He served with Josef Brass in Normandie.

A squad, Gruppe, from the Pionierzug/Stabskompanie of GR 916. Centre front is Edouard Schötz. To his left is Grenadier Josef Fuchs. The assistant Gruppführer, standing centre behind Schötz is wearing the early war pattern cap and tunic. The others wear standard M43 caps and a mix of early pattern two pocket HBT drill jackets, M40 and M43 tunics. St Paul, April 1944.

depth by a fire hose pump. At the beginning we experienced problems because the pump would clog with sand. A soldier suggested that we place someone on the pump to regulate the amount of sand flowing through it. The entire project was completed in very little time.

As many obstacles were to be placed on and behind the beaches as possible, but lack of materials did not allow preparations to the depth and strength prescribed by Rommel. It was left up to the Pionier-Bataillon 352 under the command of Hauptmann Paul to remedy matters with expedient measures in the field. One good example of their work was in the area near St Pierre du Mont, part of the coast with steep inclines above the beaches. Obergefreiter Josef Brass was one of the men assigned to this task:

> We had a stockpile of 240mm shells and since the artillery could not use them they were given to us. With them, we would make a new kind of anti invasion obstacle. We buried them in the sides of the hills with trip wires attached to them. When triggered, the shells would roll down to the beach. The fuses of the shells were set so that they only would explode when they reached the beach. Others were set to roll over cliffs and explode in midair. With the large blast range these shells had they would be very deadly. By the time of the invasion we had placed one of these 'Roller Grenades' about every 100 metres along the divisional front.

Several more items were promised to the 352nd but in most cases they would never arrive and those that did came too late. An example of this is the 'Goliath' (a miniature tank vehicle) packed with explosives and sent off into enemy lines or strongpoints by wired remote control, then detonated. Found to be very effective on the Eastern Front, the shipment for the 352nd would arrive on 5 June 1944 – without the explosive charges.

Ordered to lay extensive minefields by Rommel, the Pioniere ran into several problems. First they had to replace all of the mines that the 716th had laid. These mines had been in the sand and saltwater for two years and corrosion had rendered them useless. Secondly the Feldmarschall decreed that the minefields be five kilometres deep along the division's entire front, which would require ten million mines; an impossible number for the existing supply systems. In fact, none of the anti-tank mines had arrived yet. Despite this, by 1 June the Pioniere managed to place 11,000 mines along the coastal front. This number does not include the 'Roller Grenades' and other extemporised measures.

Natural obstacles were also exploited within the 352nd's sectors. Areas were flooded in expectation of airborne landings but care was taken not to flood too much of the local farmers' pastures so the local food supply was not hindered. The warm weather of May dried up many of these areas.

Still under orders to prepare for the defence as far south as St Lô, Kraiss had to compromise plans for this entire area, which ran from Caen west to Brevands, then along the Vire river in a rough line to St Lô, then back to Caen, basically a triangle. Kraiss's secondary line behind the coast would incorporate within it the same basic types of works as were along the coast, centring on strongpoints, minefields and anti-tank obstacles primarily within areas where the threat of airborne landings or important objectives existed. After some analysis Kraiss chose three main locations to commit the time and effort to build anti-airborne defences. They were Bayeux, the Vire Estuary and the clear areas just behind the coast. Kraiss felt that any airborne landings would come close to the beach landing, therefore justifying his decision not to build obstacles inland and around St Lô.

Infantry training
exercises, prior to the
invasion. Photograph
from Martin Eichenseer
who is one of the
figures in the distance.

The primary structure used in this type of defence would be Rommel's *Spargel* (asparagus). These were two-metre stakes, sharpened at the end, set up in various patterns two to three metres apart at possible landing sites. Between each stake was strung barbed wire, to entangle those men who were not impaled. Gliders would break into pieces when landing in one of these fields. Any survivors of the crash would be easy targets as they tried to make their way to safety. Luckily for the Allied airborne units, the supply of barbed wire was insufficient. Only the sites around Bayeux were completed. The other two areas remained only partially covered by the time of the invasion.

The construction of inland bunkers presented its own problems. First and foremost there was a complete lack of organisation of the available work force. This was because of the many forces within the 352nd's area of responsibility. Units from the Luftwaffe, Kriegsmarine, independent army construction battalions, RAD units and men from the Organisation Todt (specialised construction units named after the late Dr Fritz Todt, engineer and senior NSDAP figure). All of these different factions were, in theory, to work side by side to build the Atlantik Wall and other sites but more often than not they were in each other's way. For example, some units were building their living quarters in the fields of fire of other unit's bunkers and different groups were sent to build the same bunker but each with different plans. It was not until the Düsseldorfer Baufirm, a civilian construction company, came into the picture that things were straightened out. They coordinated all the units' efforts and made good progress, but it was all too late.

Oberstleutnant Ziegelmann made a report to 7. Armee Quartermaster Corp regarding the building supplies for the inland defences. These were separate from the coastal supplies with a lower priority and drawn from different depots. The depots were also part of different services, sometimes the Luftwaffe or Kriegsmarine. Even when supplies were available, the distribution was handled poorly. In several cases rear echelon troops, such as Luftwaffe units, were building their structures in cement while infantry units had to dig earthen bunkers along Kraiss' second battle line. Most of these positions suffered from poor drainage because of their close proximity to the coast and were therefore flooded or muddy. One of the reasons for this misallocation of materials was that the troops stationed in Normandy the longest received their supply request first. Despite the complaints filed by both Generalleutnant

Officers of GR916 at II Bataillon HQ in Formigny. Left to right they are Leutnant Maas, Zugführer for the Pionierzug/ Stabskompanie, Oberleutnant Dr Bahr, Regimental Surgeon and Leutnant Heinze.

Kraiss and Oberstleutnant Ziegelmann the Quartermaster Corps would not change its way of operation, regulations must be adhered to at all times was the reply.

By June things looked bad for the defences along the coast. On the 1st Kraiss received the Staff Engineer's report from Ziegelmann and was not happy. It stated that only 45 per cent of the bunkers could withstand artillery fire and only 15 per cent of these could withstand air bombardment. The rest were not strong enough to withstand direct hits from either. The verdict was in; Generalleutnant Kraiss would have to depend on his soldiers' abilities rather than the non-existent wall on which the Generals in Berlin had placed their bets.

Despite all the missions assigned to them, it was still the predominant opinion that the 352nd would be sent to Russia some time during that summer. This was still the main emphasis in the training. This was harsh and tough because it had to be. Many of the recruits were shocked at the physical demands made of them after working a good part of the day on bunkers and obstacles. Karl Wegner read in disbelief the many letters he received from family and friends telling him how lucky he was to live the easy life in France and not be in Russia. But it was known that well trained men could accomplish much in battle even with limited resources. Leutnant Heinze, who was training Nr. 5 Kompanie/Grenadier Regiment 916, was determined to train his men 'until they could shoot their weapons in their sleep.' Generalleutnant Kraiss had this same ambition for the entire 352nd. He decided to concentrate all the training on two central themes. The first would be individual training. Combat experience in Russia had shown that single soldiers or small groups could inflict large numbers of casualties, holding up a more powerful enemy force. And these men were more likely to fight their way through enemy lines rather than surrender.

More importantly, the second theme was the counter attack. On the Eastern Front this was an everyday mission. German units counter-attacked continually to retake ground or plug gaps in the lines. And of course it would be the 352nd's mission to make counter attacks against any Allied landings in France. The 352nd would train from platoon up to divisional level in this type of operation. Kraiss would still be under orders to maintain the Korps Reserve, which now consisted of Grenadier Regiment 915 and Fusilier-Bataillon 352 under the overall command of Oberst Meyer (CO of GR 915). He would have to coordinate their training schedules in order to keep it on a par with the rest of the division. He decided that the reserve should practise making counter attacks on the coast from the village of Seulles. Oberst Meyer agreed. Kraiss visited Meyer in late May to get an assessment of training. Meyer stated that the main problem was with the volunteers – not the Russians or Ukrainians, but the French. All of the drivers from the transport unit assigned to drive Meyer's men were French volunteers. Meyer told Kraiss that they were lazy and untrustworthy, but if handled properly could get troops to destinations quickly with their knowledge of the area and its roads. They had caused some delays in training, but nothing that could not be over-come. The two officers discussed various landing scenarios and amended the training to centre on the Colleville–St Laurent area. They did not know how prophetic their discussions had been.

All preparations had come a long way since Leutnant Heinze and Hauptmann Grimme had toured the coast earlier that spring, even so problems persisted that never would be overcome as Heinze recalls:

> A large percentage of the machine guns in the bunkers were captured weapons that did not fit our standard ammunition. At several points the barbed wire and trenches were not complete or manned properly. Close to Vierville we did have one of our dependable 88mm guns. Still much work had to be done to finish the coastal works before an attack. Although with some luck and a large amount of sweat from Leutnant Berty's Nr. 8 Kompanie we accomplished much in the short time allotted to us.

In the final analysis it can be said that, despite all of the difficulties, the 352nd was the most prepared and best trained of the infantry divisions along the Normandy coast. An NCO in Grenadier Regiment 916 summed up the situation. Leutnant Heinze, who had just been reassigned as Ordinance Officer for II Batt/Grenadier Regiment 916, heard his forthright analysis:

> Two days before the invasion, I was on an inspection tour with a major from the staff of LXXXIV Armeekorps. He was the officer in charge of our munitions supplies. We went from strongpoint to strongpoint. He looked in them and asked questions of the men, mostly getting the correct if uninspired answers. At one strongpoint a veteran Feldwebel stepped forward and spoke to him. He said 'Herr Major, we have enough ammunition to stop the first, second, third, fourth, and maybe even the fifth wave of Tommies. But after that they're going to kick the door in on top of us and then all is lost.' The bewildered officer stepped back and stated he would ensure that enough ammunition was available. I don't think he believed that Major. We didn't know that within 48 hours his words would ring true. Again and again in the days that would come I would hear those words. I can still hear him to this day.

two

LITTLE TIME FOR SLEEP: A SOLDIER'S DAY

I N the blackness before dawn, the shrill blast of a whistle followed by the harsh voice of his *Feldwebel* woke Karl Wegner from the deep sleep that engrossed him. Amidst the grumbling and shuffling in the bunker he caught a glimpse of his friend, Willi Schuster. Willi looked exhausted, Karl felt very much the same, and yet the day had just begun.

This day, like the many that had preceded it, was one in which there were more duties to be done than time would allow – despite the belief in Germany that duty in France meant a life of ease. The regular duty day began at 0400 hrs with wake up call followed by the first formation, *Appell*, after which the men would be marched off to morning mess. The meal in itself was not appetizing or very nutritious, mainly because of the supply problems. Obergefreiter Brass states that breakfast consisted of 'Ersatz' coffee, which was not always hot, *Kommisbrot* (army bread) and a small portion of some sort of meat. The meals did improve when the 352nd began to purchase eggs and dairy products from the local farms. It was the practice that those fed first were the men still on guard duty. It was felt that since they had been up longer than the rest it was only fair.

While the young Grenadier sat crunching on his Kommisbrot, liberally spread with sweet Norman butter, across the English Channel, other young soldiers began their day. In the vast tent cities that had grown all over southern England thousands of men were roused from their rest. In some places it was the call of a bugle and at others the bellowing of 'Sarge!' While the ever present smell of canvas hung in the air, GIs and Tommies rushed about to shave, shower and get dressed for their first formation of the day.

Then they too would be marched off for the morning meal at the mess hall, most likely another, bigger, tent. Even with the tirade of complaints the meal fed to them was fairly good and always nourishing. The breakfast menu included hot coffee, milk, eggs, biscuits, butter, bacon and sausage, or even hot cakes with maple syrup for the GIs. There was a degree of gastronomic monotony – the simpler the menu the easier it is to prepare – but it is certain that none would have traded it for what their enemies were getting across the Channel.

Obergrenadier Karl Wegner during his time of service in the RAD. He is shirtless, sitting on the left.

Typical German NCO inspection. He is checking that all buttons are present.

German recruits have their weapons inspected.

Life in a four-man *zeltbahn* tent pitched next to a camouflaged vehicle.

Recruits during a break in bayonet training. Note they all have First World War issue Mauser G98 rifles fitted with Second World War bayonets. The Gefreiter instructor is a decorated veteran with the Iron Cross 2nd Class and wound badge. He walks with the aid of a cane. Photograph taken *c*.1942, Germany.

The standard German Army field kitchen, *Gulaschkanone*, which would feed a whole company of soldiers. This could be used when stationary or on the march.

Grenadier Alois Meyer – Angers, France 1944, while with the
Armee Pionier Schule, learning basic combat engineer skills.

With morning mess complete, the soldiers of both
armies would be assigned their duties for the day. The
American in southern England and his native comrades
could expect any number of various assignments. They
could be sent off for tactical training on the moors of
Devon and Cornwall, or to classes that covered first aid,
rifle marksmanship or map reading, amongst dozens of
other topics. Sometimes the drudgery of army life set in
and he was assigned guard duty or some other fatigue duty.

For the Grenadiers in the 352nd, life was not so pre-
ordained. Overburdened with tasks and having a limited
ability to perform them, plans were drawn up to achieve the best results from any expenditure of time and resources. The overall plan was to combine training with assigned duties.
The mornings were mostly allotted for construction of defences. In general this meant
filling sandbags, digging trenches and the like. But when wood was needed for any construction, tactical training was worked into these details. The only place to get the wood
was 30 kilometres away, the Bois de Bretel, and the lack of fuel required the soldiers to
walk to the area. Because of this, the Grenadiers were given a forced march with full gear
and packs under combat conditions. After the wood was cut down and to length, it was
then loaded on transports to be taken away and the men marched back. This march would
incorporate counter attacks against various objectives. The system worked well enough,
toughening up the new men considerably.

Another example of combining training with mission requirements is illustrated by
the job performed by the Divisional Pioneer School in Angers. Here, men from Pionier-
Bataillon 352, Obergefreiter Brass amongst them, trained men from infantry regiments in
basic engineering such as bunker and bridge building. This training also included courses
on landmines and their proper use. Hauptmann Paul, the Pionier Bataillon's CO, decided
not to waste the training effort. Lacking the proper manpower to place and build all the
obstacles required, he decided to have the students place real minefields all along the
352nd's coastal front. This worked very well. So well in fact, that this programme was
extended to all courses taught at the school.

After a full morning of duty, the men of both armies would be fed their midday meal.
For the GI this might mean going back to the mess tent. If in the field, meals would
be trucked out in thermal containers called Mermite Cans. The menu was varied, anything from hotdogs and beans to fried chicken with mashed potatoes. Although it was not
mother's home cooking, the meal was, as far as the US Army was concerned, more than
sufficient for an active man's nutritional needs. To receive the meal, the GIs would line up
and get the food ladled out. For this the soldier had his two piece oval mess kit that had
everything 'slopped' into it. When faced with the accumulated pile, many GIs realised why
it was called a 'mess' kit. One was Sergeant Richard Quaterone of the US 2nd Armored
Division, but he added 'It was all going into our bellies that way so, what the heck, we
ate the stuff.' They got an introduction to English dishes, as units were sometimes fed by
British Army mess halls or field kitchens.

The German Grenadier got something less satisfactory for his midday fare. He would be fed in his bunker or where he was on detail, the food being sent to him from the unit's cookhouse or field kitchens. Sometimes the horse-drawn kitchen, nicknamed the *Gulaschkanone* (Goulash Cannon), would come to feed the men.

This at least ensured them a hot meal. However, diversity was not on the menu. The main meal was a stew or soup called *Eintopf*, literally 'one pot'. The practice was to put whatever was on hand into the same pot to cook, the most common ingredients being potatoes, turnips and noodles. Throughout the German military, times were lean. Most rations that could be were replaced by artificial substitutes, ersatz goods.

At least in Normandy the men were able to enjoy the fresh butter, milk and eggs procured from the locals. Even meat was more plentiful here than in Germany itself. Those men that had served in Russia had eaten things much worse and some nothing at all for long periods. They told the recruits that times were good and not to complain as it would only get worse. Yet occasionally incidents would occur that put doubts in these young men's minds as to how good times really were. Grenadier Gockel, to his dismay, was part one such drama:

> Our post was an underground bunker, some 100 metres away from a house in which our kitchen was set up. [Gockel was stationed to WN62 just north of Colleville]. At noon each day a French farmer would pass by on his horse cart. On this day I hitched a ride with him to bring up the mail and our meal to the bunker. After reaching there I prepared to ladle out the soup to my Kameraden, who had lined up in anticipation. All of the meat and vegetables had settled to the bottom so I gave the pot a strong stir then to my surprise and horror, I pulled up a dead rat in the ladle. 'How is this possible?' I thought to myself. In the second canister another rat was found. The cook was sent for immediately and was greeted by several threats and insults when he arrived. To our officer he explained that the rats must have gotten into the containers while they were stored in the dark cellar of the cookhouse.

When the cooks filled them up with the hot soup they were not noticed, and boiled. The cook was relieved of his position on the spot and his assistant promoted. This was a rare event but caused many a rumour to circulate. It caused men to take more of an interest in what meat was actually being put in their meals.

After the noon meal, those not already in tactical training or on all-day jobs would begin their combat training. The younger men, called *Grünschnabel* (greenhorns, or more literally 'green beaks') by the veterans, found it hard to believe that they were required to do back-breaking work all morning then strap on a full pack to make a forced march of 20 or 30 kilometres to mount a mock counter attack or dig rifle pits. The veterans took everything in their stride; most were used to such demanding routines. They took delight in telling the Grünschnabel that the fighting in Russia was more demanding than this training ever could be, though it is safe to say that some of the tales told by the veterans were exaggerated.

Generalleutnant Kraiss did manage, with the help of the Düsseldorfer Baufirm, to get many construction jobs done by the labour units in order that his troops could get in training exercises of longer duration than just an afternoon. It takes a huge effort and a great deal of time to train units to combine in large-scale operations. This involved training with live ammunition, when in supply, to ensure the recruits would not freeze when the bullets started to fly for real. In reality, several amongst the ranks of officers and NCOs

Three members of 321. Infanterie-Division with a confiscated vehicle, enjoying a smoke during occupation, 1942. Photograph taken by Obergefreiter Josef Brass.

Oberleutnant Hans Heinze in the autumn of 1944. A Stalingrad survivor who served with Jäger Regiment 54, he still wears his Jäger badge as a commemorative on his lower right sleeve. He is also wearing mountain troop trousers and climbing boots. This is not regulation for an infantry officer, however as an officer he was given some choice of clothing since he had to purchase all of it.

Officers and NCOs enjoy some sport shooting during the occupation. Maybe they bagged something extra for the pot.

did not have any confidence in the 352nd reaching any sort of acceptable level of combat effectiveness, despite what Berlin might declare. Leutnant Heinze was amongst those who felt this way. A survivor of the battle for Stalingrad, he had been wounded three times there before even being allowed to go to an aid station. Even then he refused to leave his unit, fighting in the ruins of the tractor factory. Complications then set in, and while unconscious he was evacuated out of the pocket on Christmas Eve 1942. His experiences had shown him what a well trained unit could do despite the lack of equipment. When posted to Grenadier Regiment 916 his study of the men within it was not encouraging to the young officer. Within the regiment, just over 10 per cent had experience of combat, but this number included 75 per cent of the NCOs. He found the recruits lacking in physical endurance and training. A large number of the regiment, 30 per cent, were draftees from Alsace and the Polish Corridor or volunteers from the various regions of the Soviet Union. Heinze knew that many of the volunteers in the German Army were good troops, after all he fought side by side with Croatians in Stalingrad, but these men were not the most reliable. It was a general consensus that they would disappear or surrender once the fighting actually started. With this came speculation as to whether these men would shoot their German leaders in the back. Within the 352nd, they comprised a large percentage of the troops, around 20 per cent. Heinze and those of his mind believed that the 352nd would not even reach the level that Berlin had already assessed them to be at. In his words, the 352nd was a 'tossed together heap'.

Despite the opinions of their officers, the enlisted men seemed to get along with the foreign volunteers quite well. *Obergrenadier* Martin Eichenseer, Stabskompanie/GR 916, stated that most were very amiable fellows, always eager to please and quite willing to do almost any work. He and several others stated that their unit field kitchen even had female Russian volunteers working in it.

The US Army did not have a problem with foreign volunteers but did suffer from racial and cultural differences. Some soldiers, both from the north and south, forgot that the American Civil War had ended some 80 years before, wanting to take up where Lee and Grant left off. Different religious and ethnic backgrounds caused some friction but nothing that would affect the course of any battle. There was some truth in the stereotypical GIs found in war movies: characters such as the Tall Texan who would always declare that nothing was as big or good as it was in Texas, or the New Yorker with the Brooklyn accent and streetwise ways, though in the years after the war Hollywood did its best to exaggerate every localised trait.

Of the two divisions slotted for the landing on Omaha Beach one was veteran and the other was not. The 1st, the 'Big Red One,' had landed in North Africa. The 29th, 'the Blue and the Gray', had been stationed in England for two years, even beginning the war with wooden rifles back in the US.

The evening brought the weary soldiers back to their billets to be fed. This meal tended to be, in both armies, the biggest of the day. The GI was fed a full three-course meal that might feature pork chops or Yankee pot roast. On holidays the army gave the troops a taste of home with turkey dinners and all the trimmings.

The German Grenadier would receive his largest portion of meat with this meal. Again, noodles and potatoes were the usual staples. Like his American counterpart the German cook tried to give the men a home-style feast with desserts and cakes on holidays. Most often, though, it was only on Sunday that the Grenadier got a dessert.

Grenadiers mount formal changing of the guard ceremony in garrison. Guard duty was one of the most necessary but also one of the most monotonous parts of a soldier's existence.

When the meal was finished the soldiers were then required to clean their weapons, gear and uniforms. When this was done, a final formation was held either for them to be dismissed for the evening or assigned night duties. If not on night training exercises the Allied soldiers could expect guard duty at their billets or some other post. Fire watch was required in all billets and there were several other menial assignments that could be given to fill up the nights. The Grenadier had all of these same responsibilities and several others not required in England.

There were security patrols. These were of course important because the Grenadiers were on occupation duty and expecting an invasion. These patrols, done every night, were not well liked by the men. It was not so much the danger but the boredom and fatigue of walking several kilometres in the dark instead of sleeping or getting some time off.

Some patrols went from strongpoint to strongpoint along the coast checking for activity. Other routes went through towns and villages that the *Feldgendarmerie* did not patrol. Some unlucky fellows were assigned to stare out into the English Channel looking for signs of an approaching invasion fleet, and as one veteran, Obergrenadier Martin Eichenseer, recalled, you looked out into the dark 'until your eyes hurt'.

The patrols lasted for about three hours. The detachment would leave their *lager* (billet), then follow a specific route to an objective, and take another route back. For example, a nightly patrol from GR 726 went from their lager on the coast inland to the town of St Laurent, returning on a different route, and these routes varied each night. When assigned to this unit, Franz Gockel was very nervous on his first patrol, not knowing what to expect. During the course of the night he saw a small glowing light in the distance along the side of the road. He thought that it might be the tip of a commando's

GR 916 patrol on anti-invasion exercises, April/May 1944, hedgerows on either side of the road. Photograph taken by Obergrenadier Martin Eichenseer.

cigarette, laying in wait to ambush them. An older veteran calmed him down. It was just a glow worm; Gockel had never seen one before. But what about the screaming in the distance? Again the older man was amused; that, he told Gockel, was the 'call of Normandy', a braying donkey. While these comic moments served to break up the nightly drudgery, sometimes action did happen and on the same patrol route months later Gockel got a taste of combat:

> During the latter part of 1943 we were on our regular patrol route, this time we had dogs along with us. One of them began to bark pulling the man who held its lead towards the beach. We first thought that the dog had got the scent of a rabbit but when a shot rang out we knew differently. All hell broke loose and a firefight ensued. Our patrol leader fired a flare into the air, which signalled to all of the strongpoints to begin to fire in support of the strongpoint, which was under attack. It all stopped as quickly as it had started. When the smoke cleared, it was discovered that an English Commando team had been sent in to gather prisoners and information. Some of their dead were on the beach, in fact the first Allied soldiers to die on that beach. We gave them a decent burial, leaving some white crosses in the cemetery of St Laurent as reminders of that unlucky mission.

Of course these patrols were put to good use by some of the more 'entrepreneurial' men; they used them to scrounge for extra food or other items. Buying and trading with the locals could bring a fellow some good food or extra money. Of course there were those that stole outright what they could from the farmers and other units. The units most often robbed were the rear echelon, ones for whom the Grenadiers had a general dislike.

Left 'Where to Go in Paris?' guide for German troops visiting the city on leave.

Right French photographer advertising portrait services to German soldiers in a German guide to Paris.

After the completion of the patrol the Grenadier's duty day was not finished. There would still be an obligatory shift of guard duty before a man could get to bed. Those just coming in from patrols had shifts of one hour instead of the normal four. Either way, remembered Obergrenadier Wegner, it was very demanding on a man's endurance to come back after a long patrol, preceded by a full duty day, to stand guard or stare out into the blackness of the English Channel. Wegner admits that once while leaning against a bunker wall he fell asleep looking through a pair of binoculars. He stayed that way until his relief came.

With luck, nothing would happen during a man's shift. If something did occur, it only served to pass the time quicker, provided no one was shot at. Most often the guards were there to keep intruders from getting into restricted areas, but once Franz Gockel looked the other way:

> While on guard in the chateau that served as our unit's command post I encountered a French girl sneaking across the garden. I stopped her and told her it was too late to look for work, as we sometimes hired civilians for certain jobs. I then asked what she was doing here. She replied, in very bad German, 'My boyfriend has very much love for me,' at the same time motioning towards the chateau with her hand. Since it was not uncommon for us to have French girlfriends, as well as being young and sympathetic, I let her pass.

With all duties completed it was finally time for the enlisted man to get some sleep. The Allied soldiers went back to their barracks or tent to settle in, the former in narrow bunk beds and the latter in canvas and wooden cots. Those in the field on exercise had to sleep in their small 'pup' tents on the ground. This could cause some problems apart from sore backs and stiff limbs. Private Don Van Roosen, serving in the 115th Infantry Regiment/29th Division, slept on the cold wet ground of the Devon moors, awaking to find that side of his face that lay on the ground paralysed. He had to endure a long period of therapy with a very determined nurse before regaining normal speech and muscle action.

German Grenadiers were spread over a large area and a wide variety of lagers. The four-man zeltbahn tents – a longstanding shelter design with standardised dimensions and button holes that could be locked together to make larger tents – were the most rudimentary quarters. The tent slept three comfortably, the idea being that the fourth was on duty. When four were in the tent it was exceedingly cramped. With only his issue blanket for comfort the Grenadier froze on many a cold night. Larger tents accommodating 15-20 men and their equipment were available in small numbers, these being hoarded by rear echelon units. Those men with more luck found themselves billeted in large chateaux. The enlisted men were quartered in the servants' rooms or in the barns and stables.

With a little work the latter became quite comfortable when a unit set up housekeeping. Stoves, field beds, even 'borrowed' civilian beds were amongst the articles used to make the best of this accommodation. Officers and senior NCOs occupied the formal suites and

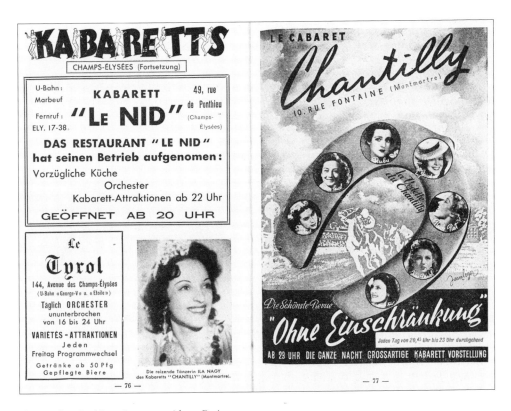

Shows advertised in a German guide to Paris.

bedrooms. Other officers enjoyed more private settings. Leutnant Heinze lived in a room of a house near the rectory in Formigny, which afforded him a much more peaceful atmosphere to rest, when given the opportunity. Even local farmers had soldiers billeted with them, if there was room and the farm was close to the soldier's duty station. Gefreiter Hein Severloh, along with several men from his detachment, I Batterie Artillerie Regiment 352, was in such a situation. The older couple that owned the farm put up with them, the wife even became something of a substitute mother to the young German men.

A soldier in 352. Infanterie-Division could alternatively find himself in one of the prepared positions along the coast, officially called *Widerstandsnest*; a resistance point, better known as a strongpoint. Each one was numbered in sequence along the coast and was referred to in this way, for example, WN (Widerstandsnest) 62. Each WN would have several gun positions, an observation bunker or two, infantry positions and enough *Mannschaft* (personnel bunkers) for those stationed there. The average bunker had rows of bunks, some built directly into the walls, three-high. Each bunk was narrow and contained a thin mattress with blanket, sheet and pillow. Tables and chairs were supplied along with a wood or coal stove. Electric lights were available, but most used kerosene lamps.

The chateaux and farmhouses had latrine and washing facilities readily available. Those in other locations had to provide latrines for themselves. In the WNs there were modern latrines while elsewhere the traditional hole in the ground with a multiple seat made of tree limbs called a 'Thunder Pole' was in use. As for bathing, streams, ponds and the English Channel made this easy though army showers were quite sought after and in short supply. In Wegner's company the men turned a gasoline tank from a tractor into a shower. This tank was heated by a fire, allowing for hot showers. For a time the bathers smelled of gasoline, despite the multiple cleanings given to the tank.

The GIs in the tent cities of England were in similar conditions but not so for those stationed in English barracks. These varied in size and age but had all the facilities found in barracks around the world. Private Milton Burke, K Co./116th Infantry Regiment, 29th Division, was fortunate to be assigned to barracks in the city of Plymouth. His barrack was directly across from the 118th's regimental headquarters. His comments are typical of those so blessed with these accommodations:

> The British barracks we had were pretty old but we had all the comforts of home plus one extra advantage. We were close enough to town so we could walk into Plymouth every night, provided we had the time off and the money.

Time off duty is very important to every soldier and when it came, the usual thing to do was to get to the nearest town and find some entertainment. The towns of England near large groupings of GIs found themselves invaded at every opportunity. Some men looked for a drink and female companionship, while others sought a quiet night of going to see a film and getting a civilian meal. Private Burke would usually go into town for a beer then go to the local cinema. He was surprised at the difference between American and English theatres:

> In England we discovered that people were allowed to smoke; it was a fire hazard back home. The theatres ran quite a few commercials and public service announcements between the films. I remember one in particular of this fellow, putting row upon row of toothpaste on his

Fine example of zeltbahns used to make an eight-man tent. Mess kits hang on the right next to two large ration sacks. Laundry hang out to dry on the left.

Officers in the field enjoyed more comforts than the enlisted man. Along with tents constructed from multiple zeltbahn sections are tables, chairs, liquid refreshment and even cots for sleeping.

Standard four-man zeltbahn tent. Only three men could sleep comfortably inside. One man would be on guard duty at all times.

Standard German infantry platoon baggage wagon. The German Army in the Second World War had more horse flesh than motor 'HP'.

Two members of Pionier-Bataillon 352 stand next to their vehicle. Note the Divisional insignia on the door and the damage to the spare wheel. The Pionier on the left wears a captured British battle dress and trousers dyed black for use by mechanics and others who would deal with machinery. Photograph taken by Josef Brass.

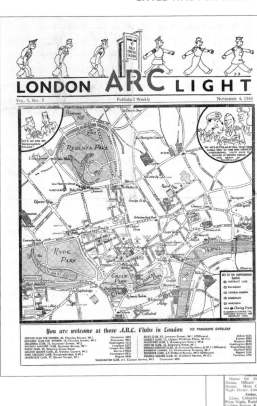

London *ARC Light* (front), the American Red Cross newsletter for US troops stationed in England. It contained information regarding what shows were on and things to do when off duty.

ARC Light (back).

The *Sternenbanner*, the US military's *Stars and Stripes* newspaper printed in German to drop on enemy troops as propaganda.

toothbrush with the narrator telling everyone that we all should use it sparingly since it was in short supply. I was puzzled by this, since we had more than enough of it and the PX had more. Sometimes we would take in a play because during the intermission the theatres would open up a bar, which was well stocked and fairly priced. Some of the pubs charged us more, which wasn't right, but in general I liked the British and we got on well with them.

The relationship between the English populace and US troops was, for the most, very good. Thousands of GIs met English girls and married them whilst others had their sweethearts amongst the locals. This, sadly but inevitably, was a sore point between English and American soldiers. The 'Tommy' began to resent the better paid and provisioned 'Yank' who was able to draw away the women in the pubs and dance halls. This, on occasion, did lead to fights amongst the Allies. Of course one might wonder where this energy came from after being put through such exhaustive training, but according to Private Van Roosen, 'We could always find the strength to go into town for a beer at the pub!' Anyone who has served in the military will know how men will muster up their last ounce of energy when told they have the night off. Any chance of getting away from army life was never passed up, although a portion of the men would stay behind in the empty quarters to savour the peace and quiet. The US Army provided books and magazines such as *Yank* or *Stars and Stripes*. Men without any money could enjoy a film for free at the camp theatre.

If the USO (United Services Organization) was around there was the chance of a good show with 'real live dames' and stars such as Glenn Miller, Jack Benny or the devoted Bob Hope. Americans did all they could for their men overseas. Finally, there was no stopping prostitution with so many men about. Despite counselling against it on moral grounds the US Army realised that it was going to happen and made a 'Pro-Kit' available to GIs, containing condoms and disinfectants.

Obviously the German Grenadiers sought the same types of entertainment. Things in the German Army were different, especially since they were a hostile occupying army. The Grenadiers' relationship with the local population dictated any extra activities. One of the first things that comes to mind when wartime France is discussed is the Resistance, the *Maquis*. Within the 352nd's area there was very little active resistance prior to the invasion. Most of the Maquis' activity here seems to have been information gathering. The 352nd recorded no combat incidents with them during their occupation. There are several reasons for this but perhaps Obergefreiter Josef Brass explains it best:

I was first in France during the early part of the war and then sent to Russia. For the most part, both before and after my service at the front, the French people were amiable towards us. Some hated us and were probably in the Maquis, others supported us, the collaborators, but most were just concerned with getting on with everyday life. Of course we heard stories of German soldiers being attacked by the Maquis but these troops were usually older men of supply and garrison units. Then there were those foolish enough to venture down dark lonely roads to get robbed and killed. Our units were never attacked by the Maquis because we were a combat unit with machine guns and support weapons. These men may have hated us but not enough to ensure death by attacking a well armed and trained unit.

Left German troops amuse themselves on bicycle patrol in occupied France 1942. Photograph taken by Obergefreiter Josef Brass.

Right Landsers have fun with straw boaters, an umbrella and French flag. This was the lighter side of occupation duty.

Left Obergefreiter Josef Brass, whilst a member of 1st Squad, 1st platoon, 1st Company of 321 Pionier Bataillon. Taken during the summer of 1941 at Le Touquet, France.

Right Josef Brass as a Private in 321 Pionier Bataillon enjoying the peaceful days of his occupation duties in France, 1942.

A SPECIAL LOW RATE TO THE ARMED FORCES ABROAD

1261

EXPEDITIONARY FORCE MESSAGE

WESTERN UNION
CABLEGRAM

CHECK

EFM

ACCOUNTING INFORMATION

TIME FILED

A. N. WILLIAMS
PRESIDENT

NEWCOMB CARLTON
CHAIRMAN OF THE BOARD

J. C. WILLEVER
FIRST VICE-PRESIDENT

Send the following message, subject to the terms of the Western Union Telegraph Company, which are hereby agreed to

PLACE   DATE   194___

EXPEDITIONARY FORCE MESSAGE (E.F.M.) available between the United States and Other Countries to and from members of the Overseas Forces.

To **EFM**

(RANK)   (FULL NAME)   (SERIAL NUMBER)

E.F.M. SERVICE

Address **APO** ___
(ARMY POST OFFICE NUMBER OR CODE)   (CODE WORD FOR DESTINATION)

Sender may select as many as three of the numbered texts shown on reverse side for transmission abroad as one message.

Via ___
(NEW YORK OR SAN FRANCISCO)

Texts Desired No.___ No.___ No.___
(Select and Indicate by Number)

MADE OR AMOUNT
UP TO 66 INSERTED

FLAT CHARGE 60 CENTS per message

(Signed) ___

(plus Government Tax of 6 Cents)

Name of Sender ___

Address of Sender ___

YOU MAY WISH TO TAKE YOUR CHANGE IN WAR S

Western Union form (front). Used by servicemen to exchange short-form messages with loved ones at home. PFC Merle Hescock.

Western Union (back). A list of useful standard form messages was available if the correspondent was in a hurry or had difficulty writing.

A German Soldbuch showing typical contents: French and German money, a photograph of a sweetheart and an unused brothel pass.

FIXED TEXTS FOR EXPEDITIONARY FORCE MESSAGES

(A) CORRESPONDENCE
1 ☐ Letter received. Many thanks.
2 ☐ Letters received. Many thanks.
3 ☐ Telegram received. Many thanks.
4 ☐ Parcel received. Many thanks.
5 ☐ Parcels received. Many thanks.
6 ☐ Letters and parcels received. Many thanks.
7 ☐ Letter and telegram received. Many thanks.
8 ☐ Telegram and parcels received. Many thanks.
9 ☐ Letters sent.
10 ☐ Parcels sent.
11 ☐ Letters and parcels sent.
12 ☐ Many thanks for letter.
13 ☐ Many thanks for parcel.
14 ☐ Many thanks for telegram.
15 ☐ No news of you for some time.
16 ☐ Writing.
17 ☐ Urgent.
18 ☐ Please write or telegraph.
19 ☐ Please write.
20 ☐ Please telegraph.
21 ☐ Please reply. Worried.

(B) GREETINGS
26 ☐ Greetings.
27 ☐ Loving greetings.
28 ☐ Fondest greetings.
29 ☐ Love.
30 ☐ Darling.
31 ☐ All my love.
32 ☐ All my love dearest.

33 ☐ All our love.
34 ☐ Fondest love.
35 ☐ Fondest love darling.
36 ☐ Best wishes.
37 ☐ Greetings from us all.
38 ☐ Loving greetings from all of us.
39 ☐ Best wishes from all of us.
40 ☐ Fondest wishes from all of us.
41 ☐ Best wishes and good health.
42 ☐ Kisses.
43 ☐ Love and kisses.
44 ☐ Fondest love and kisses.
45 ☐ Well.
46 ☐ All well at home.
47 ☐ Best wishes for Christmas.
48 ☐ Best wishes for Christmas and New Year.
49 ☐ Loving wishes for Christmas.
50 ☐ Loving wishes for Christmas and New Year.
51 ☐ Loving Christmas thoughts.
52 ☐ Happy Christmas.
53 ☐ Happy Christmas and New Year.
54 ☐ Good luck.
55 ☐ Keep smiling.
56 ☐ My thoughts are with you.
57 ☐ Many happy returns.
58 ☐ Birthday greetings.
59 ☐ Loving birthday greetings.
60 ☐ Happy anniversary.
61 ☐ You are more than ever in my thoughts at this time.
62 ☐ Best wishes for a speedy return.
63 ☐ Good show. Keep it up.
64 ☐ Best wishes for New Year.

(C) HEALTH
68 ☐ Family all well.
69 ☐ All well. Children evacuated.
70 ☐ All well. Children returned home.
71 ☐ All well and safe.
72 ☐ Are you all right?
73 ☐ Are you all right? Worried about you.
74 ☐ Please don't worry.
75 ☐ Hope you are improving.
76 ☐ Please telegraph that you are well.
77 ☐ Are you ill?
78 ☐ Have you been ill?
79 ☐ Illness is not serious.
80 ☐ Illness is serious.
81 ☐ I have left hospital.
82 ☐ In bad health.
83 ☐ Health improving.
84 ☐ Health fully restored.
85 ☐ Son born.
86 ☐ Daughter born.

(D) PROMOTION
91 ☐ Congratulations on your promotion.
92 ☐ Very pleased to hear of your promotion.
93 ☐ Delighted hear about your promotion.

(E) MONEY
98 ☐ Please send me.....pounds.
99 ☐ Please send me.....dollars.
100 ☐ Have sent you.....pounds.

101 ☐ Have sent you.....dollars.
     NOTE: The actual amount in words to be inserted and transmitted immediately following the text number.
102 ☐ Can you send me any money?
103 ☐ Glad if you could send some money.
104 ☐ Have received money.
105 ☐ Have you received money?
106 ☐ Have you sent money?
107 ☐ Thanks for money received.
108 ☐ Have not received money.
109 ☐ Unable to send money.
110 ☐ Sorry cannot send money.

(F) CONGRATULATIONS
115 ☐ Congratulations on anniversary. Best wishes.
116 ☐ Congratulations. Lasting happiness to you both.
117 ☐ Glad and proud to hear of your decoration. Everybody thrilled.
118 ☐ Loving greetings and congratulations.
119 ☐ Good luck. Keep it up.
120 ☐ I wish we were together on this special occasion. All my best wishes for a speedy reunion.

(G) NOT AVAILABLE

(H) MISCELLANEOUS
135 ☐ Very happy to hear from you, dearest. Am fit and well.
136 ☐ Hearing your voice on the wireless gave me a wonderful thrill.

Members of 321. Infanterie-Division obtain essential supplies from surly looking Frenchmen. The wine and beer will be appreciated by their Kameraden back in garrison. (J. Brass)

There are many documented attacks attributed to the Maquis throughout France. Obergrenadier Wegner offers a different view:

> In our company there was an Unteroffizier who was in France before being sent to Russia. He told us, the new men, that while serving here before he had been involved in some actions against the Resistance. But that most of the time the dead and prisoners turned out to be English Commandos. It was his opinion that most attacks were done by the English but the General Staff told everyone it was the Maquis because it would not be good for morale if everyone knew that the Tommies could come and go in France any time they wished.

As to the off-duty life of the Grenadier in Normandy, it should be remembered that the men of the 352nd and other regular units of the armed forces were not on the same footing as SS or Police formations. Those troops responsible for enforcing the regulations of the occupation were just as harsh to any German soldier that broke the rules as they were to the French. The majority of Grenadiers in the 352nd were young men from the farming areas of Germany, and had much in common with the local French. The veterans of the 352nd state that there were strict instructions from the divisional commander, Generalleutnant Kraiss, to be proper and polite at all times when in contact with the locals. This meant on and off duty.

This is not to say that every man in the 352nd was a paragon of virtue. There are many French who can recall being maltreated by the Germans, but one or two pub owners in England might have said that of the Allied soldiers. Since he was stationed in France the longest, Franz Gockel had many contacts with the local people:

> We enjoyed contact with the French in Colleville and St Laurent, mostly with the families whom we paid to do our laundry or the farms where we bought milk, butter and eggs. In St Laurent there was a family with two 'life happy' daughters, 17 and 18 years old. These two took in our laundry. One day a 17-year-old friend of mine from Köln had returned from gathering our washing. He told us that one of the girls was very much in love with him and had even given him her ring.

A light-hearted moment of celebration for a Kamerad's birthday, before the invasion, breaks the monotony of security patrols and endless drills.

In Colleville we would hang around this farm where we bought butter and milk because the farmer had a very cute daughter. She spoke German very well and was much courted. Here we would cook our meals in an old fashioned fire place, but at another farm not too far away there was a big modern kitchen. Also in Colleville were the Company Headquarters, the armoury and the canteen. At the canteen one could buy up to 30kg of meat and some butter when going on leave. Close to the canteen was a pretty cafe that we would frequent and often talk with the villagers.

From Gockel's account it would seem odd that there was a shortage of meat for meals but that a soldier could buy it at the canteen. But only a soldier going on leave could purchase this ration. This was more of a propaganda decision than one based on common sense, to persuade those at home that the war was going well. This ration was much appreciated when a soldier brought it home regardless.

The canteen, *Kantina*, was similar to the US PX (Post Exchange). Here a man could buy food and everything from a flashlight to spare socks. Films were shown at special soldiers' theatres, *Soldatenkinos*, and passes were issued for local civilian theatres. All were free to soldiers. Books and magazines were provided. Periodicals such as *Signal* and *Die Wehrmacht* and newspapers were available. These were saturated with political propaganda but the pictures were entertaining. *Signal* even had a 'pin-up girl' in every issue. The most sought-after magazines were pre-war French pornography. Despite their prohibition according to National Socialist doctrines, everyone seemed to be able to get them if they wanted them. There was also a German version of the American's USO or the British ENSA (Entertainments National Service Association, or 'Every Night

Something Awful') with travelling groups of entertainers. These troupes had both German and foreign acts.

One 'entertainment' supplied to the German Grenadier was unavailable to the GI or Tommy. This was the military brothel, in all its German regimentation. These establishments were separated according to rank, officer then senior NCO, and finally the enlisted men. In most cases senior officers did not frequent such places. A high percentage of these officers were from the 'Old Prussian' school of thought where such things were simply not done. For the younger officers the brothels were required by regulation to be more 'hotel like' in their atmosphere, with women of higher 'quality' and dining available. In the other brothels the men were segregated by rank and status. But for all, there was a regulation procedure for admittance. Obergefreiter Josef Brass:

> When one of the men wished to visit one of the local military brothels the first thing he had to do was go to the medical Feldwebel and get the proper pass. This was a small form which certified that the soldier, after a short but embarrassing examination, was free from any sexual diseases. It also contained the name, number, and location of the establishment. But most important was the space where your partner would have to sign her name. In this way the army would know where and who had given you a disease, and who else might have been infected. With this pass you were given a condom and a small spray can of disinfectant, then sent off with the Army and the Führer's approval. At the brothel the pass was checked by the Military Police in order to be let in.

The man would then pick a girl or wait in line if there were too many men and not enough women. Afterwards the girl would only sign the pass after he had disinfected her

Paris in the spring of 1944. Leutnant Heinze (left) and Leutnant Maas (right) enjoy a day horse riding.

Der Polizeipräsident
4.Polizei-Revier.

Düsseldorf,den 25.10.1943.

<u>B e s c h e i n i g u n g !</u>

Dem - Der Ehefrau - Frl. *Ogfr. Hans Braß* wohnhaft gewesen *Oberbilker Allee* Str.Nr.*157*, jetzt wohnhaft *Silberg br.Olpe* str......., wird auf Wunsch bescheinigt, dass seine - ihre - die Wohnung - der Eltern und Geschäftslokal, infolge eines feindlichen Fliegerangriffs am *12.6.* 194*3* durch Abwurf von Brand- und Sprengbomben, beschädigt - vollständig zerstört - wurde und geräumt werden mußte. *Totalschaden.*

Nur gültig zur Vorlage beim Wirtschaftsamt - Ernährungsamt - Arbeitgeber - Kriegssachschädenamt - N.S.V. - Truppenteil - Standortältesten.

J.a.

Fisk
(Stempel)
Meister d. Sch.

Zum frommen Andenken

an unsern innigstgeliebten, hoffnungsvollen Sohn und unsern herzensguten Bruder

Hans Braß

Gefr. in einem Gren.-Rgt.
Inh. des Verw.-Abz. und des Kriegsverdienst-
kreuzes mit Schwertern.

Er fand im Alter von 20 1/2 Jahren bei den schweren Abwehrkämpfen im Osten, westlich Brest-Litowsk am 28. Juli 1944 den Heldentod.
Wir erfahren durch seinen Komp.-Führer, daß er als tüchtiger, pflichttreuer Soldat jedem ihm aufgetragenen Befehl gerecht zu werden versuchte. Wegen seines vornehmen und bescheidenen Wesens machte er sich bei seinen Vorgesetzten und Kameraden sehr beliebt. Alle die ihn kannten können unsern Schmerz verstehen. Der Glaube an ein Jenseits gibt uns Kraft.

Gebet.

Herr, auch das ferne Kriegergrab ist ein Stück Heimaterde, liebend schaust Du drauf hinab, bis ertönt Dein göttlich Werde. Bis die große Ewigkeit endet alles Erdenleid. Amen.

H/0011

Ach es ist ja kaum zu fassen,
Daß du nicht mehr kehrst zurück
So jung mußt du dein Leben lassen
Zerstört ist unser ganzes Glück.
Ein jeder der dich hat gekannt
Und auch dein gutes Herz
Der drückt uns nur noch stumm die Hand
In diesem tiefen Schmerz.
Du gutes Herz ruh still in Frieden
Ewig beweint von deinen Lieben.

Opposite above Notification certificate, dated 25 October 1943, from the police of his home town, sent to Obergefreiter Josef Brass, informing him that his parents' house in Düsseldorf had been totally destroyed by incendiary and explosive bombs during an air raid.

Opposite below Death card of Josef Brass' brother Hans, killed in action in Russia, 28 July 1944, the same day Josef arrived in the US as a PoW.

Obergefreiter Josef Brass (left) on leave in 1942 visiting his brother Hans, in the Kaserne at Herford. Hans was killed in action fighting the Red Army at Brest-Litovsk in Poland.

genital area with the contents of the spray can, which once empty had to be brought back to the medical Feldwebel. If a soldier did not do this he was subject to harsh punishments. With such stringent formalities many of the younger, sexually inexperienced men did not go to the brothels at all and others went to the traditional civilian ones. However, if a man were infected with a venereal disease from a non-military brothel, punishment came in the form of service in a penal battalion.

The Medical Service regulated the brothels; indeed each brothel had a medical station in it. But enforcement was by the Military Police, the Feldgendarmerie. The 'Chained Dogs,' so called by the soldiers because of the gorgets that hung around their necks, were an unsympathetic outfit. Men were arrested for such trivialities as holding the hands of a woman in public, forbidden by military regulations unless the woman was a spouse, relative, officially engaged, or when dancing. Men came back to their units bruised and beaten after their short visits with the Chained Dogs. Obergrenadier Wegner recalled that it seemed as though the more combat decorations one had, the more punches one was given. Needless to say, these troops were despised by the common soldier.

The GI and Tommy had to contend with their own MPs but they did not enforce the regulations with such brutality, although it may be hard to convince some of this. The combat soldier could not understand why these MPs would bother him about not wear-

This photograph was brought home amongst the souvenirs of an American veteran. It is captioned on the back 'Gefr. Lerbiske AR 1 716'. It clearly illustrates the older, less physically fit men that typically comprised Artillerie Regiment 716, stationed in the vicinity of the Omaha sector. Note the lack of leggings and belts, which indicates that the photograph was likely taken in or near their billets, otherwise a belt had to be worn.

ing a tie or for wearing a uniform that was just a little dirty. After all, sooner or later he would be in battle and the enemy did not care whether he was properly attired or not. Overall the Military Police units of both armies played important roles but were held in low regard by those over whom they watched.

As stated before, in spite of all the official rules about fraternisation many soldiers developed relationships with the locals. The young men began to miss the life left behind so very far away. For a lucky few a chance posting or meeting gave them a second family. Gefreiter Hein Severloh was one. When he was billeted at the farm in Angers the farmer's wife was very much a mother to him and the other young men there. She cooked all their meals with care, making them sit and eat like a family. She mended uniforms and cared for them when they were sick. He was heartbroken when the 352nd moved up to the coast; 45 years later while visiting the area he found the old farm once more. To his astonishment his French 'Mother' was still living there. She instantly remembered her 'Hein'. Once more he slept in the bed he had occupied so many years before, one pleasant memory of Normandy. This was the same for some American lads and the kindly British folk that took them into their homes as one of their own.

Mail Call was the only connection with home the soldiers enjoyed. Naturally with the amounts of mail being handled, delivery was slow. Families sent cakes, extra socks and photographs, all of it deeply appreciated. For the German, mail from home meant more than just the possibility of presents. To those that lived in or near large cities it meant that

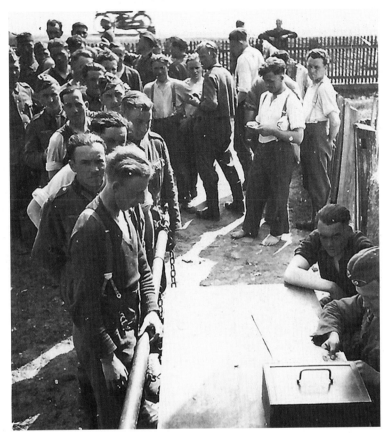

The day soldiers
most looked
forward to – pay day.

someone in the family was still alive. At this stage of the war Allied air raids were devastating German industrial centres. The fear of many Grenadiers was getting the official letter from the local police or town hall; they always brought bad news. Obergefreiter Brass, who lived in Düsseldorf, received one such letter. When he got over the initial shock he opened it and was relieved to learn that his parents had been bombed out but were alive and being relocated. He had lost his home but not his family. When a soldier received no mail for a long period of time the worst was assumed, that his family had been killed in the bombing but that the bodies had not been found or identified.

For the American or German soldier, sending mail home, providing they had the time or energy to write, was simple. Mail services were free no matter the size of the item. It is interesting to note that at this point in the war, there were more packages sent home than received by the German soldier, primarily due to the rationing in Germany. Soldiers sent home what they could to aid their families. Karl Wegner did not smoke, but got a tobacco issue just like everyone else. He sent his ration home to his father. His father received enough every month to enable him to trade the surplus for other items. Of course, all mail was censored. Germany was much stricter than the Allies. Many a soldier and family opened letters to find blacked-out passages. Security was the main reason for this but in Germany the wrong statement could get you arrested.

Extended leave was a rich prize on both sides of the Channel. A three-day pass was welcomed by men as a high award for services rendered. Many GIs went to London or other

Oberst Ernst Goth's *soldbuch*. Regardless of rank every member of the German Army was required to carry a soldbuch that contained a full record of weapons, uniforms and items issued. It also included authorised awards and medals, military medical history and pay grade status. In the back was a pocket used to hold orders, passes and other paperwork. (M. Galle)

large cities where there was plenty of nightlife such as clubs and theatres. A smaller number travelled to England's country resorts for rest and solitude.

German soldiers were able to travel home when given leave; leave durations were from 10 to 21 days, the average being 14. However, it was not as simple as getting a pass and hopping on the next train home; it was a rather involved procedure. When a Grenadier had his name come up on the leave list, he reported to his company headquarters. Here he would be given all the pertinent paperwork and his *Soldbuch* (identity and stamped pay book). This was a very important document, containing all of the bearer's military history, all written orders issued and the destination and length of his leave. If the soldier was not in possession of this book with its orders and was far from his unit he could face trial as a deserter by the military police.

With all the formalities complete the Grenadier was on his way, and he could go to the Kaserne to purchase anything he might wish to bring home. The military also provided a parcel of foodstuffs for returning men called a *Führergeschenk* (Gift from the Führer). Then one final check of paperwork and uniform before leaving the company area and he was on the first leg of his trip to the local train station. Upon reaching the station he was required to report to the officer in charge of the depot. This meant another check of paperwork and registering that this soldier did in fact get on his train. While waiting on the platform he was under the watchful eyes of the 'Chained Dogs'. One small infraction of regulations could mean a soldier's leave delayed or cancelled, and Grenadiers often watched in silent contempt as their comrades were dragged away because of an improper haircut or dirty

A wedding ceremony in the field. The soldier's bride would be performing the same ceremony at the same time back home in Germany.

Example of a military marriage eligibility certificate showing that the union of the soldier and would be wife would not be a 'detriment' to the German people.

Amtsärztliche*)
Ärztliche **Bescheinigung**

über die Untersuchung auf Eignung zur Ehe

Ich bescheinige hierdurch, daß

Herr — ~~Frau~~ x x ~~Fräulein~~   Obltn. L e t t o w   Klaus

wohnhaft in   Feldpostnummer L.- 14 217   Lg.P.A. Wien

Kreis ....   -.-   ....   Nr. ....

von mir auf Eignung zur Ehe untersucht worden ist.

Nach den Angaben des — der Untersuchten und den angestellten Ermittlungen besteht kein Verdacht für das Vorhandensein von vererblichen geistigen oder körperlichen Gebrechen.   Es bestehen bei dem derzeitigen allgemeinen Gesundheitszustand ärztlicherseits auch sonst keine Bedenken, die seine — ihre Verheiratung nicht als im Interesse der Volksgemeinschaft liegend erscheinen lassen.

Ich versichere, die vorstehenden Angaben nach bestem Wissen und Gewissen gemacht zu haben.

O.U.   29. November   19 44

                        Stabsarzt und Truppenarzt.

*) Nichtzutreffendes ist zu durchstreichen.

S. 111. Waisenhaus-Buchdruckerei Kassel (1938.)   Din A 5

Unterschafühher Freddie Schmidtz (right) who served as a member of the 17th SS Division 'Goetz von Berlichingen' in Normandy. He was on furlough, which saved him from being returned to the Eastern Front to fight against the massive Soviet summer offensive of 1944. His brother Peter Schmidtz (left), a tank crewman, was killed in action during this Soviet thrust. The badge that Freddie wears on his tunic breast pocket is a Flak badge of the Luftwaffe pattern, not the authorised German Army pattern.

A group of men from GR 914 visit Verdun just prior to the invasion. On the right, pointing, is the company Hauptfeldwebel (1st Sergeant). On his right is Obergefreiter Paul Kalb.

uniform. Any sort of a protest would result in the onlooker being taken away as well. With a little luck the train came soon.

The longer it took to get home the shorter the leave. From Normandy, excluding any delays caused by bombings, a man could be home in about two days. If the train stopped for the night or the Grenadier had a changeover delay to get another train he was required to report to the Army transport and control office at the depot. Here, for overnight stays, he would be allotted sleeping quarters and rations.

If an emergency arose he could be called upon to assist the local army command. This also applied whilst travelling on the train. The German soldier always travelled with his weapon and full pack. In the morning he would line up at this office once more to be checked out, and long lines caused many men to miss trains and connections. Experienced men rose very early or slept out in front of the office to ensure a swift departure.

At any of these offices or stops, bad news could wreck plans. Men from larger cities would be told that travel to them was suspended until further notice because of bombing. Those travelling to them would have to be given another destination, perhaps a rest camp or the town of another relative. Most towns had a *Soldatenheim* (soldiers' home) where these luckless fellows could rest, hard to do if one had family in the bombed city. It was not uncommon to find men wasting their leaves waiting for trains that never came or cleaning up debris from air raids. Others would give up and go back to their units where at least they would have the company of their friends. The majority did get home, of course reporting to the transport and control office before their loved ones, but being home could be more of a burden than a relief. *Unterscharführer* Ferdinand 'Freddie' Schmidtz was home on leave in Köln from his unit, 10. SS Panzer-Division 'Frundsberg', awaiting transfer back to the Ostfront.

> This was the first time in two years that I had been home, basically since the invasion of Russia. It had been a long journey back from the Eastern Front and not a peaceful one either. Where my unit was there were many Partisans so when we travelled to the rear it was in a tank and you could hear the bullets bouncing off its side. Back home it was much worse, the English by day and the Americans by night. To tell the truth I wished I had stayed in Russia.

For those who did not go home, Paris was a magnet; one could get anything one desired there. The black market flourished but it was expensive, and a few men opted to stay with their units and relax, making short trips, especially those with French girlfriends. At the end of a soldier's leave the trip back had all the same requirements as the one home, but it was not minded as much since smart men could extend their leaves officially by a day or two.

Private Milton Burke of the US Army came back from a pass at the end of May 1944 when he and the rest of the 29th Division were sealed in secluded camps to be briefed on the invasion:

> We didn't believe it was true, we thought they were crazy or that it was a drill because we had landed at places like Slapton Sands. After a day or two it gradually sank in that this was IT. We weren't too worried then, but hell – I didn't know what I was getting into anyhow.

three

THE STORM BREAKS

S UMMER was still officially a month away, but the final days of May 1944 let those in Normandy feel that it was almost upon them. The nights were still chilly but the days were sunny and warm. The weather mirrored the mood of Generalleutnant Kraiss. The progress report he had received from Oberstleutnant Ziegelmann showed results better than expected. Of the three main missions assigned to it the 352nd had attained, in Ziegelmann's view, the following levels:

1 The 352nd was prepared for combat actions in either offensive or defensive roles.
2 The battle area assigned to them, both coastal and inland, had been greatly improved despite all the persistent problems but Ziegelmann made it clear that this area was not properly fortified to withstand a major enemy attack. This was echoed by Generalleutnant Kraiss in his reports to LXXXIV Armeekorps.
3 The individual and small unit training was progressing well with all of the units rating a combat-effective status far above the other units in the area. However, the goals set by Generalleutnant Kraiss had not been reached as yet.

Nevertheless, the shortages of supplies and ammunition had greatly affected the training of specialised troops. To illustrate this, consider the *Panzerjäger* (anti-tank) companies. These units were armed with PAK anti-tank guns and a few *Panzerschreck* (bazookas). The munitions supplies allowed them only five rounds per month per company for target practice. The large array of foreign guns in their inventory of varying calibres made the situation worse. The guns were not alone in this. A good portion of the 352nd's motor transport was also non-German with replacement parts either hard to get or unobtainable. Kraiss knew quite well the equipment limitations so he redoubled his efforts with regards to his men.

So far he had forged young men who could meet and beat the Russians in battle when the 352nd was sent east. Further study of the Normandy situation convinced him that his division would remain in a defensive posture there. Very few of those in the Officer

A rather exposed and incomplete coastal artillery position along the Atlantik Wall. Positions like this suffered heavy casualties during the invasion.

Corps agreed with him but Kraiss followed his intuition. He changed the orders of the Korpsreserve, under Meyer, to practise attacking the village of Crepon from the Seulles river, a move that might be important in the defence of the coast.; there were small indications that this might happen for real very soon.

When the first day of June rolled around, Major Block, 352nd's Intelligence Officer, had received several reports of low-level air reconnaissance/photograph flights by Allied aircraft. Carrier pigeon traffic to England had increased heavily. The sharpshooters placed along the coast had brought down a large number of them, far more than normal. The cryptic messages the birds carried were sent to Major Block to be deciphered. One message from the Maquis in Criqueville stated that the positions along the Normandy coast had been greatly strengthened and that a landing there would be very difficult. Others detailed, to the surprise of many German intelligence officers including Block, the strength and dispositions of units along the coast. For every bird brought down many more got through. However, it appears that none of the messages pertaining to the 352nd's new position got through to Allied intelligence officers, since the presence of the 352nd on the coast was a total surprise to the forces that landed there.

Most of the low-level passes by Allied aircraft had been on or just behind the beaches. Occasionally these flights were followed by bombers attacking certain targets that included the batteries of Artillerie Regiment 1716, Heeres Küstenartillerie Abteilung 1260, Kriegsmarine and Luftwaffe gun and range-finding emplacements. Rumours abounded of a vast fleet just across the English Channel waiting for the order to sail. Something was happening, but not all agreed on what. Grenadier Franz Gockel remembered that just before the invasion the men in his strongpoint, WN62, had a discussion with the officer of the artillery observation team there. The officer, Oberleutnant Frerking of Artillerie Regiment 352, was convinced that the Allies would not land there because it would be too

Major Werner Pluskat, in centre holding a riding crop, Kommander der I/Artillerie Regiment 352. By all the accounts of the surviving men of WN62's Artillery OP, he was not on the beach on 6 June 1944. Second from left, wearing a peaked cap and riding breeches, is Oberleutnant Frerking, Batterieschef der 1 Batterie of I/Artillerie Regiment 352. He was with Hein Severloh directing the fire of his guns onto the Americans who landed. He was killed in action on 6 June 1944. (Hein Severloh)

costly in lives to take the stretch of beach. He said he knew the Ivans from his service in Russia and even they would not decide to land there. Most of the older men in Gockel's company disagreed with Frerking, bringing up memories of the raid on Dieppe two years before. No one was sure of the details, but Generalleutnant Kraiss and his staff also felt that some sort of invasion would occur shortly and wherever it occurred, the 352nd would be involved because of its reserve missions. Even so, it was not until 1 June that Kraiss had any solid information with which to initiate action.

In the morning an officer in the Maquis was captured in Brittany. At his interrogation he revealed that the invasion force was to land in Normandy some time during the first week of June. When notified of this, Kraiss compiled it with all his other findings in a report to his superiors. He requested permission to put all units along the coast on alert. OKW in Berlin turned him down as being too alarmist; after all they had solid proof that the Allies would land at the Pas de Calais. These generals had been fooled completely by a masterful Allied ruse. Kraiss was positive that Normandy was the place; even General Marcks, his superior at LXXXIV Armeekorps, agreed with him but did not have the authority to override OKW. The remarkable – not to say astonishing – story of the intelligence garnered from the Maquis officer is found in US Army Intelligence Document MS-B 432 (a series on 352. Infanterie-Division, 1947) which was the series of debriefings of Oberstleutnant Ziegelmann in captivity.

This left Kraiss in an invidious situation; if he put his division on alert, the correct thing to do he believed, he could be relieved of his command. If he did not, many of his men would be caught off guard and needlessly killed. Kraiss discussed the matter with his staff and Ziegelmann found the answer to this problem. The whole of the 7. Armee was having scheduled war games for the entire first week of June. All the local divisional commanders were required to report to Rennes for these operations. Most units would not be taking part, the games being carried out by the generals with their maps, but some units would stage actual operations with blank ammunition. Ziegelmann noted that this would give them the excuse they needed to put the 352nd on alert, enabling Kraiss to declare that it was part of 7. Armee operations. But he strongly recommended to his General that he tell his men the truth about it being a real alert, noting that soldiers unsurprisingly did not take war games as seriously as real action.

On 4 June, a Sunday, 352. Infanterie-Division was on full alert, the only unit in all of Normandy waiting for the real Allied invasion. Generalleutnant Kraiss elected to stay in Littry at the 352nd HQ; he would stay with his men and not go to Rennes. If he was right, this was the place to be.

From Isigny to Caen, the Grenadiers of the 352nd looked out onto La Manche, *Ärmelkanal*, hoping that they would not see the Allied fleet they were told would come. Between the little villages of Vierville and Colleville all was calm. Reports to Oberst Goth, Commander of Grenadier Regiment 916 and this sector, stated that all was normal. As his men stared out into the Channel from the heights above, a beach that would forever be known as 'Bloody Omaha' now lay quietly before them.

Beyond the sight of all the Germans on the Normandy coast the preparations of the Allied armada were in full swing. Vast numbers of men were assembling. Amongst them was Private Don Van Roosen:

Oberst Ernst Goth briefs his officers on Omaha Beach prior to the invasion. (M. Galle)

Our preparations really began in Camp Raleigh near Bournemouth where we were isolated in late May. On Sunday 28 May we boarded boats and were ferried out to the LCIs [landing craft infantry] in the harbour. There we would stay for the next six days in very cramped quarters, with poor food and little to do but sweat out the time.

We did get some exercise in on a couple of days and that helped pass some of the time. The weather was good so we sat on the decks and waited.

While the Tommies and GIs sat on decks or were crammed in below them, boredom was their worst enemy. The Grenadiers of the 352nd did not enjoy this luxury. Even though on alert, construction work continued and those units not directly on the coastline kept training. Oberst Meyer and the Korpsreserve kept training on attacking objectives from inland positions. Oberst Goth and his regiment were responsible for the coast from Vierville to Colleville inclusive. He inspected his unit, including the I/GR 726, which was assigned to his command, and found several of the coastal positions lacking manpower. He would have to bring his regimental reserve closer to the beaches but still would require some extra manpower in order not to have any gaps in his lines. To his left was GR 914 under Oberstleutnant Heyna. Their lines began just outside of Vierville so Goth met with Heyna to request the use of some men. Heyna was already down one company that had been sent to LXXXIV Armeekorps to guard their headquarters. After discussing the area and strongpoints, Heyna agreed that it would be to his tactical advantage to have a stronger right flank, and sent Goth two platoons, roughly 90 men, to assist in manning beach strongpoints. Goth agreed to shift his reserves closer to Heyna's lines so that if a breakthrough occurred there, Goth could send immediate help. The two officers both felt that the reliability of their foreign troops was low and that there would be very little prospect for reinforcements other than Meyer and his men. They adjusted all their defences accordingly with Generalleutnant Kraiss approving of all the changes.

At lower levels, the NCOs were pushing men to finish local defensive work in the coastal strongpoints. Grenadier Gockel remarked that his Feldwebel was eager to finish the trench that connected their quarters to the bunkers. Without this trench they would all have to cross a wide open area devoid of cover. The prospect of doing this gave the tired men a second wind. The question was whether or not they would beat the start of the invasion.

In accordance with Goth's new plan for the defence of the coast all the other companies of Grenadier Regiment 916 were moved to within one kilometre of the beach. Obergrenadier Peter Simeth, Pionierzug of Stabskompanie/GR 916, recalled this move as one of the more agreeable moments he had in Normandy:

Since May we were stationed in the village of Treviers, some six kilometres from the coast. In this area we had built bunkers and obstacles. May passed very quickly and before we knew it June was upon us. Then one day we were given an order to prepare to leave Treviers because of the invasion alert. It was Sunday, 4 June, a day I will not forget because on this day I was promoted to Gefreiter [Lance Corporal].

We packed our tornistors [canvas packs], rifles, and equipment to move to a spot just one kilometre from the beach. Here we put up our tents under some large oaks. In each tent there were four of us. Running through the lager was a picturesque stream in which we went swimming after our noon meal. We were not alone because many of the young people from the surrounding villages joined us. We passed a sunny and enjoyable afternoon.

GR 916 MG squad poses in Cerisy during the early spring of 1944. (Martin Eichenseer)

Leutnant Heinze, acting in his capacity of *Ordnanz Offizier* for II/GR 916, was swamped with requests for more ammunition from the companies in his battalion. All ammunition except emergency reserves was given out and no more was on hand. Perhaps theFeldwebel had been right after all.

Feldmarschall Rommel held the belief that the Allies would land at Normandy but Kraiss could not reach him to confide in him about his decision to put the division on alert. The Feldmarschall had left early that Sunday for Germany. Rommel went both to argue the point with Hitler and to visit his beloved wife Luci on her birthday, 6 June.

Failing to contact Rommel, Kraiss tried to convince – with the tacit approval of General Marcks – the divisions on his flanks to put their men on alert. Generalleutnant von Schlieben and his 709. Infanterie-Division were on the 352nd's left, while Generalleutnant Richter and 716. Infanterie-Division were on the right. Both officers refused. The issue was settled; Kraiss prepared for the invasion and the others prepared for games.

Far away from the 352nd HQ in Littry a certain Major Hellmuth Meyer, intelligence chief of 15. Armee in Calais, had scored a major coup. His organisation had broken the Allied codes, and knew that when certain verses of a poem by Paul Verlaine were broadcast the invasion would begin within 24 hours.

Les sanglots longs
Des violons
De l'automne
Blessent mon coeur
D'une langueur
Monotone.

The poem translated as 'The long sobs of the violins of autumn wound my heart with a monotonous languor.' There wouldn't be much languor over the coming weeks. The broadcast was heard, and 15. Armee was on alert.

Monday 5 June dawned. Weary eyes stared out onto an empty English Channel, straining to see if the armada was on the horizon. Obergrenadier Karl Wegner, 3 Kp./GR 914, was one of those sent to the coast and on watch that morning:

> I was on guard in my position, which was near Vierville. It was the last hour of duty for me when dawn arrived. My eyes hurt from the strain. I was tired, cold and hungry. Soon our relief would be here. I pushed aside the MG I was resting my chin on in order to take another look with the field glasses. I had never been in combat before so I was pretty nervous. I was actually afraid to see anything, for two reasons. One, because if I sounded the alarm and it was nothing my friends would be mad at me for disturbing their precious sleep, and two, if it was real I was worried that I might freeze up stiff. With thoughts like these running through my mind I peered out the view slit onto the water. Suddenly I saw something out there.
>
> In the early morning darkness I wasn't sure what kind of boat it was but it was heading straight at us. It wasn't German and all the French were restricted. Seized by a momentary panic I thought to myself that this was it, the invasion. I knew that I should tell someone, when I turned to pick up the phone I saw Unteroffizier Radl coming with our relief. I waved to him to hurry, pointing out into the Channel. He ran up quickly and jumped into our bunker. I handed him the glasses and pointed. After a long look he turned and stared at me. It was very strange; he was mad, but was laughing. Then he said, 'Not much of a fleet, that is if the Tommies are using fishing boats.' I felt like such an idiot. I think Radl noticed this because on the way back he told me he was glad that we had been alert in noticing such a small boat in the dark, adding that the Frenchman would be in serious trouble for breaking the restrictions. Nothing else was ever said about the incident, but I still felt very embarrassed.

Wegner was not the only soldier uneasy that morning. Major Block was concerned about the quietness along the coast. The reason for this was simple – because of the information communicated by him and his men, Generalleutnant Kraiss had put the 352nd on alert, disobeying a direct order. If his assessments were wrong his commanding officer would be in serious trouble. The Major spent the day monitoring all reports that came into headquarters. He was, perhaps, the only German officer who prayed, reluctantly, that the invasion would come.

The level of tension rose rapidly during this first full day of alert, and there were several instances of anxious troops overreacting. Oberstleutnant Ziegelmann suggested that some troops be given the afternoon or evening off instead of training. Kraiss agreed but only after he had doubled the guards on all the strongpoints and patrols. The number of men given time off was small, mostly those behind the coast. Gefreiter Simeth was one of the blessed few. Since they had worked most of the 4th for the regimental move they were given the rest of the next day off. With his new stripe sewn to his left arm he went with some friends to the Varieté, a theatre in Treviers. When this was over he collected his laundry from the washerwoman. Back at the lager he found everyone but the sentries asleep. He crawled into his tent, settling down for some much needed rest. As he nodded off he did not know that it would be the last sleep he would enjoy for some time to come.

While Gefreiter Simeth had enjoyed his night off, Grenadier Gockel was delegated guard duty all day. In WN62 he was on watch near an MG42 set up for anti-aircraft use. The last night of peace for the men on the beach was much the same for all:

After my relief from duty I was with some Kameraden at the entrance to the bunker trench. We had managed to connect the gun bunker to our quarters. It was a hard job with picks and shovels to dig in this stone-filled earth. We only managed a few metres a day. The connections to many other bunkers were not done yet.

I looked through the sights of an MG at the sea. Here, several months before, I had first seen the English Channel. Nothing disturbed the surface of the water, the fishing boats from Grandcamp and Port en Bessin were anchored in the harbour. Most of the time they still had been able to go fishing but now the sea was lonely. These were the many hours in which no one thought of war. As the sun set on the horizon, its reflection on the surface of the water would let one forget. But there were the messages from home about brutal experiences, which showed us that the front was not just here. We waited every day for mail. Many men lived in the big cities and some had already lost their homes in air raids. The fellow that just relieved me at the MG post had received a letter stating that his sister and grandmother were lost in the last raid. This was among the last letters we received. In such cases a special leave was granted but to our shock all emergency leaves were cancelled. When he relieved me I had said 'At anti-aircraft post nothing to report.'

Sometimes, especially in the last weeks before the invasion, there was something to note. Many low flying planes had been seen over the coast. Once we saw a burning Flying Fortress pass overhead. Three men jumped out but one landed in the sea where the weight of his flying suit pulled him under and he drowned. The waves washed his body onto the beach. We found six others in the wreckage; only two were saved by their parachutes.

The guards had been increased recently and all stood within calling distance from each other. From the bunker we could hear the rhythm as the guards walked along their post, the hobnails clacking on the ground. The password had already been given out for the evening. Our company commander was busy overseeing last-minute preparations. In our quarters we were reading and re-reading the last letters from home, a few wrote letters that would never be mailed. In a corner two men played cards, on a bed near them an old wind-up gramophone played 'If You Once Gave Your Heart Away' and 'When the White Lilies Bloom'. We had all heard these records more than a hundred times, perhaps more. A Kamerad sat on his bunk wrapping a parcel he was going to send home in the morning mail. There had not been any electricity for weeks, only the flickering light of candles, and the weak light from oil lamps that smelled bad. Soon one after another of these would go out as men went to bed.

In stacks of three our bunks stood, with narrow intervals between. I slept in the middle; underneath me was an older man of 35, already ancient to us 18-year-olds. Heinrich, his name was, had spent the last weeks in Bayeux at the dentist getting a set of false teeth. These did not fit very well and each evening he placed them in a glass of water on the edge of the headboard of his bunk. There were others who would normally be unfit for duty with us, the *Invaliden*. One 18-year-old had lost an eye as a child and now wore a glass one. Another was hard of hearing; sometimes we were envious of him.

Later on in the evening I had to go on guard again; how often this duty seemed like an eternity until relieved. I ran back to the bunker to get a few more hours of sleep because I

The entrance to the personnel bunker of WN62, just after being reopened in May 1989. This was home to Franz Gockel and his kameraden.

still had another shift of watch to stand. On the way back I met a friend who had also been relieved. We left together and went to our bunker. We both hoped there would be no test alarm, which had become more frequent of late. Just in case we decided to sleep fully dressed, complete in tunic and boots. Sleep came upon us quickly.

Operation *Overlord*, the invasion of France, had begun. Thousands of ships cut through the dark waters making their way towards assembly points off the southern coast of England. On one of those ships, Private Van Roosen stood on deck catching a glimpse of history:

Finally we set sail, just about dark and headed out into the English Channel. I was on guard duty with a navy gunner on one of the starboard 20mm guns at about 11:30pm, when the C47s [carrying paratroopers] came over at about 1500 feet. We could see lights on inside the planes while they quickly passed overhead. We wished them luck. I went below after my watch and managed to get a few hours of sleep.

The C47s were over France in a very short time. Obergrenadier Wegner had been asleep when the drone of planes awoke him. In the candlelight he strained his eyes to see his watch. It was just after midnight. He still had four hours to go before his next watch so he shut his eyes and rolled over. Then he heard planes pass over again – someone was going to get pounded by bombers this morning. He pulled the blanket over his head and went back to sleep. Moments later thousands of Allied paratroopers were falling silently towards the earth.

four

ALARM!

OBERSTLEUTNANT Ziegelmann had gone to sleep a few minutes before midnight. Before he was able to nod off, his telephone rang. He jumped up and grabbed the receiver. On the other end was an officer from the staff of LXXXIV Armeekorps HQ. 'Oberstleutnant Ziegelmann, enemy parachute troops have landed at Caen, all units Alert stage II.' With a loud click the line went dead. Ziegelmann pulled on his uniform jacket then telephoned to wake his General. This was it, the invasion, they had gambled and won but this was just the first hand. With Kraiss informed, Ziegelmann set about having his staff notify all the subordinate units of the 352nd. Before this was begun, reports from them began to arrive at divisional headquarters. The commander of GR 914 called first. Heyna reported that his men were engaging enemy paratroopers on the Carentan Canal near the emergency bridge west of Brevands. Major Block requested a situation report with all available information at once, including enemy strength and probable objectives. It was then that Kraiss appeared at the headquarters, knowing that by daybreak he would have a fully fledged battle on his hands.

Again Wegner was shaken from his sleep, only this time it was the boot of Radl kicking his bunk. 'Raus, Raus! Everybody up, full combat kit, this is it – the invasion!' Wegner rubbed his eyes as Radl's words sank in; he was now wide awake and it was no dream. Once more Radl bellowed at them, 'All men report to your stations, quickly!' Amidst a clattering of hobnailed boots, Grenadiers rushed to their assigned places.

Wegner and his close friend, Willi Schuster, who was also his Nr. 2 on their machine-gun crew, followed closely behind their gun commander. He led them to their battle station near the village of Vierville. Once there, they made the gun ready to fire then looked out into the Channel for targets. It was dark and there were no ships in sight, not a single one. They were puzzled; was it another drill or test alarm? Their gun commander told them that they would know soon enough, and to relax while he kept watch. Then Radl appeared at the entrance to the bunker. In low tones he told them the situation. Enemy paratroopers had landed around the Carentan Canal and other companies of GR

Gefreiter Hein Severloh in a photograph taken on his return from the Eastern Front, about the time he was assigned to the newly formed 352. Infanterie-Division. He wears an early war tunic and insignia but a late war issue cap.

914 were engaging them now. It was suspected that the Allies would land troops on the coast by dawn. This meant another long wait staring out into the blackness of the Channel; only this time they would eventually see something.

It was just before 0200 hrs when Oberst Goth received his call from Ziegelmann; it was a short call. The experienced Goth sided with Rommel in his stance that the outcome of the entire campaign would be decided on the beaches – and this was his area of responsibility. He placed a call to Hauptmann Grimme, his II Bataillon commander. He ordered Grimme to get a full report on the status of all units and strongpoints on the coast. This order was relayed to Leutnant Heinze, who, like most, had just got to bed. He was to go up to an observation post near Colleville and have a look at the coast. Heinze was briefed on the situation of GR 914, but still wondered if he was wasting his time on another false alarm as he headed off with his orderly.

Major Block finally received information from Oberstleutnant Heyna. At least two companies of paratroopers were in action against Heyna's men and that enemy strength was growing as stragglers joined their units and more drops occurred. Two companies of Heyna's II Bataillon were mounting a counter attack to throw them back across the Carentan Canal. The Oberst also requested the return of his Nr. 3 Kompanie, which was on guard at Generalleutnant Marck's Headquarters. Block said he would relay that message but could not guarantee their release. Shortly after this call, the Major received a call from a Luftwaffe detachment, Flak Regiment 1. The officer on the line stated that American paratroopers had landed between Grandcamp and Isigny and were sending light signals to aircraft. These were US Pathfinders. Security detachments from the Flak batteries were engaging them, but help was requested. Block told them to do the best they could until help arrived.

Those men in the divisional Headquarters were kept busy compiling reports and working on radio and telephone transmissions. Along the beach the darkness had begun to recede, giving them glimpses of the Allied armada. The first sightings of the fleet came in the form of a frantic call from an observation post near Port en Bessin, so far other strongpoints reported nothing.

Based on this one confirmed call, Generalleutnant Kraiss ordered Oberst Meyer to take his units through the Forêt de Cerisy to St Jean de Daye, but to report to the divisional Headquarters for the rest of his orders. This was done because Kraiss needed Marck's permission to move Meyer's men and the radio traffic might be monitored. Oberstleutnant Heyna was then ordered to send out patrols to determine the situation along the Vire river south of Carentan. Hauptmann Paul was sent orders to move Pionier-Bataillon 352 into reserve positions near the town of Isigny. Obergefreiter Brass peddled along with most of the non-motorised elements of his unit. Upon reaching Isigny they heard of the parachute landings around Carentan. The Pioniere took shelter under some trees and tried to relax. While waiting, Brass was called for by Leutnant Leischner. From the officer he learned that he was now in command of the 5th Gruppe (squad) Zug (platoon) 2 of Nr. 1 Kompanie. His combat experience in Russia during the Kursk offensive was a factor here, since the rest of the squad had never been in combat before.

By 0300 hrs Meyer had met with Kraiss and had his *Kampfgruppe* (battlegroup) under-way towards St Jean de Daye. This move away from St Lô would put them much closer to the fighting and when Kraiss did 'officially' get permission to move they could enter the battle from here. Plus, they would be in a position to prevent Allied operations against Carentan. The problem was that the unit would arrive in separate parts. Trucks driven primarily by French volunteers would transport I/GR 915 along with the *Stabskompanie*. The rest of GR 915 and Fusilier-Bataillon 352 would make the trip on bicycle. Some minor problems with the drivers were experienced but these were easy to solve with the right kind of 'persuasion'.

Meyer had been given a special band on the radio net and been ordered to keep in per-sonal contact with Generalleutnant Kraiss at all times. The coast was filled with Germans still waiting at their guns; it was no different with Franz Gockel in WN62:

> Out of a deep sleep we were ripped by the call of 'Alarm!' A Kamerad stood in the bunker entrance and roared out 'Highest Alarm Status and you'd better damn hurry!' The man was still in the entrance when our Unteroffizier yelled from behind him 'Boys, it's for real!' In a short time we had our rifles and the MG crews were in place, all the tiredness had gone away. The guns were loaded and made ready to fire.
>
> Here we stood at our weapons, like many other nights that passed before but then came the reports from the company command post. St Mère Église was under direct attack and ships were reported near Port en Bessin. Still nothing happened. No ships showed themselves on our part of the coast, all was peaceful. Was it another false alarm? The minutes passed slowly. In our lightweight uniforms we stood shivering at our weapons. The cook came and gave us hot red wine, the 'spirit of life'. We were awake again.

A few metres away from Gockel in WN62's artillery observation post, Gefreiter Hein Severloh sat behind his MG42. With him were Leutnants Frerking and Grass. Frerking was on the telephone reporting the situation to the *Batteriechef*, Major Werner Pluskat. Pluskat was actually, according to Severloh (the only survivor from this post), in a chateau some kilometres away. He relayed Frerking's reports to Oberst Ocker, commander of Artillerie Regiment 352. Severloh saw the early morning mist was beginning to clear. Then he saw them; ships everywhere. He was not the only one.

Leutnant Heinze was in an observation post just to the west of WN62, almost at the centre of what would be Omaha Beach. Since his arrival, the darkness had prevented him from seeing much of anything. Like many others, he was beginning to believe it was just another false alarm. The mist was rising and there was a faint glimmer of light from the east. One more look through his field glasses should suffice before he made his report to Hauptmann Grimme. As he scanned the horizon a shape emerged from the mist; it was a masthead. Then another and another until the sea was full of them. Soon entire ships appeared, then an entire fleet. The young officer cleaned his field glasses and looked again, on to see more ships. The observer next to him was just as shocked and, as if it would make

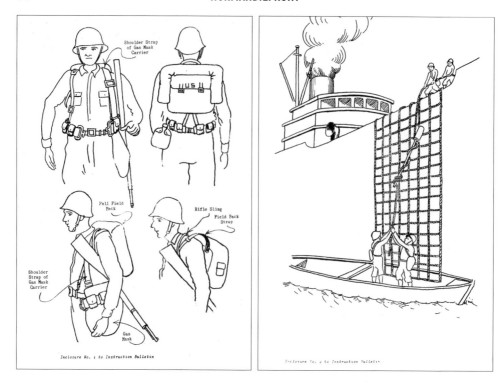

Left US Army instructions on how to wear equipment to facilitate embarking onto troop transport. Note how the cartridge belt is shown unbuckled, to enable quick abandonment of field gear in case of an emergency at sea. (PFC Merle Hescock)

Right Instructions on unloading heavy equipment from transport to landing craft. (PFC Merle Hescock)

a difference, they switched glasses and looked again. The ships did not go away. Heinze then realised that he should inform his commanding officer. He scribbled out a message and gave it to his orderly; it read, 'Thousands of ships in front of us, the invasion is at our doorstep.' The orderly headed off, Heinze called after him to bring back his 'parade hat' (helmet). As the man sped away Heinze realised that his commander would read his message and think that he had lost his mind. With the veteran Feldwebel's words in the back of his mind he fixed his sights on the mighty armada arrayed in front of him. He would never forget this sight.

On the troopships the men had been awake, making last-minute preparations for some time now. Soon they would be loaded into the landing crafts. When most of the troops were allowed up on deck it was still dark, but as light gained the upper hand they too were awed by the size of the fleet they were in. Private Van Roosen simply said, 'The sight was breathtaking!'

Major Block was briefing Generalleutnant Kraiss on GR 914's actions against US airborne forces. The fighting was heavy with I/GR 914 taking severe casualties but gaining all their objectives, even bringing in some prisoners. All of these were from the US 101st Airborne Division. From one of these it was learned that dummies were dropped with pyrotechnics to sound like gunfire. Kraiss ordered that GR 914 make contact with 709. Infanterie-Division because all the landlines were out and their situation was unclear to

Instructions on use of cargo nets for debarkation and embarkation from and to transport and landing craft (front). (PFC Merle Hescock)

ARMY SERVICE FORCES
NEW YORK PORT OF EMBARKATION
Brooklyn, New York

INSTRUCTION BULLETIN   1 November 1943

USE OF CARGO NETS FOR DEBARKATION AND EMBARKATION

1. *NET SCALING:*

a. General. It is important that the method of net scaling be taught as prescribed below. The net drill of the soldier must be emphasized until a state of perfection is reached. There must be no hesitation on the part of the individual during the movement from loading station into small boats. The following instructions will govern.

b. Method.

(1) The method used for ascending or descending nets will be referred to as the "three rope method". The climber uses the outside ropes of a set of three vertical ropes for his hands, and the squares adjacent to the center rope for his feet.

(2) Personnel will be taught by demonstration that long steps slow the progress of descent since, where his feet are too far apart, the individual has difficulty removing his feet from the squares being used as steps. The best practical distance between feet has been found to be two squares of the net.

(3) Personnel who have never practiced net scaling before will first be taught the proper method without equipment. After all such personnel have mastered the technique of net scaling, both descent and ascent, further training will be given wearing full field equipment.

(4) When climbing or descending, the individual should look up—not down.

(5) Keep hands above head when climbing or descending.

(6) After thorough training in net scaling with full field equipment has been completed, instruction should be given in climbing the net in darkness.

(7) The net is not a ladder for single file purposes, but a means for simultaneous movement of groups of men from ship to small boats.

(8) Nets are usually of sufficient width to accommodate 4 to 6 men abreast. Three or four lines of men abreast can be on the net at the same time.

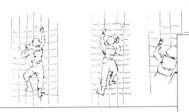

Instructions on use of cargo nets (back).

INSTRUCTION BULLETIN, 1 Nov 43, Subj: Use of Cargo Nets for Debarkation and Embarkation, Page 2 Cont.

(9) Speed in debarking from the transport is attained by utilizing the nets to their fullest capacity.

(10) The boat team commander should be the first man to go down the net in order that he may direct personnel and equipment to their proper places in the boat.

(11) The second in command remains on deck, directs the personnel down the net, and finally accompanies the last group down the net.

2. *METHOD OF WEARING EQUIPMENT:*

a. The first piece of equipment put on is the gas mask. Place the shoulder strap of the mask over the left shoulder; do not fasten the waist strap. The pack is then slung in the usual manner. The cartridge belt remains unbuckled to allow the equipment to be dropped in an emergency. The rifle is then slung over the left shoulder, sling to the rear, butt in front of the shoulder, muzzle down. This method of slinging the rifle keeps it from fouling the net while climbing up and down. It must be tied or fastened to some part of the removable equipment to prevent slipping off the shoulder. One method is to engage the sling in an "S" type wire hook, the other end of the hook being around the strap of the pack harness. Another method is to unhook the field bag strap, pass it outside the rifle sling and rehook it. (See Inclosure No. 1)

b. The equipment, when worn in this manner, provides the maximum in safety and, at the same time, keeps the equipment at hand for immediate use.

3. *LOWERING EQUIPMENT (LIGHT) OVERSIDE INTO BOATS:*

a. The caliber .50 AAA machine gun will be broken down into the following loads in preparation for loading:

1. The three tripod legs.
2. Pedestal, water hose, spare part kit.
3. Cradle and pintle.
4. Gun, spare barrel, cleaning rod.
5. Water chest and one ammunition chest.
6. Ammunition chests.

b. Crew operated weapons, ammunition boxes and other equipment are transferred by hand to and from boats by use of loading nets and loading lines. The procedure is as follows:

(1) Secure equipment with firm knots easily untied such as the clove hitch, bowling and square.

(2) The first two or more men, including the commander of the boat team, enter the boat to handle the guide lines and equipment and to pull the cargo net into the boat. Men on deck lower the equipment contained in a net or tied on a line, down the side of the ship and into the boat aided by a guide line. This guide line prevents the equipment from fouling the climbing net or from missing the small boat. In raising equipment the same process is used. Selected personnel carry lines up the side of the ship and draw up the equipment, guided by personnel in the boat with guide lines. (See Inclosure No. 2)

(3) In loading equipment it is necessary to load the bow and stern of the boat simultaneously. While the equipment is being loaded, the gun crew will be coming down the net into the boat.

General Marcks. Contact had been maintained with the 716th, from whom it was learned that British paratroopers had landed in the sectors north of Caen and seized the small bridge over the Orne at Bénouville. Units of the 716th were making preparations to counter-attack to regain this crossing.

Wegner had fallen asleep while resting his head on the butt of his machine gun:

Violently my arm was shaken by Willi. I sat straight up and looked at him, his face was pale. I asked him what was wrong. He just pointed towards the sea. After my experience of the other day I was not going to be disturbed by another fishing boat sneaking out in the mist. I looked out and saw ships as far as one could see. I'm not ashamed to say that I was never so scared in my life. But the sight was so impressive that no one could help but just stare in amazement. Just then Obergefreiter Lang burst into the bunker, he had gone back to the latrine. The look on his face was serious, no more games. This was real, some of us will not be here when the sun sets today. [Wegner recalls Lang as the name of his new gun commander but since he was from another unit and only with Wegner for a short time this could be wrong. His diary of the campaign does not list the name, only the notation 'Obergefreiter "L"'.] Lang looked out of the view slit with his field glasses and said something about the 'idiots' in the navy bunker firing recognition flares at the fleet, any fool knew that they were not ours. That's when we heard the planes again.

Gockel heard them too, but he had clear sight of them from his post:

The silence weighed heavily upon us, the tension inside grew. Soon came a noise from the air, waves of bombers approaching us. At first we did not worry since many flights had passed overhead in the days before, but the peace was to be no longer. In Port en Bessin we saw the first bombs fall. Another wave approached us. I stood in the bunker behind my MG, which sat on a table pointing out the view slit towards the sea. I checked the ammunition belt, attempting to concentrate on my weapon to take my mind off everything else. The bombers were over us; all the others had thrown themselves into the dugouts we prepared for this. I had waited too long; all I could do was squeeze under the table on which my MG stood.

The bombs landed in the sand and rocks, roaring and whizzing. Dust and smoke surrounded us. The earth trembled. Eyes and noses were full of dust. Sand gritted between our teeth. We had no hope of help, our planes stayed away and we had no flak. Unhindered, the bombers could drop their deadly cargoes. Wave after wave flew over our sector of the coast. Debris buried much of our strongpoint. I saw bombs score a direct hit on a nearby strongpoint. Several bombs hit them throwing dirt, wire and parts of the bunker into the air.

For those men inland the situation was worse. Many bombers had overshot their targets hitting spots inland. Some of these were empty meadows, others where troops were stationed. The Stabskompanie of GR 916 had the good fortune to be missed by most of the bombs although some landed very close. This was their first taste of the awesome Allied air power, something Gefreiter Simeth would not forget:

Shortly before 0500 hrs the Feldwebel was calling 'Alarm!' We crawled from our tents and saw the fire show. Bombs of all types were hitting the ground. All sorts of bombers filled the sky; a couple were on fire. We got dressed and fumbled with getting our gear on. The Feldwebel

Lieutenant Don Van Roosen with Micky Rooney during one of the latter's jeep tour stops, Germany 1945.

yelled for us to dig one-man holes for cover as fast as we could. When we finished it was daylight and we could see the black smoke belching out of the fiercely burning village of Treviers. 'Where would those pretty girls stay now?' I thought to myself. More planes appeared, smaller single-engine ones. These flew lower, bombing and shooting us with machine guns. Even a single man was a target.

The Mustangs and Typhoons, along with others, would become feared and hated. To the Germans they were known as 'Jabos' which was short for 'Jagdbomber' (fighter/bomber). The Jabos instilled the greatest fear in the men in the rear areas who did not have concrete bunkers for protection.

Despite the ferocity of the air bombardment, damage to the coastal defences was minor. The miscalculation that caused the bombers to over-fly their targets was the main reason. This would not bode well for the GIs that had to cross the beaches. But this was just the overture. Next was the naval bombardment. Guns of all calibres were busy finding their assigned targets, in anticipation of the order to open fire.

Private Van Roosen saw the USS *Texas* open up first at about 0600 hrs, noting that her 16-inch guns 'were inspiring at our end'. The other end was as close to hell as anyone would want to be, at least that's how many Grenadiers felt about it. These were desperate moments for all, including Grenadier Gockel:

But that [the air bombardment] was not enough. In the grey of the morning the fleet moved closer to us, bringing more trouble. We all knew that this was the beginning of a hopeless struggle and, perhaps, because we shared this feeling we would fight with much tenacity and bitterness. As if on parade an unsurveyable fleet stood before us. The sight was unique, but a horrible experience for those that would survive. With mighty flashes and deafening thunder they opened fire upon us. Salvo after salvo hit our positions. Throughout the bombardment the fleet moved closer to the shore. We watched as the fleet grew bigger. The rain of shells fell on us seemingly without end. Fountains of earth shot into the sky and fell back again. Many of the obstacles on the beach were blown apart. Everything we had seen so far indicated to us the considerable amounts of material that the Allies possessed in contrast to us, with only a few strongpoints. The anti-tank gun in our bunker was already firing at the fleet. For the rest of us the wait was still on.

On the other side of WN62 Oberleutnant Frerking was watching the fleet close in. The coastal artillery batteries had begun to engage some of the smaller craft that were closer in to shore. He waited to give the order to fire: when he yelled this into the field telephone receiver, all of the guns of his I/Artillerie Regiment 352 would let loose. Next to him Gefreiter Severloh just waited behind his MG watching the show.

Wegner, Schuster, and Lang were still lying flat at the bottom of their bunker. The ground shook violently; dust and sand in clouds were covering everything. So far they all were unhurt, but for an eternity of minutes the shelling continued.

The larger calibre guns, especially those on the battleships, reached targets far inland. These monstrous shells rained down upon vital road junctions and suspected supply points. Unluckily, Gefreiter Simeth was near one of these road junctions.

The artillery fire from the ships had been crashing into Treviers when the Feldwebel came and said that Gruppe 6, which was my squad, had to go and support the *Sturmgeschutz Abteilung* [assault guns]. We were to keep the roads clear for them and help to camouflage them. We made our way over a hedgerow and found them waiting for us. We rode them as we made our way through Formigny. All this while the naval guns battered the town. I was hit by a piece of shrapnel in my back. The wound was minor in nature so I went on. After passing through the town we took up positions under some big trees. These gave us good cover while poor Formigny was being devastated. A farmhouse was next to us, in front of it stood an old woman who cried bitterly that all her cows and horses would be killed. We tried to console her and asked her for something to drink. She brought us some Calvados, apple brandy.

The barrage slackened, then stopped. It was an eerie silence. The shelling of the beach proper had not yet begun. The Allies were confident of quick victory. Only elements of the poorly trained 716. Infanterie-Division were holding this beach and they had just been bombed flat by the Allied Air Forces. GIs from the 1st and 29th Divisions were disembarking into their landing crafts for the beach.

Oberst Goth was pleased none of the lines to the coastal strongpoints had been cut by the bombardment or shelling. He issued orders to Hauptmann Grimme and Major Korfes. These were clear and concise. All men would hold their fire until the enemy infantry had disembarked onto the beaches. The only exception would be the artillery, who would be ordered to engage troopships and landing craft ignoring all other ships unless in immediate danger.

Willi Schuster was the first one on his feet when the shelling stopped. Lang and Wegner followed. The three peered through the view slit. No words were said; nothing could express their emotions about what was in front of them:

We saw the landing craft, it seemed like hundreds of them. They rocked back and forth in the wake of the larger ships. Suddenly they all turned and began to come straight in towards the beach. We jumped behind the MG Lang yelled to hold our fire until he gave the order. He was on the field phone, but I didn't hear it ring. The sweat rolled down my brow as I as I watched these boats come closer and closer. My stomach was in knots.

Oberleutnant Frerking watched and waited in readiness to give the proper command to open fire. All of his guns were sighted onto predetermined targets along the coast. The code word 'Dora', which meant the beach line at low tide, was the target choice for the opening German salvo. On their left *Oberfeldwebel* Pieh was making sure his men were getting things ready for the landing, clearing away debris and wounded from the barrage. Gockel shook off the effects of the explosions:

Officers and NCOs of I Abteilung AR 352 in St Lô in the spring of 1944. Seventh from left in the centre is Oberleutnant Frerking, Battery Commander of the 1st Battery. Facing the camera wearing an armband and peaked cap is Major Werner Pluskat, the Abteilung's commander. With his back to the camera, wearing spurs, is Hauptmann Wilkening who was commander of 3rd Battery..

The barrage, along with the air bombardment, destroyed some of our strongpoints. However, casualties had been very light so far. We took this advantage to deliver help to our wounded. We didn't know if we would have a way out of this chaos, so we were happy for each moment we won. Throughout this time the fleet had moved closer to the beach. Now we could see all the ships clearly. The barrage had ended some time around 6 am and an eerie quiet had ensued, but not for long. We had just begun the work of clearing away things when once more the ships fired at us. This time it was directed at blowing a path through the obstacles on the beach. The mined stakes near us were torn apart, steadily the wall of fire pushed nearer and nearer. A rolling pin of smoke, dust, and flames came towards us, cutting down everything in its path with howls, whistling and hissing. The wall of destruction took its time; they knew we could not get away from it. We sat small and helpless at our weapons, here we prayed and took refuge. The first shells landed among us. Over and around us it drummed and pattered. Splinters shot through the air clanging against the concrete of our bunker or hitting the ground.

Immediately the Jabos were upon us, strafing our bunkers. There were six of us, and including the last attacks nothing had happened to us yet. The sea was now alive with activity, the landing crafts closing in on the beach.

With the second barrage over, every Grenadier still breathing rushed from cover to man his weapon once more. Wegner brought his MG42 to bear down his length of beach:

I tucked the butt of my MG into my shoulder, resting my cheek on it. I braced myself for the recoil. I checked the view down my sights but, somehow, I just couldn't watch what was happening. I closed my eyes and waited for the order to fire.

five

BLOODY OMAHA

A T 0630 hrs, the first landing craft hit the beach in front of 352. Infanterie-Division. Men from the US 1st and 29th Divisions rushed onto the sand and began a dash across a 300m-wide kill zone.

Seaman Wesley Hoer was a crewmember of one of the landing craft. The boat was packed with infantry and a ton of explosives. Everyone's nerves were frayed because one hit and it would all be over in a blinding flash. As they neared the beach, everyone on board tensed up. In a few moments they would hit sand, and the ramp would go down. This would expose them all to machine-gun fire. If all went well the GIs would be off quickly and they could reverse engines to get out of there, only to make another trip. The Chief was yelling at the men in front not to lean on the ramp, because if they did, when if dropped they would fall out and get sucked under it. The landing craft struck bottom and the ramp went down. Some poor fellows either didn't pay heed to the Chief or were pushed by those in the rear because Hoer saw a couple of men fall out and go under the ramp. They never came up. Machine-gun fire ripped up and down in front of them, but it was over fast and they were backing away from the beach. Hoer knew that he would have to make this trip many times but was glad he didn't have to stay on the beach. He looked back; smoke was beginning to cover the heights above the beach and the sounds of the fighting were clearly audible. The moment Wegner dreaded was now upon him:

'Feuer, Wegner, Feuer!' Lang yelled at me. I was frozen, I saw all those men in olive brown uniforms splashing through the water towards the sand. They looked so unprotected in the wide open space of the beach. Lang took the butt of his pistol and crashed it down on the top of my helmet. The metallic clang brought me to life and I pulled the trigger up tight. The MG roared, sending hot lead into the men running along the beach. I saw some go down, I knew I hit them. Others dived for whatever cover was out there. The bullets ripped up and down the sand. This 19-year-old lad from Hanover had just cut down several men. My mind rationalised it; this was war. Even so it left a sour taste in my mouth. Now was not the time to think of right or wrong, only of survival.

When Severloh opened fire with his MG, Frerking gave the order to fire on target 'Dora.' His fire pinned down the GIs in front of Severloh. When he stopped to reload or change the barrel, one or two would brave the open and make for the cover of the seawall. Some were lucky and others were not. Severloh was not the only one with an MG in WN62. The surviving PAK guns began to pour direct fire onto landing crafts as they came into range. Without these little boats the Allies would lose despite the size of the fleet.

Grenadier Gockel was ready when the first wave of troops stormed ashore near him:

> The troops sprang forth from the first boats. They sank into the water up to their knees, sometimes even to their chests. For them it was a wet walk over the wide, uncovered beach. They headed for the seawall where the best protection could be found. We sprang into action; up till then it had been useless to do anything against the air or sea bombardment. We were all thankful for our lives; our bunkers had saved us. The troops from the first landing craft made the first few steps in close formation but broke apart under the first burst from our dependable MG42.

In Littry, the headquarters of 352. Infanterie-Division was choked with reports from coastal strongpoints. Some were calm and others were more frantic in nature. It was crystal clear to Generalleutnant Kraiss and all his men that this was the real invasion. The Generals in Berlin refused to believe it. The whole thing was a ruse; the real landings would come at Calais. Kraiss knew that until these men were convinced of the fact that this was the actual invasion of France no reinforcements of any substantial size would arrive in Normandy. For now the 352nd was quite alone. Shortly after 0700 hrs a message came into the 352nd HQ from one of the units of 716. Infanterie-Division. It was the German commander of one of their Ostbatallions. He reported to Major Block that an enemy force with armoured support was advancing on Meuvaines, and they had repulsed another smaller force at Asnelles. Major Block asked why the officer did not report this to his own divisional command. The answer was simple, the officer had no contact with any other unit in his division and felt that the 352nd was in danger, with these Allied advances into its right flank. Block reported this to Kraiss immediately. The Generalleutnant was angry; the 716th was beginning to disintegrate and the battle had just begun. Far worse was the prospect that his flank was in danger of being turned. Since he had officially obtained the release of Meyer's Kampfgruppe from LXXXIV Armeekorps he would be able to throw them into the right flank to shore it up and gain contact with larger elements of 716. Infanterie-Division. He told Block to inform the commander of the Ostbatallion to hold the line until Kampfgruppe Meyer arrived. If they caved in, the roads to Bayeux would be wide open. With this move Kraiss was sending one third of his division against the western end of the British beaches – and tangling with three more enemy divisions, although he didn't know it at the time.

The attempts to reach Oberst Meyer and redirect him would not be successful until 0900 hrs. Then he would be ordered to move his units into positions around Esquay, just about three kilometres east of Bayeux. When ready, he was to counter-attack towards Crepon, a manoeuvre well practised by his men, thus throwing a wedge into the advancing enemy units threatening the division's flank.

Oberst Goth's men were heavily engaged along the coastal front. The I/GR 916 was already engaged on the beach plugging gaps in the lines caused by the shelling. The only reserves Goth could muster at the moment were his own Stabskompanie under the command of Hauptmann Steneck. The command bunker of GR 916 was just outside Formigny and the Stabskompanie was stretched from Treviers to Formigny. Steneck was ordered to divide his company into small groups for specific missions that would include counter attacks against any enemy breakthrough. The company itself was divided into four Zugs (platoons). Each Zug had a specific function. First was the Stabszug, which contained all of the administrative and supply personnel, including the medical orderlies. The Regimental Surgeon, Oberleutnant Dr Bahr had his aid station near the command bunker. The other three Zugs were signals, pioneers and *Aufklärungs* (reconnaissance). The latter two were comprised of infantrymen who had taken the proper courses needed for that specialty. Gefreiter Georg Seidl and his close friend Grenadier Alois Meyer were members of the *Aufklärungszug*. Both were still in the lager around the command bunker. Gefreiter Seidl had a relatively easy start to the fight:

> I was a member of the Aufklärungszug. This was not as glamorous as it appears. One might think we had armoured scout cars or motorcycles, but we were 27 men who rode around on bicycles looking for the enemy. We had three Gruppen [squads], each of nine men. The strength of the Gruppe was one MG42, one *Schiessbecher* [rifle with grenade launcher], one MP40, which was carried by the Gruppe leader, one semi-auto rifle and the rest with K98s [bolt-action Mauser rifles]. I carried the semi-auto [identified by him as a G41, however G43s were more common].
>
> On the morning of 6 June, our Zug was with the Stabszug at the regimental Headquarters. Hauptmann Steneck then ordered each of our Gruppen on different missions. My Gruppe, Nr 3, was detailed to stand guard at the command bunkers. We were lucky; we didn't have to pedal anywhere. Nr 2 Gruppe was sent to secure the telegraph and phone offices in Treviers. Nr 1 Gruppe was sent to the front as battle reserves. So the first part of the Invasion day I spent standing guard at the bunker entrance, listening to the sounds of heavy fighting coming from the beach.

While Gefreiter Seidl listened to the gunfire the situation had not changed very much. The first waves of American forces had landed but had made little headway. Most of their efforts were simply to get to the cover of the seawall. A good proportion of the GIs had lost their weapons and equipment when landing craft were hit or capsized. The chain of command was broken and paralysis had started to set in amongst several of the units pinned down or huddled behind the low stone wall at the edge of the beach. Private Milton Burke, 116 RCT/29th Division, landed amidst this confusion:

> While waiting our turn to go in we attempted to see what was going on, at least with the ships. The ships firing those broadsides with rockets were the most impressive to me. Then we finally headed in to the beach. I was a little nervous because I had just been assigned as BAR man [Browning Automatic Rifle] but I had been trained as the platoon scout. I was wearing an eye patch over my left eye because in Basic Training I learned that I couldn't close that eye to look down a rifle sight correctly. The sergeant gave me this patch to wear and if I was going to hit anything with the BAR I was going to need it. When the ramp went down

Omaha Beach 2009 view from bunker at WN62. (P. Botting)

Omaha Beach 2009 looking toward WN62 from low tide line. (P. Botting)

Omaha Beach 2009. Taken just to left of WN62 down bluffs toward beach with tide coming in. (P. Botting)

Omaha Beach 2009. View from edge of beach up bluffs up toward WN62. (P. Botting)

Omaha Beach 2009, viewed from the general area of Hein Severloh's MG position. (P. Botting)

Bunker at WN62 marked with construction date. (P. Botting)

we all jumped out and ended up in chest-deep water. We struggled and fought the weight of our equipment but we did get ashore. When I got out of the water I saw all these men lying down behind this stone wall at the end of the beach for cover. So I just ran up and got down with them. All of the officers and even the Regimental Commander were wounded. The guy next to me even got his picture in *Life* magazine. Ed Reagan is his name [Bob Capra's famous blurred photo of a GI lying in the water]. We were at that wall for a long time to come. You just couldn't move without being hit.

Another man in Burke's unit was not so lucky; his landing craft did not make it ashore. Private Don McCarthy had the misfortune to be assigned to a British-made landing craft., which were not as stable as the American versions because of their low sides. On the way in towards the beach McCarthy's boat began to rock and sway in the wake of the other boats. Then without warning it dipped, rolled and capsized. Most of the occupants were trapped underneath the sinking craft. McCarthy had been one of the blessed few who were thrown clear. Still he struggled to keep afloat, laden down with his heavy equipment. Somehow he managed to shed his gear, except his helmet. First he trod water, and then decided he best make for the shore.

He let the ingoing tide do much of the work, the waves pushing him closer to the beach. Only his head was above the water. All around him he could hear the throbbing engines of incoming and outgoing craft. This was bad news. The crews would not be able to see him and even if they did they would not be able to avoid him. The thought of being run down by a landing craft kept him turning and searching the sea any time he heard the sound of engines close by, hoping he would be able to dive out of the way in time. After an eternity the toes of his boots touched the sandy bottom. Private McCarthy had reached Omaha Beach, without the help of the US Navy. He knew then that he would make it. In the water he made his way forward, keeping only his eyes and nose above it. He was crawling on his hands and knees when he neared one of the criss-crossed steel beach obstacles. A hand reached out and grabbed him. It was another GI. The soldier said not to move, even an inch, or German machine guns would cut him down, adding that he had been stuck there for quite some time now. McCarthy surveyed the scene on the beach for the first time. Dead and wounded everywhere, the other fellow was right. He would stay here for a while.

Sweat made tracks through the dirt and dust caked on Wegner's face while he kept pressure on the trigger of his MG42. The wads of cotton stuck in his ears blunted the sharp report of the firing; the constant pounding of the butt caused a numbness:

After the first few moments had passed my mind became automated. I would fire as I had been trained to do, in short bursts 15 to 20 cms above the ground. When the gun jammed I would clear it quickly because every second counted. Willi kept the ammunition clean, as dirt would jam the gun, ready to load. Lang yelled out orders and targets but we really didn't listen to him; we couldn't really hear much anyway. Besides, we knew where to shoot. He was just as scared as we were but tried not to show it. When I pulled back the bolt for what seemed to be the thousandth time, I paused for a good look down the beach. I saw Amis [German slang for American troops] lying everywhere. Some were dead and others quite alive. Landing boats were backing away from the beach. Some of them were burning, hit by our PAK guns or they had struck mines. I saw one of the boats hit a mine while it backed away from us, sending shrapnel into the sea and a group of men who had just landed from it. What I saw convinced me that, for the moment, it was worse there than where we were, although we had taken – and still were getting – a pounding. Smaller ships had come closer and fired at us with quick firing cannons making us duck while their shells smacked the outside of the bunker. One burst hit our view slit. A chunk of cement struck Lang in the face. He violently swung around and hit the floor. Willi went to his aid. He had a deep gash on the side of his face, the blood made it look worse than it was. I kept up the fire by myself while Willi bandaged him. He then went back to his spot, picked up his battered field glasses to scan the beach for targets. He straightened up immediately, intensely looking out. Then Lang said 'Another large force of boats approaching.' More Amis would land on the beach against us.

Leutnant Heinze was still at the observation post he had been sent to in the early morning hours. He was sending back reports to Hauptmann Grimme on the situation. To the young officer it appeared that the Americans were in complete disarray, the result being the slaughter of many fine soldiers. He never thought the Allies would expose their men to such folly as to land at low tide against his division. What Heinze did not know was that the Allied commanders picked this beach because apparently it was only manned by one battalion of poorly trained troops from GR 726. In his last report he noted that the Americans had not made any significant gains past the seawall. In fact, most units were stopped there. Heinze surmised that many of these young men were leaderless and paralysed by fear, something he had experienced at Stalingrad. He noted the approach of more landing craft but felt that the addition of more men into the current conditions on the beach would do no good for the US commanders. Heinze' assumptions were correct. Command and communications had broken down or ceased to exist amongst the first waves of GIs. Only individuals and small groups attempted to gain ground or take objectives. If things did not change, the prospects for a successful landing were slim.

Once more Heinze took up his worn-down pencil and wrote another report to his commander. As he did he rubbed his tired face, realising he hadn't shaved. He thought to himself that if the fighting continued on the present course, it would all be over by nightfall. With this in mind, he decided he would shave after the Americans had been driven back into the sea.

From behind his gun, Grenadier Gockel watched the second wave approach:

Now came the second wave of landing boats and again another wet walk for the Amis. We defended our bunkers very well but with every casualty we weakened. More and more Kameraden were killed or wounded. One of our men fired round after round from his 75mm PAK gun and this was returned by heavy fire from the ships in the bay. The view slits were covered by smoke and dust from exploding shells. Some rounds made it through and put the gun out of action. The crew only suffered from light wounds and made it to safety. I fired two short bursts at the first landing craft near us, but the ammunition belts were dirty because of the bombardments and this jammed the MG. Quickly I pulled out the belt and cleaned it. Just as I had reloaded a burst of fire from one of the landing crafts shot it from my hands. It is amazing that I did not even get a scratch from this. Some of the Amis had reached the seawall. Here they thought that they had reached protection from our fire. But this was short-lived. Our mortars had waited for this moment and now lay down a terrible shelling on them. showering these men with splinters and rocks, inflicting heavy casualties on the men who sought shelter there.

Far away from the carnage on the beach, Oberst Meyer had his own set of problems. In the early morning darkness he had led his men off towards Carentan because of enemy paratroopers. That now was being handled by GR 914. So he was turned back the way he came and then given orders to bring his men a further 80 kilometres from their original start point to Crepon, then mount a counter attack. Most of his units were on bicycles and had travelled 55 kilometres without rest or rations. The motorised units had overcome the problem of 'hesitant' French drivers but now suffered from overloaded, overworked trucks starting to break down. And with daylight, 'Jabos' attacked every unit. With just over 25 kilometres to reach their new assembly area, and casualties mounting, Meyer made the decision that the rest of the way would be covered on foot. Hugging the tree line and cutting through streams, Kampfgruppe Meyer made its way towards Crepon. They became strung out along the road and runners appeared before Meyer requesting morning rations; he had none to give. His men were exhausted and had not even fired a shot yet. Despite everything, the leading elements of his unit did begin reaching their objective.

Generalleutnant Kraiss was briefed by Ziegelmann on the situation at HQ in Littry. Oberst Goth reported that some penetrations along his front had occurred but these either had been contained or were made by small, unorganised groups.

Off the beach, Goth noted that parts of his II/GR 916 had engaged and stopped Allied units advancing westward from Meuvaines at the La Gronde river; a stream in reality, adding that this small detachment was needed back on the coastal front but would wait until the arrival of Kampfgruppe Meyer. The main fighting was centred between Vierville and Colleville. Here, Goth had a detachment from GR 914, all of his own regiment including I/GR 726, a scattering of Ostbatallions, Kriegsmarine and Luftwaffe troops. The area as far inland as the N-13, the main road to Bayeux, was under constant shelling from the larger naval guns; this included his own command bunker. Goth asked his commander to allow him 15 minutes to assess the reports just brought into him and call back with an updated picture of the fighting. Kraiss agreed and turned his attention to the situation of GR 914. Ziegelmann informed him that no significant changes had occurred with these units, but

GIs sheltering under the cliffs at Fox Red, the far east sector of Omaha Beach, on D-Day morning. No weapons or equipment can be seen. (USA National Archives)

that Heyna could not contact any units from 709. Infanterie-Division, and units sent out to do so reported that the 709th was withdrawing to the south. This was not good news; both of the 352nd's flanks were now in danger of being exposed. Then a message came in from Meyer. His men were now engaging enemy units near Crepon and Meuvaines, having relieved the elements of GR 916 in this area. The right flank would now be secure. If Heyna used the Vire and Taute rivers as natural obstacles in the event of flank attacks by the Allies, this would give Kraiss sufficient time to organise any counter operations.

Goth reported once again but could not talk to Kraiss, who was busy with Heyna. He reported that there had been enemy penetrations into Colleville and Vierville. Kraiss was informed and demanded confirmation. Goth suggested that they call WN76 at Pointe et Raz de la Percée. This position was west of the beach and offered the best unrestricted view of the situation. On a joint line Ziegelmann and Goth spoke to the strongpoint commander, who reported the following:

> At the water's edge at low tide near St Laurent and Vierville the enemy is in search of cover behind the coastal zone obstacles. A great many motor vehicles, and amongst these ten tanks, stand burning on the beach. The obstacle demolition squads have given up their activity. Debarkation from the landing boats has ceased; the boats keep farther seaward. The fire of our battle positions and artillery was well placed and has inflicted considerable casualties upon the enemy. A great many dead and wounded lay on the beach. Some of our battle positions do not answer any longer when rung up on the telephone. Hard east of this position one group of enemy commandos, one company, has set foot on land and attacked WN76 from the south, but after being repulsed with casualties, it has withdrawn toward Gruchy.

Goth felt the landings had been 'frustrated' all along his coastal front, noting that *NebelwerferBatterie* 100, mobile rockets, dug in around St Laurent, had been very successful against the enemy troops. Prisoners had verified that the effect of these was both physical and psychological because of the distinctive screeching noises of the incoming rockets. The prisoners noted that the noise caused men not even in danger to take cover, holding up offensive actions.

Goth reaffirmed the reports of US troops in the coastal villages of Vierville and Colleville. Casualties had provided new information on this situation since the Regimental Aid Station was near the command bunker. If a counter attack were to be victorious, added Goth, more troops would be required since he had received a call for aid from the artillery detachment at Point du Hoc, which was under attack by US Rangers. This was the first Ziegelmann had heard of this and was very sceptical of this report since he knew the area well. It would be impossible for anyone to scale those cliffs. Goth countered this with reports of US troops using special cannons that fired rope ladders up the cliffs and that they had scaled them under fire from the artillery security detachments. In any event Goth could not spare any men and left the problem in Ziegelmann's hands, then went to plan counter operations against the pockets in the coastal villages. After hearing of the remarkable feat at Point du Hoc, Kraiss ordered 40 men from GR 914 to assist the artillerymen – since the guns were not even in place as of yet. This detachment would be from the company in St Pierre du Mont.

Oberst Meyer crackled in a report over his special radio frequency. The news was encouraging. Most of his Kampfgruppe were in positions for their attack with elements

Oberst Ernst Goth wearing the General Staff trousers
c.1939. (M. Galle)

repulsing an attack by Allied units just west
of Maisy. Some of these landing craft were
on fire and adrift or caught on obstacles but
most had pulled out to sea, heading farther
westward. Kraiss' right flank was now secure
and contact was also now made with his left-
hand neighbour. Observers from I/Artillerie
Regiment 352 called in with information that
US troops had landed north of Pouppeville
(Utah Beach) against 709. Infanterie-Division.
They had directed some fire in assistance, as
it appeared the artillery of this division was
ineffective or had no forward observers still
in service. This token support was ineffectual.
Heyna confirmed that his men had cleared the
rear area of all organised resistance from enemy
paratroopers save one small pocket along the
inlet near Brevands, which was actually in the 709th's sector. Here contact was made with
Falschirmjäger Regiment 6 (German paratroopers) who were assisting the 709th against
these US paratroopers. Through them, and the forward observers, a tenuous link with the
command of the 709th was achieved. Kraiss would now attempt to coordinate defensive
actions with his fellow generals.

Utter confusion reigned amongst the clusters of GIs seeking cover of any kind from
the withering German MG fire. They lay or crouched along the seawall waiting, hoping
someone would do something. The battle for this bloodstained strip of sand might be over
quickly if Goth mounted an attack along either end of the non-existent flank defences of
these demoralised men. One company might be able to accomplish this. Pionier-Bataillon
352 was still fresh, and his reserve behind the beach. For several reasons this attack could
not occur. First, Kraiss was not sure of the tactical situation of his entire division, especially
with regard to his flanks. Secondly, experience gained from the journey of Kampfgruppe
Meyer showed that any movements of troops would bring attacks from the air and heavy
naval bombardment down upon them. And finally, any commitment of reserves had to be
calculated against when more reinforcements would arrive. Suffice to say, the 352nd did
not have a company to spare.

While his commander struggled to gain a clear view of the tactical situation, Wegner
and his comrades had front-row seats. The picture was crystal clear; the Atlantik Wall was
beginning to crack:

> Lang was looking at the situation along the beach, despite the rifle fire that peppered the edge
> of the view slit. The bandage that Willi put on his face, a very poor job, made him look as
> though he had a great toothache. If it wasn't for our predicament I might have laughed about
> it. Then he saw something. He moved back to the bunker entrance with his pistol drawn. We
> feared that the Amis had gained our rear and were going to finish us off. We continued our fire

but watched Lang, just in case. Then we heard cries of 'Nicht Schiessen! Ich bin Deutscher!' Lang cautiously peered out then reached out pulling someone back in with him. Like us, he was a young Grenadier but was bruised and bloody about the face with a deep gash on his right leg. He pleaded for water; Willi gave him a canteen. Lang cleaned and bandaged his wound, then asked what he was doing out there. He said that in his strongpoint most of the men were Volksdeutsche, Alsatians and Poles. Things went well until the Amis fired directly on them. Most then refused to fight and demanded that their Gruppe Führer surrender the position. This man, an Obergefreiter, became infuriated and threatened to execute anyone who did not fight. From behind, one fired a shot and killed him. And since he was the only 'German' in the Gruppe the man before us was disarmed and beaten up. They kept him pinned to the floor. Helmuth, his name, then said when they came under fire again he leapt out to get away and no other men would let him in, fearing a trick by the Amis. He scrambled up to us but was hit by a piece of shrapnel on the way. He thanked us again and again, saying any longer and he surely would have been killed out there. Lang had become very angry at this story. He brought Helmuth to the entrance and ordered him to show where his former position was. It was about 100 metres off to the left. No firing was coming from it. Lang picked up the receiver of our field phone only to throw it down in a fit of rage; the line was now dead.

He picked up several grenades, we knew then of his intent. Willi began to say something but was cut short with an order 'Deckungsfeuer' (cover fire). Lang crouched in the entrance, we fired, and he was gone. We watched as Lang made his way to the other bunker. Shrapnel and bullets were flying everywhere but he made it. We saw him throw in the grenades and fall to the ground. Explosions followed, levelling the place. When the dust settled Lang got up and ran back towards us. Fate was not with him this time. Fire from one of the landing craft cut him in two. We were horrified, this was the first person we knew who had been killed and right before our eyes. He would not be the last.

The support units of the 352nd, behind the front, were fighting a different kind of battle. The Nachrichten-Bataillon (signal) had the monumental task of maintaining all inter- and extra-divisional communications. Radio operations were still fully functional, but many of the landlines had suffered from the bombardments or Maquis activity. By now several of the coastal strongpoints had been cut off from contact by the shelling or advancing groups of GIs. By mid-morning all but a few lines had been restored within the divisional sector. A major part of this accomplishment was owing to the survival of the civilian network. This fact did not go unnoticed by the 352nd. Subsequently, detachments were dispatched to take control of the civilian networks, to which the military lines were then switched. The radiomen even managed to get onto the Allied radio network, gathering valuable information. Some of this information was dismissed as ruses, such as the dummy paratroopers, because it conflicted with the known tactical situations. This was probably not the case since they were hearing radio transmissions from other beaches where the situations were far better for the Allies than on Omaha. The signalmen were, literally and metaphorically, holding their line.

Artillerie Regiment 352 was having a string of good luck as well. The Allied bombardments had not been as effective as the GIs on the beach might have hoped. Many of the batteries had been missed completely, either because they had been moved or the bombardiers had overshot. As of 1000 hrs no casualties had occurred in any of the gun crews stationed inland. Well camouflaged, these guns had not yet been discovered by the Jabos.

German Falschirmjäger tank hunter team moves through the hedgerows. The anti-tank weapon is a *panzerschreck*, the German version of the US bazooka.

Oberst Ocker had all of the most likely places of troop concentrations and cover pre-plotted before the landings, which was now greatly aiding the shelling of the beach. Casualty figures were not known, but his forward observers reported to Ocker that the Amis had gone to ground under the shelling of the regiment's guns. Ocker had only one problem to bring to Kraiss' attention, and it was a serious one. The regiment had only one day's supply of munitions, this because of the unique status of the division. Kraiss was further informed that the available stocks were low and a resupply would not arrive until 9 June at the earliest. There were barges with munitions on them in Port en Bessin and Grandcamp. However, these had either been evacuated or destroyed except for two still in Port en Bessin. Ocker had no way of getting in contact with them or transporting the munitions to his guns from the barges. Kraiss was furious. Without sufficient artillery support the well armed American units would overwhelm his infantry. He had no choice but to agree to Ocker's order to start conserving ammunition. This would in effect give the Americans a total mastery of artillery, and they already possessed air superiority. Ziegelmann then reminded his Generalleutnant that Flak Regiment 1, Luftwaffe anti-aircraft troops, was in their sector. Kraiss contacted the commander of this unit and ordered him to use his heavy guns, 88mm and 37mm in calibre, in ground support roles. The Luftwaffe Oberst protested, stating that the mission of his unit was to sweep the skies of enemy aircraft and not fight it out with tanks. The Generalleutnant exploded at this officer reminding him that he was just given a direct order from a senior officer and that if he disobeyed he would face charges. Kraiss added that his lighter guns would still be used in their primary role, but they too might be drawn into support if needed. Perhaps in an attempt to cool the General's anger the Luftwaffe officer noted that his men had brought down six Jabos and two heavy bombers. Unmoved, Kraiss repeated his order, then ended the conversation.

These additions would bolster the immediate strength of his artillery, but not enough to stem the tide of the invasion. The news that eight enemy aircraft had been shot down was a sour reminder to Kraiss that he had been requesting air support since dawn and had received none. Only two German planes had shown themselves over all of the invasion beaches that morning. Major 'Pips' Prüller and his wingman had this honour thrust upon them. They strafed and bombed with little effect, getting away intact despite the massive numbers arrayed against them.

The lifeblood of soldiers is their supplies. Cut them off from these and it will hinder their performance, no matter the quality of the soldiers. The supply units of the 352nd had established depots behind every regiment within the divisional sector. This was done to speed the replenishment of ammunition, rations and medical supplies. Large amounts of equipment and stores had been destroyed so far in the fighting. But this system proved effective in distributing what *was* on hand, even with the constant interdiction of Allied airmen. The short distances limited the amount of time supply columns were exposed on open roads. However, the supply units were in much the same shape as the artillery units. Once again, owing to the 352nd's multiple missions, only minimum amounts of stores were on hand, what these units could carry with them if the division were ordered to another sector. Rations and replacement clothing could wait, small arms ammunition was a different story. The staff of the 352nd was informed by the larger depots that all supplies would be brought up with the arrival of nightfall. Every vehicle on the roads had been attacked, including horse-drawn field kitchens. The only exception to this, save for some indiscretions by Allied pilots, were ambulances, which would continue making the journeys including the bringing up of rations. The main concern for Kraiss was whether or not his men had sufficient reserves of ammunition to prevent a successful establishment of a beachhead and make counter attacks, before a re-supply.

US troops started landing armour on the beach, despite earlier failures. Ziegelmann informed Kraiss that a problem would arise if sufficient amounts of American armour got ashore – hardly the most startling apercu one would have thought. Most of the division's anti-tank guns were in fixed positions already engaged against landing craft and armour, or destroyed. Beyond the efforts of individual Grenadiers with panzerfausts and grenades, Kraiss possessed within his organisation a *Panzerjäger* (Tank Hunter) Abteilung, which was numbered, as all the division's support units, 352. The compliment of this unit was 26 *Sturmgeschutz*, assault guns, of the Mk III and *Marder* class. These were turretless tanks mounted with anti-tank guns. Their low profiles allowed them to take on enemy armour from easily concealed positions, a significant advantage against the very high Sherman that was the mainstay of the US armoured units. The 352nd was the only infantry division in Normandy on 6 June to have this type of heavy support unit. Generalleutnant Kraiss decided to split up this unit, sending half to Oberst Goth and half to Kampfgruppe Meyer. GR 914 was still engaged against lightly armed American paratroopers and did not need this support. Goth and Meyer were preparaing for major counter-thrusts.

The situation on the beach was fast approaching breaking point, though it was still a question of who would break first. It had been three hours since the first GI splashed ashore. Nothing seemed to be going right for these men. It was now up to individuals to act or it would end up a humiliating defeat. When Private McCarthy finally reached the seawall he discovered that no one could contact anybody for orders or support fire because all the radios had been lost in the landings. Having lost all of his equipment during his swim to shore, he was scanning the area to see if he could get some discarded weapon or pack. Then he saw a man down, like so many others, but this fellow had a radio on his back. Knowing that it had to be retrieved, the young man sum-

This spotter's manual was more or less redundant on the beaches of Normandy. The Luftwaffe was conspicuous to the angry Grenadiers by its absence.

moned up his nerve and ran back down the beach. Despite exposing himself to a hail of machine-gun fire he reached the spot. He pulled the radio off the back of its unlucky owner and began to strap it to himself for the dash back. Another burst of fire raked the spot hitting McCarthy twice, once in the hand and once in the lower leg but he got the radio to where it was needed. The wounds were minor; by nightfall he would be back on board a ship out of action for just a few days. This selfless act was a prime example of many like it, which helped US troops begin to organise their efforts to get off the beach.

The tide was rolling in, forcing those men under obstacles on the beaches to make for the seawall. It also allowed landing craft to get closer to it, minimising casualties. The added risk was that now obstacles intended to damage landing craft were being covered by the sea. Not being able to see them, the crews could not manoeuvre around them.

The landing craft was heading in for the beach; the crew had lost count of the trips. Suddenly it crashed to a halt with a metallic crunch and all the occupants lurched forward. Seaman Hoer heard the engines clang to a halt. They had hit an obstacle, which had ripped through the hull, smashing engine No. 2 to pieces. Parts of it had jammed into engine No. 1. They were stranded on the obstacle and much too far out to drop the ramp and go ashore. Their only hope was a tow, very unlikely, or to wait until the tide lifted them off so they could drift ashore. As a stationary target, it would be an unpleasant wait.

Contact with the headquarters of 709 and 716. Infanterie-Divisions had been established by the Nachrichten-Bataillon some time after 0930 hrs. Kraiss was now able to confer with his fellow generals and get a proper tactical picture of his own unit's situation. The IA of the 709th stated that American forces had succeeded in landing a large force on a wide front and expected further landings to take place. He also confirmed that US paratroopers had taken the crossroads at St Mère Église, and several other pockets of them were being engaged. The officer requested aid from Kraiss, who refused and withdrew the support of the artillery battery now assisting the 709th. This was done because of the munitions shortage and Kraiss knew that the 91. Luftlande-Division (air landing) was moving to engage the Americans in support of the 709th.

As Kraiss had speculated, the 716th was in the worst shape. The conversation with Generalleutnant Richter was sombre to say the least. British forces had established a large bridgehead and were in position to cut the main road from Caen to Bayeux, the N-13. Richter's entire left was collapsing. His Ostbatallions stationed along that part of his flank had disintegrated or retreated headlong to the south. If this front were not shorn up, it

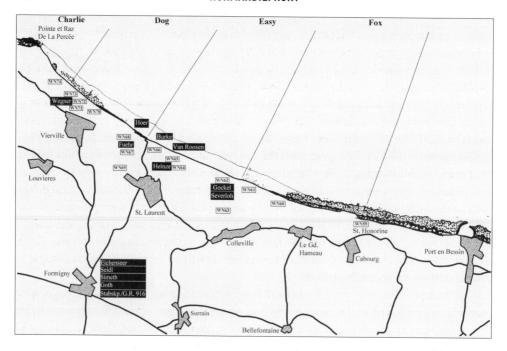

Map showing the known locations of veterans in Omaha Sector on 6 June 1944.

would spell disaster for both divisions. The only bright spot in the conversation was confirmation of a large-scale attack against the British by the 21. Panzer-Division on the 716th's right flank. The attack was making good headway, shifting Allied attention for the moment. It was decided that Kampfgruppe Meyer would attack towards Caen to secure the N-13 while Richter tried to regain control of units. There was also an agreement that Meyer could absorb, for tactical purposes, any units from the 716th that he came upon. After this call, Kraiss informed General Marcks of the seriousness of the situation. Marcks backed Kraiss' plan of attack, but ordered it done immediately.

Oberst Meyer was still getting his men into positions for his previously ordered mission when he was summoned by his radio operator. Kraiss gave him his new orders. Meyer protested, stating that at least half of his men were still strung out along the line of march. Kraiss insisted that he attack whether he was ready or not. Meyer requested permission to wait until the arrival of the assault guns; until then he would mount probes into the British lines. This compromise was acceptable. Kraiss was dispatching with the assault guns Nr. 3 Kp./Pionier-Bataillon 352 to give Meyer a reserve of fresh troops to draw upon. Nearby, Meyer had located the II/Artillerie Regiment 1716, which he could now have under his control for artillery support. Even while he was talking to the General, several companies of infantry from the 716th had crossed into his lines. Upon hearing this, Kraiss ordered Meyer to shift his I/GR 915 to the left until they linked with Goth's GR 916. This allowed Goth to shorten his lines for the counter attack against the beachhead. Harassing fire and probes would suffice for now, but as soon as the assault guns arrived Meyer was to attack with every man he had or had found.

Major Block had been very busy. He was elated when he reported to Kraiss that additional artillery was not very far away and ready for use. A railway artillery detachment, as yet uncommitted to the fighting, was at Torigny. Although this was farther south than St Lô their long range guns could be brought up by rail close enough to engage very quickly. Any opportunity to get artillery could not be missed. Ziegelmann placed a call to LXXXIV Armeekorps to obtain permission to use this unit. Marcks agreed and went one step further. He gave Kraiss authority to absorb and use all troops, military or paramilitary, within the divisional boundaries. This order gave Kraiss a large pool of manpower upon which to draw. The older men and foreign workers would be put to use in the rear, building defensive positions and helping with the dispersal of supplies. Some of the units would be of questionable fighting quality but if used as replacement pools dispersed among experienced troops they would be as adequate as any new recruit. And there were several RAD units in the area, which meant a pool of fit young men. These lads were going into the army anyway, however just a little bit sooner than they had anticipated. Making the transition easier for the RAD troops was the fact that their training and organisation was along military lines. All other regular military formations absorbed would be used as complete units under officers from the 352nd.

It had not been an hour since his last call from Generalleutnant Kraiss when Meyer was once again summoned to the radio. Kraiss had further changes. The I/GR 915 must head directly to Surrain and its commander was to report directly to Oberst Goth in Formigny. The rest of Kampfgruppe Meyer would mount its main effort from Villiers le Sec to Crepon. The plan was to have Goth and Meyer mount their offensives at the same time in order to give the appearance of a large-scale operation against the invasion forces. Kraiss wanted the attacks to begin at 1200 hrs as all units should be in place by then. Last but not least was a change in artillery support: the II/Artillerie Regiment 1716 and III/Artillerie Regiment 352 would support the attack of GR 916 since they were closer to the coastal front. All other artillery, including the railway artillery, would fire in support of Kampfgruppe Meyer. The Oberst acknowledged the changes and hoped that these were the last.

Kraiss also checked in with Goth on the situation. Everything here was set. II/GR 916 was to launch the attack against the beach and coastal toeholds in Colleville. Leutnant Heller's Nr 6 Kp. would spearhead the offensive. His was the strongest company having absorbed the survivors of Nr 7 Kp., which had been mauled while defending the beach. Oberleutnant Hahn's Nr 5 and Leutnant Berty's Nr 8 companies would follow in support. Both units had sustained casualties but were still fully operational. Goth already has his assigned 'Stugs' (assault guns) in place. They had a much shorter distance to travel. The plan was set.

Weather has a way of upsetting plans. The morning of 6 June had been damp and rainy with low clouds. This had prevented Allied fighters from attacking German units moving through woods and dense terrain. With limited visibility, they had concentrated their efforts on the roads and were doing an excellent job of it. Now with the sun getting higher in the sky the low cloud cover and mist were burning off. Jabos pounced upon any movement spotted, no matter where it was. This was affecting Meyer's plans for the noon attack on Crepon. Most ground fire was ineffective against the fast fighters. Only south of Grandcamp, where elements of Flak Regiment 1 were still in anti-aircraft operations, was travel relatively safe. Jabos attacked I/GR 916 while it was preparing for the attack. Physical damage was light but morale was shaken. Complaints about the missing Luftwaffe were being voiced very loudly. The air attacks had broken telephone lines and repair parties sent out to fix them had suffered tremendous losses. New lines were now being laid through the woods, but this was taking time. They had to rely on radio, but just as they could hear the Allies, so then could the Allies listen in on them; something the Allies were very good at. Nevertheless, Meyer still planned to attack at noon, provided the Stugs arrived.

The situation along Omaha Beach was slowly beginning to change. More and more men had been able to push inland, some a few metres, and others a few hundred into the coastal villages. GR 916 was hard pressed trying to maintain its main battle line, counter small penetrations and prepare for a counter attack, all while being shelled from the air and sea. This was just too much. Goth asked for permission to shorten his lines even further than the move of I/GR 915 had allowed him to do. Kraiss agreed but only because he was lucky enough to have troops on hand to allow it. The 1/GR 916 could move eastwards because the companies of GR 914 had returned from their anti-paratrooper missions. Heyna would not have to shift his regiment since these companies would just take up GR 916's old positions in Vierville that his I Bataillon already bordered.

Oberst Ocker called back with another update on the artillery. He noted that some of his men, fighting as infantry, had repelled an attack by British troops from Crepon on their gun positions in the hamlet of Pierre Artus. That was the good news; the bad news was that his entire regiment was out of ammunition except for the emergency reserve. Kraiss pressed for an explanation; how could they be out of ammunition after five hours of fighting and what about the shells allotted for the attack of GR 916? Ocker stated that those shells were on their way to III/Artillerie Regiment 352 from the depot at Bussy, but after that it was emergency reserves only, then asked for further orders. The Generalleutnant told him to wait for further instructions. Emergency reserve meant that Ocker's guns could only fire three rounds each in defense of a unit that was in immediate danger of being overrun; this included the guns themselves. Luckily the depot at Bussy was closer to III/Artillerie Regiment 352 than to any of the other batteries. A short trip gave them a chance of avoiding the Jabos.

Major Korfes had sent a runner to the command bunker of Oberst Goth. The exhausted man handed the message over to Hauptmann Steneck and was told to wait for a reply outside. Goth read the communique. Korfes and his battalion had repelled two more large thrusts by the Amis but his ammunition was almost gone and he needed reinforcement desperately. Alongside information regarding the pockets in Vierville and Colleville growing in strength came this message and another that St Laurent was now under attack. His men still held a solid line along the coast. Goth sent back word to Korfes to hold on as long as he could and a counter attack was coming to his aid at noon. Or at least Goth hoped it would.

Heyna was having his problems too. The company sent to attack Point du Hoc had not reached there yet because of the Jabos. He had lost contact with several of his coastal strongpoints between Vierville and Point du Hoc, sending runners out in an attempt to re-establish it.

All along the length of Omaha, things were occurring faster than could be reported to higher commands. Firing from strongpoints began to slacken as they were destroyed, captured or the Grenadiers in them started to conserve their dwindling stockpiles of ammunition. This was the moment US commanders realised that they had to get their men off the beaches before enemy troops from inland could reinforce the defenders in front of them. The small thrusts inland were not enough; a concentrated push was needed. Private Milton Burke was about to witness – and participant in – one of the most famous incidents on Omaha Beach:

We had been pinned down for a long time, I don't know how long exactly, but the tide was coming in while we were there. A short way away from us was a big work of obstacles blocking the exits off the beach. If we could get through it we would have plenty of cover from the German bunkers firing at us, pinning us down along this wall. Then we saw General Cota [Assistant Divisional Commander, 29th Division] hurrying up and down the length of our part of the wall. He yelled out to us. I couldn't hear most of it but caught the part that we were to follow him. Later we read what he said. [General Cota is reported to have said 'Two kinds of people are staying on this beach, those that are dead and those that are going to die. Now let's get the hell out of here!'] I saw some engineers make their way to the big obstacle; many didn't make it. Soon enough they blew that thing all to hell. All in a rush we made a mad dash through that hole and up the hill. On the way up we saw our first dead German. He was just lying there, we all looked at him as we stepped over him. It was the first dead man I'd ever seen. We kept going inland. We didn't hit much German resistance although there still was heavy fighting down on the beach. We could still hear it. We made our way to the outskirts of this village, taking up positions in a hedgerow along the road. We were all exhausted.

Burke and the rest of Cota's group had made it inland. This gain served to put off, once again, Goth's attack. The hole had to be plugged and the lines reconsolidated. However, Meyer was going to attack with his men at 1400 hrs, two hours past his jump off time, but he had decided to wait for the Stugs. Grimme and his battalion would now have to make efforts to control this breakthrough before starting any kind of attack. In doing so they had large numbers of casualties inflicted upon them, especially among the officer corps. Leutnant Berty was killed and Oberleutnant Hahn was seriously wounded in this fighting. Only Leutnant Willi Heller remained. It was imperative that Grimme get his company commanders replaced. There were no ready replacements within the companies themselves since they only possessed the one officer. The only officer available was Leutnant Heinze. Grimme sent for him with the intention of giving him command of Nr 5 Kp. Heinze had served in this company as a platoon leader and knew many of the men already. It would be his first combat assignment as an officer, though his experience as an enlisted man in some of the hardest fought campaigns in Russia would pay off. He would need all of it.

As to the effect of officers lost, the 352nd was in a much better shape than other units in the area. More than three-quarters of the senior NCOs were combat-experienced, a fact that would aid units cut off from higher commands because of the breakdown of communications. These NCOs would generally make the correct tactical decisions. Contrary to this, the vast majority of the American leaders were only now experiencing their baptism of fire.

Heinze and his orderly did not have far to travel to find his new company. It was still in relatively sound shape but included a sizeable force of Volksdeutsche and Russians. He would also have the bulk of Nr 8 Kp. under his control and work in cooperation with Heller, a close friend. The young officer was confident that he would do a good job and listened intently to the reports of the unit's two most senior NCOs, Oberfeldwebels Pfennigsdorf and Nielen. Morale was a major problem. Constant attacks by Jabos had made the men jumpy, in particular the Russians. With no air support and short of supplies, Heinze sensed a similarity with the beginning of the Stalingrad Campaign. Amis brought in as prisoners accelerated the deterioration of morale. All had new equipment, semi-automatic rifles with plenty of ammunition and were laden down with ample supplies of food and tobacco. Although some GIs found it hard to believe, the Grenadiers were envious of the American K Rations. The German Army did not have anything close to these pre-packaged meals. Karl Wegner recalled that one man in his company traded two bottles of Calvados for six boxes of these meals and still wonders who got the better deal, the hungry German or the Amis who needed a stiff drink. Perhaps, in retrospect, it was an even deal. More importantly for Heinze, all of these men had seen the Allied fleet in the bay. Having been among the first to see it himself, Heinze understood their feelings. From his ordeal in Stalingrad he knew that these men must only focus on their immediate situation – since they could not fight against a whole fleet. The achievement of small victories in the face of such odds could turn morale around. This officer had a great deal of work ahead of him.

Some encouraging news was coming in by messenger to Generalleutnant Kraiss. The units preparing his second line of defence were making excellent progress, despite the constant attacks from the air. In the key areas that surrounded Bayeux several strongpoints had been built. Most of the primary and secondary roads under his control had been mined and obstacles were being put in place. If the order to withdraw had to be given, the 352nd would not be routed along with the other divisions in the area. They would fight every inch of the way, then go into new bunkers to hold until Rommel came with his Panzers.

The problems within the supply and communication systems of the 352nd had given the momentum to the Americans. Since all efforts to bring the battle to the Americans along the beach had been delayed or thwarted, all the 352nd could do now was to contain them. Units were beginning to get ashore intact with all their equipment, not having to face the withering machine-gun fire the first waves had. There was still much confusion within the American ranks, but these fresher units separated themselves from it. The 115th Infantry Regiment/29th Division was landing. Private Don Van Roosen had watched much of the show, now he was joining it:

The landing craft were circling, getting ready for the second wave and we could see that they were in trouble with six-foot waves. The small craft were shipping water badly, Amphib tanks were sinking, and some LSTs were coming back from the beach listing and burning. Time disappeared and then it was our turn. We headed in and I was inordinately curious. After all, I had never seen an invasion or a war and I wanted to see everything. Some officer with more caution than brains made us kneel down on deck and put our heads down. One shell and we would have died one way or another. As we started the run-in I could see MG fire coming down from the cliff-top positions around Les Moulins right into the LCVPs when the doors opened. In close to the beach there was a lot of mortar fire. The destroyers were in as close as they could go, giving support fire.

I later learned that we were diverted at the last minute from Dog Red and Easy Green to Easy Red Beach. We all stood up and braced for the landing, which was remarkably smooth. A sailor scrambled into the surf and secured a line which helped us get through the deep water. He came back to the ship in one big hurry, pushing people aside to get back on deck as quickly as he could.

We went down the ramps in orderly fashion and waded through the waist-deep water and stepped out onto the sand. We had a short walk to the shingle, which was a high mound of rocks the length of the beach. The rocks were about 3 to 4 inches across and the tanks found it nearly impossible to get through. One landed just beside where we first gathered, fired a few shots at the cliffs to our right, moved forwards, and hit a mine; a short way for all that effort. The company joined the rest of the battalion in the middle of the beach and someone ordered us to lie down. Why, I have no idea. I had so much gear on that lying down was a luxury so I stood up. I was still very curious and wanted to see all the action along the beach. Several sergeants yelled at me to get down, so I got down. My basic load is worth mentioning. I had a pack with the usual rations, spare underwear and socks, mess kit, raincoat, and personal gear. I carried a carbine and six extra clips of ammo, two boxes of .30 calibre MG ammo in canvas bags with straps that rapidly became rope-like, another canvas bag with five rounds of 2.3inch Bazooka ammo, and the Bazooka. I must have been carrying over 100 pounds. I didn't see how I could go fast, even if I fell over a cliff. After Colonel Slappey, Regimental CO got his orders, the battalion commanders took over and we moved. Colonel Warfield was a mover and we started up the cliffs at once. I had to change my wet British socks for a dry pair and we had no sooner got inland when we went through a short marshy, stinky area and I got wet all over again. We filed up a narrow path. Half way up we passed a soldier lying beside the path with one foot blown off at the ankle. He was very calm, he had on a tourniquet, was smoking and warning people to look out for mines. It was a very graphic warning to say the least and we were even more observant when we got to the top where 'Achtung! Minen!' signs abounded. Sniper fire and MGs could be heard on all sides as we moved towards St Laurent. Having landed well to the east we had to double back to reach our objective. We went along densely shaded paths and passed small groups of 1st Division men headed in the other direction towards their own objectives.

It wasn't long before we began running into pockets of Germans and progress slowed while a few people tried to deal with the local situation. It was to happen many times in the future as we learned to fight. We had all the firepower but were slow to use it. The trial and error learning began at once. We were very conscious of being alone. No tanks, no artillery, poor communication with the naval guns early on, so we had to cope by ourselves. I remember stopping and looking back at the scene just off shore. I had never seen so many ships, ever. I began estimating and stopped at a thousand, as a guess.

With the penetrations and masses of new troops landing, it was apparent to Generalleutnant Kraiss that the entire object of Goth's counter attack would be changed. The fighting was still on and directly behind the beach, with Goth's men offering very stiff resistance, especially those units still supplied with ammunition. It would only be a matter of time before American forces overwhelmed them. Kraiss still ordered the attack but its primary objective would be to throw the Americans off balance and buy him time to establish his division in their second line of defence. He also ordered all troops not involved to fall back to this line and to gather any stragglers found during the move. His goal was to be ready to contain the beachhead by the following morning.

Major Block had been gathering intelligence information from incoming prisoners. In a short meeting with his staff he concurred that the 352nd was actually engaged against several Allied units. Meyer's men had brought in prisoners from Crepon and Port en Bessin. Those from the former were members of the British 50th Division and the latter were Royal Marine Commandos. GR 916 was known to be fighting against units from the US 1st and 29th Divisions. On the left flank and inland GR 914 had encountered elements of the US 82nd and 101st Airborne Divisions. Block relayed this report to Generalleutnant Kraiss. While it is true that the defender has the tactical advantage,

Infantrymen and
Coast Guard crew
prepare to head
into the beach
in their LCVP, 6
June 1944. (USA
National Archives)

Kraiss was, overall, impressed with the performance of his division. For all its shortcomings, the 352nd was still holding against no fewer than three Allied divisions. Perhaps
victory was on the horizon. Those still fighting on the beaches had no such optimism.
Karl Wegner had survival uppermost on his mind:

> The mood was very grim after the death of Lang. The fighting persisted. We could see smoke
> belching from some of our strongpoints, while others had fallen silent. We had no way to
> contact those that still resisted or to get further orders since our field phone was out. We felt
> quite alone. We kept up our fire at the Amis on the beach but only to keep them away from
> us. I only fired when I saw them coming towards us. I did not shoot at anyone that was not
> moving; my thought was simple, do not shoot at me and I won't shoot at you. And no need
> to shoot at dead or wounded men. Willi finally spoke to me. Between bursts he said, 'I guess
> you're in command now.' 'In command of what?' I thought to myself. We were three scared
> kids in a bunker in the middle of one of the biggest battles in history. Yes it was true that
> I was the highest ranking soldier there, an Obergrenadier, which was a Private First Class
> in the US Army. Now two lives were dependent on my actions. This was a great weight I
> did not want and was not ready for. Any decision could mean life or death. The first thing
> I did was to think of what Lang would have had us do. Then I gave my first 'official' order.
> Helmuth was to take Willi's rifle and guard the entrance. This I did in case we had any visi-
> tors. I told them we would stay here and fight until it wasn't safe anymore. This could give
> me time to think of something or perhaps someone would reach us and relieve me of my
> burden. If we had to we would try to get out and find our company. I should state that at
> this point we were actually more afraid of leaving our bunker than to stay and fight because
> of the Führerbefehl. Getting shot by the 'Kettenhund' ['Chained Dogs' German MPs] for
> retreating was something the veterans had told us about in the fighting in Russia and I didn't
> want to find out if it was true or not.
>
>   As it turned out, the matter was decided for me. I finished up a belt of ammunition and
> waited for Willi to load another one into the gun. He pushed through the starter tab and I

A dead GI beside an obstacle on Omaha Beach. (USA National Archives)

noticed it was only a 50-round belt. Normally the belts we had linked together for about 200 rounds. I told him to get some more since this would not last long. He simply said that there wasn't any more to get. I looked at him in disbelief, then realised we were standing in a pile of empty ammunition cans, belts and spent shell casings. All that was left of 15,000 rounds. The two of them looked at me. I can still see those faces silently asking me 'What should we do now?' I was angry, mad at myself for not being sure what to tell them. I looked out the view slit. The Amis were gaining ground and from the sounds of the fighting some were up in the village behind us. My eyes caught Lang's body and I remembered one of his stories of Russia. In the few short days we had been together he had talked much of his experiences on the Ostfront. In death he still helped me. We would use the firepower of the MG42 to get us out of here. First we would put all the rounds we had in our pouches into belts for the MG. For the carbines we left what was already loaded in them, five rounds. While they did this and I told them of my plan I fired the last belt in short bursts to keep the Amis at a distance. The final count was 64 rounds, a number I never forgot. We put them all in one belt. Each belt held 50 so we just broke off enough links and added it to the other. Rummaging through the mess Helmuth found two grenades. This was an added benefit. The plan would go, we hoped, like this. The two of them would throw out the grenades, one left, and one right. Then I would go out with the MG and make for the trench that was not too far away. From here I would cover them while they ran across. Willi could run, but Helmuth would be hampered by his wound. Instead of a rifle I gave him my pistol so he would have an easier run. For now, Willi carried two rifles.

We all crouched in the entry way. I took a deep breath and nodded to them. Both grenades flew out at the same time, explosions followed. I sprang through the doorway. Fearing the worst, I tensed up as I emerged into the open.

Collar tabs of German soldiers killed in action on 6 June 1944, cut off by a veteran of the US 1st Infantry Division. *Top left*: Enlisted man M36 tunic collar with mid war pattern general service collar tab. *Top right*: NCO collar from M43 tunic with dark green material added to enhance the appearance of the tunic. *Mid left*: Luftwaffe Flak NCO collar, probably from the 1st or 15th Flak Regiment. *Mid right*: M36 tunic collar with enlisted man early war general service collar tab. *Bottom*: M36 tunic with red piped collar tab indicating that the wearer was in the artillery.

The bloodstained and battered photograph wallet of a German soldier killed in action, retrieved by a veteran of the US 1st Infantry Division on Omaha Beach, 6 June 1944.

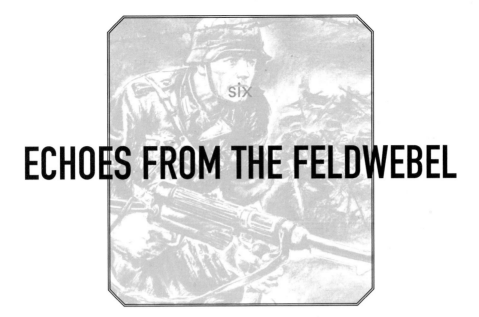

six

ECHOES FROM THE FELDWEBEL

SMALL battles raged between handfuls of GIs and Grenadiers. The length of the beach had erupted as each strongpoint became an individual battleground. The fighting was close and bloody. The hiss of a grenade as it flew through a bunker view slit, detonation, then muffled cries followed by silence. Figures clad in olive drab scrambled over the seawall and started up the hill only to be greeted by a scythe of machine-gun fire. The twang of ricocheted bullets, the hammering of Tommy guns and above, shells screamed as they passed over to land on GI or Grenadier. Shouts and screams passed in a strange blur. These were the sights and sounds one encountered, no flags or bugles playing taps.

There were few German positions still offering determined resistance. Those that were still fighting held on by their fingernails. WN62 was one of these. The fighting had swept back and forth across the open ground between the bunkers several times. Each time the defending Germans had been able to regain ground lost or hold onto the bunkers. The price was high on both sides. The GIs brought their wounded, if they could, back to the aid stations at the seawall. The Germans could not evacuate theirs. In Gockel's bunker the lightly wounded were patched up and send back into the fray. Those with serious wounds were treated as best as could be and placed out of the way in the rear of the bunker. These men were still in danger of being hit once again. Ammunition was low, but there was still enough to fight on for a while yet. Off to Gockel's right Gefreiter Severloh was still behind his gun. With rivers of sweat running down his face he repeated his grim task, sweeping the beach in front of him with fire. He could see the number '1' painted on many of the GIs' helmets. His MG42 was exacting a heavy toll on the US 1st Infantry Division. Oberleutnant Frerking was still calling in fire missions on targets, but not much of anything was coming from their guns. Severloh knew that most of the shells falling around them were from the Allied fleet. He also knew that sooner or later they would have to evacuate the bunker. Their only hope was the counter attack they were told to expect, but that should have started long ago.

Freshly captured German PoWs, still in shock. Omaha Beach Sector, 7 June 1944. The man on left is an infantry man, most likely from GR 916; the man on the right is a Naval Coastal Artillery soldier from one of the shore batteries. (USA National Archives)

With a grind of metal, the landing craft floated off the obstacle that had held it firm. Seaman Hoer was relieved, but only for the moment. The waves pushed them, painfully slowly, in towards the smoke and fire of the beach. They were no longer a sitting target, just a slow moving one, and they were taking on water. Would they sink or hit shore first? That was the question on all the occupants' minds. Then a scraping sound and movement stopped. Luck was with them; they had made it ashore. The ramp crashed down, and they all, soldier and sailor alike, scrambled down it onto the beach. Hoer and his fellow crewman had no weapons. In their wet denims they headed up the beach. At the seawall Hoer sat down. This was as far as he intended to go. The fighting wasn't over but now it was the Army's job. All he and his fellow sailors planned to do was watch and wait.

Obergrenadier Martin Eichenseer was tired as he sat down for a rest outside GR 916's command bunker. He was a runner for the Stabskompanie and Hauptmann Steneck had kept him busy much of the morning. He had just returned from bringing a message to Leutnant Maas, the Pionierzug leader. This was no easy task because of the constant attacks by the Jabos. So far, two other runners had been chased down and killed. While resting, he put together the situation as he knew it. The messages he had delivered relayed that a counter attack was being planned. He watched Steneck come and go from Goth's bunker bringing in maps and messages, noting that the Hauptmann's face looked tired and pale. Tension was in the air. Catching dribs and drabs of the conversations of others, Eichenseer heard that even though there was a terrible slaughter happening on the beach, the Amis had managed to start pushing inland, gaining toeholds in some of the coastal villages. The situations on the division's left and right didn't sound so good either. This prompted him to consider the fate of his mother. She was all alone; his father was long dead. His older brother was serving in the Waffen SS in Russia. If he and his brother were killed this would leave her in a terrible situation. He remembered how upset she was when he had found the Allied propaganda leaflets that had fallen on their home. She was so afraid that he would be arrested and executed. She had made him burn them in the stove. Eichenseer's thoughts were interrupted by the call of his name. From the entrance of the Signals Bunker an officer was calling him. Once more he was needed. He took the dispatch and trotted towards the sound of the fighting, one eye looking skywards.

British 7th Armoured
Division tank destroyed
in the fighting that
raged on the right
flank of 352. Infanterie-
Division.

Once again the counter attack by GR 916 had been replanned and rescheduled but a breakthrough between WN62 and WN64 had been reported. This had to be contained first, the task falling to Leutnant Heinze and his company. Oberst Goth ordered him to contain the pocket and wipe it out while establishing the old main battle line. Heinze led the hastily planned attack. They encountered minimal resistance in certain pockets, not enough to prevent them from achieving their objective. It was apparent that this reported breakthrough was nothing more than some isolated groups pushing inland. This small victory served to revive morale within his company, but had thrown off the crucial counter attack. Heinze informed Goth of this and in order not to delay the attack any further, the rest of II Bataillon would follow Nr 5 Kompanie, since they were already engaged. Leutnant Heller would lead this element while Heinze pressed forward. Heinze acknowledged his orders and pressed on. Goth contacted Kraiss via radio and told him the counter attack had finally begun at 1400 hrs. Shortly after this Major Korfes called in on the radio to request that I/GR 916 attack towards Meuvaines and St Côme to take pressure off the remaining strongpoints in that area which were in imminent danger of falling. This would mean that Goth would have to commit all his reserves at the beginning of the attack. Goth said he would do all he could. Major Korfes, by all accounts a fine officer, must have realised the predicament that his commanding officer was in since he did not press the issue, stating only that he and his men would hold out for as long as possible.

Meyer, who had hoped to start his attack at a much earlier hour, was still having no luck. He had no idea where his II Bataillon was and had no contact with them. His attempts to get his remaining men into position for the beginning of his operation were hampered by the Jabos. Generalleutnant Kraiss finally reached the beleaguered officer by radio. When informed that Goth was already attacking, he told Kraiss that his attack had not yet begun. Kraiss was not in the mood to hear any more bad news but listened to Meyer's problems. He then asked if Meyer could attack with what he had on hand by 1430 hrs. He stated he could, and was ordered to do so. No sooner had he took off the headset than British troops attacked his positions. It was a large push towards Omaha Beach with armour and air support. Meyer's men were not caught off guard since they were in readiness for their own attack. The Grenadiers held their ground at first; the British were surprised at finding any

A US 2.5-ton truck arrives with German PoWs fresh from the fighting. Most are looking down at the beach in amazement at the vast amount of men and supplies being landed. (USA National Archives)

serious resistance after slicing through 716. Infanterie-Division. The weight of the attack began to push back Meyer's lines. The Oberst was in danger of having his force cut in two. The timing could not have been more dramatic: just as Meyer was about to order a general retreat, II/GR 915 with the assigned Stugs from Panzerjäger Abteilung 352 appeared on the British spearhead's flank. They launched an immediate assault.

The stunned British fell back disorganised. There were not supposed to be any German tanks in this area, according to intelligence. Kampfgruppe Meyer retook its lost ground and extended it. Meyer would not go further until he regrouped his command and re-plotted the support artillery's fire missions. The tactical effect of this attack was probably greater than the actual gains. British commanders were faced with reports of German armoured units making attacks on both ends of their beachhead. On the right 21. Panzer-Division had made good gains, even reaching the beaches in some spots. Now reports indicated another armoured offensive coming in from the left. This could mean a major German effort to destroy the bridgehead. Even though Meyer attacked with only 13 Stugs one must remember that in the heat of battle, reports, especially by the time they reach the rear, can become exaggerated. In any event the British hesitated to consolidate their beachhead, instead of pushing on to Caen, their primary objective. This is only speculation as to why the British stopped their advance – but it makes psychological sense. Caen could have been in British hands by nightfall, but this hesitation allowed German troops to reach it. The British would pay dearly to enter the city in the future.

When Meyer resumed his offensive, he found himself halted after only a few hundred metres. The British had dug in and were determined to stop them. It would then only be a matter of plastering Kampfgruppe Meyer with bombs and shells. Information from prisoners brought in told Meyer that the British would attack as soon as they received more troops from the landing ships. His only option was to attack westwards to link up with GR 916. He radioed Kraiss for approval. The Generalleutnant consented, telling Meyer to create a stronger main battle line to help Goth contain the beachhead within the division's sector but to watch the flank. This would also give Kraiss more control of his units when he pulled back to the secondary line of defence. For now he would hold onto what he had of the coast until the last possible moment; he was still depending on Rommel to come.

II/GR 915 would lead the move westwards followed by all the other units of Kampfgruppe Meyer. However, just as Meyer feared, the British attacked just as he began to move. His exhausted men began to fall back once more. This assault proved too much for the men of Fusilier-Bataillon 352. Their lines shattered, leaving men in small pockets trying to gain the lines of GR 915. They too, were in trouble, with the flank ripped open. The commander of the Fusilier-Bataillon and the commander of Panzerjäger Abteilung 352 were both killed when their command post was overrun. Meyer tried to organise his units into a 'rolling pocket', where one side attacked while the other defended. This was going well, almost in textbook fashion. But he delayed moving his command post in the hope of picking up elements of the Fusiliers. Out of nowhere, Tommies with tanks appeared and the reaction was fast. Shots, shouts, explosions and all was over in a short time. Oberst Meyer was dead.

A small band of lucky men, including the Regimental Adjutant, fought their way through to GR 915's lines. He called Kraiss to report the death of Meyer. That was not all; on Meyer's person when he fell were maps showing the 352nd's placement of troops in detail. Of course all the infantry lines had changed, but not the supply and command centres. Kraiss ordered that a company be dispatched to retrieve Meyer's body and the maps. The Adjutant led them but they made no headway against overwhelming British forces. In the space of an hour the 352nd had lost three of its most senior commanders and vital maps – if the British had found them.

Leutnant Heller and Heinze made good headway against the US troops they encountered. A few bunkers were retaken and others were relieved. The lines were solidified and they managed to link up with elements of GR 915. This was better than Goth expected, since he knew his forces did not have the strength to reach any of their over-ambitious goals. The Americans had firmly established a beachhead; now the objective was to get off it.

A sense of desperation began to set in amongst the men in strongpoints still fighting but not reached by GR 916th's efforts. In WN62 the ammunition was all but gone. It was time to leave and Franz Gockel knew it:

> Enemy troops had driven into and around our bunker and our ammunition was low. We had to retreat. As we made our way back Oberfeldwebel Pieh was hit by rifle fire. With two others I made the cover of the left side of our bunker. We still had rifles and a light MG, I noticed before we left that Heinrich's false teeth still sat in the glass on the edge of his bunk. After all that had happened they remained untouched while Heinrich was long dead. As we made our way through the communications trench another in our group was killed by a shot through the head. Pieh, though hit again, still managed to crawl to the rear with us. A short time later I was hit. A bullet shattered my left hand. The Amis were in the trench with us and all around for about twenty metres or so. A Kamerad, who applied my first bandage, said that I had a

good *Heimatschuss* [Blighty wound, one that isn't so severe but bad enough to get you sent home to recover]. Crawling and running with our weapons clutched tight under our arms we headed towards Colleville. We could hear the sounds of battle from there. Outside the village I met another wounded man who had got out of our strongpoint. We had gathered at the command post of a company still fighting in the town. [Heinze's Nr. 5 Kp/GR 916.] Here we heard that the Amis had been in Colleville for several hours and had made their way inland between here and St Laurent. We were told that the commander of this company had been killed when they had been attacked by Amis from inland. [Most likely a member of Leutnant Berty's Nr 8 Kp. absorbed by Heinze.]

For us wounded there was no protection here. Enemy planes flew over and attacked anything that looked like it was carrying troops. A truck brought us to the rear, about 15 of us in all. We also had a captured American with us. At breakneck speed we made our way along the coast to St Honorine. On our left was the sea, two kilometres away. We could see the invasion fleet with its barrage balloons arrayed above them. Dead cows lay in the road and meadows. Rubble littered the road. Dead men were being collected for burial, but the rear area troops had to stop their 'Harvest of Death' many times because of the Jabos or shelling. Finally the truck could go no further. Those of us that could walk were told to make our own way to Bayeux where the hospital was; on the way some farmers in carts picked us up. They had lost everything but helped us. Even in these we were not safe from Jabos.

Severloh and his group also had to fall back from WN62. All shook hands, and Frerking told Severloh to go first. Through craters and enemy fire he made the opposite side of the rise near his position. A radioman joined him but then they heard gunfire and screams. The others, including Frerking, had been caught in the open and cut down. The pair headed inland but they too drew fire. The signaller was hit in the buttocks. The shot passed through him and into Severloh's hip knocking him three metres away. The shot even pierced his Soldbuch. Eventually they made the German lines and were treated for their wounds. Severloh was issued a rifle to guard four captured GIs, one of whom spoke excellent German. With his prisoners and other badly wounded Germans he tried to make contact with German troops around Colleville. Getting shot at some more then becoming lost in the hedgerows proved enough. He told the German-speaking GI that they were surrendering. For Severloh the war was finally over. He was apprehensive about the fate that awaited him as a prisoner of war.

At his headquarters in Littry, Generalleutnant Kraiss found himself nearly blind and deaf because most of his communications had broken down. Only fragmentary reports were getting through. To prepare for his next moves, he needed a clear picture of the state of his division. Ziegelmann suggested that patrols of officers from the staff be sent out to each of the regimental sectors to get situation reports. This idea was approved at once, with the first detail sent to the last known position of Kampfgruppe Meyer. This unit had not been heard from since they reported the failure to recover Meyer's body. The other two would be sent to Goth and Heyna within the hour. Each team was to have a radio with allotted frequencies and an ample supply of dispatch personnel, some mounted on horses and others with motorcycles or bicycles. Within two hours, Kraiss would have the information he needed and begin regrouping his division. When the first team called in, they stated that the surviving elements of GR 915 and Fusilier-Bataillon 352 along with the remaining Stugs were now under the command of Major Korfes. With the remnants of

I/GR 726, they were ordered to solidify the right flank by establishing a main battle line. This line would extend from Coulombs to St Gabriel along the Suelles river to Esquay, then to Batzonville. The latter had a prominent point, Hill 64, which commanded the view all around. From Batzonville they would extend to strengthen their loose ties with GR 916. Behind them, elements of III/Artillerie Regiment 352 serving as infantry, along with stragglers picked up by the Feldgendarmerie, would be positioned to defend against any thrust towards Bayeux.

In the centre sector, GR 916 was still engaged in intensive fighting, which had not let up by the early afternoon. It was tough, inconclusive combat. The unexpected arrival of the leading companies of GR 915 had enabled Goth to establish a fairly continuous front that included some individual bunkers still holding out.

Heyna had bottled up the Rangers at Point du Hoc and secured the beachhead's left flank outside of Vierville. Here he had linked up with Goth. Inland there had been no further actions against Allied paratroopers save for the small pocket along the canal. Here it was stalemate, just as at Point du Hoc. All American attempts at breaking out were thwarted, but so were the German attacks on these positions. At least it kept the Amis in check.

Kraiss decided that he might possibly have one more chance to actually destroy the beachhead. He reasoned that if he could hit the Amis hard between Vierville and Colleville that night with everything he could muster, he could split them in two and roll up one side of the beach at a time. In the dark no Allied air or artillery support would be accurate enough to be effective. On the other hand, his artillery had every spot along the coast pre plotted so they could fire blind. And he still had the Brevands Canal as a bulwark against the rapidly advancing US forces from Utah Beach. This could work, and Kraiss felt that he was once again in firm control of his men and their operations. Elsewhere, one small group felt many things, but secure was not one of them. Wegner and his 'command' were lost and scared:

When I had got out into the open the bullets were flying all about. With some luck I made it to a slit trench a few metres away. It was actually dug for our protection against air raids only two days before. I had just landed in the bottom when my Kameraden toppled in on me. They did not want to wait for me to say it was alright. Both looked as scared as I felt. I asked if they were unhurt. Out of breath they just nodded. We now had to reach the ditch that led away from the beach. I sent them to it while I covered the rear. Willi went first, then Helmuth. When I felt it was safe I followed, keeping care to watch behind me. Abruptly a cascade of rifle fire landed around us. I saw Willi's helmet fly off and his body snap back. I jumped over Helmuth and crawled to him. He was not even scratched. When we picked up his helmet we saw that a round had gone through the rear skirt of it, knocking it off his head. Naturally, he did have one great headache. Without further mishap we made it to where this ditch ended. It was not too far from a road. This was not good because we had to cross a large open area to get cover. Again, I decided to go first. We looked around and up in the sky, just in case a Jabo was around. When I felt sure it was safe I sprang across the road as fast as my legs could carry me. On the other side I jumped into a drainage ditch, which ran the length of the road. I waved and the others followed. In the ditch I said it would be best if we stayed in it and made our way towards Vierville. We didn't know then that the Amis were already in the village. After a short walk we came upon a group of dead soldiers, our own. There were five or six of them strewn across the road. It looked as though a Jabo caught them in the open. After getting over a bit of queasiness we took the ammunition that these poor souls still had on them and another rifle for Helmuth. Willi had dropped the other one while he ran across to the trench. This gave us just over 500 rounds, of which 300 were in belts for my MG.

We pushed on and encountered more dead, both ours and some Amis. For a while it felt as if we were the only ones still left alive. But the sounds all around us of heavy fighting reminded us that we not alone.

Willi, who was in the lead, saw them first. Around a bend in the road we saw some soldiers, Germans. It was a great relief. We jumped from the ditch and ran up to them. They were not a proud sight but then neither were we. Some were wounded, all were dirty and tired. A Feldwebel came up and asked what our situation was. I told him everything that had happened up till then. He told me to have my group fall in with his. They were going back to the *Gefechtstand* [command post] of their company where there was also the *Truppenverbandplatz* [first aid station]. From there we could find out where our company was. He told me to be wary of the Chained Dogs because they might accuse me of cowardice and desertion. This bothered me and I spoke up defending what we had done. He said that I did do the right thing but they might not see it that way. Adding that if they were stopped to keep my mouth shut and he would do all the talking. I felt better about that. The last thing he said before we moved off was that I should only give a full report to my own officers, besides since the lead was flying around here we probably wouldn't see any of those bastards. He obviously did not like them. We fell in with the others and started to walk through the trees. I felt very much relieved. Then my stomach began to growl. I realised then that it was yesterday when we had eaten last. From my bread bag I pulled what little I had, only a chunk of stale bread. I bit a piece off and handed it to Willi. He took it in silence.

Oberst Goth studied the maps in his bunker. Silently he contemplated his situation. Back in May, Rommel had told him, just as he had Kraiss, that the Allies would land here because it was just like the bay at Salerno. And all Goth had to do, would be to hold them for 48 hours until he could arrive with his panzers to throw them back.

Oberst Goth was an experienced and highly decorated officer and thus could not be fooled with inspirational talks or propaganda. He knew that there were not enough German armoured units to throw the Allied armies back into the English Channel in all of Normandy and none that could get there within 48 hours. If by some chance they did arrive, they did not have a chance against the powerful Allied air forces that would destroy them from above. Yes, there was always the chance of a victory against the odds but even so the mood in Goth's bunker was sombre. Hauptmann Steneck relayed the latest information regarding the counter attack. Grimme's II Bataillon was successful in keeping the front contained. Heinze's company had made a concentrated effort against Colleville but had only been able to cut off some American units that had advanced south of the village with two of his MG teams. The rest of his men were in stalemate positions. The commander of WN69, Leutnant Backhaus, continued to mount a good defence and had used his reserve troops to push through St Laurent and relieve some survivors in WN67 that were still holding out. In the process he picked up many stragglers and the remnants of a Landesbau Pionier-Bataillon, older men used for construction. The news of casualties was bad. Goth had lost most of his officers and the numbers of dead, wounded and missing Grenadiers rose steadily. Goth was an officer who was close to his men and knew many of them personally; it did not make this job any easier. It was clear that he would have to reinforce his

Even in the field, the military must complete paperwork. Company clerk and Trossführer maintain personnel records.

regiment. Steneck was ordered to take all the remaining men of the Stabskompanie and form them into small battlegroups. These would be assigned to the weakest sections of the front. Only a handful of officers and signallers would remain behind.

Steneck divided his company into five sections. These were led by Oberleutnant Pill, Leutnant Maas, Leutnant Lang, Oberfeldwebel Janeck and Feldwebel Winter. Each section numbered between 20 and 30 men. Given their missions, they headed off towards the fighting. Gefreiter Seidl was in Lang's group:

> After being rounded up and put into groups we were sent towards the fighting on the coast. I seem to remember that we were supposed to contact a company that had not been in touch with the command post for several hours. The Signals platoon leader was also with us. We had heard the sounds of the fighting all day long. But luck was with us as the fighting appeared to be subsiding and we made it without incident. When we reached that company's command post we saw the vast fleet in the bay for the first time. As you can imagine, we were grateful that it was peaceful where we were.

Leutnant Maas put Obergrenadier Eichenseer into the group lead:

> After a day of running all over Normandy – well that's how it felt to me – I was ordered to fall in with a detachment of men from our company that was going to the front. I grumbled at the thought of another long walk, but then this was the Army. Added to our already cumbersome field gear were vast quantities of ammunition. The troops at the front were low on supplies we were told. I was loaded down like a pack mule with about seven belts of MG

ammunition around my neck, twenty 'Egg' grenades stuffed in my pockets and twenty stick grenades, which I tucked into my belt, boot tops and pack. With my rifle slung on my back and a 500-round ammunition can in each hand, I headed off to the fighting. I was positive that if one bullet struck near me they would have to sweep up what was left in a dust pan.

Eichenseer made it to the front without being shot at. Here he was reassigned as a machine gunner: 'Now I had something else heavy to lug around the countryside.'
Ziegelmann called Goth to inform him that Hauptmann Paul was reporting to him with his Pionier-Bataillon 352. They would be used in a night attack on the beach, and were to coordinate the attack with Paul. Flak Regiment 1 would be supporting the operation with all their remaining guns, and would be under the direct control of Goth. With these fresh troops a night assault might have a chance of success. Goth mulled over the best routes of attack while he waited. Obergefreiter Josef Brass was amongst the first troops of Pionier-Bataillon 352 to reach GR 916: 'By the time we reached the front, much of the day's fighting had begun to die down. So we settled in positions along the road that lead to St Laurent.'

Generalleutnant Kraiss was to be the beneficiary of an event that many commanders pray for but never get – and he would benefit in the same way twice. Around 1000 hrs a battered landing craft drifted close into the shore near the village of Maisy. Some Russians in an Ostbatallion attached to GR 914 waded out to take a look in it. Unknown to them, it was a Beach Master's boat. This boat contained the Army and Navy liaisons administering command and control of invasion beaches. Amongst the debris and bodies they found several copies of orders and maps. Although not understood by them, the Russians recognised their importance. They turned them into their immediate superiors. In due course, these papers came into the hands of Oberst Heyna. The officer was shocked when he realised what he held: the complete Operations Order of the US VII Corps. At once he dispatched them to Littry. With all the traffic and attacks by Jabos they only arrived in the late afternoon.

Although higher commands would later dismiss them as a planted ruse, Kraiss was certain of their validity and had a copy made for his use before sending them on to LXXXIV Armeekorps. Despite the fact that this was not the US corps that was facing them, Ziegelmann and Kraiss could obtain priceless tactical information for defences over the next few days. Ziegelmann appraised the value of these orders:

> From the captured document, which drifted ashore, it was seen that the invasion had been started with three Corps, the 30th English and the V and VII American. The demarcation line between the V and VII Corps was the mouth of the Carentan Canal. We had to reckon with the employment against us of at least two divisions of each Corps, and presumably each division disposed of an armoured battalion. In connection with the parachute divisions (one English north of Caen and two American divisions north of Carentan) we might very well presume that on 7 June the bridgeheads of the 30th and V Corps were to be enlarged and united for the conquest of Bayeux, in order to thrust forward from this large bridgehead upon Caen and the Cotentin Peninsula. Accordingly we had to reckon with heavy attacks on the right wing and in the centre of 352. Infanterie-Division on 7 June.

This gave Kraiss good information on which to base his deployment of his troops for the Allied attack, but in shifting them he would upset his planned night operation with

GR 916. The question was whether his division had the strength now to hold any line against the units that this order stated were arrayed against them. The only possible hope of increasing the number of his troops was from the growing number of stragglers that were showing up along the newly established front. If enough men were regrouped, and all the moves prompted by the captured order could be completed, the attack could still take place. Most of these moves would take place after dark to avoid the Jabos and Allied artillery. The attack had its best chance of victory at night for several reasons. First, it would be the time when the Americans were at their weakest; after this they would only grow stronger. Secondly, if the Allies fired their ships' guns in the dark there was the chance of hitting their own troops, a chance Kraiss felt they would not take. And finally, the Jabos could not operate at night. But for now it would be a waiting game. Singly, and in groups, men kept coming into their unit's lines, displaced by the great confusion all about them. The stragglers that Wegner had attached himself to were joined by others as they made their way to what they thought was the rear:

After we headed out, away from Vierville going back part of the way we came, several others joined our little band. Some were wounded, and others were like us, lost. We all came to a stop when we ran into a group of officers who said they were from Divisional HQ. [Probably one of the 352nd's roving officer patrols.] I noticed that there were several groups stopped by these men. We gathered under some trees, cover against Jabos. They ordered us to divide into groups by unit to be sent to where we belonged. We ended clumped together in bands varying in size. There were Grenadiers, Kanoniers [artillerymen], Signallers, along with some Luftwaffe flak troops and even some Kriegsmarine. The group from our regiment, GR 914, was not very big, numbering about 15 to 20 at the most. One officer asked what we were doing here, where another regiment was supposed to be, ours was further west. No one spoke. I suppose we were all afraid of getting in trouble for the wrong answer, or worse, being shot for desertion. He went up to this Obergefreiter, who was the highest grade in our group, and asked him directly. The man stood stiffly at attention and bellowed out that we had been assigned from GR 914 to assist the coastal defences. The officer left to consult the others with this information. Apparently he was satisfied, because when he came back he placed the Obergefreiter in charge of us, then showed him a map. We would be sent off towards St Pierre du Mont. Here we would find our unit in operations against Point du Hoc. Shouting loudly at us, more for the benefit of all the officers present, he headed us off down the road. We kept close to the tree line. A few kilometres later we reached our regiment. This Obergefreiter was glad to be rid of us 'tag alongs'. We were posted to Nr 4 Kompanie as replacements. We managed to stay together, Willi, Helmuth and I, because we were a complete MG team.

A meagre meal was given us. We devoured it in seconds. After this I was sent to this farmhouse to get some more ammunition for the MG. There, I was handed about 1000 rounds of mixed tracer and regular rounds and, to my surprise, 500 rounds of wood-tipped practice rounds, blanks. We used these in war games because the wood burned up before it left the barrel, and worked the MG like regular rounds. This was useless in combat so I angrily asked the Feldwebel why he gave me this stuff. I didn't want to carry it around. He was not mad but his tone indicated he was not pleased with my protest. He said 'Now listen up! The Amis are not like the Ivans because they value lives. So if you need to retreat, save the live rounds and fire a belt or two of this stuff at them, because they will always take cover and give you time to get away. I know this because we have been doing it for a good part of the day.' I had just

learned a valuable lesson. Taking all the ammunition, I headed back to my friends and hoped
I would get some rest.

Several kilometres away from Wegner another young soldier ended the first day of fighting. Private Van Roosen:

> We eventually made our way in and out of St Laurent and moved into a field where we dug
> in for the night. The hedgerows gave good protection at once and we dug slit trenches for
> further cover. Later on there was a call for anyone who could speak German. Our assistant S2
> had been killed and we had a German prisoner that had to be interrogated. He was so scared
> that I couldn't make head nor tail of what he was babbling. In retrospect I think he was telling
> me that the 352nd was on manoeuvres but at the time I didn't get it. By that time the damage
> had been done so it was of little value except to confirm why the landing was so difficult
> in our area. I still remember the smells of Normandy, like the inside of a dairy that has been
> washed out but still has that heavy, almost greasy smell. Everything was so 'European', old,
> odd-smelling. The water was yellow and the people looked liked peasants. They were very
> stolid and showed little emotion, at least in our area. When we were shot at later [D+4], we
> began to wonder who we were liberating. The black market was strongly entrenched here,
> and the farmers were making a good profit selling to the German Army, who trucked it to
> Paris and resold the food again on the black market.
>   We came across an abandoned MG position during the advance in the afternoon. There
> were wooden bullets in the belt. It started a good rumour about how the Krauts were shoot-
> ing wooden bullets at us. The rumour persisted even when we shot them at a cardboard box
> and they disintegrated before they even got to the box. The first night was strictly to be on
> adrenalin; jumpy at every noise: impressed by the amounts of tracers being fired by the ships.
> We were inland only 100 yards or so, our beachhead was hardly enormous but we were ashore
> and knew we would stay.

The 1st and 29th had paid a high price for that strip of beach, over 3000 men killed. However
the other US beach, Utah, was a very different story. The troops of the US 4th Infantry
Division had made deep penetrations inland with limited casualties. PFC Merle Hescock,
Cannon Company, 12th Infantry Regiment, was typical of the men that landed here:

> We landed real early in the morning. The Germans appeared confused and their fire was
> sporadic. When the landing craft got to the beach, we ran off of it and then just walked up the
> beach. I saw many gun positions and bunkers but these were empty, some looked like they
> were not even finished yet. If these had been, and were manned, there would have been quite
> a different story on that beach when we landed. As we drove inland the real fighting began
> and the German artillery began to hit us in a more concentrated way. The Germans were get-
> ting over their shock.

For both sides operations of the day were winding down. In this calmer period, Kraiss
wanted an update on the actual condition of all his subordinate units. Ziegelmann briefed
him on the status of artillery support. Oberst Ocker had reported in that due to the
ammunition shortages, only harassing fire could be brought to bear on any attack against
352nd's front. The only exception was GR 916, which had Flak Regiment 1 in direct sup-

port for Kraiss' precious counter attack. Major Block had finally contacted the commander of another Luftwaffe unit in the area, Flak Regiment 15. Kraiss spoke with this Luftwaffe Oberst; to his chagrin the Generalleutnant found him protesting like the commander of Flak Regiment 1 had previously. Kraiss was in no mood to hear this again or explain his orders; he let Ziegelmann do this. When this Luftwaffe officer heard all of the orders and likely punishments for disobeying, his only option was to back down and request assignment. Ziegelmann transferred the call to Oberst Ocker. In contrast, the commander of Flak Regiment 32 called Generalleutnant Kraiss, offering his surviving guns for the division's use, then offered all of his surviving men without guns as infantry replacements. It was clear that this officer understood the predicament that the entire front was in. All of this unit's heavy guns were sent to aid Major Korfes in anti-tank roles and the lighter pieces were assigned to the control of Artillerie Regiment 352. This was a rare case of cooperation, since most officers would stand behind the rigidity of the German command and regulation structure and demand proper written orders and authority, a major hindrance throughout the campaign.

Oberstleutnant Ziegelmann did voice his doubts as to the quality of these Flak troops as infantry replacements. Kraiss pointed out that when they were dispersed amongst regular infantrymen they would be as good as any replacement from Germany – perhaps better since they had already been under fire. In any event the men were accepted. Kraiss had a few more men for his battered infantry regiments.

The status of the front line was fairly good. With the approach of darkness, the shifting of units in relation to the information from the captured order was begun. On the right flank Major Korfes now commanded the remnants of Kampfgruppe Meyer, his own battalion, and several stragglers from 716. Infanterie-Division. The primary mission of this unit was to defend against any drives towards Bayeux. Units were being sent into the city, but no real defences had existed before today. They could expect no help from the 716th, nor did they have any contact with them.

Oberstleutnant Heyna and his regiment had bottled up the US Rangers at Point du Hoc but could not make any headway against them. A large attack was planned for the next day. Goth wished to use GR 914's I Bataillon in support of his planned night attack. Kraiss thought this would work, until Heyna pointed out to him that if this battalion was to arrive in the area Goth needed them, they would have to travel in the remaining daylight over open roads. The losses from Jabo attack and artillery would be too high to risk, and Heyna stated he could not hold his lines against any attacks from across the Vire without them. Kraiss could not afford these losses. If Goth attacked, it would be without the support of I/GR 914.

GR 916 had taken the brunt of the fighting during the day. Casualties were high, but countermeasures had stabilised the front throughout the afternoon and into the evening. Goth had been given Pionier-Bataillon 352 for the upcoming night attack, but the shifting of units meant that his lines were extended and he would need more men. Ziegelmann had called to say that Feld-Ersatz-Bataillon 352 was being sent up to help. But Goth knew that the divisional training battalion had its companies scattered all over the rear and would arrive the next morning at the earliest, and piecemeal at best. His only hope was to have a sufficient number of missing men regroup within his lines. Each hour brought more of them in. Hauptmann Grimme reported that one officer and his company where still unaccounted for; the officer was Leutnant Heinze:

Der Angriff auf Europa

Berlin, 6. Juni

Auf Anfrage des Deutschen Nachrichtenbüros gab Reichspressechef Dr. Dietrich heute morgen folgende Äußerung zum Beginn der Invasion:

„Heute früh sind unsere Gegner im Westen zu ihrem blutigen Opfergang, vor dem sie so lange sich gescheut haben, auf Befehl Moskaus angetreten. Der so oft angekündigte Angriff der westlichen Helfer des Bolschewismus auf die Freiheit Europas hat begonnen. Wir werden ihnen einen heißen Empfang bereiten. Deutschland ist sich der Bedeutung der Stunde bewußt. Es wird mit ganzer Kraft und mit leidenschaftlicher Entschlossenheit kämpfen, um Europa, seine Kultur und das Leben seiner Völker vor dem Ansturm der Barbarei zu bewahren."

Die Meldung des Feindes

Berlin, 6. Juni

Ein vom Hauptquartier des USA-Generals Eisenhower am Dienstag ausgegebenes Kommuniqué besagt: „Unter dem Kommando von General Eisenhower haben Marinestreitkräfte mit Unterstützung starker Luftstreitkräfte mit der Landung alliierter Armeen an der Nordküste von Frankreich am Dienstagmorgen begonnen."

Kein Wort

Berlin, 6. Juni

700 000 Worte und kein Wort! Die Invasion startete kurz nach Mitternacht. Die Londoner Nachrichtenzentrale wollte täglich 700 000 Worte zur Invasion über den größten Nachrichtenapparat der Welt verbreiten. Bis 9 Uhr früh fanden die Angloamerikaner keine eigenen Worte, Reuter verbreitete nur die deutschen Meldungen. Deutsche und angloamerikanische Invasionsvorbereitungen scheinen zweierlei zu sein, auch in der Nachrichtengebung.

Im Atlantik versenkt

Stockholm, 6. Juni

Die USA-Marine gibt bekannt, daß der nordamerikanische Geleit-Flugzeugträger „Belock Island" durch Feindeinwirkung im Atlantik im Mai versenkt worden ist.

Sein oder Nichtsein

Berlin, 6. Juni

Auf einem Kreistag der NSDAP in einer vom feindlichen Bombenterror schwer getroffenen Gauhauptstadt sprach Reichspropagandaleiter Reichsminister Dr. Goebbels zu Zehntausenden von Volksgenossen, die sich inmitten der von den feindlichen Luftgangstern geschändeten historischen Bauten auf dem größten Platz der Stadt zu einer eindrucksvollen Massenkundgebung versammelt hatten.

Diese Stadt und ihre Bevölkerung habe, so sagte Dr. Goebbels, wie alle anderen vom Luftterror heimgesuchten Städte des Reiches den feindlichen Versuchen, ihre Moral zu brechen, eine hochgemute Tapferkeit und ein standhaftes Herz entgegengesetzt. Wenn der Feind geglaubt habe, die Heimat würde in dem Augenblick, da sie unmittelbar in das Kriegsgeschehen einbezogen wurde, ihre Zähigkeit und Ausdauer verlieren, so habe er sich darin gründlich getäuscht. Im Gegenteil sei die Kampfentschlossenheit des deutschen Volkes durch den feindlichen Terror nur gehärtet worden.

In diesem Sinne forderte der Minister das gesamte deutsche Volk auf, auch in den kommenden entscheidenden Wochen und Monaten die gleiche hohe Kriegsmoral zu beweisen, die sich bisher so hervorragend bewährt habe. Jedermann wisse, daß ein Volk für ein großes und edles Ziel auch schwere und manchmal unerträglich scheinende Opfer bringen müsse. In diesem Kriege werde nicht um strategische Grenzen oder territoriale Vorrechte gekämpft, sondern es gehe um Sein oder Nichtsein unseres Volkes. Die weltgeschichtliche Auseinandersetzung, in der wir stehen, werde über die Neuverteilung der Machtverhältnisse auf den Kontinenten entscheiden.

Ein Volk, das dabei versage, sinke in ein geschichtsloses Dasein zurück, ein tapferes, standhaftes und entschlossenes Volk aber werde den Sieg und damit endgültig sein Freiheit und sein Lebensrecht erkämpfen.

„Die deutsche Nation", sagte Dr. Goebbels unter begeisterten Beifallskundgebungen der versammelten Massen, „hört nur auf ein einziges Kommando, und das ist das Kommando des Führers. Er ist der stärkste moralische Faktor unseres Sieges. Unter seiner Führung haben wir noch alle, auch die schwersten Krisen überwunden. Ich bin der festen Gewißheit, daß aus den gegenwärtigen Belastungen dieses Krieges für uns der Sieg hervorgehen wird.

Clipping from the Hamburger *Abendblatt* newspaper, dated 6 June 1944, reporting news of the invasion. It notes that the invasion was begun by the 'Western helpers of Bolshevism against free Europe'. It also states that these 'helpers' are in for a 'hot' reception. (M. Galle)

We had launched our attack to retake WN62b at about 1300 hrs. I split the company into three groups. One stayed in the wood line as reserves, and I led the other two in the attack. Moving like rabbits, hopping from one bush to another, we retook the position, and with it some prisoners from the US 1st and 29th Divisions. They looked depressed and tired; this gave us hope. Men from Leutnant Berty's company had been here. They had retreated and left their dead. We did not have time to care for them either. Soon the Americans bombarded us with all they had. After a long time I knew we couldn't hold out any longer. I ordered the men to try to get out through the shelling by themselves, not in groups. This was the only possible way through that terrible fire. I told them to rally at the battalion command post. I could hear the echoes from that Feldwebel in my head as we crawled and ran through the countryside that evening.

The action Leutnant Heinze mounted was an attempt to reach the rest of the survivors of his battalion's 8th Company. These beleagured men had been holding out since the beginning of the invasion. Leutnant Fuehr had been on the beach since before dawn:

The early morning of the invasion was dark and cloudy but one could hear that something big was going on. With the first flicker of daylight we could see the ships. I surely thought it was the real invasion and immediately reported it to the battalion commander. He said it must be a feint to take our focus from the real invasion. More and more ships came, then the bombers. Some of these bombers came from an inland direction, from France. Thinking these were our planes several soldiers jumped up and began to wave. The dropping bombs covered our area with explosions. The naval guns of the invasion fleet began to fire at us. The wooden bunkers we had built began to break apart. I took the radio and strapped it to my back. I had no luck keeping in contact with battalion headquarters. After a while, from our position, we could see the first landing craft approach. Many of these struck mines and sank. We could see the American soldiers who had survived the mines waiting for the boats to flood so they could begin their swim to the beach. The fighting for the beach was fierce and in these first actions our company commander was killed. Since I was senior officer I took over command at the orders of the battalion commander. Heavy fighting continued throughout the day for our position and by the evening our ammunition was almost gone. Luckily, in the darkness the fighting slackened away to nothing.

As the time passed it looked more and more to Goth that his attack would be delayed well past midnight. Once again, all that could be done was to wait. As the final moments of the momentous day ticked away, the Grenadiers of the 352nd found themselves in various situations. Some, like Peter Simeth and Josef Brass, had not actually been in the fighting yet and waited, tensely, for the day after the 'Longest Day'. Others like Heinze were in more desperate straits. Gefreiter Georg Seidl found himself with a peculiar burden:

I had been sent up to the fighting late in the day. After I was in the line for a while my name was called out, and I had to report to the Leutnant in charge of our group. I was ordered to bring back a prisoner to the command bunker where the aid station was. He was a wounded sergeant of the famous Rangers. He had a bandage on his head and was very tall. I sat him on the handlebars of my bicycle and peddled off down the dark road. His feet almost dragged on the ground and because he had a head wound, he lost balance many times, wobbling back and forth. It was dark and I couldn't see very well with him sitting in front of me. We almost went into the ditch a couple of times. I eventually had to hold onto him with one hand and steer with the other. As we made our way along the road, I thought to myself that this was the end of his last day of fighting but only the first for me. Strange things happen in war.

Two men in different uniforms cling to a wobbling bicycle on a Norman road as they make their way from the sounds of battle. The German who was pedalling was dwarfed by his American 'passenger'. Given the chance a few hours ago, each would have killed the other in the time it takes to pull a trigger. Now they had the same destination. While this odd pair made their way through the darkness, 6 June ended. The battle had just begun.

seven

WITHOUT HINDSIGHT

COMMANDERS in history are judged by those that have the benefit of knowing the out-come, and who have the time to consider where all the mistakes were made. While it is true that inept or overconfident officers make mistakes, the decisions in battle are the result of what information, good or bad, is on hand for field commanders. These men do not have the luxury of hindsight.

The following is a record of the telephone communications of 352. Infanterie-Division and the units of the US 1st Infantry Division that landed on Omaha Beach. There was a time difference of two hours between German and Allied forces, which can lead to some confusion when reading some accounts. The times here have been adjusted to fit the Allied time frame. This is the day as they saw it. Not all readers will want to study this section throughout but it is thought useful to provide a fairly thorough record of communications; if nothing else, such a record is a salutary lesson in how complex the situation can be for any CO, who has little or no time to digest, collate and interpret such information and then must act upon it immediately.

01.00. LXXXIV A.K. to 352: Alarm Stage II, paratroopers in the 716. Divisionsector. Put all troops on alert via field phone.

01.45. 352 to 914: 50 to 60 enemy paratroopers have landed near the Carentan Canal south of Brevands.

02.00. Update of above message: 30 to 40 planes reported south of Brevands, single para-troopers encountered by II/AR 352 around Cardonville.

02.07. 916 to 352: No enemy activity in our area.

02.09. Ziegelmann to Major Korfes: What is the situation? Reply: No enemy reported in Bessin sector.

02.13 Ziegelmann to LXXXTV A.K. One battalion of paratroopers reported on 914's left sector near the Carentan Canal sc.... of Brevands. Single troops near Cardonville, other sectors quiet.

02.14. 352 to Seekommandant ..6rmandie: Enemy vessels reported 11km north of Grandcamp, verify. Reply: ..firmative.

02.55. 914 to 352: 8 – 10 enemy paratroopers reported near IV/AR 352. Near Cardonville two paratroopers in camouflage uniforms captured. Seventy paratroopers reported to have landed near Isigny.

03.10. Gen. Marcks to Gen. Kraiss: Enemy troops have landed on both sides of the Vire as well as the meadows south of Carentan. Clear them out and correct the situation. The 352, in cooperation with the 709. Division will clear the Isigny-Carentan Highway. Kampfgruppe Meyer stays as Korpsreserve.

03.20. LXXXIV to 352: Order Nr. 1200/44g. Kdos. is in effect. [No retreat order.]

03.30. Ziegelmann to LXXXIV A.K.: Position of enemy fleet known at this time. K.G. MEYER will be in position by 04.15, I Bn. in Carentan, II Bn. in Montmartin.

03.35. 916 to 352: Strong enemy air attacks on Le Guay, Point du Hoc and Grandcamp.

04.01. 352 to FluKo Caen [Luft. Area Commander]: 716. Division right neighbour, over flown by formations of heavy bombers heading southwest. Paratroopers dropped at Morsalines, St Côme and St Mère Église. Three prisoners carrying maps of Vire sector.

04.20. LXXXIV A.K. to 352: Situation still unclear at this time, maintain absolute radio silence. [This refers to traffic between 352 and other divisions and LXXXIV A.K., not within the 352.]

04.21. K.G. Meyer to 352: Have met with Fus–Bn 352 and securing area; will be complete in 3–4 hours. From sector of GR 726 we can hear artillery fire.

04.30. 914 to 352: The attack of II/GR 914 against the enemy paratroopers is going as ordered southwest of Brevands. The enemy is pushing towards the Carentan Canal from Les Moulins towards the south.

04.34. AR 352 to 352: No landing boats can be seen from Grandcamp at this time.

04.35. 916 to 352: An American 1st Lieutenant captured at St E le Guay said that they have dropped dummies, which explode when they hit the ground.

04.45. 726 to 352: WN44, 47 and 48 heavily bombarded.

05.02. AR 352 to 352: At Port en Bessin one large and four small groups of ships have been observed. Also ships reported at Grandcamp.

05.06. 726 to 352: Strongpoints, especially those around Arromanches, St Honorine and Colleville, have suffered heavy bombardment. At Sully paratroopers are reported but it is probably just planes flying over them.

05.10. 914 to 352: II/GR 914 has brought in three US prisoners who had maps and air recon photos of the Cotentin Peninsula. The prisoners cannot be transported at this time.

05.20. AR 352 to 352: OPs have reported smoke, presumably ships, 2km away in the Vire rivermouth. Point du Hoc reports 29 small ships escorted by 4 destroyer or cruiser class 6–10km away. Four planes shot down. One pilot, a Pole, has been captured. Fifty landing craft now in front of Port en Bessin.

05.22. Seekommandant Normandie to 352: Naval batteries and available torpedo boats have fired on enemy ships, one is on fire.

05.32. 916 to 352: In the bay at Colleville–Vierville landing craft are closing in on the beach. A group of five ships heading east have left more landing boats heading for the beach.

05.37. 726 to 352: Between WN's 56, 59, 60 and in front of Asnelles warships have begun a broad bombardment.

05.45. 914 to 352: North of WN88 large concentrations of landing boats are heading for the beach.

05.50. Ziegelmann to LXXXIV A.K.: Due to the reports of landing crafts and coastal bombardment Division Kdr. Request that the status of K.G. Meyer be changed.

05.52. AR 352 to 352: Some 60 to 80 landing boats have reached the coast at Colleville; our own artillery has not been able to fire on them to great effect because our batteries are under heavy bombardment at Marcouf and Maisy. The ships are too far away for counter battery fire.

05.55. 916 to 352: In front of Vierville 45 landing boats are reported, bombardment of the beach has begun.

06.03. Ziegelmann to Fus. Batt. 352: Halt your unit and wait for orders from the CO GR 915. You will wait in the Forêt de Cerisy.

06.04. 916 to 352: In the bay at Vierville since 0545 hrs over 145 ships have been counted. The coast is under heavy shelling.

06.15. 726 to 352: WN60 is under especially heavy fire. At WN37 more landing boats reported.

06.20. 916 to 352: In Vierville bay landing boats with armour have been seen, Reply: Pz. Jg. Abt 352 is being sent up to support you against landing armour.

06.30, US 1st: First wave lands on schedule on beach of Normandy and is meeting fierce resistance on beaches. Beach under heavy MG and rifle fire. No advance made inland as beaches are fully covered by pillboxes and minefields just inland from the beaches.

06.32. 726 to 352: Boats have landed between WN59, 61 and 62 and Asnelles. The enemy has laid a smoke screen from the sea. More have landed at WN65 and 69; armoured vehicles.

06.45. 914 to 352: Attack of II Bn. against enemy paratroopers is going forward but slowly. Grandcamp is under heavy fire. Some landing boats have reached the beach.

06.57. 914 to 352: Landing boats heading for the beach in front of WN90.

07.05. 916 to 352: At WN68, east of Vierville, the enemy has landed about 50 men; another small group is at WN62.

07.06. 726 to 352: At WN60, northeast of Colleville, they are engaged against about 40 men and 1 tank.

07.08. 914 to 352: II Bn. has attacked with four companies the enemy paratroopers and has slowly taken the enemy positions.

07.20. 726 to 352: The landings have been at WN60, 61, 62 and farther west. Between 61 and 62 a unit of company strength is under fire by our artillery. The 88mm gun at WN61 has taken a direct hit and is out of action. In front of WN37 and 37a more boats have reached the beach but landing forces have made no progress. WN37 is under heavy fire. WN61 has four more landing boats. one boat has been hit by the 50mm gun. Now the enemy has driven in between 61 and 62 and attacked 61 from the rear. The phone lines to Port en Bessin and 726 are out. Question: When and who can mount a counter attack to throw the enemy out between 61 and 62. [No reply.]

07.30. AR 352 to 352: At this time no contact with OP in Colleville. Landing boats between WN61 and 62 are being met with as much fire as we can give. In the Vire rivermouth there are 15 more small landing boats.

07.30. US 1st: Forward CP lands. Beach still under small arms and MG fire. No advance made inland. Casualties extremely heavy. Heavy MG fire covering all exits and the entire beach.

07.35. Ziegelmann to LXXXIV A.K.: At Arromanches on our right flank more landing ships are reported; the landing stands as before, At WN60-62 northeast of Colleville the enemy have advanced with about 100–200 men. In the bay at Vierville the enemy has not landed but large formations of boats are approaching the beach. Request that one battalion of K.G. Meyer counterattack between WN60 and 62.

07.45. 916 to 352: At WN70 northeast of Vierville three tanks ashore, at 66 three tanks within the perimeter. WN62's upper gun bunker has taken a direct hit and is out of action.

07.50. Kraiss to Korfes: I Bn. K.G. Meyer will attack WN60-62 from Colleville. Estimated time of attack 1½ hours.

07.55. AR 352 to 352: Message from II AR 352 that their situation at WN60 is unclear.

07.57. 726 to 352: On our right 716. Division reports that between WN35 and 36 that 30 tanks are ashore.

08.01. 916 to 352: At WN68, north of St Laurent, there are four tanks. Three at WN66 that are off the beach. WN65 situation is unclear. The anti-tank platoon is heavily engaged.

08.04. 716 Division to 352: The Orne river bridge at Bénouville is in enemy hands, east of there we are mounting a counter attack. Nr 1 Battery of AR 1716 is wiped out.

08.05. 916 to 352: Weak enemy at Point du Hoc, 1 platoon of GR 726 is counter attacking.

08.05. US 1st: Rear CP lands. Beach still under fire. CP established on beachhead infiltration started through right flank of area of small breakthrough. Minefield cleared out and all troops on beach commence moving off to flank.

08.20. 914 to 352: The battle with the paratroopers in the Brevands area is not over yet.

08.20. 716 Division to 352: The 30 tanks on the left flank have driven to the south and are on the outskirts of Meuvaines.

08.25. AR 352 to 352: III/AR 352 reports that by WN35, six enemy tanks have been hit by PAK guns and are on fire. Update at 0830 hrs WN35 and 36 have been overrun in 716 Division sector. The enemy is outside Meuvaines with tanks and infantry. Holding on to the high ground is Ostbatallion 642. WN37 is still holding on. WN40's PAK gun has hit three or four tanks as well as two or three landing boats.

08.30. US 1st: First four prisoners, all from 8 Kp. GR 916 352 I.D., brought in.

08.31. Ziegelmann to Korfes: I/GR 916 has attacked to the right in the direction of Meuvaines. Support them.

08.33. Kraiss to Gen. Marcks: Situation on right flank at Meuvaines and Asnelles is serious. In front of Asnelles six tanks have been destroyed by our guns. I have ordered K.G. Meyer to counter-attack with the support of Pz. Jag. Abt. 352 on right flank to throw enemy back to the sea. Sections of Pz. Jag. Abt. should plug hole until then.

08.40. Ziegelmann to AR 352: Contact with OP's is late. Have them watch for the second wave of landing, it is expected. Give Meyer the III Abt. for support as his counterattack gets underway. Reply: WN68 reports strong landings with large boats carrying approx. 150 men.

09.03. 726 to 352: I Bn/GR 915 has counter attacked at 0830 hrs at WN60 + 62. WN61 is in enemy hands, 62 is still firing with one MG. Enemy craft are driving in between 61 , 62, and 63: Further strong landings of about 50 boats at WN62, reserves from Nr. 1 and Nr. 4 companies sent there. At WN52 it is quiet. WN37 is requesting reinforcement. Enemy infantry and tanks are making further advances on Meuvaines.

09.12. 914 to 352: Landing boats are at WN92 and 99 in the Carentan Canal but landings are still not having success. Nr. 5 and 6 companies are in defensive positions in the canal opposite enemy paratroopers.

09.15. 726 to 352: At this time the enemy has unloaded some 60 to 70 boats in front of WN65 north of St Laurent. No messages from Point du Hoc. Situation at Grandcamp is unchanged. WN's 65, 66, 67, 68, and 70 are in enemy hands.

09.25. 916 to 352: 3 tanks reported east of WN38, Aufklärungszug sent out, Reply: One company of Pz. Jag. Abt 352 being attached to you, it is now in Engreville. II Batt. Will counter attack WN65 to 69.

09.25. Ziegelmann to Major Block: Enemy radio captured, one message intercepted: All goes well just a little behind schedule. ALASKA out.

09.29. 914 to 352: Our left neighbour, 709. Division, says there are tanks between WN3 and 5 and are requesting anti-tank support as they have no contact with their units.

10.00. US 1st: CP established just off beach on side of hill at 684895. Battalions are moving forward, but are out of contact with regimental CPs. Beach and entire territory still under heavy fire and companies still meeting heavy resistance. Several landing craft have received hits and troops landing on the beach are receiving artillery fire, causing medium casualties. Things are becoming organised, however and the situation is beginning to clear.

10.12. 726 to 352: WN60 stopped the enemy from taking WN61 with the support of Nr 1 and four companies. WN62 is still firing with one MG but the situation there is critical.

10.13. AR 352 to 352: Ammunition for the heavy guns, IV Abt., is critical.

10.20. 914 to 352: Situation at WN3 and 5 is critical. Large groups of landing boats on the coast.

10.27. 916 to 352: Enemy is on the high ground north of St Laurent. [Reply]: You will attack as ordered with II Batt. and throw enemy back to the sea.

10.55. US 1st: 1st and 2nd Btns/16 I.R. got contact with regimental CP and are moving forward slowly, hitting heavy resistance.

11.10. 726 to 352: Despite earlier reports WN66 and 68 are still in our hands. At Point du Hoc the enemy is there in strength of about two companies. The enemy ships are firing heavy shells on the steel reinforced bunkers. WN71 and 73 have taken heavy structural damage but engineers are reinforcing the structures.

11.14. 726 to 352: GR 916 counter attacked at 1110 hrs against Hill 22 east of Asnelles, they have retaken Asnelles. The situation on left is critical; the church in Colleville is in enemy hands. WN60 and 62 stopped them from getting any further.

11.15. US 1st: CO to CO 2nd/16th Infantry: Battalion to hold up at point 38. Do not move further forward until you hear from us.

11.20. US 1st: S-3 to S-3 1st Btn.: Hold up at point 38 Right we have contact with 2nd Btn. 5th company GR 916 reported to be at Surrain.

11.35. US 1st: Negative report to division by radio.

11.40. 726 to 352: Southwest exit from Colleville is in enemy hands. Further tanks have been successful in getting ashore at WN62. Many tanks are stopped in front of anti-tank ditch.

11.45. US 1st: S-3 to Exec. Off. 1st Btn/18 Infantry: 2nd Btn has landed. They will go in on your right. They will take your objective. You dig in and prepare for counter attack, Ok. A is on the right, C is on the left, with B Co. following. We are advancing slowly.

11.47. 914 to 352: I Batt. still has no enemy contact. In the Vire Bay there are strong concentrations of enemy ships with barrage balloons. The attack of II Bn. is going forward slowly.

11.47. US 1st: S-3 to CO 2nd Btn/16 Infantry: I talked to Capt. Smith and told him about the 18th. How soon can you move the rear part of your CP here by us forward? We have someone on the way here to pick them up and guide them forward.

11.55. 916 to 352: The enemy has one platoon on the southwest exit of Colleville. Further tanks have got ashore at WN62.

12.05. US 1st: Exec. Off. 1st Btn to CO: Can we get any tanks up to Colleville sur Mer? [Reply]: No, none of them are up to us yet, they aren't off the beach. However, as soon as we can possibly get anything up, we will shoot it up to you. Keep yelling for it.

12.05. Ziegelmann to 914: Concentrated fire of II/AR 352 has been given against enemy company at WN3 and 5. WN1 is surrounded.

12.10. US 1st: CO C Co. to S-3 16th Infantry: We must have tanks or artillery up here soon. Will you see what you can do about it for us? [Reply]: OK.

12.20. 709 Division to 352: Armour has broken through our lines 4km deep. In front of WN3 and 5, masses of landing boats and barrage balloons. Massed anti-tank weapons needed.

12.20. US 1st: Information received that the 3rd Btn, 18th Infantry was in, but location at present time was not given. Probably only a rumour.

12.23. US 1st: CO 16th Infantry to CO 3rd Btn: 2nd Btn has had units in Colleville for some time. 1st Btn landed on the left of E-1 and is pushing to assist the 2nd Btn in taking its objectives.

12.25. Ziegelmann to LXXXIVA.K: Point du Hoc is defended by two companies of enemy infantry. Counter-attack with parts of GR 726 in progress. [Reply]: The General [Marcks] has placed under your command Schnellebrigade 30 for the defence of the right flank, they are on the march to you now.

12.32. US 1st: Exec. Off. 1st Btn to S-2: A Co. is at 678892. Part of B Co. is with them and the rest in going in reserve. We are going over to Point 19 first, then towards 38. C is at 681884, moving very slowly. Capt. Meredino, B Co., lost about 12 men from pillboxes firing on them. He couldn't get contact with battalion. Major Driscoll said he wanted him over on the right, Driscoll says he is 100 yards NW of 20 and still pushing.

12.35. 726 to 352: The enemy has driven into Colleville again. WN60, 62 and 62b still in our hands, the enemy still has 61 now reinforced by 1 tank.

12.55. US 1st: In with 3rd Btn/16 Infantry by wire.

12.57. US 1st: MSG to Division CO: Prisoners stated that the CP 10th Co. 726th is at St Laurent sur Mer. CP 12th is at Grandcamp, that is 116th sector. CP 5th Co. 916th at Surrain. The 916th relieved the 915th two weeks ago.

13.01. US 1st: In with 3rd by wire.

13.12. US 1st: 1st Btn. 18th Infantry is landing and is passing through the CE area and will follow the wire up.

13.18. US 1st: Major Lauren to 1st Btn/16th Infantry Adj Lt Kolb is trying to find your CP and is following the wire up.

13.25. US 1st: S-3 to 2nd Btn/16th Infantry: Where are you? [Reply]: CP is moving forward. We are not in contact with them right now. They took a radio with them to keep in contact with us.

13.27. US 1st: S-3 to 1st Btn/16th Infantry: Are you with Maj. Driscoll now? [Reply]: No, he is at the forward CP and we can't contact him now. However I can give you the dope. A Co. is pinned down by a strongpoint, just at the head of the draw there at E-2, over by 20. West of Colleville B Co. is going along sending a couple of sections over to help out C Co. C Co. is 100 yards NW of point 20. The Naval Shore Fire Control party is out with Maj. Driscoll now. The 2nd Btn is held down. We are in the buildings S and E of 20. There is stuff all around. S-3: Artillery fire is coming in on the beach now. [Reply]: Well, I can't tell where it's coming from up here.

13.40. II/915 to 352: On the left flank of the battalion between 62a and b the enemy has driven south, the flank has been extended left.

13.42. 914 to 352: Two companies from II Bn. are in defensive positions on the Carentan Canal, also one company from W100b will attack the enemy paratroopers towards the south from Villadon.

13.55. US 1st: CO 16th Infantry to Division CO: White out by wire.

13.58. AR 352 to 352: I Abt. reports that Colleville has been retaken. The tanks in front of Asnelles have changed course to the east; there the bridgehead on the coast is already solidified.

14.00. 916 to 352: 5/GR 916 has stopped the enemy breakthrough between WN62a, b and 64 with a counter assault and is leading the attack of II Batt.

14.20. 726 to 352: Attack of I/GR 916 on Meuvaines must drive in the direction of St Côme, as eight tanks with infantry have attacked WN40a, b, and c. WN60 and 62 still in our hands.

14.26. 11/916 to 352: Our attack on the enemy strongpoints has met strong resistance and we have taken heavy losses. WN62 is still holding out, 62b has no more mortar rounds left. The enemy are in the church and southern part of Colleville, counterattack in progress. [Reply]: The enemy must be thrown out of Colleville at all cost. WN60 and 62 must stay in our hands.

14.25. US 1st: More prisoners brought in. Prisoners have been coming in by twos and threes since the landing. MSG, 2nd Btn to CO: I Co. held up at point 8.1 Co. unable to assemble forces to advance and has enemy infiltrating his position. L Co. same situation. I and L Cos are just beyond point 9. Tanks and reinforcements needed.

1440, US 1st: 1st Btn to S-2 C Co.: The same as before, and B Co. has moved up to the right of them. There is no other change.

14.55. 914 to 352: II Bn. in heavy battles with enemy in the hedgerows around Catz. At 1445 hrs another 100 paratroopers dropped NW of WN100, 23 prisoners brought in.

15.02. US 1st: S-2 [Intelligence Officer] to 2nd Bn: Have they cleaned out the town yet? A: The last report I had a half hour ago was that they were just on the outskirts of the town. I will check by the 300 set and let you know.

15.15. US 1st: 2nd Btn. to S-2: Capt. Dawson started into the town. He had a small counter attack. He had a couple of sections as far as the church. Wosenski is trying to clean up. Dogtag is going thru the town. S-2: Halftracks are in. I am sending them up, what is your location? [Reply]: The CP is at 683885. We have contact with the 1st Btn only by means of passing men. The 2nd Btn/18th Infantry is passing through. E Co. is working on the right, between G and Red. We received information from a civilian that there were about 150 Jerries in Colleville sur Mer. We have only about 200 men left: 115 in G, 2 officers and 40 men in E, and 2 officers and 12 men in F. There are possibly 20 more around.

15.40. US 1st: 2nd Btn to S-2: What is the latest with BLUE? A: Not so good. Part of I Co. didn't land. Very low in strength. 1st Btn to S-2: C Co. is moving very slowly. B is on the right, moving slowly, because of MG fire. As far as we know A Co. is on the same spot.

15.50. K.G. Meyer to 352: Have met up with I/GR 916 on our left. General axis of advance Meuvaines–Asnelles. Assault guns have linked up with us.

16.00. K.G. Meyer to 352: On the right flank of our line is Villiers le Sec, on the left is Bazenville. Enemy tanks at Creully have attacked towards the south.

16.10. 916 to 352: The enemy breakthrough at St Laurent has been enlarged; WN71b and St Laurent have fallen to the enemy.

16.12. 726 to 352. Have retaken WN39. WN38 is surrounded, however WN40 is holding against six tanks and one company of infantry. Seven tanks are in front of WN42 and more at WN44. Strong enemy landings at WN62.

16.34. 916 to 352: Between WN62 and 64 the enemy has broken through with tanks.

16.38. 726 to 352: Reyes has fallen.

16.40. US 1st: S-2 to Switchboard: Are we in with Danger Advance? [Reply]: No sir.

16.50. AR 352 to 352: IV Abt. reports strong landings of tanks and trucks between WN62 and 64, which are pushing inland.

16.58. AR 352 to 352: Between WN67 and 73 there are also further landings of tanks and trucks.

17.10. II/915 to 352: The Batt. has been able to gain the rear of the enemy on the Colleville plain but he is driving to the south. The wounded cannot be brought back to the rear any longer.

17.21. AR 352 to 352: Further strong landings on the Vierville coast reported.

17.25. US 1st: 16th Infantry to Division: In by Wire with DECOY.

17.30. K.G. Meyer to 352: At this time we believe the enemy has taken Villiers le Sec and the heights south of it with tanks and infantry. Fusilier Batt. 352, on the right, must withdraw from St Gabriel or be overrun; the assault guns cannot reach them as they are vastly outnumbered. We are not in contact with I/GR 915, which is near Bazenville. The CO Oberst Meyer, is probably seriously wounded and in enemy hands.

17.43. 726 to 352: The enemy has attacked from St Honorine towards Russy.

17.50. 916 to 352: Enemy troops have driven into Vierville, Asnières and Louvières and are getting reinforced.

17.53. Gen. Kraiss [from Korfes' HQ] to Ziegelmann: Collective report on the right sector: South west of Reyes in the hands of a Festungs Pionier Kompanie. I/GR 916 should be at this time linking up with us from the left.

18.00. US 1st: Capt. Smith, 1st Btn/16th to S-2: Major Driscoll says we need stuff up here to take out these pillboxes. If we can't get it we will be held up. We're leaving this for your consideration.

18.25. Ziegelmann to Pionier Batt. 352: Your unit along with Landes Bau Pionier Batt. 17 is ordered to report to command post of GR 916 for placement in the St Laurent sector.

18.30. US 1st: 26th Infantry started landing on the beach at 1830 hrs. A few enemy shells landed near them along the beach. Shortly after the cruisers and artillery guns opened up for a short period of time.

18.30. Gen Kraiss (From 916 HQ) to Ziegelmann: I/GR 914 has orders to clear up the situation at Point du Hoc. A counter attack from the east with detachments from Le Guay is also in progress.

18.36. 352 to Feld-Ersatz-Bn. 352: The Bn. and part of the Marsch-Bn., which will meet you shortly, are ordered to the area south of Mosles.

18.38. 726 to 352: Enemy tanks from Sommervieu are attacking towards Magny. To counter this we are attacking with six or seven assault guns in the lead.

18.40. 352 to Flak Regiment 32: Send all heavy batteries that are east and west of Bayeux to the defence of the city against tanks.

1935, US 1st: Cruisers and ships firing heavy counter battery on guns firing on beach.

19.35. 916 to 352: 15 large transports and 30 smaller ones reported 10km out heading SE. The enemy in Vierville has been reinforced by one company. [Reply]: Assault guns from St Gabriel are on the move to the west to counter the enemy tanks moving on Bayeux.
916: Our defensive line extends from the east of Colleville through WN69, 69b, and 71b. From WN74 to the west, all is in order. At Point du Hoc 9/GR 726 has held up the enemy south and east of there.

19.40. US 1st: Enemy barrage of artillery landing along the beach where the troops are landing. Casualties are light.

19.45. 916 to 352: Reports of enemy paratroopers landing at St.P. Le Guay.

20.45. US 1st: S-4 to DANGER 6: Do you have ammunition supply? [Reply]: We don't have any yet. S-4: Do you have any transportation in yet? [Reply]: No, we are getting some in on DUWKS and as soon as they come in we will send you one of the DUWKS with ammunition. It will come in at E-1.

20.48. US 1st: DELIGHT line is out.

20.59. 914 to 352: 50 transports have landed west of the Carentan Canal.

21.00. US 1st: Capt. Robbins to Major Heath: A German prisoner had two maps on him with three spots underlined. Believe they are strongpoints. These are at 659874, in the vicinity of the road; 665874, running along road to road junction and road north of it at 666875; and at Surrain they had underlined around 670859. Very little change.

21.00. 726 to 352: I/GR 915 has contacted us by radio; they are engaged around Bazenville and have captured an English General.

21.12. 726 to 352: In front of Port en Bessin, 15 large and 30 small landing boats.

21.15. US 1st: Col. Pickett, Division Signals Off, to Wiles: What is your equipment status? [Reply]: We are very short on our signal equipment. All the men that were carrying equipment were hit and we had to salvage what we could off the beach. Pickett: OK. I will try to get you another signal crew and what equipment I can.

21.35. Fusilier-Bn.352 to 352: Enemy infantry and tanks have taken St Gabriel, the rest of the Batt. has fallen back to Brecy.

21.36. US 1st: Capt. Bour, WHITE 1 to S-1: Any improvement on the evacuation of wounded? [Reply]: If at all possible, we will send them out to the ships tonight. S-1: Send them up to us as soon as you can, and we will take care of getting them out.

S-3/18th Infantry to S-3/16th Infantry: Williamson is located just north of goose egg on your map. One company at 702872, one at 702873, one at 695873, and one at 788875. They are advancing to the high ground and then will move toward the west. We are holding back our 1st Btn. Do you have anyone in Colleville? [Reply]: Not that we know. 5-3/18th: Is your 2nd Btn at 682878 and your 1st Btn at 679878? [Reply]: That is correct.

21.42. Ziegelmann to LXXXIVA.K.: From interrogations of prisoners at Sommervieu we know that the British 50th Division is there. They were landed from the transports at Port en Bessin, battleships have fired broadsides. Landings of stronger enemy units stands as before.

21.45. US 1st: DANGER 2 to S-2: What is the situation in front of you? [Reply]: Very vague. There is a pill box in the draw near Colleville and it's causing trouble. G-2: Is the enemy close to the edge of Colleville? [Reply]: The 18th is at the top of the hill south of Colleville, but our right flank is still held by the enemy. There is no enemy north of the road except at E-3 exit, where there is a pillbox. There's a heavy gun at Formigny and a few small ones at Russy. A few tanks were seen yesterday in Colleville. G-2: What about your left company? [Reply]: No reports of any today. We got prisoners from the 10th and 14th Companies. 916 is the only company we are in contact with now. G-2: There is a lot of shelling from the southeast and the Vaisy area.

G-3 to S-3: Any more dope on your two units near Colleville? The General says that place must be cleaned out by tonight. The 18th has two battalions in front of you. [Reply]: No, no dope on them.

22.10. Ziegelmann to LXXXIVA.K.: A detachment from S.B. 30 will be sent in to centre sector under GR 916. There, the situation at Grandcamp is unclear. Paratroopers have joined with Terrorists over there.

22.33. Ziegelmann to Korfes: Bns 517 and 518 of S.B. 30 are being sent to reinforce you. A new defensive line is being planned: Brecy – Esquay – Sommervieu – Pouligny – Tracy.

22.42. US 1st: DANGER 4 to S-3: Do you know where the temporary vehicle is? [Reply]: Yes it is at E-1. Capt. Fish has been out there. G-4: I'm setting up a temporary ammunition dump there. The ammunition will be rationed. Do you know anything about the 116th? [Reply]: Yes. They are getting along OK. They are southwest of St Laurent.

22.55. Fusilier-Bn. 352 to 352: Batt. is only 40 men strong, we have got 50 men from I/GR 915 as well as six assault guns.

22.55. US 1st: Capt. Toby, 7th F.A. to S-2: I had report from a medic that people in St Laurent had 29 Jerries billeted with them; they left tonight and were to meet in Louvières. S: 2 to DANGER 2: Col. Evans we had a report from 7th F.A. who talked to some civilians who said 29 officers were billeted with them in St Laurent, left tonight, and were to meet in Louvieres.

Maj. Tegtmeyer to Col. Picchy: We are not able to evacuate any of our people. There are no evacuation facilities at the beach and something must be done. [Reply]: We will try and see that it is taken care of at once.

23.07. Ziegelmann to Korfes: Part of Baupionier-Bn. 94, 360 men, are being sent to you for replacements.

23.10. US 1st: CO 2nd Btn/16th Infantry to S-2: Can you give me any dope? [Reply]:Yes, two battalions of the 18th are on that hill by you. CO: OK, people are infiltrating. We are digging in and need reorganisation.Tell the Colonel.

23.10. Gen. Kraiss to Gen Marcks:The division today has held up in a hearty defence an overwhelming enemy assault as best it could. Tomorrow we must expect new units after their heavy losses. The losses at our strongpoints of men and weapons total. Heavy air bombardment combined with strong naval artillery fire have destroyed most of the prepared positions and we must first dig in again. WN74 through 91 are still in defensive postures and holding up the enemy. At this time Pionier-Bn. 352 with 7/GR 916 will attack from Formigny towards WN68 to 70. 6/GR 916 has retaken WN65a, but now are pinned down by naval artillery fire.

II/GR 915 has taken after hard fighting the strongpoints north of Colleville, but is held up there and in need of ammunition.WN37 and 38 have fought admirably and destroyed six enemy tanks. On the left flank the counter attack of I/GR 914 against Point du Hoc is still in progress. Feld-Ersatz-Bn. and Marsch-Bn. are opposing the enemy assaults to the south in the areas around St Laurent and Formigny.The fate of III/AR 352 surrounded southwest of Reyes is not known.All the radio communication between AR 352 and their OPs is out

[Reply]:What reserves I can send to you I will, but you have to make the most of it now. Make each foot of earth as costly as you can until further reserves can be sent to us.

eight

THE PRICE OF EARTH

NIGHT had come, a cloak for both sides. A tired, breathless Leutnant Heinze arrived at his battalion's command post. Amazingly, only a handful of his men were missing. He then entered the bunker of Hauptmann Grimme to report in. The scene inside was dismal. In the flickering lamplight Grimme told him that most of Nr 1 Kp. had been cut down in an ambush and all the companies of the regiment had taken serious casualties. He ordered Heinze to relieve the men still holding out in WN78. The survivors of this strongpoint had reached Grimme by field telephone and were pleading for help. Outside the bunker Heinze gathered his men and headed out into the blackness towards the coast.

On the beach US commanders took advantage of the quiet to bring ashore as much men and equipment as they could. The 352nd was no different, using the night to bring back wounded, feed and resupply units. For some this was their first meal since the 5th. More and more men came through the lines; one of them was Oberst Meyer's adjutant, cut off in the movements during the latter part of the day. He was placed in command of GR 915 under Korfes, who was to be the overall Kampfgruppe commander.

The first real combat reinforcements had reached the 352nd's lines shortly before midnight. Schnellebrigade 30, three battalions in strength, had been ordered up to the 352nd by General Marcks. The leading elements of this unit, parts of Bataillon 517 and 518, and its commander, Oberstleutnant von Aufsess, reported to Generalleutnant Kraiss. They were dispatched directly into Oberst Goth's sector. Along with them they would bring ammunition and food. Few men were able to sleep on either side because they knew that with morning the fighting would recommence.

Along the 352nd's front it was the British that broke the morning peace first. Just after dawn, the weakened flank of Fusilier-Bataillon 352 was hit hard. The shattered remnants gave way and retreated into the lines of GR 915. This allowed the British to cross the Suelles at St Gabriel, then continue to push southwards. GR 915 also reported fighting at Esquay. Offensively, GR 916, without Heinze's company, was first into the fray for the 352nd. This was Gefreiter Simeth's first combat:

Gefreiter Peter Simeth, taken in Schlann, Germany, 1943 (now Slany, Czech Republic). This photograph was originally sent to his brother, who was killed on the Eastern Front. Note that he is wearing a well-worn early war tunic and cap. As was the practice, he was issued with new clothing before his departure to France. (Peter Simeth)

Grenadier Josef Geschwendtner, a member of GR 916 who served with Peter Simeth and was killed in action on 7 June 1944, during a counterattack against Omaha Beach, aged seventeen. The photograph was taken at Schlann, Germany, after the issue of new clothing, 25 November 1943. (Peter Simeth)

Grenadier Karl Wiesmuller, the last comrade of Peter Simeth's unit. They were captured together on 26 July 1944. Wiesmuller was wounded by a hand grenade at that time. (Peter Simeth)

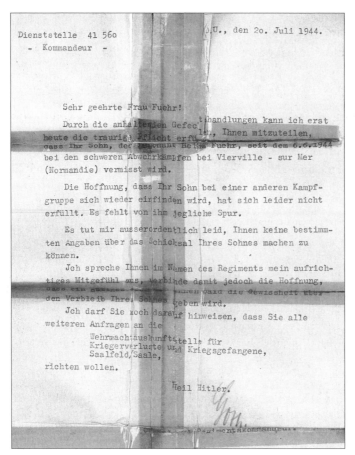

Dienststelle 41 56o
- Kommandeur -

).U., den 2o. Juli 1944.

Sehr geehrte Frau Fuehr!
    Durch die anhaltenden Gefec t handlungen kann ich erst
heute die traurige Pflicht erfü ..., Ihnen mitzuteilen,
dass Ihr Sohn, der Leutnant Heinz Fuehr, seit dem 6.6.1944
bei den schweren Abwehrkämpfen bei Vierville - sur Mer
(Normandie) vermisst wird.

    Die Hoffnung, dass Ihr Sohn bei einer anderen Kampf-
gruppe sich wieder einfinden wird, hat sich leider nicht
erfüllt. Es fehlt von ihm jegliche Spur.

    Es tut mir ausserordentlich leid, Ihnen keine bestimm-
ten Angaben über das Schicksal Ihres Sohnes machen zu
können.

    Jch spreche Ihnen im Namen des Regiments mein aufrich-
tiges Mitgefühl aus, verbinde damit jedoch die Hoffnung,
dass ein ... ...en wird die Gewissheit über
den Verbleib Ihres Sohnes geben wird.

    Jch darf Sie noch darauf hinweisen, dass Sie alle
weitere Anfragen an die
        Wehrmachtsauskunftstelle für
        Kriegerverluste und Kriegsgefangene,
        Saalfeld/Saale,
richten wollen.

                        Heil Hitler.

                             Regimentskommandeur.

Missing in action letter sent
to Leutnant Heinz Fuehr's
mother on 20 July 1944
by Oberst Ernst Goth. It
states that her son has been
missing since 6 June 1944
during heavy defensive
fighting near Vierville
on D-Day. The letter was
written on the same date as
the assassination attempt on
Hitler at Rastenburg.

During the early Morning of 7 June I was on guard duty with the MG; when dawn came it was bleak and grey. The shelling had gone on all night but now the explosive rounds began to drop closer to us and the ships' artillery began to shift farther back, a sign that the Amis would come soon.

Around 0800 hrs the Stugs went forward. My friend Josef Geschwendtner and I were on the first one. We advanced fast. Then suddenly a 'peng' from a shot rang out. I was standing on the back of the Stug and jumped off rolling into a ditch on the side of the road. Two more shots rang out and the Stug was in flames. My Kameraden went everywhere, all I saw was arms and legs flying about. I tried to go back and help, but the MG stopped me. I couldn't see if anyone was still alive because I was pinned down. I crawled back a little way, and with a shove, I pushed my way through a thorn bush and made my way back along another road. Half bewildered, I found my Gruppführer and reported to him. He sent me back to our Zeltlager. I had to go through Formigny, and the shelling there was still very heavy. I made my way as best I could through the devastated town; everything was covered with soot and black smoke. Finally, I emerged on the other side of town. I stayed in the roadside ditches while making my way along, this to give me some cover against the Jabos. Men, horses and cows were strewn all along the roads, the blood was everywhere. Telephone wire was all over the place; if you didn't watch your step you would be flat on your nose in a heartbeat. After some time I reached our camp. No one was there. Suddenly our Leutnant appeared and I told him all that had happened. He said that the other groups under the command of the Oberfeldwebel had broken through and pushed forward. He sent me to Oberst Goth to make a report. The Oberst sent me to the signals bunker to wait there for a message to take back to my platoon. Here I met another good friend, Karl Wiesmüller.

Simeth's officer was correct: the regiment was making some headway in their attack. But Heinze and his men had lost touch with the regiment for the second time in two days and Goth was furious at both him and Grimme, who had sent them out on a mission without his approval. Heinze had a problem of his own to contend with; he would worry about his commander later:

On the way to relieve WN78 we encountered two men, who literally ran right into us. They told us that they were the only two to make it out of WN78 alive and were trying to get through the Amis lines. I decided that we should return immediately. But when we reached the main road, it was occupied with a large American convoy. We too were behind the lines. With the small amount of ammunition we had, I let the convoy pass unmolested. Then another passed and yet another. When there was a break in the travel we crossed the road and used the hedgerows for cover. Since it was dark, movement was slow as we headed to our lines. I hoped that when daylight came the Jabos would mistake us for Amis since we were on their side of the line.

Despite the efforts of their fellow Grenadiers, Leutnant Fuehr and his surviving men on the beach had come to the end of the line:

Early on the morning of 7 June, my men captured two wounded Americans. I also sent out a Feldwebel and *Sanitater* [medic] to try to retrieve our wounded but these two men never came back. A little later on in the morning there was fighting but not as heavy as the day before. Our machine-gun ammunition was exhausted and I only had 15 or so soldiers left. Around midday the Americans attacked our position again. Over a loudspeaker they told us to surrender or they would use flame throwers on us. Before I could make any decision a round hit me in the helmet and knocked me out. I awoke as an American medic was treating my wound. The Americans gave me and my men cigarettes and sweets.

Nursing their wounds and with the subdued joy that comes with still being alive, these battered soldiers were led into captivity. They had put up an amazing fight against over-whelming odds. The rest of their Kameraden were still pressing home an assualt towards the beach.

In this attack, Pionier-Bataillon 352 was pressing forward, regaining ground. Under cover of the pre dawn darkness, a patrol was sent out to assess the situation around St Laurent. Obergefreiter Brass and his squad were assigned:

I took my squad, Gruppe 5, 2 Zug of Nr 1 Kp., which consisted of twelve eighteen-year-olds and a twenty-two-year-old officer, Leutnant Leischner, out to find the village of St Laurent. We also had to find out what the Amis had set up for a defence. In the darkness we came upon some houses, and Leutnant Leischner wanted me to go back with a message that the town was in our hands. But I persuaded him to let us make sure this was St Laurent. He asked

me how. My thoughts went quickly to the First World War memorial that was in the centre
of most French towns. This would have the name of the town on it. The night was peaceful
and under the cover of the MG we went forward. There was no defence, the village was clear.
They found the memorial, and a message was sent back, 'St Laurent is in our hands.' For this
action in which we had not fired a shot or even seen the Amis I was put in for the Iron Cross
Second Class by Leutnant Leischner.

Brass' patrol had slipped unnoticed through the American lines. The rest of Pionier-
Bataillon 352 began to push forward with GR 916. When they linked up with their
company, Brass and his men pushed towards Vierville to reach Germans still holding out in
the town and surrounding area. During this attack they took about 30 prisoners.
       Private Van Roosen nearly began his day with a disaster, just outside St Laurent:

The next morning didn't start out well. A G Company PFC, who had come back from the
29th Rangers, was wounded by a sniper. When I went to get him the sniper put a bullet right
beside me. He lay there until we could get counter fire going and some mortar fire so we
could evacuate him. We took too long. He died on the way back to the beach and I suffered
through my first casualty.
       We heard a rumbling coming from the direction of the beach in the mid-morning. I got
out the Bazooka, as we knew it was a tank. With all the shrubbery atop the hedgerow I
couldn't see that far. When I saw a flash of metal through a small gap I fired. The Bazooka
round bounced off the turret of a Sherman Amphib. My assistant had not taken out the
safety pin from the round. Another learning experience! It was also lucky for the guys in the
Sherman. If one has to make a mistake it is best that it occurred the way it did.

On the other side of the town, Private Milton Burke's group was suddenly under attack
as Pionier-Bataillon 352 pushed towards Vierville. Burke was farther down the column
strung out along a road when they were hit. He couldn't see much from where he was but
made his BAR ready for action:

Up front they called for the BAR to be brought forward. One of my buddies turned around
and said, 'Burkey, that's you!' I got up and started running up the road as fast as I could. The
next thing I remember was that I was flipping over in mid air and then coming down hard.
A mortar round had landed just behind me. The medics were on me in seconds and within
minutes I was on my way back to the beach to be evacuated.

Burke's wounds, although in a rather embarrassing place, were serious; his buttocks were
torn to shreds. The fighting was over for him but he was in good hands, as the US Army
possessed an excellent system to care for and evacuate their wounded. The German units
had already lost much of their ability to do this for their wounded. German medics were
relying on newspapers and rags for bandages when supplies ran out, and it was not uncommon for them to take the first aid packets of the dead of both sides, though this was not
permissible under the Geneva Convention. Movement to the rear was impossible some
days because of the Jabos so many men who could have lived if they had received proper
medical attention died without it. Several men with minor wounds opted to stay in the
line with their units because of the hazards of the trip to the rear. Wegner's new-found

A group of men from Pionier Bataillon 321 which would be formed into 352 Pionier Bataillon in November 1943. First on the left standing is Obergefreiter Karl-Heinz Voss. He is wearing riding boots and breeches because of his assignment as a mounted messenger. Sixth from left, standing in the centre is Gefreiter Fritz Klipp, the biggest man in the unit. He was killed in action on 9 June 1944. Sitting on the ground, far right is Gefreiter Josef Brass.

friend Helmuth elected to stay despite his pain. His group found themselves facing off against US Rangers at Point du Hoc on that morning:

> Our group was kept together as a heavy MG team under the direct command of the ZugFührer. I was still the Nr 1, Willi Nr 2 and Helmuth was now our Nr 3, the ammunition carrier and rear security. We were told that a new gun commander would be given us. Helmuth's wound gave him much pain but he steadfastly refused to go to the Verbandplatz [aid station]. We cleaned it and changed the bandage when we could. Since this morning, we were opposing the Americans' famous Rangers. They were far better soldiers than us. We couldn't make any headway against them and they were too few in number to make a big attack against us. If they did it would have been bad for us. For now it was just another game of waiting to see who moved first.

In Littry, Oberstleutnant Ziegelmann received a call from the commander of WN76, at Pointe et Raz de la Percée. This officer and his men were still resisting. He did confirm all of Oberst Goth's prior reports, but had called specifically to inform Kraiss that the Americans had unloaded on to the beach vast amounts of supplies and equipment during the night and were now offloading more troops and armour. The officer added that these operations went on completely undisturbed by artillery or Luftwaffe interdiction, a fact Kraiss was fully aware of, but about which he could do nothing.

The remainder of the morning saw GR 916th's advance begin to stall and then finally halt, putting them on the defensive, but not before Heinze and his men managed to get through to them. The officer went straight to Oberst Goth to inform him of the ordeal he and his company had been through:

> When I reached the bunker to report the past action of my company, I found Oberst Goth not pleased with me at all. In fact he was furious that I had not been there to be used in the last attack. Despite my arguments of being ordered on a mission by Hauptmann Grimme, he yelled at me that I couldn't fight and should be shot. I think he was going to shoot me on the spot. But without warning, the Amis attacked the command bunker. I turned and faced him, saying 'Let me go back to my men and I will show you how well I can fight.' He nodded and sent me off. At first I was demoralised by the event but then realised he was only giving me a shove in the right direction. Now I had renewed spirit.

Gefreiter Simeth was still waiting for a message to bring back to his platoon when the attack began: 'All of a sudden things got very hot. We had to defend the bunker. We were surrounded for a long time. We held, and were told help was on the way.' Oddly, during this action the US troops did not cut off any of the telephone lines that led away from the bunkers. This allowed Goth to lead his regiment even though he was physically cut off. Soon enough the siege was ended and Simeth got the promised relief: 'We fought into the afternoon and then finally my platoon broke through. The Feldwebel and some men were wounded. Four others were killed.'

Even while Goth was besieged in his bunker, Major Korfes and his battalion were falling back towards him under pressure from a massed British assault. Over the radio, Korfes told Kraiss that the British had reached the Bayeux–Caen road near St Leger, adding that III/AR 352 was using the last of its ammunition in direct fire against British armour around Reyes and Sommervieu. The new commander of GR 915 informed Kraiss that his I Bataillon had managed to get into the northeast part of Colleville in support of Goth's men, facing an American attack from St Laurent towards the south.

It looked as though all of Kraiss' lines would break under the pressure. Everything he had was already in the line, used in the morning attack. Then von Aufsess reported that most of his brigade would be arriving during the day. This would consist of the balance of Bataillons 517 and 518, the entire Bataillon 516 and all the support units. Marcks had told the Oberst that the mission of his men would be to close the open right flank and prevent the British from taking Bayeux. Kraiss called Marcks to inform him of the new situation around St Laurent and ask that part of Schnellebrigade 30 be used there. Marcks agreed; since a portion of Bataillon 517 was already with GR 916 the rest could be sent up to Goth at Formigny. Von Aufsess would proceed to Bayeux to link up with Korfes. Arrival time was a factor that only the Jabos could determine.

As he ended his call to Marcks, an explosion rocked the building Kraiss was in. Jabos were attacking the divisional command post. The headquarters occupied the buildings that surrounded the church in Littry, all of which were being attacked. The building where Kraiss and Ziegelmann were was hit particularly hard. Casualties amongst the staff members were high, and there was no doubt in the Generals' minds that the attack was the result of the maps on Meyer's body being found. The attack centred on the houses that contained tactical sections. Those that the support services occupied, only 500 metres away, remained totally untouched. After recovering from the effects of this attack, Ziegelmann was ordered to make a personal tour of the front to assess the situation for Kraiss. Despite his rank and position, he was to suffer the same dangers anyone else did while heading for the lines:

> Towards 1600 hrs I drove in the Kubelwagen to the C.P. of GR 916 and from there on a side road to WN76 [Pointe et Raz de la Percée]. The trip, which usually takes thirty minutes, consumed five hours. The fighter bombers forced us to take cover. The view from WN76 will remain in my memory forever. The sea was like a picture of a 'Kiel review of the Fleet'. Ships of all sorts stood close together on the beach and in the water, broadly echeloned in depth. And the entire agglomeration remained there intact without any interference from the German side. I clearly understood the mood of the German soldier who was missing the Luftwaffe. That the German soldiers fought here hard and stubbornly is, and remains, a wonder.

This sight made it abundantly clear to Ziegelmann what his division was up against. He would attempt to make the picture as crystal clear to Generalleutnant Kraiss; but for now he was once again crouching in a ditch while Jabos circled above.

The status of the 352nd was already in flux and would be transformed by the time Ziegelmann returned to Littry. Kampfgruppe Korfes was resisting tenaciously but this had not prevented the British from taking Reyes and finally getting into Sommervieu. When a muddied Ziegelmann made it to Goth's headquarters from WN76, he was told that II/GR 916 and III/AR 352 had been torn to pieces by Jabos and massed artillery fire. Grimme reported that he was trying to rally the survivors and rounding up stragglers for some sort of defensive line. The Amis had pushed out of St Laurent in a few spots and got into the gun positions of II/AR 352, north-east of Formigny. The gun crews were now fighting as infantry. Both in Colleville and Vierville, the tide of battle had surged back and forth many times, each side taking, losing and retaking the same houses, all the time losing more men. This was something that Kraiss could not afford.

At Point du Hoc US Rangers had broken through some of GR 914th's defences, pushing them back a short way. All these events once more focused minds on the need for reinforcements to prevent a major disaster. Schnellebrigade 30 had still not arrived. These troops had to travel a hazardous 90 kilometres, all on bicycles. The Jabos were a constant, louring presence above them. Oberstleutnant von Aufsess arrived at Littry by Kubelwagen to inform Kraiss that the bulk of his forces would not arrive before the early morning of 8 June. These men would get no rest because Kraiss wanted them sent directly into the lines once they arrived.

To Kraiss' surprise his men had stabilised the situation by nightfall. Artillerymen from AR 352 had stopped the British advance just west of Sommervieu. They had used their heavy guns in direct fire roles against tanks and had the crews without guns fight as infantry, although some small British elements did reach and cross the Bayeux–Caen road. The last survivors of GR 915 held a thin line north and northwest of Tilly sur Seulles. There was still no contact with 716. Infanterie-Division. Patrols sent out could only locate a few rearguard detachments along the road near Bretteville.

Eventually, Ziegelmann made it back to Littry. His report was not what his Generalleutnant wanted to hear – but had expected. Kraiss called General Marcks with this news and to discuss tactical options. Both felt the only real hope of destroying the beachhead was to attack the Americans in strength around St Laurent and Colleville. All the attacks made by the

352nd had been thwarted but had shown that the US troops were green and relied heavily on their air and artillery support to get them out of tight situations. This support tended to diminish in close-quarter fighting, which allowed German infantry to push forward.

It was clear that the 352nd was much too depleted for an attack that could destroy the American forces in front of it. Marcks felt that Kraiss was correct to suggest that his division go over to the defensive, the main objective being the containment of the beachhead. If the 352nd could keep the US forces to a small area it would give the Germans a better chance to destroy them once reinforcements arrived en masse. The problem was that Hitler and many of his Staff Generals still believed that Normandy was a diversion and the real invasion would come at Pas de Calais. Any Grenadier in the 352nd could have told them differently. While going over to a purely defensive role, Kraiss pointed out to Marcks that his infantry strength was only about 4800 men. These were opposed by no fewer than four Allied divisions. Their only support was the twenty remaining guns of AR 352 and the attached flak regiments, plus the six surviving Stugs. All this stretched over a front 53 kilometres in length. It would be a very thin line indeed. Marcks realised this and again stated that he would do his best to get higher commands to commit troops before it was too late.

In the darkness, the first columns of bicyclists from Schnellebrigade 30 arrived in Littry. It was the three remaining companies of Bataillon 517. They were exhausted and had lost several men along the way. Ziegelmann dispatched them directly to GR 916. After another two hours of pedalling, they reached Goth in Formigny. He sent them, by foot, into the line to relieve his I Bataillon, which was withdrawn to the rear for some rest. 517th's appearance meant the balance of Schnellebrigade 30 would be arriving soon. If they did, he could have over 2500 fresh troops in the line before dawn. That evening the intel gods would bless Generalleutnant Kraiss a second time.

During the house-to-house fighting in Vierville, an American officer was killed. His body fell into the hands of Pionier-Bataillon 352. It was discovered that he had a briefcase chained to his wrist. Easily removed with wire cutters, the case was sent back to Hauptmann Paul. A quick look at the contents, and he knew that it had to get to Division HQ immediately. He called for a dispatch rider. Obergefreiter Karl-Heinz Voss reported to him:

> I was given a large leather case with specific instructions. My Hauptmann told me that this was to be brought to divisional headquarters in Littry as fast as possible. I was not to turn it over to anyone except the IC [Major Block] or the IA [Ziegelmann]. I left the door of the command post and mounted my horse. I rode as best as I could through the confusion that filled the roads. I watched for Jabos, taking cover several times. Then, as night approached, I did not have to worry about them. But in the dark these roads were hard to follow and I got lost for a while. I met some of our men at a crossroad and asked directions. I was closer than I thought. I reached a church and then asked the men around it where I could find either officer. I was directed to a heavily damaged house. Inside, I found this officer and gave him the case. When he opened it the look on his face told me that I had been carrying something of great importance. I left to care for my tired mount. I would catch a little sleep and head back before dawn.

It was a little before midnight when Major Block was handed this briefcase. When he opened it he could not believe what he saw. Contained within it were the entire opera-

First page of Gefreiter Karl-Heinz Voss'
Wehrpass.

Gefreiter Karl-Heinz Voss'authorisation
to carry classified documents as a courier.

Gefreiter Karl-Heinz Voss' declaration
of non-Jewish ancestry, also needed for
security clearance.

Obergefreiter Karl-Heinz Voss' induction
notice.

tions orders for the US V Corps, which directly opposed the 352nd. Both US Corp plans within 24 hours! He ran to Kraiss to show him the material. These documents showed in exact detail the plans and organisation of the US forces arrayed against them. Ziegelmann was present when they arrived, and was impressed by what he saw:

When the division, towards 0000 hrs, received the captured order from Vierville the situation could be estimated in a much clearer way. In my opinion this extensive operations order disclosed that the invasion plan was far beyond the scope of the American V A.C. I admit that I, along with my divisional commander, did not have the time to study this operations order in detail. This order covered every minute item from D Day to D+17 (as far as I can remember) and continued with much data on organisation, armaments, assignments, tactical intentions, radio plans, etc. On a sketch map, small scale, it could be seen that the boundary line between the British XXX A.C. and the American V A.C. lay at Port en Bessin (British) then along the course of the Drôme.

According to the time schedule of the enemy, they intended to build a bridgehead on D-Day at St Laurent with the American VAC (codenamed 'Omaha'). On D+1 they wanted to have reached the line Isigny Bayeux; on D+3 the line St Lô–Balleroy. In this plan the area of 352. Infanterie-Division was given out as St Lô. Next to the organisation the names of the regimental commanders and their adjutants were given. Of the divisional HQ the enemy only knew the name of the Military Law Inspector [this information was dated January 1944]. After D+2 the American XIX AC was to begin pushing 30 Infantry Division between the VAC and VII AC. It showed that in addition to the army tank battalions the subsequent deployment of the US 2nd Armored Division was also planned for. Moreover, it was assumed that the establishment of a strong trans-shipment port (called 'Mulberry A') had been provided.

I must say that never in my entire military career have I been so impressed as in that hour when I held in my hands the operations order of the American V A.C. I thought that with this captured order, the German Seventh Army and Army Group B [Rommel] would reach a decision. I later learned that this captured order first lay around for days at Seventh Army HQ and reached High Command only after a long time. Even then it did not get the consideration it deserved, or else I could not account for the piecemeal bringing up of the divisions from the Fifteenth Army zone etc. in July and August. As a young general staff officer the impression was more and more as if in the highest quarters it meant 'looking, but not jumping'.

It is clear from this account and the historical record that higher commands let this opportunity slip through their collective hands with very little consideration as to the importance of the documents. Generalleutnant Kraiss realised the importance and, once more, had copies made of maps and orders dealing with the immediate situations on his front.

The condition of the men in the 352nd was prominent in the minds of the staff members. Most had been fed only one meal since the beginning of the fighting, and very few had had any real sleep. The level of losses amongst officers and senior NCOs was relatively high, but this did not create a major problem. In the German Army of this period, the ability of junior leaders to assume command and finish missions was one of its strong points. Obergrenadier Martin Eichenseer recalled the situation at this time as very tense:

I had been serving as a machine gunner since the evening of 6 June. We attacked the morning of the 7th but then we ran into a wall of fire and shrapnel, literally, from the ships and Jabos. We lost many during the day, especially our leaders. By nightfall, anyone in command was either an Unteroffizier or Obergefreiter. This attack had frayed everyone's nerves. We kept asking where the damn Luftwaffe was and when would Rommel arrive with his Panzers. We still believed this would happen. We had confidence because every time we met the Amis without their support fire we beat them back. I'm not saying that we were elite or anything like it; we just had more experienced leaders. The biggest gripe was that everyone was hungry and tired. With a good meal and some sleep things might have looked different. In any event we were quite happy when fresh troops arrived allowing us to pull back.

This was the arrival of Bataillon 517, which meant rest and food. As far as food was concerned, Kraiss gave explicit orders to the commanders of his support units that all troops at the front must be fed by midnight and that they be given rations for the next day to carry with them.

The condition of the artillery after the offensive actions of the day was poor. Most of the flak guns had been destroyed on the roads by Jabos. This was mainly because of their lack of manoeuvrability and poor camouflage. Those guns that survived the day were now at the front in anti-tank roles. AR 352 was at less than half of its pre-invasion strength with many of the remaining guns having no ammunition. The one bright spot was the six remaining Stugs, their crews having become more skilled in hedgerow tactics. Using their low profile they hid behind hedgerows, striking the taller Shermans with deadly results. They reported hitting 40 Allied vehicles, of which 11 were Shermans and 15 were armoured cars or half-tracks. Most of these were British, since four of the Stugs were operating on the 352nd's right flank.

Another noted exception to the depressing news was the actions of Nachrichten-Bataillon 352. So far, these men had kept most inter-divisional units of the 352nd in contact, and Kraiss in touch with higher commands, while at the same time intercepting numerous Allied transmissions – many of which were not in code. Major Block was able to use some of these transmissions to verify the accuracy of the captured operations orders and ascertain some immediate tactical plans of units opposing them. This gave 352's regimental commanders something of an edge, coupled with the fact that many of the US troops were still green, learning tactics on the go.

The common practice of the GI, as the Grenadiers saw it, was to fall back to cover and call for air or artillery support. In this manner German troops in small numbers could hold back much larger formations of enemy troops. While the GIs were learning, so were the Grenadiers, like Eichenseer:

Being new to combat myself I really did not pay attention to the way the Amis fought in general. But our leaders did. When we got into a long firefight the Amis would fall back and within minutes we would be pounded by Jabos or *Arifeuer* [artillery]. So, we began to fall back about 10 or 20 metres when we saw the Amis pull out, letting them hit where we used to be. Then it was something of a race to see who could get back to their positions first, us or them. We played deadly games with our lives.

The Allies had the supplies to fight tactically by using materiel rather than lives; the Germans did not. It was almost impossible for supply trucks to get to the front unmolested by Jabos. Supply at night was the only way. Wounded and prisoners had to be evacuated as soon as possible. It was hoped that the Red Crosses on the ambulances would deter any attacks by fighter pilots but artillery shells made no such distinctions. On the night of 7 June over 300 prisoners waited to be brought to the rear, and despite the constant shelling, not one was wounded.

7 June had seen a small reduction in the length of the 352nd's front, from 53 to 50 kilometres. The US V Corps was firmly established on the coast, but according to the captured orders they and the British had not achieved any of their main objectives within the 352nd's sector. However, Kraiss had lost his only real chance of defeating the invasion. The attack along the Vierville–St Laurent bulge was the last chance the Germans would have to destroy this beachhead and drive a large wedge between the other, more easily established and successful ones. The 352nd did not possess the proper support or strength to accomplish this mission. The advent of darkness would allow them to transform from the attacker to the defender, a change that would bring with it some advantages. First of all, the Germans had superior knowledge of the countryside and terrain. The 352nd had been training in it for eight months. They knew where every back road was, where it led to, where the best natural obstacles were, where the best observation post would be, and so on. The artillery had pre-plotted, as was the standard practice, all roads, crossroads, hilltops, farms and anywhere else that might have to be shelled. This would enable them to use their undersupplied guns to get maximum results. Pinpoint accuracy is far more effective than saturating an area with large amounts of shellfire. And finally, the American penetrations inland meant that the Germans could now exploit one of Normandy's best defensive attributes: the hedgerow.

The hedgerows are ancient boundaries between farm fields found all over Normandy. They range in height, averaging about two metres. Over the ages, they have been built up by farmers while they worked the fields, adding stones and ploughed-up detritus to them. These mounds have then become overgrown with trees and bushes and bound together by the roots. They surround the fields like walls, and are ideal for establishing in-depth defences. Foxholes dug in them give good protection against artillery and air attacks. The Germans even cut tunnels through them in order not to expose themselves to Jabos along the roads. Allied tanks could not push through them, at least at the beginning of the campaign, and when they went over them they exposed their soft underbellies to Grenadiers with panzerfausts or to Stugs lying in ambush. Infantry either had to work their way up along the tops of the hedgerows or across the open fields in between. Both ways were tough going. When one hedgerow and field was taken, the action began all over again.

Wegner's group received a new gun commander on the night of 7 June, the same night the 352nd went over to containment and defence:

We had fallen back somewhat since the morning, but not as much as the division to our left [709. Infanterie-Division on Utah Beach]. In the evening we were put under the command of a new leader. He was Obergefreiter Paul Kalb. When I first saw him I was impressed. He was a big man of strong build, older than us, in his late twenties. In his buttonhole he had both the ribbons for the Iron Cross II and Ostfront medal. On his chest he wore the Iron Cross First Class and the Infantry Badge along with the medal for being wounded once. He was a real veteran. The lace on his shoulder boards indicated that he was waiting promotion to Unteroffizier. With his awards I would have expected him to already be one, but found out later that his wound was serious and kept him out of service for quite a while. He placed us, and the gun, in a better position on the top of a hedgerow. He first talked to us of tactics, saying that if we kept up with these full-scale assaults without replacements we would win the battle for the Amis. He had lost a whole squad since 6 June. He left to get more specific orders for the gun from the Leutnant. When he reappeared he was much happier and more confident. He told us that our mission now was to hold the Amis in the space they were now, until other troops arrived. To do this we would dig in where we were and use the hedgerows in our defence. And according to Kalb all the way back to Divisional HQ preparations were being made for this. Kalb ended by saying that the order was 'Make every field a FORTRESS.'

All along the 50 kilometres of front line, Grenadiers with shovels and picks hacked into the hedgerows. The race now was not for ground; the Germans knew they would lose it to the more powerful Allies. The Germans had to hold them in check until Berlin woke up and sent in more divisions. It was now a battle of endurance. But who would break first, the well supplied, but comparatively inexperienced Allies, or the under-equipped veteran Grenadiers?

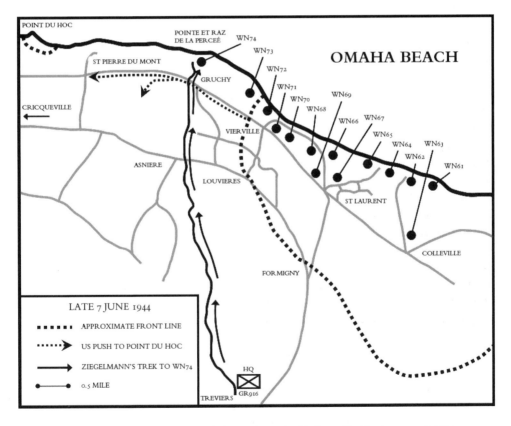

The route Oberstleutnant Ziegelmann took from Oberst Goth's Grenadier Regiment 916 HQ in Treviers to the strong point at Point et Raz de la Percee in order to view the landings at Omaha Beach. He had to evade US aircraft and troops to get to WN74. In his post-war interrogation he stated that he went to WN76 at Point et Raz de la Percee. In reality it was WN74; WN76 is east of Point Du Hoc and has no view of Omaha Beach.

nine

GREATNESS THRUST UPON THEM

P EACE did not arrive with night as it had on the previous day. Just after midnight on 8 June, British infantry with tank support sliced through the lines of GR 726, gaining a foothold in Bayeux. Intense street fighting broke out. Major Korfes finally got a message through to Kraiss at 0200 hrs. The troops from 716. Infanterie-Division were ineffective as a fighting unit and there still was no contact with their divisional head-quarters. Korfes was trying to gain control of any of their units in the area to aid him but had no success. Kraiss' only option was to use Schnellebrigade 30 in a counter attack to regain the lost parts of the city and form a new front east of it. A messenger was sent with orders for them to change direction and head straight for Bayeux rather than Littry. Oberstleutnant von Aufsess changed the direction, once more, of his exhausted men. It had been 36 hours since anyone of them had had any sleep, and now when they reached Bayeux they would go immediately into action.

Nachrichten-Bataillon 352 had intercepted several enemy transmissions; some were obviously ruses, but they got one of great importance. It dealt with the air bombardment of a suspected German headquarters at Cerisy. Since this was the place 352nd's headquar-ters was in the process of moving to, with some units already there, Kraiss ordered an evacuation of the immediate area, including civilians. With daybreak came the bombers. No lives, French or German, were lost. Kraiss continued the moving in of his new com-mand post. Oberst Goth was delighted with the arrival of Bataillon 517 but the Americans had other ideas. As the unit entered GR 916's sector, intense shelling from the Allied fleet began. The effect of these naval guns was tremendous, more powerful than land-based artillery. Some men were obliterated by the shells, others were lucky. Gefreiter Seidl was one of the latter: 'The *Schiffsarifeuer* [naval artillery fire] was extremely powerful. One of the big shells landed near us, throwing the bunch of us in the air. I was far enough away not to get hurt too badly but the others were killed.' Seidl's eardrums were blown out by the concussion and his hearing was minimal over the next few days but he would recover. He stayed in the line throughout this time.

Goth knew that this shelling was not a welcome present for 517. The strength of the barrage indicated that it was preparatory fire for a major US attack to enlarge the beachhead and to link up with the Allied forces on the left and right flanks. He also knew that at first light the Jabos would appear. This left him with the problem of positioning his troops during the barrage while it was still dark. This was dangerous and meant some kind of a withdrawal to a more defendable line. Gefreiter Simeth remembered that morning as one of quiet desperation and total exhaustion:

> The 8th of June brought another night of no sleep. With the morning approaching, the situation once again got 'hot'. The Amis were going to encircle us so we had to retreat. With light steps in the darkness we left the bunker; our officers had already left with the vehicles. We went down the road, the same one we used to travel to work and march back again. The good asphalt had been destroyed by the *Schiffsari*. Telephone wire, cars and trucks lay strewn all along the way making our travel very difficult. Finally we came to Treviers. It was all destroyed, all I saw was a dog running back and forth, whining, looking for his master. I felt bad for the children who had lived here. It took us a long time to get through; all that was left was rubble.

GR 914 was still in basically the same position as the previous day, holding against the paratroopers at Brevands and Rangers at Point du Hoc. Neither side had made much headway. The Rangers had resisted every attempt by GR 914 to take Point du Hoc. US Rangers were especially aggressive, according to Obergrenadier Wegner:

> During the night the Rangers would attack and infiltrate our lines, even though we vastly out-numbered them. Willi and I were too jumpy to try and get sleep with these men against us. When we attacked we learned that they were good fighters all around. Once we heard the familiar rattle of one of our MG42s off to our right and I thought one of our groups had broken through their lines. I looked over the edge of our hole but Kalb pulled me back, he yelled at me 'Wegner, the Amis are using MGs they captured from us, so keep your foolish head down.' And he was right.
>
> Kalb was very good to us. He was like an older brother. He watched out for us. He had a wife and two little boys at home and sometimes I think he treated us like them. Although a friend of mine in another group, Dieter Behle, said that on the day of the invasion Kalb lost his group to Jabos with six killed and two wounded. He was the only one not hit but never told us about it in detail. In any event I was glad to have him with us against the Rangers.

The first reports of Schnellebrigade 30 and their operation against the British in Bayeux filtered into Cerisy around 0650 hrs. These were sketchy, and indicated that they were having a tough time even after joining up with Kampfgruppe Korfes. At 0800 hrs Korfes himself called Generalleutnant Kraiss. He reported that the attack was repulsed and both units had been thrown back, taking up positions in the southern part of Sully but they had prevented the British from breaking out of Bayeux. Kraiss ordered them to secure all roads that had crossings over the Aure river. Then he had Ziegelmann send one platoon from Feld-Ersatz-Bataillon 352 and a section from a Luftwaffe flak regiment to secure the Drôme river crossing. The Jabos hindered them, but these two units made it to their objective by late afternoon.

Reports of Allied air attacks were coming into divisional headquarters faster than they could be logged. It appeared that on this day there were more of them than on the day of the landings. The majority of landlines went out, communications were left to radio and messengers. The vaunted Luftwaffe was still absent from the skies.

The dispatches coming in from Korfes indicated that the fighting around Bayeux was heavy and unrelenting. The British seemed intent on breaking through to link up with US troops on Omaha Beach. Their main thrust was just behind the coast, but bypassing strongpoints around Port en Bessin – the cut-off Germans could be dealt with by other units. At Longues, survivors from HKAA 1260 held up the British advance with a remarkably determined defence. Eventually, this pocket was bypassed as well. However, once this main thrust hit 352, it ground to a halt just two kilometres inside the 352nd's old lines. It was expected that the British would resume the attack when fresh troops and supplies arrived.

Oberst Goth had been correct in his assumption. The US forces attacked in three directions simultaneously – east, south and west. They too ignored the existing strongpoints on the beach. Goth's men put up a tough fight. Even so, the GIs pushed into the northern part of Formigny. US troops made good headway as they pushed west from Vierville along the road to Grandcamp. Their objective was to reach the Rangers at Point du Hoc. The entire line of GR 916 was being pushed back. Gefreiter Simeth was sent back to his platoon, reaching it just as the attack began:

> Around noon we were hit again, the Amis pushed us back until we reached a village. It was still somewhat intact, offering us much protection. Here we stayed fighting until evening in a large ditch. This protected us, with the benefit of the branches of several trees, from attacks by Jabos.

It was not just Goth's men, but also the entire 352nd that was collapsing under the collective assaults of the Allies. Kraiss just did not have adequate manpower for this overstretched line, and with his troops exhausted from lack of sleep, it is a wonder that the line held at all. Kraiss was informed that even regimental command posts were under attack. Goth was fighting with his staff members in Formigny. Oberst Ocker and the staff of AR 352 were street fighting in Tessy. It was clear that the 352nd had to withdraw to a more defensible line. He decided that GR 914 would withdraw and occupy the village of Longueville and the surrounding area, absorbing Ostbatallion 621, which was already there. The move would keep them in line with GR 916 and prevent them from being flanked. This would open the road for the GIs to relieve the Rangers, but it was no longer of tactical importance to the 352nd. The main problem for Kraiss was not the Allies but rather the Führerbefehl. He needed to shorten his front and to do so meant that he would have to withdraw to a position where he could properly link up with the divisions acting on his flanks. Failing this, the 352nd would cease to exist by the next day. He placed a call to General Marcks to explain the division's situation and request permission to fall back. Marcks said that he would be at Kraiss' command post by 1500 hrs to discuss the matter. This left the Generalleutnant cold, all he could do was wait while his men fought on and died.

A call came into Kraiss from von Aufsess at 1400 hrs. The Oberst calmly stated that his men were being pushed back towards the southwest from Bayeux and that he and his command post were under direct attack by British infantry and tanks. Hearing the sounds of battle through the receiver, Kraiss told him to hold on as long as possible, but if he had to, he could fall back to the new line Kraiss was establishing. The Generalleutnant had no authority to give this order, as it was in direct contravention of the Führerbefehl.

General Marcks arrived. In a steady tone, Kraiss told his commanding officer of his division's situation. He went on to declare that he had already authorised Kampfgruppe Korfes and Schnellebrigade 30 to withdraw to his planned line. He ended this briefing by noting that if the Führerbefehl was reaffirmed by Marcks, the 352nd would not be able to hold and its collapse would open the way for an Allied advance on a broad front to the south. The decision now lay with Marcks.

There was a long silence, with Marcks contemplating the possible repercussions of a decision that he knew to be tactically correct; Kraiss silently hoped that his commander would not be cowed by the generals far away in Berlin. Marcks spoke, authorising the withdrawal, but with conditions.

First, all of the remaining strongpoints on the coast must remain in operation in order to hinder the landing of supplies and tie up US troops. They could only withdraw when their ammunition ran out. Secondly, Kraiss and his staff must prepare an operation to support a planned armoured assault against Bayeux on 9 June. Kraiss readily agreed. Marcks did not know that 352 had no contact with any of the remaining strongpoints. These were on their own with regard to further resistance, withdrawal or surrender.

Ziegelmann and his staff went to work right away. By 1800 hrs all units had been advised of the new plans and issued orders for the attack on 9 June. In all likelihood, it would be a fighting retreat because of the US advances. This new main line of resistance, HKL, or *Hauptkampflinie* – literally 'main combat line' – would run just north of the Aure river and south of the N-13. Kraiss also ordered that all troops in the rear be rounded up to form a secondary line behind the Aure.

The night of the retreat gave Leutnant Heinze time to contemplate the past few days:

> The withdrawal was hasty, the men were in a state of total exhaustion. The prospects of sleep this night were dim as well. All of the signs showed us that this new line would not hold against the strength of the Amis. The words spoken by that Feldwebel to the Major rang in my head this whole time.

Generalleutnant Kraiss felt that his front would not be able to hold for an extended period because of the condition of his division. This move signalled that the 'door' had been kicked in all the way.

Some minor successes had been achieved during the withdrawal. Oberstleutnant von Aufsess had rounded up over 500 stragglers and 5 Stugs from GR 915 to add to the 352nd's depleted strength. On 8 June divisional losses totalled over 2000. Ziegelmann credits the lack of a major enemy breakthrough to the endurance of the German Grenadier. It must not be forgotten that the GIs and Tommies were just as tired, and Allied troops had had orders to take specific objectives on that day, which they did. This was the first step back towards St Lô and proof that the 352nd would fight every inch of the way.

Filthy, tired and hungry, Obergrenadier Wegner headed off towards the Aure river line:

> Since the late afternoon we had been on the move. Earlier we had withdrawn from the coast to Longueville. All the day we were harassed by Arifeuer and Jabos. The roads were littered with dead horses and burning vehicles. All around was the din of battle. Even though we fell back, other parts of our regiment were still fighting in the hedgerows. Sometimes it was only a handful of men, but here that could hold up a company. We always looked skywards searching

Josef Brass (centre) in St Fosse, northern France, May 1942. On the left is Theo Zeinbold, killed in action 9 June 1944 while leading a squad as an Unteroffizier. He is buried in La Cambe military cemetery.

for the Jabos, which came time and time again. It was always the same, dive into the ditch and keep your head down. For the most part, it was useless to shoot back because they were gone as fast as they appeared. We did see some shot down by flak soldiers. But always we asked the same question; '*Wo ist die Luftwaffe?*' This question got many answers but the most common was, 'They're all back home protecting Fat Hermann's [Goering's] medals.'

From Longueville, we went back farther to a new HKL. The march was one of numbness; we were so tired we didn't feel our feet. The only thing we wanted was some food and to lie down and sleep. I still carried the MG over my shoulder but Willi carried his load and that of Helmuth. His leg was much worse; every step he took was painful. Kalb helped him along but he still refused to go to the Verbandplatz. At a rest stop Kalb told us that if he did not get medical attention soon he would lose the leg, and maybe even his life, adding that his chances would be better if the Amis took him prisoner, since our medical troops were in a state of disarray. At the first chance he would be left so that he could surrender and live. If he stayed with us death would be his only reward.

Through the darkness came sounds from the rear that gave heart to the disgruntled Grenadiers: the neighing of horses and the muffled clanging of pots. The 'Gulaschkanone' (goulash cannon) field kitchens had come up to feed them. The meal was meagre but warm, giving them renewed strength. Even field rations were given out. Officers realised that sleep was now more important than digging foxholes in the dark. They allowed their men to rest. The lucky ones got as much as four hours straight, their first sleep in two days.

9 June arrived without the fanfare of the previous day. It was four hours into the day before Ziegelmann was awakened by the first report of action along the front. Oberstleutnant Heyna had detailed Ostbatallion 621 to protect the bridges across the Aure at Isigny, with orders to destroy them in the event of an American attack. Under the cover of darkness a US armoured column penetrated the town. Most of the Russians ran in total confusion across the bridges to escape the onslaught. Only the German NCOs and a handful of more stalwart volunteers stayed to fight. They were no match for the GIs, and within minutes most were either dead or prisoners. Those that survived made it across the river and tried to rally the Russians on the other side. The bridges were lost and Ostbatallion 621 had ceased to function as a unit. Then Major Van Dem Bergh and his I/AR 352 were on their way to cross these bridges with his guns. They spotted the US column on the road advancing to Isigny.

Undetected, they left the road and headed for an emergency bridge built by Pionier-Bataillon 352 just north of the town. This bridge could not support the weight of the guns, and the river was too deep to ford. Van Dem Bergh had to destroy his guns but took his 400 men and their horses across the Aure to safety. This group reached the command post of Heyna and reported the situation to Ziegelmann. Kraiss was enraged, he now had only 14 guns left to cover a front of 40 kilometres. And with the loss of Isigny it was clear that the Americans would drive towards the vital crossroads of Carentan. Heyna was given orders to move into this area and hold the line along the N-13 around La Madelaine, stopping any advance towards Carentan. Wegner was abruptly awakened from sleep. His company was sent on another forced march, the third in 24 hours.

The men of Goth's regiment were putting up a dogged resistance, and now took some time to lick their wounds. II Bataillon had only three officers left, Hauptmann Grimme, the Battalion CO, and Leutnants Heller and Heinze. Heller was senior to Heinze in grade and a particularly able combat officer. Originally commanding Nr 6 Kompanie, now he had absorbed the remnants of Nr 7 and Nr 8. This was now known as Kampfgruppe Heller. Heinze still had his Nr 5 Kompanie, although greatly diminished in number. This battalion now held positions around Mandeville, Treviers and Rubercy. Goth's I Bataillon was in much the same shape. Hauptmann Loges was not as aggressive as Grimme and Goth had to keep him under a firm hand.

The night of respite benefited 352's right flank the most. With dawn came the massed attack of the Panzer-Lehr-Division. This was the attack that 352 was supposed to have supported. However, under the current conditions it could not be done. Panzer-Lehr took the pressure off Kampfgruppe Korfes, giving them time to regroup and form their front. Luckily, over 100 men and five artillery guns, cut off since the day before, came through their lines. Amongst them was the Kampfgruppe commander, Major Korfes. He and his staff had fought their way through the Allied lines after being surprised by British infantry at their command post the previous night. Attempts to contact Panzer-Lehr-Division by radio and patrols failed.

East of Isigny, another American attack was stopped at Monfreville by GR 914. The GIs could not get across the Aure. If the armoured unit that took Isigny had not halted outside of the town, a major hole in the 352nd's front could have been opened. This delay allowed Heyna to get his men into position to prevent any further movement forward. GR 914 also made attempts to contact the new division on the 352nd's left, the 91. Luftlande-Division, again with no success.

Unteroffizier Werner Knapp's Nahkampftage document noting his service at WN69a and Mandeville whilst serving in GR 916. It states that he received a bullet wound to the leg on 9 June 1944 and was sent to hospital in Paris to recover. He rejoined his unit on 7 August 1944. Werner Knapp survived the war. (M. Galle)

Somehow, Gefreiter Peter Simeth struck lucky again. His platoon had ended up in the village of Rubercy. During the night he found a barn that looked inviting. He crawled into a stall and amidst the hay, just as soft as any bed, he fell asleep. His wake-up call came in the form of an artillery barrage that shook him from his well deserved slumber. The shells landed all around the farm but amazingly no one was hit. It did mean that sooner or later the Amis would come:

Around midday the Amis attacked. Then we went right into the defence. The first four squads went to the right of the main road, I was in Nr 6 Gruppe, which went to the left along the road but keeping in the ditch. We reinforced another platoon. Overall it went this way; once a man was wounded, one of us took him back while another took his place. If he was killed one of us just went up and took his place. Soon it was my turn. I went up and got down next to a fellow with a head wound; his brains were shot away. Lying next to him I brought my rifle to bear and fired back in the general direction of the Amis. This was some bushes far away, I could see their muzzle flashes as they fired at us. This didn't last long because the Amis brought their mortar and Arifeuer to bear on us. Our numbers began to shrink, then they attacked our flanks. We had to go back or be cut off. One man went this way, another went that way and suddenly I was alone. I heard something in the bushes. When I investigated I found six men there that I did not know. I ordered them to fall back with me. We did so together, firing and fired upon as we went.

Simeth was not alone; all of GR 916 was being pushed back. US forces made and crossed the Tortonne river, keeping the pressure on Goth and his men. At the same time an attack from Isigny towards La Madelaine drove back GR 914 towards there. Parts of I/GR 916 were heading for Voully as well. Goth and Heyna ordered these unit commanders to mutually support each other for the time being. Nachrichten-Bataillon 352 once more intercepted a message, one which would save their own lives. Late on 8 June the battalion moved from its exposed position in the town of Vaubadon to the Forêt de Cerisy. Here, they picked up an American transmission stating that there were large troop concentration in the Forêt de Cerisy, which would be bombed that afternoon. The signalmen moved and reported this to Kraiss. The raid hit an empty forest, allowing the men to watch the show and take great comfort in the fact that they were not engulfed in the firestorm.

In the early afternoon Kampfgruppe Korfes was hit. Masses of British infantry had broken through on the roads from Bayeux, pushing towards the west and south. A newly promoted Oberst Korfes was compelled once more to defend his command post. Luck was not with him this time. He and most of his surviving staff were taken prisoner. Responsibility for the right flank now passed to von Aufsess. He went into action at once, organising his Schnellebrigade 30, GR 915 and I/GR 726 into a cohesive combat command. He built a new line of defence just south of his previous positions. Here they stopped the British advance. The armour supporting this drive was halted on the road to Le Molay by two 88mm flak guns placed there by von Aufsess. The British tanks could not even get within range to fire at the German guns.

This ability to constantly regroup to defend or attack under most circumstances was one of the primary reasons why the outnumbered Germans could maintain such a formidable resistance. The Kampfgruppe was born out of this need and had learned during the campaign in Russia. By the time of Normandy campaign, it was something that German troops were expected and their commanders were trained to do.

First page of Unteroffizier Werner Knapp's Soldbuch. (M. Galle)

GR 916, using the hedgerows as a base for their defence, had stalled the American push. However, the attack had shifted some of Goth's men towards the west, causing several men to become cut off and lost. Such was the case of Gefreiter Simeth:

> After we fell back from Rubercy we continued on until we found a farmhouse. At the door stood a pretty girl. We asked her for something to drink. She spoke with us then brought us a pail of milk. There wasn't a drop left when we had finished. We bid her goodbye and left. Eventually we came across a road. On it was a whole column of destroyed vehicles and ugly bomb craters. All the cows in the meadows that bordered the road were killed. By nightfall we reached Isigny. We were met here by other men from our unit in retreat; it was my platoon and our platoon leader. He wanted to stay and fight in the town but soon there came a motorised flak unit. He stopped them and yelled at us, 'Raus, Alle aufsitzen.' We hurried and all sat down on the trucks and guns they towed. The flak soldiers said that the Amis were right behind them. We left in one big hurry and soon the town was in flames. We drove through a wood. Here we had to blow up some of the trucks and guns because they were out of gas and we had no more. The rest of us in the overcrowded trucks drove through the night.

Gefreiter Simeth and his men could not have gone to Isigny. It was too far to travel on foot in the time allotted and was already in American hands. The town was most probably Bernesque, as US troops had attacked Bernesque that afternoon pushing the Germans out. Many of the buildings were set alight by the fighting. Outside of the town is the wood where the flak troops stopped, the Bois du Molay.

At La Forêt the supply depots were in danger of being overrun. Kraiss had no troops to spare. He sent out an officer patrol, which rounded up stragglers and rear echelon troops from the areas south of Isigny to stop the American advance on the depots. Despite the inexperience of these troops, they did hold up American tanks long enough for the depots to be evacuated. No supplies were left behind or destroyed.

With GR 914 split in two, Heyna was facing a dilemma. In order not to cause a large hole in his and the 352nd's front he ordered his I Bataillon to fight their way south through the American lines. The goal was to have them link up with the rest of GR 914 defending the area south of Isigny. During this drive I/GR 914 found lost detachments from both AR 352 and III/AR 1716. The latter had lost all the transports for their guns and had to destroy them in place. The entire manoeuvre was a success, with I Bataillon taking up position in the small bridgehead still occupied by the Germans south of Isigny. The men from III/AR 1716, 300 in all, were absorbed as infantry replacements for GR 914. This allowed Heyna to extend his line and regain contact with GR 916.

As a defensive move, Kraiss ordered the bridges that crossed the Aure along his front to be destroyed when the last of his men got across. Obergefreiter Brass and his Gruppe were detailed to one of the smaller bridges:

> We prepared the bridge, which was somewhere around Treviers, for destruction. We could see the Amis off in the distance, as our position was a very good one for defence. We did fear that we would be bombed from the air, but that never happened. The Amis wanted the bridge intact. We just had to wait for the order to come to blow the bridge. Units and small bands of troops were still crossing it.

In the late afternoon the first indication of large-scale troop movements into the front from the German side arrived at 352 Headquarters. It took the form of a rather conceited officer, Commander of the Aufklärungs-Battalion (reconnaissance) of 17. SS Panzer-Grenadier-Division 'Goetz von Berlichingen'. He presented himself to Oberstleutnant Ziegelmann and informed him that he was going to reconnoitre the area north and north-east of Balleroy. Ziegelmann told the officer that this sector was already in Allied hands. The officer shrugged this off saying he would go in the direction of Tilly sur Seulles–Bayeux–Bernesque. Ziegelmann gave the officer permission to move within 352's area, but felt that he would have done so regardless.

Amongst the men with this detachment was Unterschafführer Ferdinand 'Freddie' Schmidtz. He was an artilleryman driving one of his unit's officers. They were here to plot fields of fire for their Artillerie-Bataillon, which would be the next unit from their division to arrive at the front. Freddie was new to this unit; he had been home on leave in Köln after serving in Russia with 10. SS Panzer-Division 'Frundsberg'. It was bad: American bombers by day and the British at night. He was glad when the news of the invasion came and he was ordered to report to France and join the 17th:

> Somewhere along the way from Tours I picked up this mongrel pup. My commander was tolerant and let me keep him as sort of a mascot. I called him 'Pierre'. I was assigned as a driver and took the dog in the car with us to the front. On the way, with our division, nick-named the '*Kuss mein Arsch!*' (Kiss my Ass!) division, my officer and I were sent ahead with the Aufklärungs-Bataillon to prepare and coordinate fields of fire and targets for the guns. So he, I and Pierre went up to the front.

The SS unit, with cars and lightly armoured scout vehicles, reached the Seulles river. They were advised by men from GR 915 not to cross. The warnings were ignored. Along with the rest, Freddie and Pierre crossed the river:

> All was going well and the officer stood in the back of the car, making notes on the maps and looking through his binoculars. Then Pierre became agitated and jumped from the car, run-ning to some bushes about 100 metres away. I looked at my commander and he said to go and get Pierre. I reached the dog and turned to go back when all hell broke loose. A round hit the car, obliterating it and the officer. I lost a good Kamerad but that little mutt saved my life. But getting back to our lines was going to be tough. With Pierre clutched to my chest I made for the other cars as they sped back to the river.

Shot up, missing men – but not Pierre – and with damaged vehicles, the SS men came back across the Suelles, not so cocky as before. GR 915 reported this much to Ziegelmann.

Regardless of this little foray into Allied lines, the arrival of these SS troops meant that fresh troops in numbers were coming to take up the fight. With luck this would mean the 352nd would be able to shorten its lines to a much more reasonable length, per-haps 15 or 20 kilometres. General Marcks, who knew firsthand of the 352nd's problems, ordered Kraiss to have his division fall back to the southwest. Here they would take up a front beginning at Berigny, following the Vire and Elle rivers to the Carentan Canal. 3. Falschirmjäger-Division would move into the open right flank of the 352nd, shortening the front to a length of 35 kilometres. Kraiss insisted that his division did not have the men to cover that much front either. General Marcks refused to hear the argument, ordering the 352nd to be in the new positions by 0600 hrs on 10 June.

At 2300 hrs the task of informing all units and commanders of the move was complete. All bridges across the Aure would be destroyed when the troops of the 352nd finished crossing the Vire and Elle rivers. Then the Pioniere would have to take out these bridges as well but there were adequate supplies of explosives. If no explosives were available, the Pioniere were instructed to dismantle them by hand, a difficult task, to say the least. These bridges had been of benefit to the 352nd. All troops crossing them found themselves 'transferred' into the division. Some flak guns that had avoided service with the infantry were grabbed. Even with these added men the numbers were not good. The total combined strength of infantry which 352 could muster was just over 2300 men. For support they now possessed 30 guns of various calibre with limited munitions. Even knowing the Allies' general plan of attack could not help Kraiss if either the British or Americans launched a major assault. With this knowledge, the conduct of the Allied commanders puzzled the Germans, in particular Ziegelmann:

> We noticed that the enemy troops had gained confidence in themselves, feeling that they were getting the upper hand. This particularly applied to the 29th Infantry Division, which had been reinforced by one armoured battalion. True enough, a somewhat exaggerated superiority complex could be observed, such as for instance tanks which stubbornly kept on rolling forward along main roads without the support of covering parties and the carefree way in which quarters were taken up once the initial objectives had been reached, instead of exploiting success, etc. We Germans did not reckon that the enemy would cross the swampy Aure depression. It is true that there were no German forces available to stop the enemy from doing so. The portions of the 29th Infantry Division that got across it with their special equipment did not, therefore, have a particularly hard job. It was all the more astonishing, therefore, that these enemy forces and armoured formations approaching from Isigny stopped their advance at Bernesque and turned off southwards. We had the feeling that the enemy divisions had not learned to work together properly as of yet and that liaison between them was poor. Had the thrust of the 29th Infantry Division been continued farther in an easterly direction, it would have resulted in the entire front of 352. Infanterie-Division, which was thin in any case, being rolled up.

The move at midnight masked the tired Grenadiers. All had to be done with the utmost secrecy. As quiet as humanly possible, these men headed away from the Amis. Gefreiter Simeth and his platoon were still riding southwards with the flak detachment, not knowing of any of these changes. But he, at least, could catch up on his sleep. Obergefreiter Brass was ordered to blow his bridge exactly at midnight. This order was countermanded at the last minute. He was to wait until dawn in order to cover the withdrawal. Then he and his men would head south to safety, but on their own. Leutnant Heinze was amongst the first to reach the new HKL, and now set about the job of preparing a line of defence. He learned much in the past three days about fighting the Amis, all hard lessons:

> At first we would fight in the traditional way but the material that the Allies possessed would beat us. Once we had set up positions, when American aircraft flew over my men convinced me to let the MG fire at them, in hopes of bringing them down. These planes seemed to be

well protected on their undersides as the bullets appeared to bounce off of them. Soon after-wards came the Jabos and Arifeuer. They hit us with all they had, literally driving us into the ground. After this bombardment I went to find my friend Leutnant Heller. The ground was torn apart and I found him with his men in a dugout. He was crying. He was not ashamed of his tears because he was crying for his men who had been killed. This much decorated soldier had been in the French campaign of 1940 and in Russia. He said to me 'If they would only fight us man to man we would have a chance, we can't fight their planes and bombs.' I knew he was right. And now we learned not to fire at their recon planes. Otherwise, our tactics were simple when attacked by infantry. We would hold with the aid of the hedgerows. If we saw them withdraw we then did so ourselves because in moments Jabos and Arifeuer would pound our foxholes. Then their infantry would take over our old line, thinking we were destroyed. Afterward they would advance casually and we would hit them from the next hedgerow. We lost ground, but this was a slow process. It was all we could do.

After one such action we took many prisoners. Their officer came to me and said something an American President would make famous two decades later. He said '*Ich bin ein Berliner.*' He was born in Berlin but his family had emigrated to the United States. Our men shared photos of their loved ones with each other and we traded chocolate for cigarettes. The Amis were, overall, very chivalrous, as many of us were, and we tried to keep it that way. On the first day of the invasion I met an officer from one of our replacement battalions. I briefed him on the tactics to use. He was appalled and thought it was cowardly. He would adhere to the aggres-sive tactics. This was fine when supplies and men were plentiful but not now. I then met him again a few days later. I was glad that he was still alive. He immediately apologised to me for his previous behaviour. He said that through much bloodshed he had learned that I was right.

At 0200 hrs another call from General Marcks came into the 352nd's command post. Kraiss was ordered to strengthen the left flank of his line on the Vire, west of Isigny, so that the Americans could not unite beachheads north of Carentan. Emphatically, Kraiss told his commanding officer that if he placed all of the men in his division in this sector it was still doubtful if they could repel a concentrated effort by the Americans. Those already on the way there were on foot and would reach the area by dawn. The only other alternative was for Kraiss to shift his artillery so that he could bring all of it to bear in that sector. Even so, they could not be in firing positions west of St Jean de Daye before midday. Then he boldly asked to have detachments of 91. Luftlande-Division placed in that sector. The answer was no, they were unavailable. After the call, Ziegelmann, who had listened in on an extension, agreed with Kraiss that Marcks must have been given these orders from higher com-mand who did not know the true condition of the 352nd. Soon after this the telephone rang once more. It was Oberstleutnant Creigern, Marcks' IA. The officer told Kraiss that a Kampfgruppe from 275. Infanterie-Division was ordered up to them, courtesy of General Marcks. This group, under the command of Oberst Heintz, was being subordinated to the 352nd. They were expected to arrive some time in the early morning. This was the type of news that Kraiss wanted to hear and just in the nick of time. The command post was being evacuated again, this time to the village of Le Mesnil-Rouxelin just north of St Lô. If Creigern had called minutes later the line would have been dead. Elated by this news the staff moved quickly and were fully operational by 0500 hrs on 10 June.

Of course, with this move they had lost contact with subordinate units for a short period of time. Attempts at regaining all contact were meeting some difficulties. In order to expedite this, Ziegelmann sent out his officer patrols once more, only this time larger signals detachments would accompany them.

While making their way to the new command post of GR 914 one of these patrols encountered some remnants of Ostbatallion 621. These men were brought to Oberstleutnant Heyna, who, despite their questionable worth in combat, assigned them to his II Bataillon. The Russians and Poles in many cases proved to be unreliable. In order to dilute the problem in his company, Leutnant Heinze dispersed them amongst the German troops, but several of them ran away in groups when the first shots were fired. Heinze does note that 'perhaps they saw that our star was sinking.'

When Oberst Goth's new command post had been located, Generalleutnant Kraiss headed there to confer with his senior regimental CO. Before he left, he was forced to send one of his staff officers on a dangerous mission. With all of Pionier-Bataillon 352 spread over the sector destroying and, in some cases, building bridges, no one was available when this new task came to light. In view of the current tactical changes, the bridge over the Vire at Neully had to be taken out.

This job fell to the divisional staff's Chief Pioneer Officer. With volunteers from the remaining enlisted men of the headquarters troop, he set off with the last few boxes of explosives in the 352nd's inventory just before sunrise.

Far away from Le Mesnil–Rouxelin the first rays of sunlight were streaking across the eastern sky. Obergefreiter Brass turned the handle of the detonator. A bright flash, a cloud of debris and then splashing as chunks of stone and wood fell into the Aure river as the bridge was blown. Brass and his men mounted their bicycles and quickly pedalled away. They headed south, keeping in the shadows of the trees as they rode, in hopes that this would hide them from any Jabo pilot flying this early. In the lead, Brass saw some men in the distance. He signalled for them all to stop – it was what he feared the most: 'In the fields up ahead were US troops, everywhere. We ditched the bicycles and on foot made our way quietly through the woods. The movement was slow but we would not have to worry about Jabos. Here they would think we were Amis. It was going to be a long, treacherous day.' Gefreiter Simeth was awakened by the jolt of the gun he rode on as it bounced along the cratered road:

> When morning came, the Leutnant and one man still sat on the flak soldiers' truck. The rest of us were clinging all over the gun it towed. Suddenly the truck turned the other way and we had to jump off but the Leutnant and other man disappeared with the truck as it went around the bend. [Maas and the other man reached Goth's command post later in the day.] We were in the area of Le Mesnil-Rouxelin near St Lô. We met a Hauptmann and he sent us to the schoolhouse in the village. We knew it well because this is where we had trained. We got another ride with some Kubelwagens to the village. But these were attacked several times by Jabos. We arrived, finally, at about three in the afternoon. From here we went up to our company. We were all together again. My Kamerad, Eduard Schötz, was there but of our platoon, ten men were missing, six were wounded and five dead.

Otherwise, the morning of 10 June was peaceful. A large quantity of stragglers, like Simeth, came in and regiments took the time to consolidate lines and regroup. This was important because of the men from different units absorbed by 352, many had no field equipment, in particular sailors and labour battalion men. Oberst Goth now had men from over 30 different detachments and services under his command. His general theory was that if enough experienced officers and 'old hands' were in leadership positions these new men could be used much more effectively. Time would tell.

The first reports of enemy action against 352 arrived at noon. SS Artillerie Regiment 17 under the command of Kraiss until the arrival of the rest of 'Goetz von Berlichingen', announced that a strong enemy armoured force had entered the Forêt de Cerisy and Balleroy. In the town was a German forward aid station containing some 200 wounded and several medical personnel. They were trapped with no way out. The German officer in charge came to terms with the advancing Americans. The aid station was surrendered and both German and American medics evacuated the wounded. This American column advanced as far as the southern edge of Balleroy, only to dig in. The SS artillerymen were amazed at this. Even more so was Oberstleutnant von Aufsess – he only had one company of 90 men standing in their way.

At GR 916's command post, Oberst Goth showed his Commander the regiment's defensive line. The front for them was seven kilometres long. Behind this, Goth had just over 1000 men, reminding Kraiss that many were not regular infantry or even German Army troops. Whilst these two officers were discussing tactical options, a message came in for the General. First, a small expedition of US troops had crossed the Elle, just west of St Jean de Savigny. This was pushed back across without much of a problem, but another larger force crossed just east of the first group and was successful in holding their bridge-head against counter measures. Kraiss ordered Goth to wipe out this bulge in the lines, and then left for his own command post.

Heyna's move had not been executed very well. He had lost contact with his II Bataillon and now held a very weak front of four kilometres manned by 500 men. Most of these were Major Van Dem Bergh's artillery troops. It was hoped that the II /GR 914 would reach their expected positions west of Isigny soon. Altogether only 18 kilometres of the 352nd's 35 kilometres front were actually covered. The peace was holding, and this was good for the lost groups trying to find their new positions. Wegner and his team were amongst them:

At this point we were not quite sure where we supposed to be going. The officer in charge led us down one road, then across a field, then another road and a field once again. We were lost. Kalb was disgusted, in addition he was carrying all of the spare ammunition for the MG and Helmuth's rifle. Willi had to help Helmuth along now, the poor kid could hardly walk any more. While we stopped for a rest Kalb looked at the leg, he showed it to me. It was all infected with pus oozing from the gash. It made me sick to look at it. Kalb, as always, was straightforward when he spoke to the boy.

He said 'Helmuth, your leg is very bad. You can't walk any more, both you and I know this to be true. The only way to save you and maybe the leg is to leave you behind for the Amis.' Helmuth was startled by this. Kalb saw this and put his hand on the boy's shoulder and again said, 'It's the only way.' Helmuth looked at Willi and me. We both said it was a good idea and all for the best. Willi joked, saying that tomorrow he would have a full belly and warm bed while we still wandered lost through the countryside. Kalb went off to find a good spot to leave him. When he came back he told us to pick up Helmuth and follow him. The spot he found was well protected from Jabos and Arifeuer, overlooking the road. We placed him in a small depression, giving him the last of our water and chocolate. From his pocket Kalb pulled a small white flag with a red cross on it. This he tied to a stick and gave to Helmuth. Along with it he gave clear instructions. He said, 'Listen up, when the Amis come they won't see you but you can see them. Let the first groups pass because they will be a little nervous and may shoot. When the next group comes keep low and wave this flag. You'll be OK because the Amis aren't like the Ivans. Now take this and send it back to me when the war is over, on the back is my address. Good luck.' Kalb had given him a picture of him and his family. We, too, scribbled our addresses on the back of it, then said goodbye. Many times as we walked away we looked back at the spot where we left him. There was nothing else we could do.

When Karl Wegner returned home from captivity in 1948 there was a letter waiting for him. It was from Helmuth Wittner. The letter described how he was found by American GIs and they had saved his leg at the US hospital. Out of gratitude he was going to America to become a citizen.

When the Generalleutnant returned to his headquarters he was informed that contact had finally been made with 91. Luftlande-Division. Kraiss asked to speak with Generalleutnant Falley. He was told that Falley had been killed in action on 6 June by American paratroopers. Now in command was Oberst Konig, who explained to Kraiss that his division was in no shape to take over the defence of the Vire river bend. He listed the strength and conditions of the 91st's units, and they were in worse shape than the 352nd. As expected, IV/AR 352 took up position west of St Jean de Daye just after noon. This detachment was re supplied with munitions the night before, and thus able to bring the GIs advancing from the bridgehead at Auville under fire, slowing their move towards Carentan. After a short time, this detachment was joined by several guns from II/AR 352 who had been lost on the back roads in the area. These guns then began to bring the main road from Isigny to Moon-sur-Elle under fire. Another message was sent to the munitions dump in this sector, and before the end of the day a second supply of shells was brought up. This gave both detachments ample ammunition for sustained bombardment of targets.

Heyna was also lucky enough to acquire one lone 88mm gun from a flak unit that was driving through his zone. This may have been the one Simeth had been riding on, since it headed that way when it turned off the road. Heyna used this as a cornerstone in his line, giving him a solid punch against any advancing enemy armour. Along with the re-establishment of artillery support, which seemed too good to be true, the left flank became quite defensible.

The promised Kampfgruppe from 275. Infanterie-Division was having difficulty getting through to Kraiss. During the late afternoon this unit's commander, Oberst Heintz, arrived in Le Mesnil-Rouxelin. He told Ziegelmann that only Fusilier-Bataillon 275, travelling on bicycles, would arrive by the morning of 11 June. All other detachments were on foot and would arrive piecemeal from 12 June onwards. These units were I and II/GR 984, one company from Pionier-Bataillon 275, III/AR 1275 and the appropriate signal and supply personnel. The 352 needed them to fully man the front immediately. He ordered Ziegelmann to do anything he could to get transportation for the rest of Kampfgruppe Heintz.

An exhausted messenger reported to Heyna from II Bataillon. He said that his unit was going into line as ordered, and the battalion CO had left a detachment to guard the ford they had used to cross the Vire near the destroyed bridge at Neully, the main reason for their tardiness. The Chief Pioneer Officer and his volunteers had done their job but in blowing the bridge they had cut off II/GR 914. This battalion's arrival could not have occurred at a more opportune time. The Americans at Auville had been joined by large armour and infantry groups and had pushed as far as Catz. Here they linked up with the elements of the US 101st Airborne, bottled up there since 6 June. This advance was being held up by AR 352 who maintained fire along the route of attack.

The divisional staff was still in the process of attempting to get any form of transportation for Kampfgruppe Heintz when a Luftwaffe officer arrived. He was the liaison officer from 3. Falschirmjäger-Division and was there to inform Kraiss that his division would be moving onto his right flank that afternoon. This was excellent news for the 352nd. Now the front could be shortened, creating a stronger line, even before the arrival of Heintz. The move coordinated by Ziegelmann and this officer would have GR 916 and Kampfgruppe von Aufsess move several kilometres to the west, but leave the artillery from 'Goetz Von Berlichingen' in place to support the Falschirmjägers until their own guns arrived.

This realignment was a welcome change for the regimental commanders. All of them had misgivings about the large number of rear echelon and paramilitary men serving with their companies. Even dispersed amongst veteran infantry, these men could not be expected to hold a thin line on such a wide front. Shifting westwards allowed these commanders to have defences in depth around their core combat troops, though the problems did not go away, especially concerning command, as the following cases demonstrate.

When Wegner's group reached GR 914 and were placed along the front, they also received some new men:

With the loss of Helmuth and the mounting casualties, it was getting tough to carry all the ammunition and gear we had around. We were supposed to have five other Grenadiers with us but for one reason or another we were used as an independent machine-gun team. Most likely because we still had all of our equipment, tripod, sights and so on. Then we also had to carry panzerfausts and lots of grenades. Needless to say, we were delighted when the Leutnant, this officer was an artilleryman if you can believe it, brought over a group of men and detailed three to us. These men – actually most were boys of 16 – were the survivors of a RAD detachment. Many had no weapons. Some of their leaders were in their twenties and thirties. The Leutnant said 'Kalb, these three are assigned to you, get them some weapons and divide out what you have for ammunition.' Kalb saluted and the officer left with the rest. He then turned and began to give orders to the three while Willi and I began to shed some of our excess load. All of a sudden we heard Kalb and the older RAD man arguing. Both were about the same age, in their twenties. This fellow was yelling that he was a RAD-Truppführer, or something like that, which was equal to the rank of Unteroffizier in the Army. This was a grade higher than Kalb and so he demanded to be treated with proper respect at all times. This enraged Kalb. He stood face to face with this guy, pushing his finger deep into his chest as he said 'I don't care what rank you say you are, as of now you have been assigned to me as a Grenadier and that's the way you will be treated.' The RAD-Truppführer was going to have none of this and was going to get the Leutnant. Kalb grabbed him with both hands and threw him into the ditch. He landed right next to us. Then he was told to pick up several cans of ammunition and do as he was told or Kalb would put a bullet in his brain. The younger two were eager to follow any orders after this, even calling us 'Sir'. Kalb later told Willi and me that if this fellow caused any trouble we should shoot him in the ass and leave him for the Amis. He was never a problem because the next day he was caught out on the road by the Jabos and cut down.

The new arrivals had a worse effect in Heinze's company:

With the influx of new men in our units some problems were bound to occur. One new man was a Feldwebel who also held a high rank in the SA [Brown Shirts]. I had my own trusted NCOs whom I placed in positions of command. He was senior in rank to all of them and I finally had to make him an assistant group leader. Then one night I heard some shooting and went out with my runner to see what was happening.

This Feldwebel came running up to us shooting wildly saying that the Amis had broken through. I calmed him down and sent him back with my runner. I went forward to check on the rest of his men. They were very glad to see me. They said that the Feldwebel went crazy. He even had them dig in facing our own lines. I'm not sure he was really crazy or not, maybe he just wanted to get out of the fighting. Anyway they took him to a 'nuthouse'.

This man may have cracked under the strain of combat or he was feigning insanity; it will never be known for certain. However, signs of stress were apparent in many men in 352. Heinze noticed this with his new Battalion commander. Hauptmann Grimme was reported missing in action after the last barrage, which was particularly heavy. Hauptmann Loges was transferred from I/GR 916 to take over the job. Loges was, by profession, a school teacher and probably not the kind of man suited for a combat command or constant bombardments. Neither Heller nor Heinze were impressed by the man or his actions:

Hauptmann Loges was not able to deal well with his new command. He stayed most of the time in his bunker. It was rare that he ventured outside. Once a piece of shrapnel came through the bunker's roof. It landed right between his feet. Instead of being happy at his good fortune he just broke down. This was too much for him to take. For an officer his outburst was disgraceful. After this he became even more of a recluse.

Loges' conduct would affect command and control for II/GR 916 during the remainder of the campaign. He would merely relay the orders to his companies that Oberst Goth sent to him. He did not reply when contacted for orders during the fighting, but only relayed such requests back to Goth. Within a few days the command of II Bataillon fell on the shoulders of Leutnant Heller, aided by Heinze, leaving Loges as nothing more than messenger boy for Goth.

The sun was low in the sky when Obergefreiter Brass and his men stumbled into the 352nd's lines, a great relief. Leutnant Leischner sent them to the rear to rest for the remainder of the day. This break was well deserved. Obergrenadier Martin Eichenseer had lost many friends, some close and some just men he had shared a hole with since 6 June. Luckily he was still in one piece. He was glad that his brother serving in the SS was not in Normandy. He did not know that his brothers unit – 9. SS Panzer-Division 'Hohenstaufen' – was already on its way.

In Le Mesnil-Rouxelin, Generalleutnant Kraiss and Oberstleutnant Ziegelmann mulled over the reports given to them by Major Block. These contained intercepted radio broadcasts. The officers were puzzled at first because the information in them did not correspond to those on the captured orders. Ziegelmann suggested that the Allies were most likely beginning to deviate from the original plans. All the moves up to and including those on 10 June identified the next US objective as Carentan, a vital crossroads, and the joining of Utah and Omaha beachheads. The weakened state of the 352nd would give the US V Corps an easy route into St Lô if they chose to pursue it. As long as the inactivity of the Americans continued on their front, the 352nd could continue to strengthen their defensive capabilities. If Kampfgruppe Heintz arrived, Kraiss would be in a much better position to repel the attack he knew would come. It was just a question of time. Since they knew that St Lô was the primary objective of any Allied offensive launched against them it only made sense to place the bulk of his troops on his right flank. From here, his men could hold up concentrated drives into St Lô, aided by 3. Falschirmjäger-Division, which was a top quality unit. All that was needed for the 352nd to accomplish this was for the Germans standing in the way of the US V and VII Corps to fight long enough for the redeployment of these German paratroopers and the arrival of Kampfgruppe Heintz. Ziegelmann summed up the day:

> It may be said without exaggeration that 352. Infanterie-Division forced the enemy to change his time schedule through the commitment along its coastal front at Bayeux, the enemy thinking the division to be in St Lô at that time and describing it as an 'offensive' division. The enemy intended to be on the line St Lô–Balleroy by D+3, in order to be on the line Avranches–Domfront by D+17 [or D+19]. It is true that the 352nd was no longer on the coast by D+4 (10 June) and that it could no longer be considered a full infantry division, but it had successfully fought with the old soldierly virtues and given the US V Corps anxious moments, even making the success of the invasion itself seem in jeopardy, as it was expressed in an American service newspaper that subsequently came into our possession. It [352. Infanterie-Division] received honourable mention as the Premier Division in the *Deutsche Wehrmachtbericht* of 10 June 1944.

It is doubtful whether the 352. Infanterie-Division could have prevented an enemy break-through on the new front in the direction of St Lô. It was too sorely in need of rest and reinforcements. If the enemy failed to take advantage of a moment of weakness which must have been known to him, it demonstrates once again that he was working to careful – yet excessively long-term – plans and his reconnaissance left too many gaps.

In every way 10 June was a watershed for 352. Infanterie-Division. From Generalleutnant Kraiss down to the youngest of Grenadiers, the day provided a much needed respite from the fighting. By the time night had fallen, this division had been transformed from a battered, hungry and exhausted band of men to what it was supposed to be, a functioning combat command, ready once again to engage the Allied forces in battle.

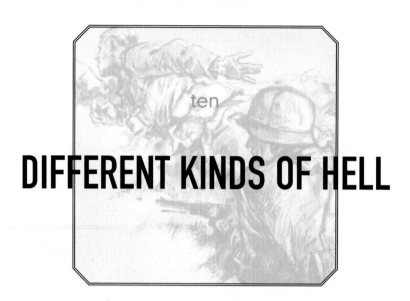

ten

DIFFERENT KINDS OF HELL

THE ability to replace men and equipment quickly and effectively, that is before the enemy can do so, is of course one key aspect of warfare. Initially the Allies were only able to offload supplies from the surviving landing craft until the Mulberry Harbour system was complete. With little notable interference from the Germans, vast mountains of supplies were unloaded onto the beaches of Normandy. In general, it would be a rare case if a GI endured a long period of time lacking equipment or clothing. For his German counterpart, scarcity was an everyday situation. Allied air superiority had destroyed or delayed the entire German supply system.

Other than ambulances moving to transport the wounded – and many examples exist of these being attacked and shot up by Allied fighters – all the German resupply had to take place at night, another duty which cut into a soldier's sleep. Obergrenadier Karl Wegner describes one of these nights:

It was the 15th or 16th of June and the day was ending. The sun was almost gone from the sky and exhaustion had gained the upper hand of us all. After we set up our position for the night we looked forward to having something to eat and some sleep. We were waiting for our food to arrive when I was ordered to report to Feldwebel K. I had just settled in comfortably too. A large group of us gathered around the Feldwebel. He formed us into columns and we began to march to the rear. Being curious I asked the Gefreiter leading my row what was going on. He said that we had been detailed to bring up the munitions and supplies.

After a time, we reached a spot in the dark and stopped. Then we heard the rumble of trucks. Dark shapes approached us then halted with a screech of brakes at a signal from the Feldwebel's service flashlight. These lights were great little things. You could adjust the lenses with different colours to signal or see at night without giving off too much light and we could button them to our uniforms and use both hands for work and the like, which is what we did this night. We piled up crates and cans of ammunition onto the carts. We had to carry this stuff

Supply convoy caught in the open by strafing aircraft. Ammunition trucks have taken hits and burn fiercely. This was why German munition movements had to be carried out at night. (Martin Eicheseer)

Jabo! A P38 fighter banks to turn back and attack Germans he has just spotted. This photograph was taken by a member of GR 916 from a roadside ditch.

around. In the end we all ended up carrying several cans and belts, easier to hang around your neck than carry in a big wooden box.

I reached my hole around dawn still in possession of 1500 rounds and ten grenades. My food, what there was of it, was cold. Kalb told me that we would be going on patrol in about an hour. He knew I was tired, so he said that Willi would carry the MG today and I could bring up the rear with his rifle. I nodded and slid down into the trench. To sleep for even an hour was at those times a luxury.

In contrast, the Allies had a more mobile all-day supply and transport system that was not hindered by enemy air interdiction. This is not to say that problems did not exist. Large amounts of repetitive paperwork and the distance to the front from the Channel ports reduced some of the speed with which requests were met as the armies advanced. The Allied expenditure of munitions convinced many German officers that a critical shortage would occur. This was based on the amount used by the Germans and their knowledge of their own system, and it didn't happen. Constantly using the already overburdened combat troops at night served to weaken the German lines, perhaps much more than realised by Allied intelligence. Manpower was a problem that would plague the Germans throughout the campaign, while the Allies, had whole divisions in reserve in England and a constant stream of replacements coming across from the US.

In Normandy, all available Axis troops had been committed within the first 48 hours. All other units were too far away with little or no motorised transportation. These units also had to face Allied air attacks whilst on the way to the front. As previously mentioned, the large number of foreign volunteers and Volksdeutsche serving in units already at the front were problematic. Leutnant Heinze tried to disperse these men amongst his ranks so that there would always be a German with a Russian or Pole. In this way these men would generally fight but the increasing number of casualties not being replaced made this arrangement difficult to maintain. As a result, during some actions the Russians and Volksdeutsche would mob together and run, although quite a few were made of sterner stuff. One Russian in Heinze's company was a prime example of this:

> In our company there was this Russian called Ivan. He was very good at 'organising' things such as food and drink. One day I saw him crying and I asked what was wrong. He said he was sad because he felt he would die here so far from home and family. I tried to console him. Well, shortly after that I met a Feldwebel from one of our other companies, he told me that they were having quite a bit of trouble with Russians that belonged to his company. I said that I might be able to help him. I sent Ivan over to him to be put in charge of his Russians. A few days later I received a box of cigars with a note from that Feldwebel. It told of the wonders worked by Ivan getting these men to fight better than they ever had.

Such instances were not commonplace and Heinze surmised that these volunteers were fearful of ending up on the losing side. If one considers the fear of the average German soldier of capture by the Russians, then one may readily conceive of the terror of a Russian who sided with the Germans after Hitler's violation of the non-aggression pact and subsequent invasion of the Motherland. If they found themselves on the losing side of the war, they would likely be sent back to Russia after the war branded as German collaborators, an uncertain but undoubtedly unpleasant fate.

In conjunction with this, the German soldier found the situation wanting with regard to replacement of clothing and lost personal equipment, especially since the existing space on the transports was only given to more important items such as food, medical supplies and ammunition. Placed all over France, however, were small depots from which items could be drawn, provided troops could get these items before they were destroyed by retreating supply personnel or advancing Allied troops. In the main, the German soldier would just have to make do with his existing uniform and equipment. The dead and wounded from both sides were relieved of anything those still fighting could use. Improvisation could also help. In desperate need of new socks and with official requests unanswered, Obergefreiter Josef Brass took matters into his own hands. Having no yarn and knitting needles, nor the ability to knit, he did the best he could. Brass took his army towel and cut from it a pair of socks, then stitched them together. Although crude they proved effective and durable, and were still in his possession 50 years later.

Others, when the opportunity arose, stole what they wanted or traded for it. The GI usually desired extras like alcohol, fresh foods or souvenirs. The German looked for basic needs. Karl Wegner notes that during the fighting Obergefreiter Kalb needed a new shirt and none were available from unit stores. He searched several deserted farms, going out of his way to look for one. He got lucky and found a wardrobe full of clothes left by a fleeing farmer. Kalb got his shirt and an extra, and gave out underclothes, socks, braces and other items to those in need in his platoon. This does not mean that the Germans did not possess supplies for their armies, but the problem was distribution. However, as the Allies advanced the supply lines became shorter and the situation improved, due to lower fuel and travel time requirements.

A well nourished man usually performs to the best of his abilities. Knowing this, the US Army put years of development into suitable field rations. The result was the famous, or as many a GI would declare, infamous, K ration. This was a pre-packaged meal provided in breakfast, lunch and dinner versions. In general, the box contained tinned meats and vegetables, crackers, cigarettes, chocolate and chewing gum along with powdered beverages such as coffee, cocoa and the not so well received lemonade. The canned food contained easily consumed items such as cheeses and jams for the crackers, or beans and stews, which could be consumed without heating. This selection, although limited, gave the GI a dependable and nourishing meal he could carry with him. Despite the constant complaints and grumblings by the men who ate them, this was by far the best field ration of the war.

The US Army did provide, whenever possible, hot meals to forward area troops. Cooked in rear echelon kitchens these would be trucked up in Mermite cans (thermal containers). Efforts were made to have at least breakfast and supper served hot, while lunch would be eaten 'out of the box'. From a central point, the platoons of any company would pick up the hot meals in Mermite cans allotted to them. Private Don Van Roosen was detailed to this duty once:

> Jim Vollmer and I were sent back for platoon rations one late afternoon. We picked up three big Mermite cans and headed back. In the field where Miller was hit we got another barrage. We heard it coming and dived into a shell hole. When it was over we climbed out to find the Mermite cans were riddled. Everyone crabbed about the destroyed meals. No one asked how we were. Priorities!

Left: Hungry soldiers wait in line for their rations from the field kitchen. Right front, soldier holds his mess tin and folding spoon/fork (spork) utensil.

Right: German Army field kitchen recipe pamphlet supplied in box of ingredients. This would be added to the field kitchen's cookbook. This one is from a powdered pudding mix supplier.

The German Army did possess canned and pre-packaged foods, but these were not as widespread as in the Allied armies. Tinned meats, powdered soups and the like were all produced, but were generally sent to troops in Russia or to the Kriegsmarine for naval operations. The policy of the German forces in Normandy was to live off the local agriculture, saving the issue rations for actual wartime operations.

The officers who devised this system did not envisage the degree to which Allied air power would fracture German supply lines. This, coupled with the virtual elimination of procurement from local sources, meant the German soldier would have good, nourishing meals only on an irregular basis at the best of times. Even at the beginning of the invasion, when food stocks were at their highest, many units actually engaged in combat were not fed for 24 hours or more, primarily because their stationary mess houses were destroyed or overrun. From this day on, it was a downhill slide for the men at the front. On average a soldier received only one meal a day, usually brought up at night. Much of what he was eating was, at the very least, unappetising to look at. Gefreiter Peter Simeth once had the misfortune to see what he was given to eat since a night action had prevented his devouring it in the dark.

> I sat down, lit a cigarette and made myself comfortable to eat. I opened my mess tin and looked in. The sight of its contents combined with the tobacco smoke made me sicker than I had ever been in my life. I threw my whole mess tin away and never smoked another cigarette.

Simeth was not alone. Most of the other German veterans interviewed remembered meals so bad no one could eat them. Even Don Van Roosen knew it:

> One day we came upon some dead German paratroopers. They had died of wounds because they were all patched up. We poked around and eventually looked in their mess kits. Whatever it was, it was sickening. And it wasn't like it had spoiled from sitting around, these bodies were still fresh.

In general, the meals served during this time to the German troops consisted of poor quality meats. This was mainly horsemeat, the fate of the many wounded supply wagon or artillery mounts, and whatever could be acquired through local sources. The Grenadiers would beg, borrow, barter and steal whatever they could to supplement their diet and quiet the hunger pangs. Farms in the area gave them ample opportunity to do this, with the farmers more likely to trade since German money was not in high demand at this point in the war.

These unofficial forays were not without danger. Stealing was still against German military law and could get one shot. Soldiers digging in an already harvested garden for some missed vegetables could find a mine exploding in their face. Obergefreiter Kalb and Willi Schuster both had to stay submerged in a stream as a Jabo circled overhead, caught in the open while scavenging. Peter Simeth was shelled whilst digging in a potato patch; luckily he and his potatoes came out unscathed. As he dived for cover he found himself staring at a small silver and pearl crucifix. He grasped the small cross and has held onto it for more than 50 years. His luck was to hold out during another foraging effort:

> One quiet day I was picked to go and get water for everyone in the platoon. I took all their canteens and headed out to find a stream or house with a well. After walking some time I found a deserted farmhouse. With great caution I approached it. Inside it was clear the inhabitants left quickly, the remains of a meal still sat on a table but was over two days old. Behind the house was a barn with a well. I headed straight for the well. While I did this the

When the field kitchens were not around, soldiers resorted to cooking for themselves with whatever could be scavenged from the immediate surroundings.

Crucifix found by Gefreiter Peter Simeth in a potato field while being shelled by Allied guns.

animals in the barn came towards me, some cows, a mule and a dog. All were domesticated because they were not afraid of me. I knew that they must be hungry and thirsty since they had been alone for at least a couple of days. I watered and grained them then finished with my canteens. With this heavy load I headed back. As I left the farmyard I saw that these animals were following me. I turned and yelled at them to scare them away. Each time I did this they ignored me. Finally I gave up and walked down the road followed by the animals.

A short time later I heard a noise that put my heart in my throat, the drone of a Jabo's engine. I looked up and saw him circle around; he had seen me. I had nowhere to go, no cover was close. I stood there, surrounded by the farm animals, watching him and waiting for the inevitable. He flew centimetres above the treetops, coming closer and closer. He still did not fire. Then in an instant he screamed over me, I turned with him and watched him fly up and around again. He was making another pass, this time it was going to be the end of me. I was so scared my feet seemed glued to the ground. Coming at me once again he began to rock back and forth. I was puzzled; then it came to me that he was waving at me. I waved at him as he flew over me then away. I was so relieved my knees went weak. I don't know if he thought I was a French farmer or not, my uniform and weapon were very obvious. In any event I thank God for the pilot's kindness.

When I returned to my platoon I was greeted with great enthusiasm. We tied the animals up to stakes near our holes. This was a smart thing to do because the Amis generally felt that if livestock were grazing no troops occupied the area. This kept the Arifeuer off of us for a time. In addition we had fresh milk and several days' supply of fresh meat.

The junior commanders in the German Army realised that despite the danger incurred during these foraging missions, they had two positive outcomes: they improved the soldiers' diet and they kept morale from sinking any lower.

The primary form of relief from psychological tension was mail from home. To hear the news kept a man involved in his everyday family life, as did seeing the familiar handwriting of a loved one or reading the stories of children not yet seen, save for the yellowing, tattered, but highly cherished snapshot sent so long ago, taking first steps or speaking a first word. The system of military mail delivery, as discussed in Chapter 2, did not change with the advent of combat, except that with the constant movement of troops it took longer for it to arrive. It was not uncommon for the men of both sides to get mail in large batches after a period of getting nothing at all.

The German soldier, despite being fairly close to home when compared to any US soldier, suffered greatly regarding his mail. The *Feldpost* faced the same supply problems as

Mail call. The company Hauptfeldwebel, known as *der Spiess*, hands out treasured mail from home.

Another view of the same unit receiving their mail. Note the happy expressions on several faces.

Fine example of an army flak personnel bunker, somewhere in Normandy.

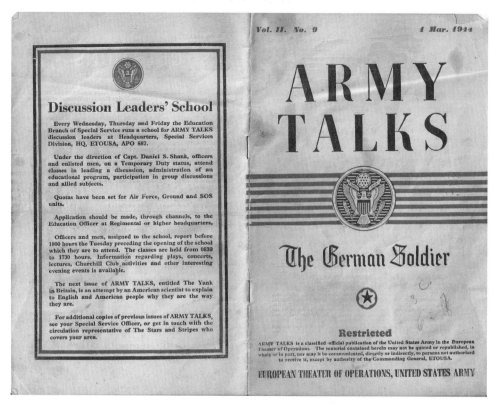

US Army manual: 'Army Talks. The German Soldier', dated March 1944. This manual was distributed to US troops prior to the invasion to give an Allied view of the German soldiers he would soon be facing in Normandy. This manual was issued to Private Merle Hescock.

everything else, as well as being a low priority. Many of the Feldpost troops found themselves caught up in the fighting or being detailed to assist in the supply distribution. This left great mountains of mail in the rear echelon areas with insufficient men to sort and distribute it. While his letters languished a Grenadier had to cope with the worry over Allied bomber campaigns – especially if his family lived in a city – massive food shortages and, later, the approach of the Red Army on the eastern frontiers of Germany. The GI, while still having great concern for his family, did not have these images to hound him.

A huge amount of physical preparation is required before engaging with an enemy. Tasks such as preparing fighting positions, troop movements, reconnaissance and the like demand much of the common soldier. Normandy required all of this, and perhaps a little more, from the armies involved. The campaign had a constant rhythm of moving then digging in. The Germans were more cognisant of this fact, knowing that with numbers against them having good secondary and tertiary lines of prepared positions to fall back on would greatly enhance their ability to hold ground. This is why German efforts concentrated on establishing these lines, when possible, before they were actually occupied. Rear echelon troops and forced labour would begin digging what would be next week's, or perhaps tomorrow's, next line of defence. Although these lines might not be finished in time, a half finished position was quicker to occupy and finish when frontline troops found themselves pushed back. This did not prevent retreats or withdrawals, after

German propaganda leaflet encouraging
soldiers to fight on and not surrender for
several reasons, including that their womenfolk
would be taken for service in Allied brothels.

Laßt Euch nicht evakuieren!

verlangt der Feind in seinen Flugblättern.

Warum plötzlich diese „Fürsorge"?
Warum diese Anteilnahme?

Er hat Deine Wohnungen ze. 5rt, seit Jahren mordet er mit
seinen Bomben — und jede Nacht kommt er noch und sät
weitere Vernichtung.

Nun ist er auf einmal „besorgt" um Dich?

WARUM?

Hier seine Gründe:

Er braucht

Arbeiter für Hütten und Gruben,
Helfer für die Kriegsindustrie,
Männer, die Minen räumen,
Männer und Frauen zum Schanzen,
Frauen und Mädchen für seine Bordelle.

Er will

schon jetzt größere Teile des deutschen
Volkes in seine Befehlsgewalt bringen,

unsere Widerstandskraft schwächen,

seine oft proklamierten Vernichtungs-
pläne zur Ausrottung des deutschen
Volkes verwirklichen.

which the infantry had to dig their own holes. Starting from scratch or not, the Grenadier had several years of experience behind him and could prepare well concealed and effective fighting positions, although it must be noted that in most cases the defender has an advantage over the attacker, and the Germans were able to use all of their hard-won knowledge and the suitable terrain to stymie the Allied advances for much longer than any of those planning Operation *Overlord* conceived.

The Allies had to learn to overcome all the barriers thrown up in their way by the Grenadiers. This began as a simple 'trial and error' system. German military training was based upon tactical doctrines used in North Africa and Italy, and the Germans had learned from those campaigns and adjusted what they felt had been done wrong. Combining this with the fact that the staff of the 352nd felt that they would be sent to serve in Russia and thus tactical training was geared for this deployment, the GI discovered that many of the Germans he ran up against did not fight in the way he had been taught they would. A new way of fighting had to be learned fast, since his very life depended on it. The GI learned of rolling pockets and to watch his rear more carefully, and how to attack well planned lines of defence. Men developed sharp eyes in the hope of differentiating between a camouflaged position and a clump of brush.

Flexibility also had to be developed within the Allied ranks. Casualties taken in sustained combat can create vast gaps in the chain of command, and privates can become sergeants or even officers during these fights. Different units can find themselves combined during heavy engagements, presenting problems with command and control. The Germans had grown quite adept at adjusting to this after five years of warfare and they could combine splintered units for quick action in defensive or offensive operations. The GIs learned all of the German strengths and weaknesses and were able to push them steadily back from the beaches, though perhaps not as fast as the higher level commanders expected. Despite all of his problems, the German soldier was still a tough opponent for any army to overcome. The GI proceeded with caution and tried not to waste life, instead relying on the firepower that was available to him. Artillery fired on any suspected enemy position, and during the campaign, the Divisional HQ of the 352nd received numerous reports of US troops shelling where there were no troops or strongpoints. For the Allies this was a case of 'better safe than sorry'. Even the amount of small arms ammunition expended by the US forces amazed the Germans. This disheartened every German from Grenadier to General, since they all knew every round must not be wasted. Materiel versus men was the order of the day, and it is much easier to expend materiel than men.

Men, despite any linguistic or political differences, are all very much the same. The average Grenadier saw much to like in the GI that opposed him. He found the Americans well trained, well equipped and in possession of a high respect for human life. In other respects they found him to be, according to German standards, lacking some forms of discipline and not used to some of the hardships of life endured by many Europeans. German officers found US commanders to be initially overconfident though this evaporated as the war progressed. In small actions, the Germans knew that the GI could do something completely unorthodox to turn the tide or complete the mission, and because of the GI's respect for life, the Germans knew that they could hold and pin down much larger forces for long periods of time. The Russians would simply press attack after attack until the objective was seized; the number of lives lost was not relevant.

The American soldiers held diverse opinions regarding Germans. Some saw them as fanatical Nazis. Whilst there were fanatics in the SS units there were very few in the German Army, which was raised by national service requirements, the draft, whereas the SS was a voluntary service. In both armies, the rear echelon troops were more likely to believe the propaganda spread about the opposing side. Those at the front knew differently. Both faced the same dangers and hardships, which allowed a sense of respect to develop, albeit begrudgingly. Sergeant Quaterone:

> We had knocked out this Mark III tank. There were two survivors who surrendered to us. They were dirty and grimy from the oil and smoke. I know they were scared and in shock, anyone would be after that. We drove back to the rear with them. They talked to us in broken English and we gave them water and cigarettes. When we finally got to our C.P. we turned them over. Well one of those 'Pencil Pushers' went right up to them and started ripping off their medals and patches. This made me furious, I took the stuff away from him yelling that these guys had earned it and they should keep it. The officer there agreed with me.

Every soldier, Allied or German, could expect one of the limited fates war assigns. He could survive unscathed, perhaps a little worse for wear. He could be wounded, suffering anything from the minor to the crippling. He could be captured, healthy or wounded. Or a soldier could be killed in action.

It is obvious to all that the best of these options is to get through the war without too much physical damage. However, what was the most likely fate of those wounded? The American soldier first depended upon the skill and bravery of his unit's combat medical corpsman, the medic. Once wounded, the medic, who did not get combat pay despite being at the front with the line infantry, would stop the bleeding, bandage, then stabilise the soldier to be moved back to the Battalion Aid Station for more treatment, and then in extreme cases farther back to field hospitals for surgery. If the wound were severe enough, the GI would find himself in England in relatively short time. Here he would have all the benefits of a real hospital: a bed, clean sheets, good food and the company of nurses. Overall, when an American soldier was wounded and could be retrieved quickly, he faced an exceptionally good chance of recovery with the best treatment.

An Allied propaganda leaflet in the form of the *Völkischer Beobachter* (*Völkisch* (ethnic) *Observer*), the newspaper of the NSDAP from 1920. It shows the differences between the war situation in 1941 and 1944. The front page shows success on the Ostfront; the rear shows that by July 1944 the Soviets were knocking on the door of the Reich at Memel.

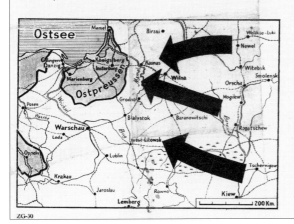

Set of escape, evasion and PoW pamphlets issued to aircrew personnel during the invasion. This set was issued to Staff Sergeant James Loftus 440th Troop Carrier Group. He was crew chief of a C47 troop transport plane that took part in the drop of the 101st Airborne on the night of 5/6 June 1944.

NOT TO BE PRODUCED IN PUBLIC

LISTS OF PHRASES

FRENCH
DUTCH
GERMAN
SPANISH

FRENCH

ENGLISH	FRENCH	ENGLISH	FRENCH
One	Un	Twenty	Vingt
Two	Deux	Thirty	Trente
Three	Trois	Forty	Quarante
Four	Quatre	Fifty	Cinquante
Five	Cinq	Sixty	Soixante
Six	Six	Seventy	Soixante-dix
Seven	Sept	Eighty	Quatre-vingts
Eight	Huit	Ninety	Quatre-vingt-dix
Nine	Neuf	Hundred	Cent
Ten	Dix	Five Hundred	Cinq cents
Eleven	Onze	Thousand	Mille
Twelve	Douze		
Thirteen	Treize	Monday	Lundi
Fourteen	Quatorze	Tuesday	Mardi
Fifteen	Quinze	Wednesday	Mercredi
Sixteen	Seize	Thursday	Jeudi
Seventeen	Dix-Sept	Friday	Vendredi
Eighteen	Dix-huit	Saturday	Samedi
Nineteen	Dix-neuf	Sunday	Dimanche
Minutes	Minutes	Week	Semaine
Hours	Heures	Fortnight	Quinzaine
Day	Jour	Month	Mois
Night	Nuit	O'clock	heures

NOT TO BE PRODUCED IN PUBLIC

ENGLISH	FRENCH
I am (we are)	Je suis (nous sommes)
British (American)	Anglais; (Américain)
Where am I?	Où est-ce que je suis?
I am hungry; thirsty	J'ai faim, J'ai soif
Can you hide me?	Pouvez-vous me cacher?
I need civilian clothes	J'ai besoin de vêtements civils
How much do I owe you?	Combien vous dois-je?
Are the enemy nearby?	L'ennemi est-il près?
Where is the frontier?	Où est la frontière
BELGIAN	Belge
SWISS; SPANISH:	Suisse, Espagnole
Where are the nearest British (American) troops?	Où sont les forces anglaises (américaines) les plus proches?
Where can I cross this river?	Où est-ce que je peux traverser cette rivière?
Is this a safe way?	Est-ce que ce chemin n'est pas dangéreux?
Will you please get me a third class ticket to …	Voulez-vous me prendre un billet de troisième classe pour … s'il vous plaît.
Is this the train (bus) for .. ?	Est-ce que c'est le train (auto-bus) (car) pour …?
Do I change (i.e. trains)?	Dois-je changer de train?
At what time does the train (bus) leave for … ?	A quelle heure est-ce que le train (autobus) part pour …?
Right; left; straight on	A droite; à gauche; tout droit
Turn back; stop	Revenez en arrière; arrêtez vous
Thank you; please	Merci; s'il vous plaît
Yes; No	Oui; Non
Good morning; afternoon	Bonjour
Good evening; Night	Bonsoir
Consulate	Consulat
Out of bounds; Forbidden	Défense de pénétrer; défendu

Detail of escape phrase pamphlet.

The German soldier who found himself in the same position faced a similar series of events. His medical orderly, the *Sanitatsoldat* – called 'Sani' for short – was of the same dedicated stock as the Allied medics. During the Normandy campaign, as with all other aspects of the German military, he faced drastic supply problems. This did not prevent him from going to extremes to save his wounded.

Even when evacuated behind the lines the German soldier was likely to find that his bandages were made from old newspaper or torn bed sheets. Only when the German wounded found themselves well out of the range of the Jabos did the medical care, in terms of supplies and medicine, improve. German ambulances were not immune from attacks by Allied fighter pilots. When Leutnant Heinze was being evacuated from Normandy, he noticed several holes in the roof of his ambulance. He queried the driver only to discover that, despite the large red cross painted on the roof, he had been attacked several times by aircraft. Once he arrived at a German hospital, usually in or near a large city, the Grenadier had to deal with the inevitable arrival of Allied bombers at some time during his recovery.

Both sides' medical corps treated their own and enemy wounded without discrimination. The doctors, nurses, and frontline medical personnel acted with professionalism and dedication to saving human life regardless of the uniform.

It is well known that certain German units, primarily those in the SS, committed war crimes by shooting Allied military prisoners. It is also a fact that Allied soldiers were also guilty of this. British, Canadian, French and US soldiers shot German prisoners out of hand. In any army the size of those involved in the Second World War, there are those amongst the many good soldiers that are heartless men of the kind who also commit crimes during peacetime; war simply gives them a wider opportunity and anonymity to act. The following accounts from Don Van Roosen illustrate the two extremes that one could encounter:

I had to deliver a message to another company. The CO was an ex-boxer and had a way of snorting out words. While I was there a Sergeant came in and asked the Captain what he wanted done with the prisoners. He chortled out that the Sergeant had five minutes to get the prisoners back to the beach. The Sergeant acknowledged this and trotted away. The fact that from where we were, even in a plane one could not get to the beach in five minutes, did not escape me. The prisoners' fates were inevitable.

The second account was more the norm:

We captured a young German Gefreiter with a new Iron Cross on his tunic. I asked him what the award was for and he said that he had wiped out an American squad trying to crawl along a hedgerow toward his MG position. Someone wanted to give him another 'reward', but this was just talk. Unfortunately, some of the men remembered the three GIs that had their hands bound with wire and shot in the back of the neck by the paratroopers in Villiers Fossard.

Unteroffizier Siegfried Sass first entered the war in 1939, was released to work in the railway service, but was called up once again in April 1941. He served on the Eastern Front, first being wounded at Demjansk in northern Russia on 17 October 1941 and for the second time in May 1943. On D-Day he found himself in Brittany stationed near Brest.

After many night marches, he was near St Lô at La Hey de Puits. For him, the fighting came to an end on 13 July 1944:

> I was taken prisoner by US soldiers. Let me say that I was already disarmed and the only pris-
> oner, when an American, about 15 metres away levelled his rifle and shot me. I think it was an
> explosive round. It hit my metal badge [Infantry Assault Badge] on my left breast. The splinters
> entered my chest and then came to rest in my right arm. I was picked up and brought back to
> an aid station by two other soldiers. While on the way I encountered other US soldiers who
> wanted to shoot me, but the two men would not let them. At the aid station I was operated on
> then sent to the beach and in a landing ship taken to England.

If wounded and captured, the Allied soldier was in the hands of the same ill-equipped medical staff as the wounded Germans and faced the same perils travelling to the rear. This included artillery barrages and air attacks on convoys. It is very demoralising to be fired upon by one's own army and it was not unusual for US troops to be wounded or killed in such circumstances. If one survived, the prospect was a dismal existence in a German Stalag.

The German soldier, during this particular campaign, faced a different and better situation if captured. He was questioned and then shipped to the rear. Sometimes he was put to work burying the dead or unloading supplies while he waited for a ship to transport him to England. In camps all over the country he was deloused, identified and fed. This meal was usually the best he had been given in quite some time. Quite a few of the men gained weight once they had a proper source of nutrition. For the Allies, convincing them that the war was lost came easily after what the prisoners themselves saw when they reached the rear areas. The mountains of supplies, the endless streams of trucks and troops head-ing inland told a tale that no propagandist could counter. Out in the Channel, an armada of ships that faded into the distance put paid to any notion that the Reich could survive. Obergefreiter Brass recalls that several 'hardcore' men, certain of final victory, were silenced forever when they saw what lay on and off the coast of Normandy.

Captivity gave the German the first opportunity to express political views without recrimination. It was a very sobering time for these young men, most notably when they arrived in the United States for internment. They were send there was for two reasons. First, the Allies needed all the food supplies sent to Europe for the armies and local popu-lations. Second, it made more sense to send back a ship full of prisoners than to send it back empty. Despite the sound economics of this decision, many GIs were resentful. The enemy soldier he just captured was going back to the US and would have a warm bed, hot food and no one shooting at him.

In the face of death, men mentally manoeuvred in order to maintain their sanity. Some called it luck, others called it fate, and many more decided it had to do with the Will of God. Many of the men quoted in this book had close calls with death, and all are remark-able, but here only a few can be related. Gefreiter Peter Simeth had, perhaps, the closest brush with death:

> One night I had taken over the MG for my spell on watch with two other men. Some time
> into our shift we heard some noise in front of us. So I fired in the direction of it. I did not
> know that the first rounds in the belt of ammunition were tracer rounds. I realised my mistake
> and stopped firing. But the bright orange streams had given away our position with the first

These newly captured German infantrymen appear upbeat as they are being searched and processed before being sent back to the beach, a not uncommon emotion since it meant they were out of the war. (USA National Archives)

D+7 – Naval Beach Battalion sailor with M1 Thompson stands guard as a new batch of German PoWs await embarkation to ships. Note the soldier is wearing Paratrooper boots that were issued to beach battalions for wear during the invasion. In the background, LSTs unload equipment and supplies. Barrage balloons give protection from enemy aircraft. (USA National Archives)

Coast Guard Second Class Petty Officer unties German PoWs that have been hauled aboard his ship. The Obergefreiter on the right wears ribbons indicating that he is an Eastern Front veteran. (USA National Archives)

Three Yanks drink a toast to a short war in the rubble of La Haye de Puits after they and their comrade captured the town. Left to right, Sergeant Robert McCurdy, of Newark, New Jersey, Sergeant Harold Smith of Bush Creek, Tennessee and Sergeant Richard Bennett of Wilkes-Barre, Pennsylvania.

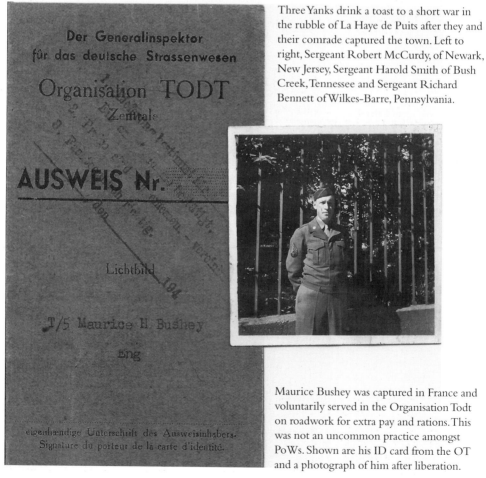

Maurice Bushey was captured in France and voluntarily served in the Organisation Todt on roadwork for extra pay and rations. This was not an uncommon practice amongst PoWs. Shown are his ID card from the OT and a photograph of him after liberation.

Dejected US PoWs in a rather sloppy formation inside a German PoW camp. This was generally the fate of any Allied soldier captured in Normandy. Photograph from Martin Eicheseer whose uncle was a guard at a PoW camp near Hannover in Germany.

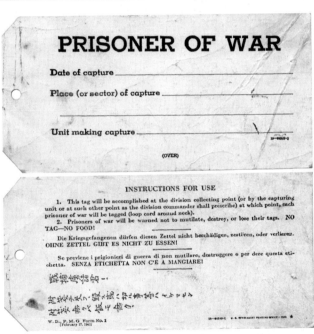

A PoW tag of the type attached to each soldier taken prisoner by the Allies, noting the date and place of capture, plus the unit making the capture, used for intelligence purposes.

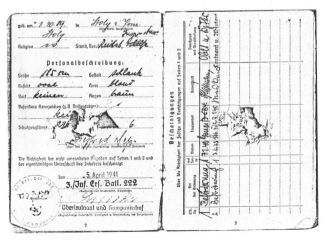

Siegfried Sass' bullet-riddled Soldbuch. Amazingly Sass survived an unlawful summary execution by US troops after surrendering in Normandy. He was the only survivor of his platoon.

FOXHOLE GERMAN

In this advanced stage of the war, many a sensible Kraut would rather give himself up than continue fighting. There are situations where a word or two in HIS OWN LAN-GUAGE may convince him that he can safely surrender — and so stop shooting at you. A cornered German will sometimes listen to reason — if he can understand.

Keep this and study the German phrases. Foxhole German may help you, but remember not all Krauts are reasonable.

Foxhole German (front). Handout given to US troops to give a very basic knowledge of simple German phrases with the aim of persuading the enemy to surrender.

FOXHOLE GERMAN

English	German
Hands up, Soldier	HEN-da hoe, LANN-ser
Call it quits, Soldier	Mock SHLOOS, LANN-ser
Drop your gun	Ga-VARE, HINN-lay-gen
Come here, Soldier	Come Here, LANN-ser
Come out, Soldier	Come RAH-oos, LANN-ser
Halt	Hahlt
Don't move	SHTILL-shtayn
Slowly	LAHNG-sahm
Quickly	SHNELL

Speak clearly. Accent capitalized syllables as in: vic-TOR-ious. Pronounce "G" as in: GET, and SH as in SHOOT.

Foxhole German (back).

mortar shells beginning to fall. One landed directly in our hole. There was a blinding flash and I felt the MG disintegrate in my hands. In a daze I realised that one man was dead and the other wounded. In the darkness I felt my body. No holes; no blood; everything seemed to be fine. The Feldwebel appeared. He said that we had to get the other man back to the aid sta-tion. We had to do it now, since we could only travel in the dark and dawn was approaching. We succeeded in getting him there just as the sun was rising. We then took the opportunity to sit down and rest. When I stretched my legs out, both of us got a huge shock. Tucked into my boot top was a hand grenade, both of us saw clearly that a piece of shrapnel had pierced the explosive head of it. I grabbed it and threw it as far as I could. Nothing happened, no explo-sion. I knew then that I had a guardian angel.

When fate twisted the outcome in other ways some men could adjust, while others avoided it. Don Van Roosen:

We had been in our position around Villiers Fossard for several days. The position was pretty good and the gun position was as good as we had ever made. A tank came up to the front line and fired ten quick shots at us. One 88 hit just in front of the gun position, jammed the impact fuse and sailed through the gun opening, and took off Jim Cooney's head. No one would go in the position to get him out so my fatalism was called on. I crawled in beside him. The body was still upright. He had been reading an overseas edition of *Time* and it was open to a page filled with big arrows showing where the big armies were headed. His blood was splashed on the pages. The price of advance.

Relaxed and cheerful, German enlisted men share cigarettes and stories with US sailors, happy to be alive and on their way to England. (USA National Archives)

Mixed grouping of German PoWs on board ship, en route to England, enjoying a sing along. Amongst this group are battle-experienced NCOs, some older enlisted men (most likely from 716. Infanterie-Division) and one Naval Coastal Artillery soldier. (USA National Archives)

Two German PoWs happily explain their circumstances to a US Navy sailor onboard ship transporting them to England. (USA National Archives)

German infantry NCO has his first meal on a US ship in the English Channel. He is one of 352. Infanterie-Division's battle-hardened NCOs with service on the Eastern Front denoted by the Eastern Front ribbon above his left breast pocket and Crimea service shield on his left sleeve. He also wears the Iron Cross 2nd Class for bravery in the field and the infantry assault badge for combat service. (USA National Archives)

An attitude developed that enabled all of these men to deal with the distinct possibility of their imminent death, one that is very succinctly summed up by Karl Wegner's squad leader, Obergefreiter Kalb:

The strain of combat was beginning to show on me, and Willi as well. Kalb saw this. He was a veteran of Russia so when he spoke to us we really took it to heart. He said, 'You can't sweat out every shell coming in as if it were aimed at you, that'll drive you crazy.' Looking me straight in the eye he continued, 'If it's your time no matter how deep your hole or how good your cover the game's over. And if it's not your time it won't matter. But this doesn't mean you shouldn't keep your head down either, you can only push your luck just so much.' I thought over many of the things I had seen and felt that he was right. I saw men run through hails of machine-gun fire and not be hit, then I saw others killed by a tiny fragment of shrapnel from an explosion metres away. I was more relaxed after that, well I should say as relaxed as one could be while being shelled and shot at most of the time.

The memories of combat are different for each man who was there. They all remember the same battle but in various ways. Some recall every detail clearly and vividly. To others it is foggy with the odd detail surfacing after some contemplation. A few have pushed these harsh memories deep into the abyss of the mind and will not allow them to resurface. Different senses make the memories, sometimes it is sight, or perhaps smell, or sound, all varying with the soldier's personal perspective of the fighting. Sergeant Quaterone in his tank saw the campaign differently to the infantry:

When the lead started to fly we buttoned up the hatches so all we really could see was things that were visible from our view slits, that is not much. Mostly it was dust and smoke through which we caught glimpses of the countryside, and other tanks. There was quite a bit of racket too. Rounds from rifles and machine guns bouncing off the hull or turret. Then there was the smell of fuel and gunpowder. This permeated everything so we smelled like it all of the time. As far as seeing the Germans close up, we never really did, other than prisoners or the dead along the roads. Whatever direction we took fire from we shot back. Once in a while we saw another tank or one guy run up and shoot at us with a panzerfaust rocket but overall it was a very impersonal way to fight. And that was good since we only had to think in terms of targets and not men.

Three members of the GR 916 take a break while practising pistol marksmanship with 9mm Radom pistols. Photograph taken by Obergrenadier Martin Eichenseer.

In the infantry, it was always the man on the other side that was foremost in your mind. An infantryman's war can be very personal. It contrasts starkly with the tanker's view. Obergrenadier Martin Eichenseer's impressions of Normandy are typical:

When someone asks what it was like in the war, it becomes very hard to give a short answer. Perhaps I am hard when I say that no one who was not there can understand but I will try to describe what I remember.

The first thing that comes to mind is the memory of the taste of sweat and dirt. We were always dirty from crawling around and digging in, and sweaty because of the heat and physical exertions. The sweat would pour down our faces mixing with the dirt crusted on them; we looked very bad. All of our bodies reeked of filth but we were used to that. Then in comparison to the rotting bodies and burning vehicles we weren't so bad. In the actual fighting, moments pass as fleeting glimpses. Figures in khaki or field grey darting through the brush or across a meadow. Blurred faces, shots, shouts, screams. The hammering of the MG into my shoulder as I fired. The hot shell casing that flew out and burned your hand. The shudder of fear that fills your body when a shell explodes too close or a round hits too near. The dryness in your throat that cannot be quenched. The pain of seeing friends die. In fact the uniforms we wore probably did not matter in this regard because I'm sure that the men on the other side felt the same, after all we both suffered the same. No one should ever have to know firsthand what we went through, but it should never be forgotten.

eleven

A TIME FOR SLEEPING
AND A TIME FOR FIGHTING

BY midnight on 10 June the Allied invasion was four days old, four very long and
costly days. Many of the Allied objectives were unmet, especially in the sectors
assigned to 352. Infanterie-Division. In this short period, this German division had
been able to thwart the invasion plans significantly, in particular against the American
V Corps in the Omaha Beach sector. The US divisions that landed there had paid an
enormous price to gain the small strip of coast and the issue was even in doubt for
some time amongst the Allied commanders. The indomitability of the US soldier won
through, and by 10 June he was pushing inland at a good speed. The units of the 352nd
withdrew under heavy pressure. A concentrated American thrust towards St Lô, one
of their main objectives, would have given them the city, but this did not happen. In
fact, the pressure against the 352nd diminished enough to let the divisional commander
Generalleutnant Kraiss and his staff consolidate his regiments and re-establish a more
or less solid front. Although stragglers from his division were still coming in, the stage
had been set. Any attempts to get St Lô would be costly for both sides. The US 29th
Division, which had paid a high price to get up Omaha Beach, would now be the first
American unit to pay for the inaction of the Allied commanders, and the next butcher's
bill was presented by accident.

In the black of the Normandy night, two columns of men had become lost along
the small, winding roads that cut through the ancient countryside. The first was the 2nd
Battalion of the 115th Infantry Regiment. This unit of the US 29th Division had had
a relatively good day, advancing and taking many of their assigned objectives. The men
were tired and the battalion commander, Colonel Warfield, decided to look for a place to
bivouac for the remainder of the night. When daylight came they would get their bearings
and press on. The second was a large group of stragglers from the 352nd and a few other
units, trying to make their way to the newly established main battle line of their division.
Their paths were about to cross. Private Don Van Roosen was tired that night; his day had
been very full:

Le Carretour, Normandy, 9–10 June, 1944. This was a memorable night for the 2nd Battalion and for me. We had put in a long day – up very early in the morning to cross an inundated area, fighting through the village of La Ballaie, the Bois de Calette, taking Voulliy and La Folie, doubling back when someone took a wrong road, ending up near Le Carretour at around 0100 hrs.

By this time we had been marching and fighting for 24 hours straight and people were asleep on their feet or by the side of the road. We finally halted at a little crossroads which we could just see by the moonlight. Companies were directed into the field on our right and our squad was stuck in the far left corner. Sergeant Hanson told me to help him set up the gun [.50 calibre MG] and we stumbled around trying to get through the hedgerow. We finally found an outlet and set up the gun in a sunken road. The position stunk, it had a narrow field of fire, about 75 feet long but it did protect the flank of our night position. A bad compromise but we saw no alternative.

Not very far away from him Obergrenadier Karl Wegner waited in a roadside ditch with his squad, alongside many others:

All day long we had stumbled around looking for our regiment. We were quite lost but our officer refused to admit it. Early in the evening we had joined up with many others from our division. We knew that we had to go south to gain the lines of our division. Night came upon us but the moon allowed us to see. All of us expressed our concerns about Helmuth [see Chapter 9] but soon other things occupied our minds, primarily our empty stomachs and sore feet. We all wanted to reach our lines soon.

Some time after midnight we stopped abruptly and were ordered to take cover and remain silent. Kalb went off to see what was going on. He came back and out of breath he whispered to us that a large group of Amis were camped in front of us barring the way. We would attack through them since our patrols had indicated that they were ill prepared for a fight. The attack would be quick and cut through them as fast as we could, regrouping, then heading towards our lines. We made ready and crawled forward into the dark to where we would set up our machine gun. In this position we were very quiet. We couldn't see much of anything but we could hear the Amis talking in hushed tones. It then occurred to me that they were almost right in front of us. I concentrated on their words trying to make out some of them in hopes my school English would not falter. My thoughts were broken by an explosion in the distance.

Van Roosen also saw the flash:

We had just got the gun loaded when we heard shouting back at the entrance where we had come in. Then came an explosion and a sick feeling that something horrible was about to happen. More shouts, more explosions, then cries of the wounded and an answer with a burp gun. Andy and I waited for something to come our way and it was not long in happening. Some Burp gunners were coming down the road spraying the hedgerows on both sides of the road. We opened up and fired 10 to 15 rounds before the damn gun jammed. Probably got dirt in the receiver.

Wegner opened fire after the second explosion:

I squeezed the trigger sending out a long burst. After some shorter bursts, Kalb yelled to move forward. We picked up everything and ran down into the place the Amis had been. There was an abundance of confusion, on both sides. We had caught them in total surprise but with us there were so many different fragments of units and officers unfamiliar to all of us that there really was no cohesion as there would have been in a regular company. Even though we had set up the gun again we did not fire. We did not know where to aim and did not want to hit our own men. Kalb told me to fire only if I was in danger, then took Willi and one of the RAD boys back to where we had passed several scattered bundles of the Amis' belongings. While they were gone several men came up and fell in around me and my machine gun, confused and looking for safety. The fighting went on in front of us. Flares went up here and there, in the moments of a somewhat eerie light I could see the dead laying still, the wounded crawling in pain and the living running all over the place. Shouts, in English and German, could be heard between the bouts of gunfire. Kalb and Willi reappeared out of the din, their arms full of American ration boxes, and in tow were three prisoners.

In the terrible minutes that passed Van Roosen tried to fix the jammed machine gun:

Since we had no tools with us, I tried to turn the driving spring rod with my thumb. This is next to impossible but I tried anyway. All I did was tear my thumbnail apart and I couldn't turn the rod. About that time several Germans rushed us, sprayed us with fire, seized the gun and ran off with it. We were so dumbfounded by the suddenness and the fact that we were still alive that we sat there for what seemed like a long time but was probably seconds. I dashed back for my pack and carbine which I had left in the field. It was gone and I grabbed another one and tried to help the wounded get to some cover. Flares were going up everywhere, firing was intense, we could hear Warfield [the battalion commander] shout that he wouldn't surrender, more firing, then silence.

With the fighting playing out its final moments Wegner and his friends feasted on the captured rations:

In the dark I wasn't sure exactly what I was eating, but it was good. We stuffed our mouths with crackers and chocolates, whatever we could eat fast, tearing open packets with our teeth and one hand. The little metal cans we stuffed into our pockets for later. The fighting was all but over so we were ordered to move on and quickly down the cleared road. An officer put Kalb and our group in charge of about nineteen prisoners including the three we had taken. We followed the officer's men down the road, we had lost contact with the company to which we had been attached. I'm sure that if the Amis had been better prepared we would have not been as successful. In any event we were not happy at being saddled with these prisoners. First it was a waste of a good machine-gun team and secondly we did not have enough men to really guard them properly. Kalb tried to argue this point with the officer, but was cut short in his protest and told to shut up. I knew he was mad, but we herded the group of disoriented Amis quickly towards where we thought our own lines would be, what we hoped would be safety.

Getting to safety was also the thought foremost in the mind of Don Van Roosen, but he found himself with much more to consider:

I gathered a handful of men in my corner of the field, and we carried the wounded to the next field back. There was a small lane separating the two fields and I thought it would be best to start reorganising there. We got the wounded secure against the hedgerow and I took out the morphine syrette that I had in my first aid kit, never having used one before I did not know that you had to break the inner foil seal. I jabbed the first patient and squeezed the tube, nothing came out but he said that he felt much better. So I jabbed the rest with the same syrette and then threw it away. One tall GI from Tennessee had been wounded in the groin and was bleeding heavily. I tried to put a dressing in place but his rather long penis kept getting in the way. We finally solved the problem but it was just another thing in a crazy night.

How long it took us to move, patch up the wounded and regroup I don't know. But I had put Abner on the corner of the bank, which was about six feet high. He called out 'They're coming!' and began firing his carbine down the road. I joined him, we fired and threw grenades at a column of Germans that filled the road. Someone shouted to stop firing and we realised that these were our people who had been taken prisoner. Every few feet they were guarded by Germans and we would have killed the lot if we had continued to fire. We stopped and looked at each other as the group filed past. What an eerie feeling that was.

Then came silence. We waited for someone to start yelling orders but there was no sound. I finally stood up and told the healthy people that we would move the wounded back towards our lines. I had staff sergeants taking orders from me and I was a great big private. But people were glad just to be doing something.

This group eventually found there way back to American lines and was able to rejoin the other elements of their unit, which had been dispersed during the attack.

The American prisoners were slowing down the column. This did not go over well with the officer in charge and at daybreak he sent word back for Kalb to come and see him:

When Kalb came back he told me something shocking, we were to shoot the prisoners. I protested and said that I would not do it. To my surprise Kalb ordered me to shut up and make the MG ready to fire. I hesitated but he yelled at me to do it. All of us were perplexed this did not seem like Kalb. The rest of our group moved off towards the south leaving just us and the Amis. They became very agitated as they saw me load the machine gun. Kalb saw this and said in very poor English that all was OK and no one would be hurt. He even tossed them some of the cigarettes we had liberated from their packs earlier. One with stripes on his sleeve was very mad and came out of the ditch yelling at Kalb. To his amazement he came face to face with Kalb's pistol. He stopped in his tracks. Then I was given the order to fire, but into the empty ditch on the opposite side of the road. I and everyone else were very relieved at this; the prisoners understood what we were doing. If we disobeyed our officer we could be shot immediately. But he would hear the firing and we would come back alone. His assumption that his orders were carried out would be enough. The one who charged Kalb smiled and winked at him, sort of an acknowledgment of the ploy. Then Kalb said, 'Bitte, quiet, vait heer, Amis komm zoon.' We turned and ran down the road, someone yelled after us 'Feelen Dunke.' His German was bad but we understood. We smiled at having put one over on that Leutnant; besides, there had been enough killing that day.

Eventually the German stragglers found themselves back at their divisional lines. Men were sent to their original units, the final stages of a major regrouping for the 352nd.

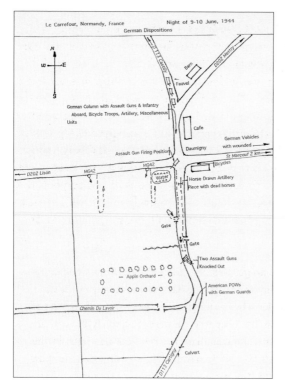

Le Carrefour, Normandy, France   Night of 9-10 June, 1944
German Dispositions

Don Van Roosen's map of the ambush at Le Carrefour, night of 9/10 June 1944. Karl Wegner was at one of the two MG locations in the centre.

Wegner and his friends were still tired, but they had rid themselves of their hunger pangs by gorging on the captured rations, still having plenty left over in their pockets and haversacks. There was still no time to sleep.

It is ironic that on one of the nights preceding this action the 2/115th encountered a German unit in much the same predicament in which they themselves had been, in a lousy defensive position through poor night discipline. But it was decided no attack would be made. Private Van Roosen spent the night watching and listening to the Germans. From Wegner's account it appears that his unit would also have avoided a fight if they could have, given their weakened state and lack of cohesion. The fortunes of war dictated that each situation played out in a different way.

This was not the only action that took place during the hours that passed on 10 June as Generalleutnant Kraiss was re-establishing his front. With the dawn came reports that US troops had reached as far south as Cormolain, deep in his right flank. Oberstleutnant von Aufsess, commander of Schnellebrigade 30, reported that his men had repulsed some attacks launched from the Forêt de Cerisy and that his patrols indicated a large troop build-up in that area. Kraiss' only hope of fending off an attack from there would be the arrival of 3. Falschirmjäger-Division. This was going to be their sector and the bridge across the Elle at Berigny had to be held and kept open for them.

The 916th was holding the line defending St Jean de Savigny, a major crossroads and Allied objective. Despite the heavy shelling, Goth ordered patrols to be sent out, he needed to assess the strength of the enemy infantry. Gefreiter Peter Simeth was assigned to one patrol:

> When the morning of 11 June dawned it was very cold but soon it was to get very 'hot'. The shelling was on. We were ordered to go out about 10 kilometres or so and find the enemy and assess his strength. We did this; it was easier than I thought. The Amis were not shelling their side of the line. We made our way back and the officer made his report. The Arifeuer became stronger and we had to dig our holes much deeper.

All the information that came into Kraiss and his staff indicated that a large-scale attack was imminent. So far, casualties had been high for both sides but as of yet no fresh replacements had arrived for the 352nd, while the Allies landed fresh troops every day. The hardest casualties to replace were experienced NCOs. Leutnant Heinze lost one such man this day, Stabsfeldwebel Nielen: 'This loss affected me greatly; he had been like a father to me. The losses in my company had been very high, not many of us were left.'

Goth's analysis was correct and at noon the American units made a thrust towards the town. The fighting was savage. Despite being exhausted and understrength, the Grenadiers of GR 916 contested every house, street, alley and yard. The GIs were just as determined to take the town and were aided by air and artillery support. Goth committed every man in the regiment to the fighting, leaving only a handful at his command post. Obergrenadier Martin Eichenseer fired his MG42 so much that it burned his hands just to hold it. He didn't have a spare barrel, nor the time to fit one even if he had. By late afternoon the Americans had taken the town. Goth ordered his men to withdraw; no reserves were left. The survivors of GR 916 disengaged, leaving behind some small groups cut off in isolated pockets. Amongst them was Eichenseer:

> We had fought as hard as we could but were no match for the force that the Amis could throw against us. We contested every metre of ground in St Jean de Savigny, mostly because it was a matter of survival for us. I sometimes wonder why we fought like that since by then most of us, even if we didn't say it, knew the war was lost. I suppose we were – especially those in the East at this time – defending our families. It is also true that since our youth, to fight for the Fatherland was branded upon our very souls. We did have some fanatics but they were soon silenced by the harsh realities we encountered. But in the final analysis our own survival drove us on. Every engagement we survived was a victory for the individual no matter what ground was gained or lost. And now on 11 June 1944, I was alone with two other men from another company with very little ammunition, cut off and not sure what to do. We crept like cats from place to place hoping to find our lines or at least other Germans with a leader among them. Stray shots, bad luck, or the Will of God, I'll never know why, but by nightfall, the others were dead. I found a place on the top of a rather high hedgerow, curled up with my machine gun, and waited for something to happen. In the end I was fast asleep.

For Oberst Heyna and his GR 914, the day was much quieter. The only actions were US probes across the Elle at the village of Moon-sur-Elle. His regiment was still reorganising and gathering stragglers and thus not strong enough to mount actions against the probes. Late in the morning Generalleutnant Kraiss appeared at 914's command post near St Jean de Daye. Reports had filtered into to Kraiss of heavy fighting in and around Carentan; now all contact with the German units in that area had been lost. Carentan was vital to the whole sector. From 914, the closest 352nd unit to the city, Kraiss had dispatch riders sent out towards Carentan and the surrounding area. None reached the city; the main road had been cut by advancing US troops. The sounds of heavy fighting could be heard at the command post from that direction for quite some time. Then they tailed off and seemed to shift farther away. An observation post of Artillerie Regiment 352 reported US troops on the outskirts of Carentan, also in the area west of St Jean de Daye and Le Mesnil. If the city fell, the crossroads and railhead there would give the Allies an enormous advantage and force a major German withdrawal from the sector. The only option was for Kraiss to secure the Vire-Taute Canal, although he did not know if it had already fallen. He was hoping that the battlegroup from 275. Infanterie-Division would arrive soon; but word arrived that Kampfgruppe Heintz was still far away. Thus Heyna was told that if Carentan had fallen, he should expect a major Allied attack within the next 48 hours. He would be expected to stop it, using all the men at his disposal. Since his regiment was not even half of its normal strength, the prospects for success were dire.

Still, 11 June, like the previous day, was giving most of the 352nd time to lick their wounds and continue improving the defensive works, GR 916 being the only exception. By nightfall the entire front had grown quiet; rumours ran rampant about the entire division being pulled out of the line. It is true that Hitler himself had ordered the withdrawal of the 352nd for rest and refitting. Rommel refused, since he still had no other unit to replace them in the line; the division would stay at the front. However, one man was to get some precious time away from the front. Gefreiter Simeth was ordered to report to his company command post:

> 'What was going on?' I thought to myself. When I got there the Oberleutnant said that I had to go to a village just 400 metres away [possibly St Marguerite] to get an American prisoner that was there. I went there and found the prisoner. I was told to take him back to the regimental command post for interrogation. As we left the village we came under heavy artillery fire but we made it to safety.
>
> After quite some distance we found a house that was deserted and decided to rest for the remainder of the night. This fellow could speak German so we talked. I told him that I was tired of the war and he said that he was not looking forward to life in a prisoner of war camp. I noticed he was slightly wounded. I re-bandaged his side and we talked some more. Then we hit on an idea. The following day we would find some place to hide and wait until the Amis came. We would take care of each other and make sure neither side harmed us. That night we were very much like close friends.
>
> In the morning we headed as if towards my command post, some 12 kilometres away. This would give us ample territory to find a good hiding spot. We did find a secluded farmhouse, well off the road. We took up residence. A short time later we saw some armed men coming our way. The American went out and waved at them. They shot at him. We saw they wore civilian clothes, Frenchmen. Could they not see he was an American? We did not wait to find out. I helped him out the rear window and we headed off into the woods. When we stopped running I gave him my canteen, he drank it dry. He needed it more than I. We walked farther on and came to a road. Here we met some SS troops [most likely elements of 17. SS Panzer-Grenadier-Division]. They questioned me about what I was doing and their sergeant came forward and said that I should shoot the prisoner and go back to the front. I said that I could not and must get him to the regimental command post quickly. He looked at me with 'fire in the eyes'. I pushed him away and we ran back into the forest. We walked until about midday, it was good just to be out of range of the shelling for a while. Then we bumped into some men and a Leutnant from the Stabskompanie of my regiment. I asked him for directions to the command post in hopes of getting on our way again. He took charge of the prisoner and told me to go back to the front with the other men. I watched them drive away. The American waved at me and I waved back, enemies but friends. I joined the others and went back to the war.

While Simeth and his new 'friend' had been on their adventure, the entire right flank of the 352nd had begun to cave in. On the morning of 12 June the US 2nd Division had smashed through the overstretched lines of Schnellebrigade 30, crossing the Elle near Cerisy and made it as far as the Bois de Elle. Amazingly, a detachment of *Festungspionier*, garrison engineers comprised of older, less fit, men, held their ground and prevented further US advances. Small and determined pockets from Schnellebrigade 30 held out, causing problems in the US rear as they rolled about looking for weak spots to cross the front. Many were able to regroup to build a new line of defence in the Bois de Elle.

Unexpected help arrived when the Aufklärungs Abteilung of 2. Panzer-Division launched an attack through the 352nd's lines and stabilised the entire front. This armoured support was well employed, upsetting the US troops' attempts at consolidating their territorial gains.

Goth's men regrouped once again and mounted their own attack against St Jean de Savigny. This operation was led by Leutnant Lang, an officer from the Stabskompanie. He was successful to a certain degree. The thrust forward took back most of the town but it failed to throw the US troops back across their bridgehead, the main objective of the attack. The losses of GR 916 would not be replaced any time soon.

On his way forward, Gefreiter Simeth encountered several of the walking wounded from this engagement heading towards the aid station in the rear:

> I walked for a while and then met up with many of our wounded heading back. They told me not to go up there because all hell was breaking loose. I went back with them to the aid station. From here I went to look for the *Spiess* [[colloquial name for a company sergeant major, the *Hauptfeldwebel* or First Sergeant]. When I found him I told him I had just gotten back from bringing a prisoner to the rear. He said that it was alright for me to stay there. The day was very 'hot' but I got a chance to rest.

While Gefreiter Simeth seemed blessed with some luck, Obergrenadier Eichenseer had little to none. Still hiding atop the hedgerow, and despite the thousands of men fighting around him, he felt quite alone:

> I had slept some during the night but it was cold and I was hungry. All I could do was make the best of it. The day arrived, and I was still confused about what to do. I could hear the sounds of fighting. But it was much farther away than I thought. My mind bounced back and forth should I try to make it back to my regiment or surrender? I did not have to ponder long; my mind was made up for me. I heard some noise and then saw American soldiers walking towards me along the road below. They were lined up in such a way that with what little ammunition I had I could have got them all; but for what reason? I decided to surrender, although this must be done right. If I called out or just stood up they might be a little jumpy and just shoot out of reflex. I had to wait for the right moment. Finally it came. I saw an officer walking with a radioman next to him. He was speaking on the headset so his attention was not on his weapon, nor were his hands. When I judged the time to be correct I slid down the hedgerow, leaving my MG and pistol behind, and landed squarely in front of the officer. With my hands held high I yelled 'Kamerad'. His look was that of a very confused man but I was so close to him that if anyone had fired they would have hit him and the radioman. The gamble worked. After much confusion, during which the officer yelled profusely at his lead men, they turned their attention to me. They called me a sniper. I denied this and pointed to the MG, still visible. The sight of this brought another cascade of shouts from the officer at his men. One of my captors seemed to enjoy this very much, the embarrassment of his commander, because he gave me a box of food then patted me on the back while he laughed. This

relaxed me as well, since during this all I was quite scared and trembled a lot. I was searched and sent to the rear. For me the fighting was over but not the war.

12 June did not bring the major offensive that Kraiss had surmised would occur on his left flank. Oberstleutnant Heyna was pleased at the prospect of another day of consolidation. American actions still went on, but at a considerably slower pace. This puzzled all the Germans, including Karl Wegner:

> Back with our regiment we now held a very weak line somewhere around La Couture or La Rousserie, near a major road. Because of our diminished numbers the spaces between our fighting holes was much greater than usual. We really had nothing to speak of behind us, just what was left of the Stabskompanie. Most of the rear echelon men of the battalion and Regiment were already fighting as infantry. Attacks did push us back, but very slowly and not far, only to our second reserve positions. Kalb said that he felt the Amis either had supply problems or lousy intelligence because one concentrated attack would sweep us aside like toy soldiers. Then to our total surprise fresh reinforcements began to arrive late in the afternoon. They only had a little dirt on them and possessed plenty of ammunition. Our company was pulled back to the area around the regimental command post, tonight we would surely get some sleep, or so we hoped.

Kampfgruppe Heintz had finally arrived. Their slow progress accelerated when Generalleutnant Kraiss ordered all available transport vehicles to pick up the lead elements of the battlegroup, Fusilier-Bataillon 275, and bring them directly to the 914th's sector. When this was completed, the process would be repeated to shuttle the entire group into the left flank. The arriving units of Kampfgruppe Heintz took up positions on the Le Mesnil–St Jean de Daye road along the railway line that split this road in two. Now any attack by US forces from Carentan would meet significant resistance. All intelligence, including the two captured US Corps Operations Orders, indicated that the major assault on St Lô would come from this area. So Kraiss sent all reinforcements to this flank, which he considered almost wide open at that point. Still, he needed to know that he would not face a large-scale assault on his centre or right flanks. To this end, reconnaissance patrols were ordered out to gather as much information as they could.

On the morning of 13 June, Obergefreiter Josef Brass received his orders; although he and his unit were technically combat engineers, he was going on a recon patrol. 'Leutnant Leischner ordered me to find ten working bicycles for a patrol. We were to go out and find the Amis and see what they were up to. Eventually we got under way with Leischner in the lead and me bringing up the rear.'

The patrol made its way along the roads and lanes in the early morning light. Brass was really not sure where they were heading or what they would encounter, since the front was not stable or secure. They reached the outskirts of a village, which Leutnant Leischner decided to patrol. Unknown to them, the 116th Infantry Regiment of the 29th US Division was about to launch an attack to seize the village of Rubercy:

> As we pedalled through the village we heard gunfire come from the opposite side of it. Suddenly through the side streets American soldiers came running out yelling 'Hands Up!' We pedalled as fast as we could to get away. Leutnant Leischner and most of my squad were lucky

enough to get away. But I and two others in the rear were not. The Americans ran out in front of us and stopped our bicycles. I won't go into our first moments of captivity but suffice to say that these were not the proudest minutes in the history of the US Army.

Brass later heard from his captives that staff officers of the 116th – shocked that Germans on bicycles would ride nonchalantly through the middle of their attack – had watched the entire episode.

Just for once, the losses incurred by Pionier-Bataillon 352 were quickly replaced. The advanced school for Pionier troops operated by 7. Armee was empty as all the men taking courses had been sent back to their original units, leaving the cadre of instructors with not much to do. These 250 experienced soldiers were sent up to the front en masse to the 352nd. Some went to the depleted Pionier-Bataillon of Hauptmann Paul but the majority went to reinforce GR 914 on the left flank. Kraiss wanted to make this his strongest point of the line for the reasons given, in the defence of St Lô. With these men and the arrival of Kampfgruppe Heintz, his division was now 'in the black' as far as infantry was concerned. Artillery was a different matter altogether. Even with the artillery that arrived to support the battlegroup from 275. Infanterie-Division, the entire front was desperately short. The 352nd's front and the front of 3. Falschirmjäger-Division, together 50 kilometres in length, were covered by only 46 guns of various calibres and with the most tenuous of links with depots for ammunition resupply. Despite this fact, he placed most of them on his left flank, leaving the rest of his front with only the bare minimum or none at all.

A fresh bag of German PoWs await evacuation by the US Navy on Omaha Beach, 7 June 1944. There are paratroopers on far right, most likely from 6 Falschirmjäger. The rest are from either 352 or 716. Infanterie-Division. (USA National Archives)

Left PoW photo of Obergefreiter Josef Brass taken at Camp Livingston, LA, US. PoW Serial No: 31G 128679.

Right German officers segregated from enlisted PoWs glumly regard the cameraman as they await evacuation to England. Note that they are wearing raincoats and the weather is bleak indicating that the date is probably 6 or 7 June. (USA National Archives)

Throughout all this, Gefreiter Simeth was doing well. His Spiess used him to help out in the headquarters, which meant he rode quite a bit instead of walking. One move of the regimental command post placed them next to a group of four houses, protected from the air by clumps of trees. After helping to camouflage the trucks against aerial attacks he went to investigate one of the barns. It was dark and cool inside; this made him sleepy again. He found a comfortable spot between two wine kegs, thinking to himself that it had been a really long time since he had any real sleep. Peter Simeth closed his eyes and closed out the war going on around him.

While the young lance corporal fell asleep, his regimental commander decided to go to the front and lead his men from there while the command post itself was in a state of transition. With only his driver, Oberst Ernst Goth set off in his Kubelwagen. Shortly after leaving his new headquarters, the driver spotted a large group of US troops apparently preparing a defensive position. Goth ordered him to stop so he could investigate the site personally; if this were true, his lines were broken already

The Colonel pressed forward on foot with his driver to discover about 40 GIs, roughly a platoon, dug into a fairly weak position. Goth ordered his driver to go back and bring up every spare man to attack this unit. After the driver left, Oberst Goth made his way to the rear of the American positions in order to cut them off. Armed only with his driver's machine pistol he pinned down the Americans keeping them from improving their positions or retreating. Leutnant Heller arrived with part of his company and took over what their regimental commander had started. But the break in Goth's line was much larger than just the 40 men he had encountered. Grenadier Regiment 916 would be forced to readjust the lines once again. The newly promoted Oberleutnant Heller did lead his company in an attack that took back the eastern parts of the Bois de Bretel by dusk. Oberst Goth, for his actions, was placed on the Honour Roll of the German Army.

Honour roll containing Oberst Ernst Goth's citation.

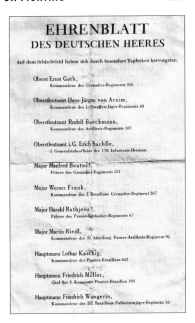

EHRENBLATT
DES DEUTSCHEN HEERES

Auf dem Schlachtfeld haben sich durch besondere Tapferkeit hervorgetan

Oberst Ernst Goth,
  Kommandeur des Grenadier-Regiments 916

Oberstleutnant Hans-Jürgen von Arnim,
  Kommandeur des Luftwaffen-Jäger-Regiments 40

Oberstleutnant Rudolf Boeckmann,
  Kommandeur des Artillerie-Regiments 187

Oberstleutnant i.G. Erich Sachße,
  I. Generalstabsoffizier der 170. Infanterie-Division

Major Manfred Beutner,
  Führer des Grenadier-Regiments 551

Major Werner Frank,
  Kommandeur des I. Bataillons Grenadier-Regiment 267

Major Harald Rathjens †,
  Führer des Panzer-Grenadier-Regiments 67

Major Martin Riedl,
  Kommandeur der II. Abteilung Panzer-Artillerie-Regiment 92

Hauptmann Lothar Kaschig,
  Kommandeur des Pionier-Bataillons 662

Hauptmann Friedrich Müller,
  Chef der 3. Kompanie Pionier-Bataillon 193

Hauptmann Friedrich Wangerin,
  Kommandeur des III. Bataillons Fallschirmjäger-Regiment 16

Simeth slept peacefully between the wine kegs, unnoticed. All good things come to an end:

I had slept until about six in the evening. I rubbed my eyes then went into the house next to the barn. Inside I met a young woman, who was the mother to a young boy and girl. I greeted them and asked about buying some milk and eggs. Right away I was given some milk and then she cooked me an egg. We came to an agreement that for as long as we were there she would cook me eggs and give me milk twice a day, the mornings and afternoons. We talked further and I found out that her father was a prisoner of war in Germany. I then heard the Spiess yelling for me. I was finally missed and needed for something.

That evening, 13 June, Major Block informed Generalleutnant Kraiss that all of the incoming information pointed to large-scale troop buildup all along the division's front and not just on the left flank. The major further surmised that a large-scale attack might occur some time during the next few days. This notion was further bolstered with confirmation from GR 916 that Couvains and St Clair sur Elle had both fallen to US forces, who had attacked in stronger than usual force.

Still, within St Clair sur Elle large pockets of men from 916th were holding out, and the southern part of the town was still in Goth's hands. On the considerably built-up left flank there was no Allied offensive action. This could be taken as a sign that a major offensive was in preparation or that Allied intentions were focused elsewhere. Either way, Kraiss would use any time he could gain to solidify the defences in that area.

The rumours of withdrawal still persisted among the ranks. Obergrenadier Wegner refused to believe that they were just rumours:

For a day or two things around us had been rather quiet and the arrival of sufficient reinforcements for once, and their taking our place in the line gave us the feeling that the talk of our being relieved was true. Willi and I began to talk of how long we would sleep and of how much we would eat, maybe even of getting a hot bath. Just these thoughts lifted our spirits. Kalb, always the realist, burst our balloon. He said, 'Look boys, the truth is right in front of you, if we were to be withdrawn it would have been at night, in fact the night the new battalion came up. We only came back as far as the regimental command post. We are in reserve. Sure we are getting a bit of a rest but we are here until they carry us away or shovel dirt in our faces.' We didn't want to believe him but deep down a small part of us knew he was right.

Leutnant Heinze also had these rumours sweep through his company and finally was able to get the full story from his superiors: 'OKW had requested that we be withdrawn for rest and refitting but the tactical situation would not allow us to be taken out of the already overstretched main line of resistance.'

No matter what army, soldiers must still wait in line. German PoWs with their possessions in used K ration crates patiently wait to board ships for England. A keen eye will detect the strings from the shoulder to the pocket that are attached to their PoW tags. (USA National Archives)

It was now the 14th and another day past meant that the 352nd was slightly better pre-pared to meet any Allied push southwards to St Lô along the Vire river, which Kraiss and his staff believed would be the shortest and quickest route to the city. This assessment was based on all of the latest intelligence on Allied troop placements and the captured Corps Operations Orders. In this sector the German over-reliance on infantry against the Allied armour-supported attacks was mitigated by the terrain of the hedgerows and mostly small, narrow country roads. The terrain greatly diminished the power of armoured spearheads. The Allied armour had to stick to major roads and towns. The advance would be painful, especially in the hedgerow country. Sergeant Quaterone, a tanker in 2nd Armoured Division:

> When we ran up against those hedgerows they stopped us cold. We couldn't punch through them so we had to go over the top of them. Sometimes our Shermans got stuck on the roots and stones but the worst was when we reached the top. Because when we did we were 'belly up' for a few seconds before the tank dropped down. Most of the time some German was waiting for you with one of their 'panzerfaust' one-shot rockets. If they hit you in the belly they would send you to Kingdom Come. Other times they would have an 88 dug in or one of their tank destroyers, low tanks without turrets waiting for us. Our Shermans sat real high and they could see us long before we could them. They only real advantage we had was the Mustangs and Thunderbolts with those rockets. The Flyboys could blast them out when we found them a target. But in the end some poor Joe with a rifle would have to put his life on the line and charge up and over the hedgerow to clear out the enemy.

Eventually American tankers would figure out a way through these obstacles but until then it would be an infantryman's war. Major Block noted that reports from the front indicated that US troops had become less enthusiastic in their attacks than they had been in the first few days of the invasion. They began to expend inordinate amounts of ammu-nition on any German position, real or suspected, before they advanced, to a point where several staff officers surmised that the Allies might develop munitions shortages. This was based on their experience of the availability of ammunition on the German side, which was reliant on a fractured and sporadic supply chain. In contrast, the Allies had huge stores with more coming over from England all the time; they could afford to waste some.

Despite being PoWs, these men are still soldiers and maintain their grooming standards while on their way to England. (USA National Archives)

Apart from the Jabos, there were small Allied aircraft that could bring a rain of shells down upon your head if they saw you: the single-engine observation planes – *Arifliegers*, literally 'Flyers for the Artillery'. They would fly above the German lines looking for troop concentrations or enemy gun positions. These pilots would commonly circle around certain areas in the hope of drawing small arms fire; many Germans learned the hard way not to fire at these 'offensive little birds'. In time the Germans learned to turn the tactics of these aircraft against them. Obergrenadier Wegner:

> For several hours we had been watching a small observation plane fly over the front. When it was fired upon it would fire back with rockets and MGs. All of a sudden the Feldwebel called for Obergefreiter Kalb. When he came back he told us to bring the gun and follow him. We went out across the field to another hedgerow and set the gun up on top of it. Kalb said 'When the observation plane returns we are to fire at it until it sees us, then pull back when it flies away.' We weren't sure why but did what we were ordered to. We got back to our line when we heard the familiar sound of a Jabo circling above. We watched as it dived onto the place where we had been, fired its rockets and then pulled up from its dive. When it did its belly was exposed only several feet above us, that's when the two other MGs we had opened fire. The Jabo took several hits, veered off towards the American lines and crashed behind them. The plan had worked and I was surprised. At the time we all felt good that we had finally brought one of the Jabos down because they had killed many of our Kameraden. It was a plan we would use every now and then, when we had ammunition to spare.

Another of the adverse effects of the Allied air umbrella was that when not actually engaged in combat, the German infantry had to spend time sitting in their fighting positions, physically uncomfortable and mentally stressful. All movement and supply work was shifted to night hours, if possible. This added more stress and loss of sleep to the soldier's lot.

Gefreiter Simeth was still with the headquarters company, although he now found himself with less free time than before. On 14 June the Spiess told him that one of his friends, Grenadier Eduard Schötz, was reported missing during the fighting around Couvains that morning. The young soldier was very much alive, but the game was up:

352.Inf.-Division.   Div.Gef.Stand..30.7.1944.
Abt. IIa.

Betr.: Anerkennung von Sturm- und Nahkampftagen.

      Dem Oberst G o t h , Kdeur Gren.Rgt.916, werden folgende
Tage als Nahkampf- bzw. Sturmtage bestätigt:

a) Nahkampftage:

    8.6.44 Aufbau einer neuen HKL. südostwärts Trevières im feindl.
         Feuer mit Teilen des II./916 bei Mandeville.

   16.6.44 Abwehr eines feindl.Durchbruchs durch Nahverteidigung
         des Rgts.-Stabes westlich Villiers-Fossard. Aufbau einer
         neuen HKL. im feindl.Feuer durch Teile der Schnellen
         Brigade 30.

b) Sturm- und Nahkampftage:

    6.6.44 Abwehr eines amerikanischen Angriffs auf W.N.69
         (Lt.Backhaus), Gegenstoß der Reserve des W.N.69 zusammen
         mit Landesbau-Pionieren über St.Laurent zum W.N.67.
         Anschliessend Abriegeln feindl.Umfassung mit 2 M.G.-
         Gruppen südl.Colleville während des Gegenstosses der
         5./916.

    7.6.44 Gliederung des W.N.69a (s.J.G.) zur Nahverteidigung und
         Abwehr des über St.Laurent vorgestossenen Feindes.
         Ansatz und Vorführen des Pi.-Batls. 352 auf Vierville
         zum Gegenangriff.

   12.6.44 Führung des Gegenstosses der Gruppe Lt.Lang, des Rgts.
         Pi.-und Radfahrzuges auf St.Jean de Savigny, der zur
         Wiedereinnahme des Ortes führte.

   13.6.44 Abwehr eines feindlichen Durchbruchs durch Nahverteidi=
         gung des Rgts.-Stabes bei Couvains. Aufbau einer neuen
         HKL. im feindl.Feuer und Ansatz und Führung eines Gegen=
         stoßes der Gruppe Heller zum Wiedergewinn des Ostrandes
         des Waldes von Bretel.

Kraiss.

Generalleutnant und
Divisions-Kommandeur.

Orders from Generalleutnant Kraiss to Oberst Goth, dated 30 July 1944, informing him which days are considered 'close combat' days and 'assault and close combat' days, for the purposes of combat decorations. 6 June 1944 is designated an 'assault and close combat day', specifically mentioning WN67 and WN69 and the fighting around Colleville of the 5th Company GR 916.

Dienststelle Fp. Nr. 41 560   O.U.,den 18.7.44

Sehr geehrter Herr S c h ö t z !

Durch die anhaltenden Gefechtshandlungen kann ich erst heute die
traurige Pflicht erfüllen, Ihnen mitzuteilen, dass Ihr Sohn, der
Grenadier Eduard S c h ö t z seit dem 12.6.44 bei den schweren Ab=
wehrkämpfen bei Couvains (Normandie) vermißt wird.

Die Kompanie bedauert sehr, Ihnen keine bestimmten Angaben über das
Schicksal Ihres Sohnes machen zu können, alle Nachforschungen blieben
bisher ergebnislos.

Ich spreche Ihnen auch im Namen der Kompanie mein aufrichtiges Mitge=
fühl aus und hoffe, dass ein gütiges Geschick Ihnen bald Gewissheit
über den Verbleib Ihres Sohnes geben wird.

Ich darf darauf hinweisen, dass Sie alle weiteren Anfragen an die
      Wehrmachtauskunftstelle für Kriegerverluste
        und Kriegsgefangene, S a a l f e l d /Saale
richten wollen.

      In Vertretung für den gefallenen Komp.-Führer

           Oberveterinär.

Edouard Schötz's missing in action letter, addressed to his father. It is signed for the 'killed in action' company commander by the veterinarian officer, *Oberveternar* Graf. This demonstrates the heavy toll on the German officers during the Normandy campaign as no regular officers were available to sign the letter.

We were in a defensive position holding out against an American attack. With the passing of time we realised we would be cut off from our lines if we did not leave soon. One of us crawled back to see if there was a way out. He rushed back over the hedgerow and told us that we were completely surrounded. The minutes passed and then we finally decided that it would be best to surrender rather than to fight our way out. We gave up to some Americans and they made us lay flat on our stomachs with our arms outstretched. The treatment was very rough at first, but we were still alive.

Schötz's father would receive that second most dreaded of letters from the government of a nation at war – the one telling of a loved one MIA. It was the beginning of a long wait, but would end well with the elder Schötz knowing his son was alive and well in a PoW camp.

Simeth was not the only man to receive bad news about a friend that day. Kraiss was informed by dispatch rider that General Marcks was dead. Apparently when the commander of LXXXIV Armeekorps heard that Carentan definitely had fallen he headed off to the front to personally lead efforts to retake the town. His car was speeding down the main road to the town in broad daylight, a very risky thing for any vehicle.

It was not long before one of the dreaded Jabos fell upon his car. With his wooden leg, a memento of the First World War, he was not able to scramble out of the car to the safety of the roadside ditch quickly enough. He did get his wish to die in battle, however. His was not to be a glorious death, but he did share the fate of hundreds of his own men. He lay, his body riddled and shattered, next to his burning staff car on a Normandy road.

This loss was deeply felt by Generalleutnant Kraiss and his staff. Marcks had always been good to the 352nd in his treatment and decisions, but there was no time to mourn. General der Falschirmtruppe Meindl, commander of II Falschirmkorps, was given command of all intact LXXXIV Armeekorps units, amongst them the 352nd. Even with the confirmation of the fall of Carentan, by the time night fell on 14 June, the 352nd was in better shape than any of the days prior. Reinforcements and supplies had been received; all the gaps in the front line had been plugged. Even more amazing was that the American units opposing the 352nd had exploited none of these gaps when they could. If they had, the battle for St Lô would have been over. Now there would be a fight for the city.

Still, there were no delusions about how the campaign would end. No matter how loud Hitler yelled or how many 'paper' divisions he pushed around on his maps of France, the truth was clear to the Generals around him and even more so to the Grenadiers dug in across the Norman countryside. The only determining factors in the length of the campaign would be the course of action the Allies took and the endurance of the German defenders. The men of the 352nd were fighting a losing battle and they knew it.

twelve

twelve

FINALLY, THEY'RE OURS!

WITH no one seeming to notice or even care that he was still at the regimental command post of GR 916, Gefreiter Simeth decided on the morning of 15 June to make the best of his situation. He would keep himself inconspicuous and get some more sleep. Far off to his right he could hear the Allied artillery pounding away at some other poor fellows, but it was much too far away to bother his slumber. On the receiving end of that barrage were the men of 3. Falschirmjäger-Division. Under the combined pressure of this sweeping artillery attack and strong thrust by US troops, the German paratroopers found themselves steadily pushed back. In between them and GR 916, Oberstleutnant von Aufsess with the remaining men of Schnellebrigade 30 attempted to maintain contact with the paratroopers and keep the front intact. All this proved futile; his lines were stretched so thin that they had been infiltrated in several places. The seasoned commander was also well aware that there was not a damn thing he could do about it.

Despite the rumbling of guns, the day was proceeding rather peacefully for the men in the 916th, but not for Karl Wegner and what was left of GR 914, now called Kampfgruppe Heyna, as they stubbornly held on to their part of the Elle river line. With the day still young, they had already beaten off several several attempts by US troops to cross the river on either side of the Bayeux-Airel road. On their left flank, help had arrived in the form of Kampfgruppe Heintz. This unit had become the extreme left flank of the 352nd. But no sooner had they set up shop than they faced a full-blown assault, complete with air and armoured support. The Kampfgruppe had no armour, nor could they expect any. Lacking combat experience, they fell back, although their relative freshness and intact chain of command allowed them to conduct a tactical withdrawal rather than a full-scale retreat. Even so, they did lose the tactically important crossroads at Montmartin, which put them in danger of being surrounded. Having lost radio communications with Heintz, Generalleutnant Kraiss dispatched a messenger with an order allowing Heintz to bring his men back across the Vire-Taute Canal and set up a new front there. He was also ordered to destroy all the bridges in his sector except for the main highway bridge. Here he was to establish strong perimeters on both ends of the bridge. This would give Kraiss a route for a counterthrust if reinforcements en masse ever arrived. If they never did, he knew what he had to contend with next.

With the information contained in the two captured operations orders and available intelligence reports from the forward units, in particular 17. SS Panzer-Grenadier-Division, it was quite clear to Kraiss and his staff that within a matter of a few days the Allies would launch the major thrust towards St Lô. He ordered his staff to plan the best course of action for the defence of the city with the limited resources at their disposal. With the last rays of sunlight, the staff of the 352nd set to work. Around them the fighting, so intensive during the day, had petered out, apart from the occasional crack of a rifle in the darkness. Those on watch fought to stay awake, others let their heavy eyelids drag them into sleep, dreaming of places they hoped to see again.

At dawn on 16 June the silence ended. Shells crashed into the earth, ripping up roots and trees, throwing dirt and rocks into the air. Hot, razor sharp steel cut through anything in its path. Obergrenadier Wegner instinctively, still half asleep, threw on his helmet and fell to the very bottom of his freshly dug hole, pushing himself deep into the soft dirt. The rest of his little band were already there.

> That morning while in positions around the village of Airel the Arifeuer was intense. Kalb yelled, in between explosions, that this was going to be a big attack. We knew we were stretched very thinly and most felt that we wouldn't hold the line. But for now all we could do was wait out the Arifeuer.

The entire front was ablaze under this barrage. Even 3. Falschirmjäger-Division radioed in to Generalleutnant Kraiss to express concerns that the 352nd's flank may be in danger of collapsing because the paratroopers were engaged in heavy fighting around Berigny and St Georges Montcocq. But most importantly they had already been forced out of St André de L'Épine – the town's roads connected with the D-972, the major highway leading into St Lô from the east. If US troops made it to this highway, 3. Falschirmjäger-Division would be cut in two, and the road into St Lô would lie wide open.

Generalleutnant Kraiss ordered the paratroopers to launch everything that was available in an all-out effort to retake the village. This was already in the works when Kraiss was being warned of the 352nd's predicament. Obergefreiter Kalb had been correct; the US 29th Division attacked their lines and they did not hold. The front collapsed under the strain. Wegner found himself in a full retreat:

> When the Arifeuer stopped the Amis came. I really didn't see much of their strength but heard the sounds of heavy fighting all around. It was not long before the Feldwebel came and ordered us to fall back across the Vire before the Pioniers blew the bridge. We picked up everything and headed down the road towards a bridge we hoped would still be there. Willi expressed the hope out loud, echoing all our sentiments. With our luck we would most likely have to swim across the river.

On a broad front, roughly from Le Meauffe to Villiers Fossard, GR 916 felt the full wrath of the American forces opposing them. Under this pressure, their lines began bending and twisting; Gefreiter Simeth's peaceful time had ended. 'Around midday I was grabbed to go

Oberst Ernst Goth with daughter Ursula Narlosh (née Goth), 1944. (M. Galle)

on a patrol under the command of an Oberfeldwebel. We were all shown a map and told that this is where we were to go and check out. With that we headed down a picturesque tree-lined road.'

The Americans had taken Les Buteaux and Hill 108, an important high point with a commanding view of the entire sector, and were now pressing towards Villiers Fossard. This was the destination of Simeth's patrol:

> We had reached the destroyed village and began to work our way through it. Immediately, we began to take fire. We made for the cover of a roadside ditch, but it soon was apparent that we couldn't stay here either. We dashed towards a damaged house, getting there only to find the Amis already in residence. Then we saw the tanks. The Oberfeldwebel ordered us to fall back as fast as we could go. It was strange that the Amis did not follow us.

While this patrol was trying to extricate itself, Oberst Goth's command post, south of Villiers Fossard, came under direct attack. Every man available was thrown into the defence of the area. The command staff itself was to withdraw while these troops held off American attempts to capture the headquarters intact. Kraiss even called Goth during this action, before the telephone lines were shut down. The sounds of close combat were distinct on the General's end of the line. The call was an order for Goth to withdraw and reform his line from La Forge to Le Mesnil-Rouxelin. Kraiss emphasised that this was to be a fighting withdrawal, holding up the Americans as long as possible. The Generalleutnant also added that an improvised Kampfgruppe was on its way forward to assist in the operation. Finally, good news for the beleaguered Colonel. He did not know that this battlegroup consisted mainly of clerks, cooks and bakers from the divisional staff, along with rear echelon support elements, although there were a handful of Grenadiers amongst them, returning from hospital after receiving light wounds. In the final tally this fighting force amounted to 30 men armed with pistols and rifles.

In the middle of the fray this group appeared at Goth's command post. The commander, a Paymaster, reported to the Oberst for orders. The simple plan was to send the Kampfgruppe into a limited attack towards La Carillon and Villiers Fossard. All Goth could do for them was furnish them with a few men who knew the area. Exhausted men in the command post watched the small band head off to the sound of the fighting, confident that these men would make no headway and only be chewed up by the Amis.

Oberst Goth's headquarters relocated in time. Now the process of regaining control of his regiment started. Just as he and his officers sat down to this task, a young soldier burst into the room. He was a clerk from the Kampfgruppe sent towards La Carillon. For a moment they feared that he was, perhaps, the lone survivor. Expecting only the worst, Oberst Goth let the young man give his report. In excited and jubilant tones the soldier blurted out that his group had pushed all the way to the Les Buteaux crossroads and his commander was now awaiting further instructions. This was very important news. First it meant that the Americans were not in the area in any kind of strength, and thus Goth could build his new front without too much interference. Secondly, if he could rally enough reserves, he could also retake a good portion of the ground lost during the morning actions. The officers of GR 916 set to work feverishly.

While Oberst Goth had this small piece of luck, Oberstleutnant von Aufsess had none. He desperately tried to put up some sort of front against the US troops pushing in at him. His men had lost all contact with 3. Falschirmjäger-Division. Now, as Goth was regaining some ground, he lost the village of Couvains. This left him only one course of action. He would have to rein in all of his surviving troops and try to establish contact with GR 916. Perhaps then a consolidated front line could be thrown up.

Along the entire front of the 352nd, except for actions by GR 916, tired, hungry soldiers were falling back with nowhere to go. If the American attack kept pressure upon them the entire division would be routed. Ziegelmann reported the sour news to his General; some sort of front had to be erected or St Lô would fall in a day or two at the most. With Goth's regiment the only one making any sort of a stand, even gaining ground, it was apparent that they soon would be cut off. The units on either flank of GR 916 were withdrawing southwards, farther and farther by the hour. The only logical thing to do was to repeat the officer patrols that had rallied and regained command and control of the division on 6 June.

Goth had exploited the advance of his rear echelon troops and then sent out patrols to further assess the situation. He relayed his remarkable news to Generalleutnant Kraiss. It was clear that US troops were taking all objectives assigned to them, then holding and consolidating, rather than chasing the retreating Germans. It should be pointed out that the Allies knew by now that German tactical doctrine was to counter-attack immediately to retake lost ground. Nevertheles it was still puzzling to the German officers why the enemy did not keep pressure on a retreating disorganised force. Ziegelmann pointed out that the Allies were now adhering to the objectives and timetables within the captured orders. Perhaps it was just problems with logistics, or a combination of the two. Whatever the case, it gave Kraiss the opportunity to regain control of his scattered division once again. His soldiers, like Wegner, would fight on another day:

> After we had been ordered to head to the bridge, we started along the road, but only for a short stretch. The road was swelled with a great throng of men surging towards the Vire. One could feel the panic in the air. I must admit that even I felt that the Amis were right upon our heels. Neither our company nor regiment existed in the minds of these men. Kalb kept us together through it all, with the road jammed and clogged he moved us well off the road and out of the way. Vehicles now added to the mess, totally forgetting the danger of the Jabos. It still amazes me that none appeared to smash this ripe target from the road. Kalb told us all to take a good look. He had seen this kind of panic before in Russia. We watched from the cover of the woods as small groups of officers and Feldwebels pushed and shoved the mob into some form of order. They were gaining control once again. Oddly enough the Amis never appeared and we found that they were well behind us, not even bothering to come after easy prey. In due time soldiers went back up the road that scared boys ran down not so long before.

In and around the town of Le Meauffe the remnants of GR 914, including Karl Wegner, took up positions.

Oberstleutnant Ziegelmann was ordered to assess the situation of 3. Falschirmjäger-Division personally. Their standing would have a direct effect on the placing of the troops on the 352nd's right flank. Upon his return from the paratroopers' divisional command post, Ziegelmann brought mixed news. All efforts to retake St André de L'Épine had fallen short, but more importantly they still had control of the D-972. Kraiss now knew what he could and could not do in the sector. He would begin a combined operation to defend his and the paratroopers' areas, overlapping his right flank behind the left flank of 3. Falschirmjäger-Division. While Ziegelmann was setting this up on the newly established landline to the paratroopers, an officer reported smartly to Generalleutnant Kraiss. It was 1600 hrs exactly when Oberst Böhm addressed the astonished General. The Colonel was the commanding officer of GR 943, and his unit, two full battalions in strength, along with a Pionier company, had been transferred from 353. Infanterie-Division to the 352nd. With some renewed hope, Kraiss immediately ordered Böhm to take his men into the line held by GR 916 and prepare for a counter attack; the objective was the rest of Villiers Fossard. The new men would move to the front when it was dark and prepare for a pre-dawn assault. Even before the Colonel left the command post, another officer entered. He was an Artillery Major in command of a 120mm Feldhaubizte Abteilung, a field howitzer detachment. His guns were now setting up emplacements near La Barre and his written orders placed him under the command of Artillerie Regiment 352. One more stroke of luck and an unexpected luxury; now Böhm and Goth would have artillery support for the attack. This also meant that large-scale reinforcements were beginning to reach Normandy.

The basic plan was to have GR 943 relieve the exhausted 916th during the night, then launch the attack with Goth's men in reserve. This allowed the majority of the 916th to get some uninterrupted sleep. A few unlucky souls were left behind to act as guides for the new regiment during the attack. It seems the fates now demanded that Gefreiter Simeth pay for his extra sleep, since he was assigned this task:

> When darkness came a motorcycle messenger came and said that we had been detailed to show a new unit where we had come from and where the Amis were. We spent the night crawling through hedgerows, bushes and across fields, every now and then getting shot at. Just before dawn we were finished and my group was allowed to go to the rear to join our company.

The loss of ground coupled with the arrival of other divisions, or parts of them, allowed Generalleutnant Kraiss to shorten his over extended front line substantially. Kampfgruppe von Aufsess was now in full reserve position, well within the rear area of the division. This was the first time in over a week that Kraiss actually possessed reserves. While the hedgerows aided in the defence of the area, they greatly hindered the efforts of troops fumbling around in the blackness looking for certain roads and collection points. Motorcycles, bicycles, horses and boot leather were all used by messengers and officers to communicate orders and direct lost companies. This large redeployment was successfully achieved well before dawn. The situation was now totally transformed from the preceding morning. As Kraiss studied the map, he knew that if the Allies had pressed forward in their advance, his division, or rather the survivors of it, would already be south of St Lô. But he now found himself in preparation for a counter attack, though he knew the regiments attacking would grind to a halt in the face of numbers and superior artillery and air power. Any ground retaken would most likely be lost again in a day or two – but the strategic aims were valid.

First, this would give the Generalleutnant ample time to plan an adequate defence of St Lô itself. Second, it might throw the Allies off balance enough to allow more time for the other divisions heading into Normandy from various points in western Europe to arrive. With these thoughts in mind, Kraiss moved his divisional staff and headquarters to some buildings in a northern part of the city.

When this was accomplished and communications with all divisional units re-established, it was discovered that II and IV Abteilung of Artillerie Regiment 352 were much further south than ordered; however, they were still within range to support GR 914 and Kampfgruppe Heintz, should Allied troops try to cross the Vire-Taute Canal. The 352nd was as ready as it would ever be, with just a short wait until dawn.

Many pairs of eyes, red and ringed from lack of sleep, kept track as their watches ticked off the seconds. The minute hand struck the appointed hour. It was 0530 hrs on the morning of 17 June. A thunder came from the rear of the German lines as every piece of artillery Kraiss could muster opened up on designated targets, something the 352nd had not been able to do since the beginning of the invasion. The barrage lasted exactly a half an hour. Even as the last shells were hurling towards the American lines, GR 943 was pressing forward. Further east, all the men in 3. Falschirmjäger-Division were doing the same.

To the west, Wegner and his little band of travellers listened to the sound of battle; for once the noise was moving farther away and to the north. The entire regiment was on alert, since an Allied offensive was expected. Unknown to these lowly Grenadiers was that the attack in the centre had drawn attention away from them. Perhaps today would pass, leaving them out of the fray. Then they heard an all too familiar sound. High above them, the drone of aircraft engines was clear; time for another drubbing from the Jabos. Wegner drew his machine gun up and waited for a plane to cross his sights:

> It was the usual thing, first we heard the engines then we either saw them or felt their sting, rockets or machine cannon fire. All around everyone was straining their necks watching the sky, I wanted to shoot at the first one I saw in frustration. Kalb told me to relax and not to draw fire. To my astonishment we suddenly saw one of our men standing out in the middle of the road. He jumped up and down waving and pointing. We were all perplexed; maybe he just cracked under the strain. Then we saw what had made him act that way. The planes had black crosses painted on their wings. Willi yelled 'Dear God, finally, they're ours!' Kalb was rather less enthusiastic, only muttering that it was about time they had shown themselves. To me it was a wonderful sight; it meant that we had not been forgotten. We cheered and waved at them as they flew off to the east.

The German fighters began to fly ground support missions in support of 3. Falschirmjäger-Division and GR 943. This was quite a surprise, and not just to the GIs who found themselves being strafed and bombed. The arrival of air support amazed all the Germans in the area regardless of rank. This unexpected gift from the Luftwaffe turned the tide, allowing Villiers Fossard and all the primary objectives of the offensive to be gained. A jubilant command staff received one positive report after another – it must be remembered that this operation had been calculated to be a tactical failure. During the course of the operation, all but 75 men of GR 916 were committed.

Kraiss did not have to use Kampfgruppe von Aufsess. The timely arrival of fresh artillery and munitions for his existing guns coupled with the air support, the first since the beginning of the invasion eleven days before, won the day. It proved to the German Grenadier that he was still capable of mounting and winning large-scale operations. Even the casualties of the attack – 500 killed, wounded, or missing – were replaced by the arrival of 1000 men from the 352nd's home station depots.

On the flank of the division not involved in the operation, defensive successes were achieved. Repeated American attacks, although not as strong as in previous days, were repulsed all through the day. No ground was lost in the 352nd's entire sector on 17 June. With the gains made and the actions of the troops opposing them, it was apparent that the Americans had been thrown off track. The question that was burdening the divisional staff was exactly how long it would take for the Amis to recover and push forward again. Oberstleutnant Ziegelmann and Major Block both felt that within 24 hours the US corps opposing them would again be mounting large-scale thrusts towards St Lô, once they were assured that the 352nd's attack was not the prelude to a major German offensive against the entire invasion front. The course of action opted for by Generalleutnant Kraiss was simple. First, he would hold all of the territory gained for as long as possible. Second, he would move his reserves back to the line he intended to build around St Lô so that work could be underway immediately. Within 24 hours he intended to have positions into which his men could fall back and, more importantly, hold onto, for a long period. In order to speed up this work, two companies from GR 916 would be detached and sent to the rear.

There was a problem with the intended front: it was not a continuous line, but disjointed because of several road junctions that were important to hold. This had to be worked out quickly, or the delay might prove fatal. Kraiss' decision was clear and concise. The right flank would be brought up to coincide with that of 3. Falschirmjäger-Division, and as it progressed westwards, it would gradually turn north until it reached the Vire river. The result would be a solid front with no gaps or bulges and – because of reinforcements – the shortest front held by the division thus far in its history.

Once again orders went out, and men moved southwards along the dark roads, each knowing that a long spell with a shovel rather than a blanket awaited them at their destination. The men from Goth's regiment took up the sector in and around Le Mesnil-Rouxelin. Gefreiters Simeth and Seidl felt quite at home here, as did any man from GR 916 who was a survivor of 6 June. The buildings and countryside were where these men had been billeted and trained prior to the move up to the coast the previous May, a thousand lifetimes ago. Their detachment was placed about 500 metres to the north of the little hamlet and shown where to start the arduous tasks of building emplacements. With service flashlights buttoned to tunic pockets, and amidst the ringing clatter of spades cutting into the ground, these Grenadiers began another day, 18 June. Amongst the grunts, groans and blisters, hunger pangs gnawed at their bellies and sleepless eyes strained to stay open in the inviting dark night enveloping them. Simeth took it all in stride; after all, he thought, are we all not well away from the front lines? Perhaps this thought was shared by others, but in true soldierly character only muffled curses and complaints occasionally wafted above the sounds of the digging.

Hauptmann Steneck, the commander of GR 916's Stabskompanie, was placed in charge of the companies preparing the new positions in the area north of St Lô while Oberst Goth stayed at the front with the bulk of his men. The morning was cool and quiet, and Goth issued an order for all troops to rest in place as much as possible. When no Allied attack materialised in the morning even Goth himself took advantage of the situation to have two hours of uninterrupted sleep. No rations had come forward in the morning but every effort was made to get a noon meal to the front. The food arrived just a little too late. None would get to eat it. At the beginning of the distribution, artillery and mortar barrages tore into the ranks of both GR 943 and 916 in a left-to-right sweeping action. The fire was heavier and more intense than most had experienced in the past few days. Leutnant Heinze knew that this was in preparation for a major attack. His new battalion commander was a man not suited to the job and sat cowering in his earthen bunker. It was a disgrace, he was afraid to show his face outside the place for fear of being hit. Leutnants Heller and Heinze, the two surviving company officers within the battalion, chose to ignore the man generally, only listening to him when he was relaying orders from Oberst Goth. Heller, the senior of the two, was in command in all but name. The young veterans conferred outside the bunker where Loges cowered forlornly, to plan measures in expectation of imminent attack.

In the middle of the afternoon the barrage ended. On its heels came a fierce attack by US troops, aided by armour and air support. The main thrust hit GR 943. Even with direct fire support from III/Artillerie Regiment 352, these men were pushed back steadily and quickly. Throwing in some of Kampfgruppe von Aufsess did manage to bolster the front, but still these units had fallen back most of the way to the new defensive line still under construction. Kraiss was beginning to enact countermeasures when two orders came through that were to disrupt his entire division once again. The Luftwaffe command in Normandy notified him that all the flak troops attached to his division were to be withdrawn immediately in order to establish air defence umbrellas along routes of supply. This would mean the loss of many support weapons, including the few remaining 88mm guns he had deployed in anti-tank roles. Kraiss was also informed that his division was now under the command of General Meindl's II Falschirmkorps.

This was not a bad thing in itself; however with this news Kraiss became aware that Kampfgruppe Heintz was still under the command of LXXXIV Armeekorps and thus he officially had no jurisdiction over them. They would stay in place for now but would no longer take orders from the 352nd. Added to this was an order attaching one battery of his artillery regiment to this battlegroup. Kraiss was furious at this development, even after General der Falschirmtruppe Meindl told him that this would only be until the rest of 275. Infantrie-Division made it to the front. At a stroke the 352nd had lost one third of its support weapons, not to enemy action, but to the paper shuffling of the rear echelon commanders. Under the current situation, the only order Kraiss could issue to his men was to hold until they could fall back to the new front.

Later in the afternoon, Kraiss once again called Meindl to remind him of his division's situation and request the return of his artillery. The Corps Commander informed Kraiss that 2. Panzer-Division had arrived at Torigny, just south of St Lô, and would come into the front between the 352nd and 3. Falschirmjäger-Division. This was good news, but the General's outlook had soured since 6 June and he made his own inquiries about the new division. His officer patrols reported back that only lead elements of 2. Panzer-Division were in Torigny; the rest of the division were strung out over kilometres of road. It would be days before it could assemble and get to the front. Once again promises were made, only to be broken.

It was something of a miracle; the Grenadiers of the 352nd held their ground throughout the day. In the dark of the evening, troops were rotated. Those digging went into the line; those in the line got to dig. Those in the line got more of a rest. During the campaign it was the norm for the fighting to wane then die down altogether with the arrival of night. Every man who could use a shovel, whether wounded or not, was set to work when darkness fell.

The GIs sent early morning greetings on 19 June in the form of another heavy barrage, this one concentrated around the road that led from Villiers Fossard towards St Lô. The barrage lasted for some time, and when it ended, an attack came that was more or less within the sector held by GR 943. Surprisingly the Germans held their ground, fending off the assaults. By noon the Americans had been blocked and all looked well. Not satisfied with this, both Goth and Böhm sent out reconnaissance patrols that confirmed what the two had suspected. Another assault force was building up behind the American lines. They were not to wait long for this to materialise. Early in the afternoon a major American thrust shot out from the north and this time they could not stem the tide. The front was rolled back, but did not break. No authorisation had come to man the new defences, however it might soon become prudent to do just that, orders or not. Oberst Goth informed his Generalleutnant of the situation and was told that GR 916 should withdraw to its new position at Le Mesnil-Rouxelin and regroup there. It would then be their mission to be in place to hold the line when the rest of the division took up their places. Leutnant Heinze remembered the sight of his regiment when they entered the tiny hamlet:

> All of us were tired, dirty and hungry. Many of the men's feet were sore and bloody from marching in worn-out boots. When I entered the village I saw Oberst Goth standing in the door of his command post, a chateau. The look on his face told me of the concern he had for the men. When we halted, several men just collapsed to the ground where they stood. Warnings of air attacks and orders to get under cover proved futile to move them. They were just too tired to care.

The balance of good and bad news tipped favourably once again. Kraiss learned from by radio that I/Artillerie Regiment 352, who had lost their guns in the first days of the invasion, had been reissued with eight new pieces and munitions from a depot south of St Lô. Even better was that they had reached the sector intact, eluding attacks by Jabos. The battery was in position, battle ready, awaiting new fire mission orders. The Generalleutnant made a wise choice. He would hold these guns in reserve to cover his division's fallback into the new positions.

Outside of this artillery complement Kraiss no longer possessed any reserves; every man was committed to the fighting or the preparation work. This was very dangerous, since any Allied breakthrough would be able to make it to the city virtually unopposed. Kraiss opted for a call to General der Falschirmtruppe Meindl, in the hope that some men could be scraped together. This proved easier than one would have thought. Meindl would have Falschirmjäger Regiment 9 holding the left flank of 3. Falschirmjäger-Division shift to the west to take over the section of front now being held by von Aufsess's Bataillon 518. If GR 943 shifted slightly to the east this would maintain a secure front and give Kraiss a battalion for reserves, though this battalion would only amount to roughly 200 men. Even so, with this unit placed in the most vital sector, behind the flank shared between GR 916 and 943, a disaster could be avoided. In conjunction the remainder of Panzerjäger Abteilung 352 went to the 916th, consisting of five 75mm PAK guns for stationary positions around Le Mesnil-Rouxelin. Also from the same detachment, three recently repaired Sturmgeschutz IIIs, low profile, turretless armoured assault guns on tank chassis, were reported to be ready for deployment. These were the only surviving armour the division now possessed. Kraiss ordered them up to support Oberst Böhm. It would be much easier for the Stugs to move when GR 943 had to withdraw to the south. The division was getting back some of its teeth.

Oberst Goth sent out runners with instructions for all his remaining officers to report at once to his headquarters in the chateau. Here, final orders for the defence of the sector would be issued. Leutnant Heinze set off for the chateau.

In the sector still held by GR 914, the day brought very little change to the front. The officers in charge welcomed arriving reinforcements from 17. SS Panzer-Grenadier-Division. This battalion of the well equipped division would bring some relief even if only for the day or two that they were expected to spend in the area. Wegner recalls that all did not welcome their presence:

> Since the episode at the bridge the past day had gone rather well. We had only lost a few metres of ground on that day and we were in the defence. This gave us a respite. Willi and I cleaned the machine gun, something we had not done thoroughly since before the inva-

sion day. Kalb was busy directing many of the new men. It was good that the Amis kept rather quiet since many of these men were Kanoniers [artillery men] or from the rear echelon troops. Time was needed to teach them something about being a Grenadier. It was, I'm fairly sure, on the 19th of June that some SS men arrived in our area. Kalb went out with the Spiess to talk with them. Soon he was back, informing us that these were troops from the 'Goetz von Berlichingen' Division and that they would teach us how to fight the war. They 'paraded' by our holes in the ground; young, fit and full of nerve wearing their splendid camouflage uniforms. The looks cast upon us were rather, I felt, contemptuous. I suppose we didn't look so glorious. We filthy, tired and hungry Grenadiers could not get cheers on the parade ground but we had seen more of this war than they had so far. Kalb just glared back at them, with as much contempt. He stood so that these young warriors could see his medal-laden chest. Pinned to it were the Iron Cross First Class, Infantry badge and Silver Wound medal; added to this were the ribbons for the Iron Cross Second Class and Eastern Front Medal. Kalb was never one to gloat about the tin on his chest but he knew these young 'heroes' were bare-chested and would look away. Most of them did. After a short time they ignored us and we them. Our lone surviving conscript from the RAD [National Labour Service] spoke up saying that they would soon find out what the Amis could throw at them. Kalb turned towards him and the poor boy just froze. A slap on the back and smile was all that he got. This officially made him one of us. Later on that day Kalb procured a cap and tunic, no longer needed, from one of the medical orderlies. We ceremoniously stripped the boy of his brown tunic and cap, then dressed him properly in field grey.

Leutnant Heinze arrived at the chateau. The trip on foot, moving from cover to cover, had taken longer than he expected. For two weeks he had been at the front and was in the same run-down state as most of his men. This too, slowed him down. He reached the building and was led into the room where his commanding officer waited. The reception from Oberst Goth was not as he anticipated:

I entered the room and informed the Oberst of my presence. He looked at me and snapped me into the proper stance of attention. I was shocked. He looked at me and dressed me down. He roared that a German officer is always clean and presentable when he reports to a superior regardless of the situation. With every word yelled I felt more and more the dirt and sweat which covered my body. He was even more angered at my beard, strictly against regulations. In that moment I remembered my thought during the first moments of the invasion as to when I would shave. The beard was not intentional; I just did not ever get the time to shave. Goth ordered me to remove myself and report back in ten minutes as a proper German officer.

Heinze left the room, going into the kitchen of the chateau. An orderly took his light-weight summer tunic to be quickly cleaned, then gave the officer a razor, mirror and basin of water:

I washed my face and hands then looked in to the dirty mirror, I did have quite a growth. The razor was dull and there was nothing to sharpen it upon or time to do it. I stared at the razor and thus also came to the realisation that my oath to shave after the Amis had been thrown back into the sea would not come to pass. I put the razor against the skin of my cheek and began to scrape the blade down my face, taking hair and skin. After all, an order is an order.

When the clock ticked off the final seconds of the ten minutes allotted to him Leutnant Heinze was standing rigidly at attention in front of his regimental commander. He was as clean as possible with all his uniform and equipment aligned in the proper place according to regulations, save for the small streams of blood that rolled down the contours of his raw face, to become dark stains upon his uniform. Oberst Goth gave his approval, and then issued him orders regarding the defence of the village and surrounding countryside. These were not complex instructions or in-depth tactical plans. One could sum them up in a simple sentence; hold this line for as long as possible.

That same morning Generalleutnant Kraiss was forced once again to move his HQ. That morning US artillery began long-range shelling of the northern part of St Lô. It was dark by the time the last trucks in the division brought the remaining men and equipment into the new headquarters, just south of the centre of the city. Thus, as far as the Germans were concerned, the defence of St Lô itself began on the morning of 19 June.

The first rays of sunlight stung the weary eyes of the German soldiers as they peered cautiously from their holes, each Grenadier straining to see the first sign of the impending attack. Yet dawn gave way to the full brightness of the day and still nothing. Böhm, Heyna and von Aufsess sent out patrols from their respective regiments. All reported the same thing; save for one or two enemy patrols, the Americans had pulled back roughly 100 metres all along the front and were digging in. Major Block was surprised to discover American radio traffic in the division's area was extremely light. With the ensuing quiet, men slept, while others dug or kept watch. Meals made it up to the front for the first time in days and the wounded were evacuated. No actions were reported to division headquarters. While the enlisted men rested and ate, beginning to almost feel human again, the officers pondered the situation. Oberstleutnant Ziegelmann, after studying the captured orders, came to the firm conclusion that major operations were occurring outside of the 352nd's sector. He was right. The Allies in this area had been fighting and pushing the Germans back since the day of the invasion. These men needed rest and their units also needed refitting. All had to catch their collective breath while preparing to crack the tough nut of St Lô. So 20 June faded away without incident for the Grenadiers, and it was another day Generalleutnant Kraiss had gained for his division in which to prepare for the eventual onslaught.

It seemed to the young Grenadiers that they had been blessed again on 21 June, until the appearance of US infantry. The alarm was raised, and everyone prepared for imminent action but no attack came. The GIs merely reoccupied the 100 metres from which they had withdrawn the day before. Standing down from the ready, they pressed their luck and got more rest, at least those not having to work on the fortifications. Those in command, as always, were apprehensive about the lack of enemy action while the common soldier took it in his stride.

The Grenadiers under Oberst Böhm did gain a major prize on this day. Around noon, on the road which led out of Moon-sur-Elle, one of the regiment's roadblocks had a bit of luck. An American communication truck blundered into them and was captured without a shot being fired. The prisoners consisted of a Signal Corps Major and two enlisted men. Even more important was that all of the radios in the vehicle were still blaring away on specific unit frequencies, and among the documents confiscated were current up-to-date code books and call signs for units of the US 29th Division. A further search of the officer produced a map with the location of these units upon it. Now Major Block had a ripe opportunity to eavesdrop and gather huge volumes of intelligence, at least until the 29th changed all the codes and frequencies. It is safe to assume that the unnamed American was not as delighted as his German counterpart. Yet another roadblock scored a truck loaded with barbed wire and American field rations, both needed for the defence of the city. These incidents also indicated that the US forces had very little idea as to the actual shape of the German front.

The captured map allowed Kraiss to readjust his front once again. Even without the map, shifts were needed since the SS troops were ordered away. The artillery, still supporting the elements of Kampfgruppe Heintz, was moved into a better position north of St Lô. The left flank, GR 914, was pushed forward into the town of Le Meauffe. This advance was unopposed. Thus, without firing a shot, the division had gained ground and was in a much better position to defend itself.

Another day gone. For the officers of the staff, a clearer picture was needed to put these events, or more properly lack of events, into perspective. Patrols were ordered out to bring in prisoners for interrogation. The roadblock that captured the signal truck yielded another truck carrying more barbed wire and a Major of the US Quartermaster Corps as a passenger. The truck was sent to GR 916 and the officer sent to divisional headquarters. Other prisoners also found themselves in front of Major Block for questioning. These were mostly infantry privates, although several artillerymen were present amongst the groups.

In a report to Kraiss, Major Block declared that the statements made by the prisoners, in particular the Quartermaster Officer, indicated that the 'Mulberry' artificial harbour was severely damaged in the last storm rendering the amounts of supplies getting ashore insufficient for large-scale operations on all parts of the beachhead. This information was quickly delivered to General der Falschirmtruppe Meindl. Kraiss further advised his commander that now would be a perfect moment to use all the available elements of 2. Panzer-Division and 3. Falschirmjäger-Division in a drive northwards. With the current Allied supply problems, this attack could gain substantial ground, throwing the entire Allied strategic plan off balance. Kraiss was adamant about this, underscoring his argument with information gathered from Allied radio traffic. He even went so far as to say his division was much too weak and too busy to mount this type of operation or he would do it himself.

Meindl agreed in principle with Kraiss but was also clear that his paratroopers were in much the same state as the 352nd and that the armoured units were not under his control. He would, however, relay all this information to his superiors at 7. Armee headquarters.

No attack, nor orders to mount one, ever came; a golden opportunity had been missed. That said, the 352nd was able to shorten its front once again, this time to a length of only 12 kilometres, since 266. Infanterie-Division was moving up to the line on the left flank, east of the Vire. This move, a dangerous chore for the Grenadiers who would have to walk over the countryside watching for Jabos, would give his defence greater depth and allow for more concentrated use of artillery. Now the only thing his division was seriously lacking was sufficient numbers of anti-tank weapons, both for crews and individuals, such as the panzerfaust. Kraiss realised that if the Allied lull went on for a few more days, even these would be provided.

Despite receiving an order to move yet again, the shortening of the left flank was a bright spot for the men in Oberstleutnant Heyna's command. The entire group was ordered to the rear for rest and refitting with all available supplies. This would greatly enhance the division's reserves, up to now still only the 200 men from Bataillon 518. Morale rose as they left the front line heading south, especially since the Amis were not in hot pursuit. Obergefreiter Kalb was happy to lead his men away from the deadly place. Wegner looked forward to some decent food.

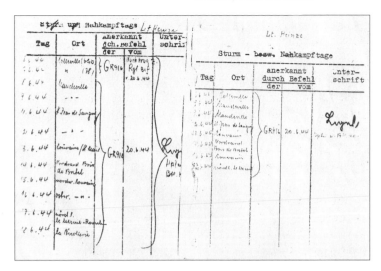

Leutnant Heinze's Soldbuch record of close combat and assault days used for determining eligibility for awards. Leutnant Heinze's actions through the Normandy countryside are clearly mapped out in this document that was signed by Hauptmann Loges.

At first we did not believe the talk that we were actually being pulled out of the line. We had heard it all before and our thoughts ranged from another retreat or to being sent to some place that was under heavy attack. One can only imagine our reaction when it was discovered to be the truth. The possibility of getting decent food, a haircut and even a bath made our spirits rise. We made all such grand plans for our time off that it prompted Kalb to speak up. Always the realist, he said that we shouldn't expect too much, especially since we were not on our way to Paris. Adding that we must appreciate what we would get because the rest of the division wouldn't be getting it. Our grand balloon had been deflated and I was rather glad he did it. Each step was heavy for us, now and then we looked back. Kalb laughed as he said to Willi that we did not have to worry about coming back here; in a day or two the front would come to us. Quite a sobering thought.

The Grenadiers had fought with every fibre of their bodies, and the recent lull had fostered a belief amongst them that the Amis had been fought to a standstill. Great for morale, but those in higher positions knew that this was only a half truth. Ziegelmann felt that the Allies would attack when they possessed sufficiently superior strength. This build-up had been hampered by the bad weather and destruction of port facilities. It be only a matter of time before sufficient men and supplies would be ashore for the resumption of the drive towards St Lô.

More troops and equipment arrived to augment the ranks of the 352nd. Two more detachments of artillery were given to the division, the III/Artillerie Regiment 266 from 266. Infanterie-Division and Artillery Abteilung Autun. This latter unit was comprised of crack crews from the artillery NCO School of 7. Armee, well trained men in possession of heavy field howitzers. The 266th was armed only with smaller calibre guns of French origin. Regardless, this allowed for a complete realignment of artillery support within the division. GR 943 and 916 would have the fire support of I and II/Artillerie Regiment 352, totalling 16 guns. III/Artillerie Regiment 266 would support the newly arrived Grenadier Regiment 897, which was taking up part of the front west of St Lô. The IV/Artillerie Regiment 352 and Artillerie Abteilung Autun would be placed southwest of the city to deal with any breakthrough that might occur at any point. For the first time since 6 June, the 352nd would have within its 12-kilometre front an indepth artillery defence for its infantry.

The days passed, each side sending out patrols and gathering prisoners. Both armies built up their armaments and supplies knowing full well that this peace and quiet would eventually come to a loud, violent end. Von Aufsess and his men were sent back into the line with GR 916 after receiving replacements. The same day, 27 June, I/Falschirmflak Regiment 2 arrived with three batteries of 88mm guns. More importantly, they were detailed to the 352nd for anti-tank use, an important addition to say the least. By the following day, the total infantry strength of the 352nd had risen to 3480 men. The bulk of these, 2000 to be exact, were in or attached to GR 916. 700 were in reserve around Les Ifs. The rest were spread out on the right and left flanks. This was not many men considering that facing them there were no fewer than four US divisions, the 2nd, 29th, 30th and 2nd Armoured. On 28 June Generalleutnant Kraiss had evacuated most of the civilian population in and around St Lô for approximately seven kilometres. Those choosing to stay were on their own. The curtain went up on the morning of 28 June 1944. At 0800 hrs a rain of shells came down on the Grenadiers in the forward positions held by the 352nd.

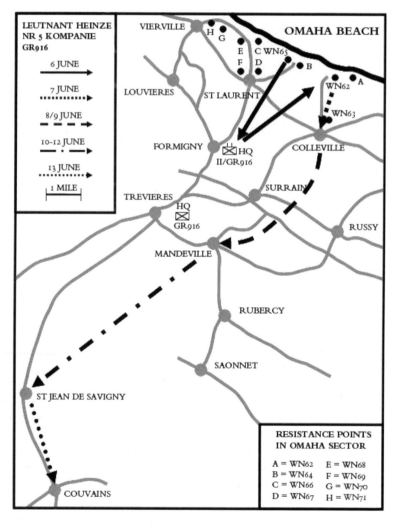

Leutnant Heinze's Nr. 5 Kompanie of Grenadier Regiment 916 was quite active in the defensive and counterattack role during the first week of the invasion. During interviews Heinze stated he led his attacks in support of WN78, based on the entries in his Soldbuch. However unit records and further study of his Soldbuch shows he misread the entry. It was actually WN63 near Colleville.

thirteen

BEYOND ENDURANCE
— THE ROAD TO ST LÔ

SOON the deadly Jabos joined the fray. They did their jobs well, hitting every known and suspected gun position and strafing both old and new supply routes. This also included the new command post of the 352nd. Actual damage was not heavy, but the GIs surged forward just as the barrage ended.

The main American thrust struck hard, with lots of armour, against GR 943. The advance was generally down the road leading from Moon-sur-Elle towards St Lô. This fighting gradually spilled over into the sectors held by the 916th and 897th. Under this initial attack, the Germans fell back but managed to recover and hold with the loss of only a few hundred metres.

Jabos played their deadly game, and prevented the reserves from moving forward via the roads. These men would find themselves travelling cross-country as they raced towards the fighting. In the mid morning, the American attack stalled and then petered out in the face of unanticipated strong resistance. No victory for the Germans, it only meant that the Americans would regroup for another assault.

Just before noon, this second thrust hit the German lines. The US troops advanced, though this was agonisingly slow going. True to their tactical doctrines, the Germans counter-attacked every time a position or road junction fell. In the village of La Forge, houses, streets and the entire village changed hands several times during that afternoon's bitter fighting.

Even darkness did not bring the peace it once had, for even though the US 29th Division had taken and held onto La Forge and Villiers Fossard, pockets of resistance held out within them. Counter attacks took place in the evening hours south of these villages. With this type of fighting, casualties on both sides were high, the losses affecting the Germans more because of vastly inferior numbers. Two more companies from Les Ifs were ordered forward into the night, one going to GR 916 and the other to the 943rd. Obergrenadier Wegner watched the columns of men head out towards the sound of battle, disappearing into the blackness:

Panzer IV knocked out by Jabo attack. Note the rear is thoroughly destroyed as Allied fighters would attack with rocket and MG fire aiming for the rear engine deck. This was the most vulnerable area of a tank.

All day long we had sat hunched over in our holes and dugouts because of the Jabos and artillery fire. Groups of men made their way forward all through that day. Very late in the afternoon we watched as messengers scurried from place to place. One didn't come to us, this was good. It meant that our company was not going into the line. We watched the others line up and walk towards the north. Kalb told us to make the best of it and get some more sleep.

Dawn brought with it a repeat performance of the previous day. Well supported and determined attacks were mounted by US forces throughout. Böhm's men were pushed back into the line that the bulk of GR 916 already occupied. This setback resulted in Generalleutnant Kraiss giving authorisation for the entire division to withdraw to the new front. This one had been constructed outside of St Lô proper, with secondary and tertiary positions. All but a mere handful of the reserves had been committed by the end of 30 June. Still, Wegner and his company waited to be called. The sound of the fighting was much closer. It was certain that the front would reach them as Kalb had predicted.

This same day, the 352nd had lost seven of its artillery pieces. Luckily, none of these losses included any 88mm guns. The surviving crews were first used to augment losses among other batteries, the rest being dispersed amongst infantry units.

Unlike the previous night, the normal pattern of the campaign returned. As the darkness rolled in the fighting ebbed, then stopped altogether. Both armies were perhaps too tired to fight through another night.

On 1 July the shrill whistle of out-going artillery cut across the sky above the GIs. The shells thundered into the German lines. Both the forward and rear areas suffered during these barrages. The Grenadiers, now in much better and safer bunkers, braced themselves as they waited for the attack, which they expected as soon as the barrage lifted.

When the last shell had made its crater upon the scarred earth, every German soldier leapt behind his rifle. The Amis did not come. They waited. As morning lapsed into afternoon they still waited but nothing happened. Every man, up to and including Generalleutnant Kraiss, was perplexed at this development since every indication was that an Allied attack was imminent. He decided to take advantage of the lull and bring up his last reserves for a night attack in order to straighten out a bulge in the line between GR 916 and 943. This time Wegner and the remnants of his company would be the ones marching off into the darkness:

Finally on 1 July our tentative peace came to an end. Late in the afternoon we received word to move forward for a night attack. We were checked for noises and loose equipment. Fighting at night, in my opinion, was the worst way to fight. No one is really sure who is who and where anybody else really is. I dreaded this more than anything else. The hedgerows were our allies during the day but at night they were no one's friends. We had made all our needed adjustments and preparations before heading out to the collection point. Our movements were quiet and quick, though time loses all meaning in actions such as these. One moved around, not really sure of how long we travelled or what time it was. Hushed orders were passed down the roads, then we all got into the ditch to wait. Up ahead were the most experienced troops, probing the Amis to find a weak spot in the line. Sooner or later we started forwards on our hands and knees, hugging the side of the hedgerow. We moved only a short distance when firing broke out ahead of us. We went into battle formation before the Amis shot flares into the sky. Firing, then moving forward, this we repeated time and time again. I could feel the splatter of the earth as rounds struck near us every now and then. The noises and flashes swelled and waned as groups of soldiers found and lost each other in the black of the night. We pushed over, along, and around one hedgerow after another. In time we reached our objective, whatever that was, because we were halted and told to dig in. Luck was with us because many foxholes were already dug in the area. We fashioned them the way we needed and tried to rest. As I contemplated the battle I recalled a few times that I was not really sure what I had fired at in the dark. Though it did not matter in the long run, we had got to where we were supposed to and all of us were unhurt.

This operation succeeded in gaining back the original main battle line held by the division on the previous day. While this attack was in progress, two full armoured companies presented themselves at Kraiss' HQ. The vehicles were all older models of the famous Panzer IV but were still capable of stopping Allied tanks. The Generalleutnant dispatched one company immediately to GR 916 and kept the other in reserve. This would give him a powerful punch in case the Allies broke through any part of his front.

At this stage neither Generalleutnant Kraiss nor his men knew that the upcoming operation against the city of St Lô would take place outside of their division's area. The main goal of the US commanders during this period was to widen the manoeuvre area around the city. The terrain on either side of the Vire river is well suited to defence. On one side of the Vire stands the Taute, which fans out into tributaries and marshlands. This had done much already to limit US troops, forcing them to stay on firm strips of ground in order to avoid bogging down in the swamps. This lost them a tactical edge, since they could not bypass or flank German strongpoints. The Germans were therefore able to use small numbers of men and materiel to halt much larger forces. The eastern side of the Vire was covered with hedgerows and hills, the Germans in possession of the highest of these, including Hill 192. From this height they could observe all movements and put pinpoint artillery fire on whatever target presented itself.

The US strategy was to clear a wide enough front around St Lô to be able to to assault the city from several directions. Major General Charles Corlett's newly formed XIX Corps, consisting of the 29th, 30th, 35th Infantry and 3rd Armored Divisions, would be responsible for mounting the operations. The 35th was fresh in the line, but this was compensated for by the veteran 29th Division. Corlett's initial plan was to clear the sector west of the Vire and seize the high ground just west of the city itself in order to support a large-scale attack from the east. The start of these attacks was scheduled for 7 July 1944, to be spearheaded by the 30th Infantry Division.

From 2 to 6 July, the Grenadiers watched various activities in the Allied lines. The GIs dug new positions and improved old ones. Both sides mounted small attacks, mainly to keep the other from gaining too much of an advantage in a few localised areas. Then something odd occurred. The Americans brought up loudspeakers to the front. Voices in German boomed out asking men to surrender and promising good treatment. Surrender leaflets dropped from the sky. Many Volksdeutsche took this opportunity to desert. Leutnant Heinze tried to keep these men well supervised, but knew that nothing could keep those absolutely determined to get out of the war from deserting.

The harassing fire from the US artillery stayed constant throughout the days that passed. Casualties, mostly wounded, began to mount once more. Since it was relatively quiet, 7. Armee Headquarters ordered Generalleutnant Kraiss to have his officers comb the ranks for any men from 716. Infanterie-Division. The unit was refitting and these men were to be sent to the rear immediately. In an unusual turn of events for this period, 7. Armee did detach one battalion of GR 899 for service with the 352nd to replace any losses. This battalion went into the line at once to relieve the decimated Schnellebrigade 30. Oberstleutnant von Aufsess pulled his unit together, now less than one-third its original strength, and ushered them into reserve positions around the village of St Croix.

7 July 1944 dawned in a dreary overcast haze, but this did not prevent the US 30th Division from launching its initial attack to get across the Vire. After a very heavy barrage, the GIs made their way across the river in rubber assault boats. Progress was good and they gained a large bridgehead. With this established, the 105th Combat Engineer Battalion feverishly worked at completing a footbridge across the river. Despite concentrated German artillery fire they were successful, and the rest of the division began to walk across the Vire.

The US attack had struck Oberst Heintz and parts of 17. SS Panzer-Grenadier-Division. Kraiss received a call from the Colonel informing him that all the support from the SS units was withdrawn since they were having problems holding back the American assault. The General's staff verified this order, leaving Kampfgruppe Heintz alone in a position to hold on as best they could.

By the end of the day the Germans had lost St Jean de Daye and were pushed away from it to the south. The rest of the US XIX Corps was preparing to cross the Vire, and for that reason General Corlett wanted the pressure to be maintained all along the 30th Division's front. He subsequently ordered 3rd Armored Division to cross the river that night and push on to the town of Pont Herbert. This town possessed many vital bridges crossing the local rivers and streams, as well as a main highway, the N-174, which led straight into

St Lô. This fact was obvious to the Germans, who acted quickly to counter any attempts at taking Pont Herbert. Kraiss did this by sending the 300 men of Schnellebrigade 30 in to defend the town. The Grenadiers would not get any of the much needed rest they had prayed for; instead they faced a night march which would end up in an early morning fight, though they would not be alone. With them would be two batteries from III/AR 266 and one battery of 88mm guns for use against the large formations of armour reported to be in the sector. While this was going on, 17. SS Panzer-Grenadier-Division was putting up a spirited defence against the US troops advancing against the town. They contested every metre of earth, constantly counter-attacking. They could not match the size and strength of the opposition and steadily fell back.

3rd Armoured's push through the lines of the 30th Division resulted in clogged roads, severely curtailing advances and allowing sufficient time for the Panzer IVs from 2. Panzer-Division, which Kraiss had in reserve, to reach the area and mount an attack on the road near St Fromond Église. Outnumbered, the Germans ran into tough resistance and lost four tanks, only stalling the American push for a short time. Still, the GIs were creating their own problems. The constant jostling between the vehicles and infantry of two separate divisions entangled together held up progress more than any German pocket of resistance. Even the arrival of daylight did not ease the problem. These snarl-ups gave Schnellebrigade 30 and its support artillery time to get into the sector and prepare for an all-out defence of Pont Herbert.

Throughout the remainder of 8 July, Major General Corlett was, despite his problems, able to widen the front giving him enough ground to deploy against St Lô. He had hoped to take Pont Herbert on this day, but had to settle for getting as close as he could while the Germans were in apparent confusion. On 9 July he would attack again.

The 30th Division was once again given the honour of leading the Corps in this operation. The division's 120th Infantry Regiment led off. All went well with the exception of the regiment's 2nd Battalion. First, they had been hit by German artillery just before they were supposed to launch their push forward. They held for some time, thinking that this was the beginning of a German counter attack. When this did not materialise, they pressed forward but were now far behind the rest of the division. From here matters progressively worsened. As the GIs approached their first objective, Hill 32, German resistance was aided greatly by accurate artillery fire, slowing them to a halt. By noon the battalion was on the defensive, fighting off German counter attacks and halting the entire regiment. The German attack was finally blunted and the 120th made ready to advance again. It was at this moment that the Regimental Commander, Colonel Birk, was visited by three Generals. These were General Eddy of the 9th Division, General Watson of 3rd Armored and General Patton. The three were first greeted by Birk, then by a German barrage, a shell landing within the 120th's command post. This was the beginning of the first major offensive against XIX Corps.

The reports flooded into Corlett's headquarters; all were sketchy and some were false, but the facts soon showed that the 120th was in real trouble. The German armour was back, and this time they were with the rest of their division, 2nd Panzer. The Germans had hit the regimental boundary of the 120th and 117th Infantry and Birk's advance was thrown back instantly. In support of them was the 743rd Tank Battalion, which fell victim to a well-orchestrated ambush.

Two Panzer IVs were reported advancing to a crossroads near them. The commander of the 743rd sent out his entire complement of B Company to squash the threat. When the US armoured column got within 200 metres of the enemy tanks they were hit on all sides by well-hidden infantry and armour. In fifteen minutes it was all over; those GIs that survived got away on foot through the surrounding woods. Every tank and vehicle was left burning on or near the road. The Germans pressed home their advantage, overwhelming some units and forcing the rest to retreat. All the companies in the 30th Division were screaming for artillery support, but none would be coming for a while. The reason was that in the haste to move the divisional command post, the remaining men at the old command post did not have the means to communicate with their own artillery. Until the new head-quarters was set up, this would be a major failing. First, the artillery that did fire was doing so only on a broad front, merely harassing the Germans as they moved quickly through the shower of shells. And second, neither command post could immediately determine the reliability of the feedback it was being sent.

Mistakes had already been made. A good example of this was a report of large col-umns of German tanks advancing up the main highway from Pont Herbert. Artillery was brought to bear on them. After some very anxious and tense moments they were able to convince the 30th Division at its new command post that they were actually units of 3rd Armored Division, who narrowly avoided a major blue on blue disaster.

By 1500 hrs, the new headquarters was again in full control and able to use the artillery batteries effectively. Still there were errors. On the highway to Pont Herbert the 117th Infantry engaged the 33rd Armored Regiment, thinking them to be Germans. The 33rd fired first because of reports of German breakthroughs west of them, and in the course of the action they lost two Shermans and were shelled before the mess was cleared up. Despite all of these and other problems, XIX Corps was able to contain the German attack by nightfall.

Although all of these actions had occurred well outside of the sector held by the 352nd, the outcome was still worrying enough for Generalleutnant Kraiss to shift some of his troops to the east bank of the Vire, just in case of a breakthrough by US forces during the night of 9/10 July. He still had standing orders for the rest of his men to continue to improve the defences, regardless of the continual Allied shelling. It was definitely the right thing to do since much of the accommodation was still rather lacking. Leutnant Heinze was unimpressed by the new battalion command bunker:

> Hauptmann Loges placed himself in a well made but poorly designed bunker. He was well behind the front but the place only had one entrance. A death trap if we had to fight in it. But Loges felt very secure because of it and never left unless he absolutely had to; as for myself I stayed in the line most of the time.

On the 10th, Corlett renewed efforts to push into Pont Herbert. But his troops were still hindered by rear area problems and German resistance was beginning to stiffen. The day produced only meagre gains. It was now apparent that the entire rear echelon had to be unsnarled and squared away before advances could proceed. He issued orders that the situation be cleared up by the dawn of 11 July.

The Germans had other ideas and struck hard at midnight. The elite Panzer-Lehr-Division slammed into the divisional borders of the 9th US Division, VII Corps and Corlett's 30th Division. Being one of the few times the Germans had mustered adequate artillery and armour support, they made good headway throughout the early morning. The element of surprise and the lack of Allied air cover helped the German advances. American casualties were high, and for the 30th it was some of the hardest fighting of the war.

Generalleutnant Bayerlein, commander of Panzer-Lehr-Division, was pleased with the initial success of his men. His main force had driven deep into the US lines and it looked as though he would gain his objective, St Jean de Daye. Elements of Panzer Grenadier Regiment 902 had torn into the 30th Division along the Vire river and had already made it to the outskirts of Cavigny. But this experienced soldier did not realise how strong the reaction would be to this assault. His division had taken on sizeable elements of two corps, not just the one division he had assumed. With the coming of daylight that would enable the Jabos to fly freely above his lines attacking at will; it would only be a matter of a few hours before his advance would be stopped, pushed back and even destroyed. And so it came to pass.

When the sun set on 11 July, Panzer-Lehr-Division had lost almost all the ground it had gained, taking a severe drubbing in the process. Bayerlein and his junior commanders were astonished at the speed with which the tide had turned against them. The day was over and Corlett's men had gained Hauts Vent, a hamlet with a major crossroads atop Hill 91, which gave them a view of the entire operational area. They had also reached the first few buildings of Pont Herbert. XIX Corps now had all the room it needed to manoeuvre against the walled city of St Lô.

The Grenadiers sat waiting, knowing that soon the Amis would come barrelling down from the north. This time they would run into strong defences and bog down. The positions were good and the terrain favoured the defenders. However, each man knew that there simply were not enough men in the 352nd to hold the line indefinitely. The front was 12 kilometres long, and held by fewer than 3000 Grenadiers, or those pressed into the infantry role. Reserves amounted to 400 men, all from dissolved rear echelon units. Morale was beginning to ebb even amongst the division's most stalwart men. Kraiss himself was worried about whether the units on his flanks would break and melt away, as had the 709th and 716th one month before.

On the other side of the line, it is safe to say that the GIs had also seen their fair share of fighting. A joke was making the rounds through the 29th Division: the US Army had three 29ths – one in the field, one in the hospital and one in the cemetery. By the end of the war the figures would bear this out. Now it would be this division leading the assault in the morning, a fact that did not go unnoticed by Major Block. His interception of radio transmissions proved invaluable. The most important ones dealt with the change of attack times. The earliest given was 0435 hrs; as the Germans were one hour ahead, all units were put on alert to expect Allied attacks beginning at 0530 hrs. The first report of fighting reached Major Block at 0538 hrs that morning.

The American plan was to have the 29th and 35th Divisions drive on and around St Lô, then have the 29th attack the city from the east, supported by all the divisions in the Corps. The 35th had been held up because of the assault of Panzer-Lehr-Division the previous morning and their continued presence in the line. The regiments of the 29th jumped off on schedule, led by the 116th Infantry Regiment. Their initial objective was the high ground west of Martinville, which became known as Martinville Ridge. The 115th Infantry Regiment would advance on their flank to take La Luzerne and the 175th Infantry Regiment would follow up as reserves. The preparatory barrage lasted only twenty minutes, but was only concentrated on their axis of advance, roughly the 352nd's right, and the left flank of 3. Falschirmjäger-Division. The 116th Infantry ran directly into the men of Falschirmjäger Regiment 9. The resistance given by these German paratroopers verged on fanatical. The GIs' first obstacle was a sunken road that they managed to cross after hours of tough fighting. The road itself was well mined and always under heavy small arms fire. When they reached the other side, the GIs found only dead or wounded paratroopers; the rest had fallen back to secondary positions. The going was horribly slow as the Germans clung to every hedgerow with dogged determination.

Even at this crawl the 116th made excellent headway in comparison to their comrades in the 115th. The latter regiment's trouble began when the German paratroopers opposing them launched their own attack just prior to the American barrage. They made no headway but disorganised the 115th, throwing them off their timetable. Even when the GIs began to advance, they found themselves slugging it out with the German main line of resistance. Prospects for any gains were slim. The 115th was attacking the boundary of two divisions. The 352nd had been allotted ample time to prepare and were warned of the impending assault by Major Block, so when it came the Grenadiers were ready. The first wave struck into the sector held by GR 943, in particular where the remnants of GR 914 were dug in. Wegner's machine gun was waiting:

> We had got very used to the way the Amis would fight. First would come the Arifeuer and when that would shift to the rear we knew the infantry would come, usually with tanks. Of course the Jabos were somewhere above hitting what they could see. We would fool them by putting out captured marker flags; they wouldn't shoot thinking us their own men. In our new holes we had done a splendid job of improving them and the Jabos could not see us. We just waited for the infantry to arrive. The first sounds of fighting came from our right, the east. After what seemed a considerable amount of time the battle came to us. There were many tanks in this one, of course none we saw were ours. Some looked odd this time, like great monsters with large horns sticking out in front. A new tactic from the Amis. These ones would charge a hedgerow and plough through it. If this did not work the Amis would put explosives in the hole that was made and try to blow a path through the hedgerow. Naturally all of our anti-tank efforts were focused against these steel monsters and our fire prevented the infantry from placing explosives in any of the holes made. In this way we held the ground for quite a long time. Eventually the Arifeuer and the Jabos would compel us to fall back, though when we did it would be to another front just like this.

These tactics had paid off for Kraiss; the 29th US Division was making almost no gains on his front. His main concern was the ability of the lightly supported paratroopers to hold out against such heavy attacks.

The 35th US Division finally mounted their assault against the 352nd, attempting to push down to the edge of the Vire river to its bend northwest of St Lô. Like those of the 115th Infantry Regiment, these GIs ran headlong into well prepared German defenders. Two of the division's regiments pushed forward abreast. One regiment, the 137th, took the rest of Le Meauffe and made the outskirts of St Gilles. Here they ran up against the 352nd's main battle line, and despite heavy air support, were halted. The other regiment, the 320th, had very little luck striking the 352nd at La Carillon and Le Mesnil-Rouxelin. Here were some of the best defences held by the men of GR 916. They made up for diminished numbers with battle experience. The units of the 35th Division were green by comparison, having only been in France for about a week. From their positions in the hills north of the villages, the Grenadiers fought the novice GIs to a standstill. Gefreiter Georg Seidl, one of the survivors of 6 June, remembered the fighting while walking through the now serene countryside 45 years later and how vicious it was during those days of July 1944:

> We had lost many good men, very few of my Kameraden were still with my regiment. Always we were under some sort of bombardment, either mortars or artillery. When the attacks came against Le Mesnil-Rouxelin it was a slaughter for those Amis. They lost many good young men for a small piece of earth. It was to get worse as the days wore on, for all of us, both sides.

Seidl's words are born out by the facts. The 320th Infantry really took it on the chin. Its E Company got caught in a trap laid down by Goth's Regiment and was pummelled by mortar fire and raked by machine guns. Of the elements of this company involved, only 14 men survived the retreat. With the onset of night, the 352nd could claim the day. Despite losing a minute chunk of ground, all the attacks against them had been thwarted, though a realignment of the flank was needed because of the ground lost by 3. Falschirmjäger-Division. This was only a minor shift southwards, but a major concern if the paratroopers continued to lose ground every day. Kraiss needed a secure flank.

The predictable barrage and the continued thrust towards St Lô came with the dawn of 12 July. The 116th Infantry tried to cut their way through the weakened German paratroopers, running into even more tenacious resistance. This was complicated by rear echelon problems similar to those that had plagued the entire XIX Corps a few days before. Some German tricks bore fruit for the beleaguered paratroopers. Thanks to Major Block, they were able to break into the 29th's radio network and order the 747th Tank Battalion to turn around and report back to the 116th's regimental command post. This disrupted forward moving traffic and of course delayed the arrival of armoured support.

This time the 115th Infantry fared better, though not much. Its 1st and 3rd Battalions gained some ground but the 2nd was facing disaster. These men were fought to a standstill at their own jump-off line, and in the confusion of a German counter attack one platoon retreated without orders, generating a rumour of a general retreat. Other men began to fall back. Officers and sergeants avoided total disaster by keeping men in place and getting others back into the line. Don Van Roosen, now a sergeant, was nearly killed during this phase of the campaign:

> I had a close call as we were getting close to St Lô. We were on the crest of a hill looking across a valley towards the 116th's line of advance. Germans spotted and started to mortar us heavily. I spent a few minutes clearing a path through the hedgerow and had not dug a slit trench when the rounds started coming in on us. I fell to the ground and an 80mm round hit an arm's length away. I was knocked out. When I came to, I could hear a popping sound in the distance. As I really came around I realised that it was the MG ammo boxes by my head. They absorbed most of the blast and the hot metal was cooking off some of the rounds. My canteen was wrecked on my cartridge belt and my jacket, which I had hung on a bush beside me, was shredded. The slight depression I was in (6–8 inches deep) had allowed the round to burst just over me.

The operations against the 352nd north of the city crashed into the same wall of resistance they had met the day before. Despite all its efforts, the 35th US Division had not been able to breach any point in Kraiss' front. The Grenadiers were paying dearly for this; Gefreiter Seidl notes that during these days his circle of close friends had dwindled down to a small number, 'not even enough for a game of cards'. Once again, it proved to be the extensive earthworks that had given the Germans the tactical edge. Passageways and tunnels through the hedgerows had allowed for quick movement of troops under cover from air and artillery attacks. Wegner personally benefited from these several times:

> This area in which we now were fighting was the best we had been in so far. Our gun was able to cover every possible approach the Amis could make. And behind us we could say the same for anywhere we might have to withdraw. Roads and tunnels had been cut through the countryside so that we could move in daylight without being seen. When we did have to retreat we would blow up the tunnels behind us in order not to be followed. We, of course, did not have every place fortified but the Amis did not know this. Yes they were good soldiers and did not want to lose men if they did not have to, which is why we knew they would not cross certain types of terrain without blasting it to hell first. The Pioniers made phoney gun positions and those took quite a bit of the shelling off us. The final most important thing was that we were holding off the American Juggernaut.

It was inevitable that something had to give way under the pressure brought to bear by XIX Corps. Gains in ground were not large where the 352nd held the front before the city. It was the 29th that came through for Corlett once again. The men of the 115th Infantry finally took the town of La Luzerne and in doing so pushed back the men of Falschirmjäger Regiment 9. This, as Kraiss had feared, opened up the entire right flank of the 352nd. The Generalleutnant scrambled to get troops into the void and regain contact with the paratroopers, but it would not be until very early the next morning (13 July) that sufficient troops could be in place. If the Americans took a bold step, they would be in St Lô by morning. The American commanders did not know this and thus settled for consolidating their gains in expectation of German counter attacks and making preparations for the next move. This hesitation kept the city in German hands, but they were merely forestalling the inevitable.

One more reason for the lack of a quick move south into the city was the condition of the US troops; having been on the offensive in heavy fighting for several days, the men needed some respite. But 13 July would be another day on which the drive towards the ruin of a once great city continued.

The plan once again called for the 29th Division to lead the way, running along the major highway that led into St Lô from Bayeux, the D-972. While they did this, the 35th would try yet again to crack the ring the Germans held around the city. Like clockwork, the US artillery greeted the waiting Grenadiers. This barrage was of no small significance, inflicting casualties on the 352nd of 840 wounded and 137 dead. It should be noted that the majority of these casualties were German artillerymen, the result of counter-battery fire, or rear echelon troops whose jobs did not allow them the same cover as dug-in infantry. III/Artillerie Regiment 266 lost six of its remaining twelve guns during this one barrage. Even during this rain of death, small detachments of men made their way to a new flank around Martinville and established contact with the remnants of 3. Falschirmjäger-Division. Individual Volksdeutsche scurried across the lines to surrender. Though the problem was not new, now the exhausted and demoralised Germans did not try to stop them. In any event a continuous, though weak, front was in place.

Left The last order from Oberst Goth to Hauptmann Loges on 13 July 1944, instructing him to form a defensive line around La Carrillon (front).

Right Goth's order to Loges, showing his signature (back).

This time the attack of the 29th was led by the 175th Infantry Regiment, which had been held in reserve until this point. They advanced through the lines of the 116th towards the villages of La Boulaye and La Madelaine along the D-972. This highway was pre-plotted by the artillery of both German divisions just in case this occurred. The 175th was under fire as soon as it jumped off at 0800 hrs. Avoiding exposure on the road they ran into Germans dug in amongst the hedgerows on either side. After tremendous efforts, the GIs were only able to force a bulge 500 metres long and 100 metres wide, not even reaching their initial objective of La Boulaye.

The 35th Division fared no better, and was bounced back after throwing itself once more against the 352nd. It was stalemate for XIX Corps. Major General Corlett knew he would have to regroup and rethink his plan to take the city. The 29th would have its divisional area decreased owing to casualties, while the 35th took up the slack. While this was done, 3. Falschirmjäger-Division was fully regrouped and brought into proper alignment with the 352nd. This allowed Kraiss to put those men holding that flank back into the front north of St Lô. The Americans resupplied and brought in replacements. The Germans scrounged for a few more men and just kept digging.

No attack materialised on 14 July; only the smashing of artillery shells into the German lines broke the silence. Then, quite surprisingly, the remaining men of Schnellebrigade 30 and guns of the artillery detachment sent with it to support the units of LXXXIV Armeekorps reported in to Generalleutnant Kraiss. The returning guns included the deadly 88mm anti-tank guns. The infantry was placed just behind the front as firefighters in case of a breach in the line. The 88mm guns were placed on routes that Allied armour would have to take, while the rest of the artillery was sent to firing positions in the rear.

Oberstleutnant von Aufsess's return was welcome as well. His able leadership was needed at this point. Oberst Goth, after issuing orders to Hauptmann Loges regarding the defence of La Carillon and alternative actions, collapsed in his command post. The older officer was just not able to go on with no sleep and little food. The highly respected Colonel was evacuated to a field hospital.

Hauptmann Loges was now the senior officer in Grenadier Regiment 916, but was in no way capable of taking over command. Kraiss decided that since most of von Aufsess's unit were already mixed with this regiment, he would be given command of the entire battlegroup. He would assume command with his own staff company. Hauptmann Steneck and the Stabskompanie of Grenadier Regiment 916 would be removed to St Lô. Here they would rest and help plan the defence of the heart of the city.

It was clear to Kraiss and his staff that with the current situation around Pont Herbert, deep penetrations would occur along the division's left flank bordering the Vire. Even the positions around La Carillon were somewhat exposed, and this would force their eventual withdrawal to the south. The 352nd was in no shape to mount any countermeasures against a major loss of ground, they were simply holding on to what they had at the moment. Every German soldier knew that when the Amis stopped it was more likely because of problems on their own side of the line or just that they needed a rest, rather than German counter thrusts – every German line had been broken eventually. For the remainder of the day the GIs were just catching their breath.

Sun up brought a massive attack by the 35th Division; artillery smashed every spot within the 352nd's sector. Generalleutnant Kraiss was forced to take cover when the divisional command post came under fire. The newly arrived Stabskompanie of GR 916 was in the area near him. Elsewhere in the sector, not knowing the extent of the shelling, Wegner longed to be somewhere in the rear and safe:

> When the Amis began the final push towards St Lô they began to shell us. This was the worst it had been since the day of the invasion. They threw everything at us, big guns, tanks, mortars and the Jabos. Between explosions Kalb spoke up saying to us that if we didn't get several new divisions soon we would not hold the front for long under this strain. When it finally ended we were all alive except for some minor cuts and scrapes. Moments later we saw large groups of tanks and men approaching. We cleaned the dirt off the MG and waited for them to get within range.

That morning a Lieutenant in the 29th Division was waiting to move out with his men when the hand of history reached out and touched him:

> 'Are you Lieutenant McNutt?' a runner said as he laid his hand on my shoulder. When I owned up, he told me I was wanted at Divisional Headquarters. Upon arrival at the command post in the Bois de Bretel I was told to report to General Cota at his tent. When I reported he was sitting at a field table studying some papers. He looked up, gave me the 'once over,' and said 'You'll do.' With this enthusiastic acceptance I became the acting Aide de Camp of Brigadier General Norman Daniel 'Dutch' Cota, Assistant Divisional Commander, 29th Infantry Division.

Captain Lawrence McNutt's Bronze Star citation.

HEADQUARTERS, 28TH INFANTRY DIVISION
APO 28, U. S. ARMY

13 February 1945.

C I T A T I O N

THE BRONZE STAR MEDAL

is awarded to Captain LAWRENCE E. MCNUTT, 01305622, Inf,
U. S. Army, for meritorious service in performance of
duties as Aide-de-Camp to the Commanding General from 14
August 1944 to 11 January 1945.

During this period, Captain MCNUTT, as my senior aide,
rendered invaluable service and by his tact, foresight,
and courage greatly aided me in the execution of my duties.
During the first month of this period, Captain MCNUTT was
the only Aide and as such was charged with the duties normally executed by two officers. His work was rendered
more difficult than usual by the rapidity with which the
division was moving at the time, being engaged in the
pursuit of the German Army through Northern France,
Southern Belgium and Luxembourg. Captain MCNUTT's high
sense of duty and industry enabled him to discharge his
many functions in a manner which reflected great credit
upon himself and the Armed Forces of the United States.
Entered military service from Ohio.

NORMAN D. COTA,
Major General, U. S. Army,
Commanding.

This new posting would see Lieutenant McNutt take a role in the final act of the taking of the city.

By 0500 hrs the telephone wires leading to the 352nd's Headquarters were humming. The entire division was feeling the brunt of XIX Corps' massive assault. The 29th pushed headlong to take Martinville Ridge, less than three kilometres from St Lô, and work around La Luzerne down the Isigny to St Lô highway. On a parallel drive, the 30th Division was on the western side of the same road. Some of the 30th was on the west side of the Vire attacking German units there in order to take pressure off of the 29th and 35th Divisions.

HQ 7. Armee sent orders through Generalleutnant Kraiss to the men of the 352nd, the kind of order that makes your mouth dry, the sweat pour down your dirty face, and gives you a queasiness in the hollow pit of your stomach. Make every round count and defend to the last man.

In the strictest military sense, this order was not subject to any interpretation, however it did mean different things to different men. Very few at this point of the campaign would take it literally. Most, including officers, felt that to surrender when any further defence was impossible or futile was not an abrogation of this command. A mood of defeat was in the air but this was still the German Army and with their training and discipline they would fight to the best of their ability with what they had, a fact soon to be realised by the GIs in XIX Corps. Even under this heavy bombardment and total American superiority, the lowly Grenadier was giving as good as he got.

The 116th Infantry of the 29th Division was the first to grind to a halt. When they had moved out against Martinville Ridge, they were immediately spotted by German observers. Every gun within range fired upon them, including a battery of 88mm guns dug in on Hill 101. From here, Kanonier Thomas Förster witnessed the devastating effects:

I was just 17 years old and in the flak troops of the Luftwaffe. I came up to the front on 14 July 1944 as a replacement. The entire trip from Paris had been rough but nothing like I was to encounter on those few days of July I spent in Normandy. My job, since I was new, was to run back and forth bringing shells for the gun. Those 88mm shells are pretty heavy too. The gun was well dug in, better than I had seen in my training. We had a clear view of the valley, roads and hills opposite us [Martinville Ridge]. The day after I arrived, the Amis came forward to attack. Within seconds we were in action. Between my trips for ammunition I snuck peeks through the camouflage. Far away the ground was filled with smoke and explosions. I tell you I would not want to be in the middle of all that. Once I saw a large dark shape moving against the smoke; it turned out to be a tank. Gunner Number 1 looked through the sights

Fragment of newspaper found in the bottom of a German soldier's bread bag/haversack that was brought back by a US veteran. This section has an article titled 'Night on the Invasion Front' which details the German point of view of the fighting in Normandy. While seasoned with a good dose of propaganda it does quite clearly state that Allied aircraft are actively seeking German columns to attack but that 'the German soldier is not fazed by this' – a tacit admission of the loss of air superiority.

and adjusted the gun. A deafening crack followed. I saw the tank explode, popping up all the hatches, shooting flame and smoke. Several men around me threw up their arms, indicating that they had seen the 'kill'. I did so as well. Then off for another shell. I pushed out of my mind the thoughts of the young men who had been inside the tank. It was something one had to do to get through war.

What Förster had seen was the pinning down of the US 116th Infantry Regiment and the loss of one of the 747th Tank Battalion's Shermans; six others were also hit. The GIs called in air strikes on the German gun positions, but these had little effect on the well concealed and protected artillery.

Despite the problems with the 116th, the 115th launched their own attack as scheduled. Bumping heads with Falschirmjäger Regiment 9, the GIs gained 500 metres, then were stalled. The 29th's divisional commander, General Gerhardt, knew that something had to be done to get both of his regiments moving again, especially the 116th, which was taking heavy casualties. The General ordered the 2/175th Infantry to attack westwards along the D-972 in the hope of alleviating the pressure on the 116th's left flank. This advance floundered as had the 115th's, checked after approximately 500 metres. For the time being, the German paratroopers had stymied the 29th Division.

Kanonier Thomas Förster, 3rd from left, with a group from his replacement unit. As with many German servicemen during the war years he did part of his training in Germany and then as Occupation Forces while finishing advanced courses.

Camouflaged 88mm flak position in Germany. Kanonier Thomas Förster served with this gun crew before his transfer to France as a replacement.

A Luftwaffe medical detachment enjoys a sing along at the training camp where Kanonier Thomas Förster received his basic training, early 1944.

The US 134th Infantry, jumping off at the same time as the 115th, ran into the survivors of GR 916 and Schnellebrigade 30. Oberstleutnant von Aufsess had expected such a move and his men were well placed. The fighting centred around the hamlet of Le Mesnil-Rouxelin. Each side fought doggedly, neither appearing to gain the upper hand. Individual acts of heroism won small gains for the GIs.

The Germans possessed men of the same calibre. Leutnant Maas, the leader of the pionier platoon from the Stabskompanie/GR 916 had just returned from St Lô when a familiar alarm was heard in the German lines – 'Panzer!' Out of the dust and smoke a group of American M4 Shermans were approaching. No anti-tank guns were near or quickly available. Maas ordered the men around him to keep the American infantry busy, and the firefight that ensued kept both sides heads down. Meanwhile the tanks still rumbled forward. The young officer, armed with all the grenades and panzerfausts he could lay his hands on, launched his first attack, fully exposed to enemy fire. The rocket struck its mark and the Sherman halted, belching out black smoke. Grabbing his arsenal, Leutnant Maas ran around this one then calmly fired a second rocket, scoring another hit. Oily smoke covered the field and road. The remaining Shermans withdrew but Maas did not reappear from amidst the smoke, and some of his men ran out into the havoc to save their officer. His body was found near a third wreck, which had been blocked from view. Maas had stopped this attack almost single-handedly, but it was a victory that only won his men some time.

East of the village of Emelie the surrounding countryside was erupting in battle. Wegner hoped to get through another terrible day:

Our hole this time was just north of the village of Emelie. From here we could cover the road that led into the village, roughly south to north, with our machine gun. In front of us was a weak skirmish line, only Grenadiers with some panzerfausts.

There was an artillery observation team too. As usual the Amis struck this line right on the heels of their artillery. From all the noise we heard we speculated that this was a large attack. Several men came running back, wounded men who could get out under their own power. In twos and threes they passed us heading to the aid station. I can clearly recall the looks of pain and fear of these men, only boys in reality. Then the sounds of shells passed over us. These were from our guns, and the same piece of earth was once again torn apart, only this time none of us were in the middle of it.

A soldier emerged from one of the groups passing us. It was one of the company messengers, I think Müller was his name. He asked for water. Kalb gave him some and asked what the situation was, between swallows he said he was sent back with an urgent request that NO troops be sent to reinforce the skirmish line. That they should wait for the Amis to come to them. It was a sound plan, to weaken anywhere for a line that would not hold anyway was very foolish. As these men fell back they would fall into our line and strengthen us. Just before he left he told us that when his boys fell back they would go back to the hill on the other side of the village [Hill 122] and Kalb said that it meant we were not expected to hold either. He was very good at tactics and the like. Willi and I often pondered why he wasn't a sergeant by now. I felt that this had to do with his attitude to leaders above him if he found them unworthy of his respect. Anyway we watched silently as Müller headed away, crunching on some stale bread I had given him. It was just too hard for any of us to eat but he had teeth that could crush anything.

A German combat patrol with fixed bayonets moves through a rubble-strewn French street still smouldering from bombardments.

The US 134th Infantry made slow, painful progress towards Emelie, hampered primarily by effective German artillery. However, some of these guns now raining shells on the 134th were supporting 3. Falschirmjäger-Division in their efforts to keep the 29th hemmed in on Martinville Ridge. This enabled the 116th Infantry to regain some momentum and start pushing forward. This also showed the US commanders that a lightning-fast regrouping was vital before continuing the overall operation. While this was done, all available air support was brought to bear on the German lines to keep them pinned down. This included some P-47 Thunderbolts loaded with 500-pound bombs, on a mission to get the German 88mm guns on Hill 101. Kanonier Förster would soon find out how lucky a man he was:

We heard the Jabos but were confident that they had not seen us, especially after the last attack, so we didn't have too much a concern. I was on my way back for more shells with this other kid, he was from Hamburg. Well, we heard a whistle and he knew that sound from back home. He pushed me into a ditch, before we hit the ground a huge explosion ripped apart the gun and all those behind us. My God I had never felt anything like it before or since. The shockwaves hit us and the air was ripped from our lungs. I knew we lost consciousness since it was a while before we got up. We went back to find an ugly smouldering hole. The only thing left of the others was a few cracked and broken helmets, an unforgettable sight. We couldn't stay here any longer. We found two usable rifles and headed off towards St Lô. We felt we would find someone in charge on the way.

Regrouping was also the main task for Kampfgruppe von Aufsess. The US attacks had opened several cracks in the lines, though both Emelie and Le Mesnil-Rouxelin still held out. This

Not yet the full
nine yards.

was the result of small groups of determined men out of the same mould as Leutnant Maas.
Leutnant Heinze was both a participant in and witness to many of these actions:

> Our lines were thinning out, the dead and wounded grew in number. My men fell back in
> good order to wherever the next position was, a field or hedgerow. Remarkably many of the
> wounded opted to stay, fight and perhaps die with their Kameraden. Those that could be
> evacuated would be, others we could do nothing for we left in hopes that the kindness and
> humanity of the Amis would prevail.
>
> We would launch small counter attacks to stem the enemy advances. However, very soon all
> of us that were left became exhausted. Then another counter measure was needed, this time
> it was against tanks. I asked for volunteers. A man from the Panzerjäger detachment came for-
> ward. His feet were a bloody mess but he did know how to knock out tanks. All of his friends
> joined him; this was good since they had to support him. Others stepped forward to join our
> band. We held up the Amis for as long as we could, falling back with a few losses, the brave
> Panzerjäger being carried by his stalwart friends. This allowed a new main line of resistance to
> be put up. Then this would all begin once more.

As the hours passed, the 134th maintained the pressure on the German line and reached
the outskirts of Emelie. Wegner caught sight of figures in khaki, drawing up within range:

> Through the telescopic sight I could see them very clearly. Soon our line would explode. I
> was not to fire unless Kalb ordered it. Willi was ready with his rifle and Gunther, the RAD
> youth, was ready to feed me belts of ammunition. Watching men approach you through that

sight is an eerie thing. I could see them yelling and pointing, moving forward as the inverted V of the sight swept across their bodies. I wondered what they would say to me if they knew I had them in my sights, and I wondered about the reverse.

At times like these odd things run through your mind. Kalb thundered out his order to fire. In seconds I had sent 50 rounds into the advancing Amis. Some fell, others went for cover. It was not long before their mortars began to drop shells near us. I would fire at anything that moved. When we stopped to change a belt or if we had a misfire I would hear the clear single reports of Willi's rifle. Then an explosion that was much too close rocked us; it was a grenade. That was a clear indication that we had been spotted and it was time to get out of there. We picked up everything and fell back in good order, but quickly.

Emelie fell to the onrushing GIs. Wegner and his group made it to Hill 122. Both sides regrouped for the next phase of the fight.

Another thrust late in the day by the 116th Infantry began to take ground from the tattered companies of Falschirmjäger Regiment 9. General der Falschirmtruppe Meindl scrambled to put any troops he could scrape up into the ever thinning front. 7. Armee Headquarters told him that parts of three new divisions would arrive shortly, being elements of 272 and 342 Infantrie Divisions and 11. Panzer-Division. Their expected arrival time was not known. Luckily for Meindl, General Gerhardt ordered his 29th Division to dig in and hold, to finish preparations for the next day's mission. Whatever the reason, this halt gave the Germans vital time to reorganise yet again.

The 29th did encounter one major dilemma with this halt. The 1/116th held up as ordered, but the 2/116th had been pushing forward faster than the rest of the entire division, having found a weak spot in the German lines. This battalion's commander, Major Bingham, only discovered the issue of the halt order while checking up on the rear elements of the battalion. At this time he had no radio communications with the forward and still advancing companies, so the Major set out on foot to stop them. Upon reaching these men he discovered that they had reached the D-972 near La Madelaine. This was the main highway leading into St Lô from the east. The German paratroopers were quick to react to this threat, launching an attack that cut off the vast majority of the battalion. Bingham and his men were in a pocket that straddled both sides of the highway. Though the Germans had cut all the wires laid by the US signalmen, radio contact was still available, and Bingham relayed that he was in a good defensive position. This prompted Gerhardt to order him to hold and not attempt a breakout. He planned to relieve them in the morning, consolidate the rest of Martinville Ridge and then push into St Lô. He even sent out a detachment with supplies for Bingham, hoping they could slip through the German lines at night.

Other than this success and the fall of Emelie, no significant advances were made against St Lô. The 134th still planned to make a night assault on Hill 122 at 2100 hrs, with hopes that a more effective barrage would make the taking of the hill easier than that of Emelie. Wegner and his dwindling company would come under the American guns once again:

After we reached the top of the hill we took up in a hole on the slope facing the village. Then came another bout with the artillery and the Jabos. This meant an attack would happen soon and it did. When it came it appeared to us that this was not on a broad front but just to get us off the hill. The Amis came late at night and were very cautious, having learned from the previous days of combat. They did push us back up the hill a bit. When the fighting ebbed away for the night some of our stragglers came through. They told us that hundreds of Amis were just waiting to get up to the front. We believed them, since St Lô was just behind us.

The Americans were just under three kilometres from the centre of St Lô. News relayed to Kraiss spelled out the impending disaster. The loss of Pont Herbert and retreat of Panzer-Lehr-Division had opened up the 352nd's entire left flank. The fall of Emelie threatened to cut off the bulk of his men fighting at La Carillon and Le Mesnil-Rouxelin. The choice was abundantly clear, retreat or face destruction. He ordered his men to pull back to the final defensive line outside the city, roughly Hill 122, to an area just south of the US lines at Pont Herbert.

Unknown to Bingham, the German paratroopers facing his forces had made their way around his battalion then back along the ridge that he had cleared the day before. Thus, when units of the 115th Infantry and the remainder of the 116th moved forward in their attempt to link up with Bingham's men, they ran headlong into determined German resistance. The encircled GIs found themselves under attack, with armoured support, to destroy the pocket and seal the road. Taking heavy losses, the GIs held out. No one got in, but no one was getting out either.

16 July brought a renewed effort by the 134th Infantry to take Hill 122. This time the direct assault was coordinated with a flanking movement to the east through Les Remains. From the besieged hill, artillery observers directed effective fire upon the American forces. The dismal weather also kept air support away; good fortune for the Germans.

The 115th Infantry's attack was faltering as the morning wore on. All attempts at break-ing through to Bingham had been thwarted. By afternoon it was apparent that no further attempts could be made and the exhausted Americans went into defensive positions. This was not good for Bingham. His shrinking band of men was short of everything – ammu-nition, rations and so on. Some men needed to be evacuated as soon as possible. The German paratroopers pressed upon them yet again and this time one tank with some infantry support broke through the perimeter. Disaster was narrowly avoided when the tank was forced to withdraw after intense anti-tank efforts by the GIs. Casualties were shockingly high from this action, and under the constant German artillery fire Major Bingham doubted his men could withstand another full-scale assault.

General Gerhardt was frustrated with the progress of his division. He had hoped that 16 July would have been the day he made it into St Lô, but this could not be done until Major Bingham was rescued. The General did not know that with this day's effort, 3. Falschirmjäger-Division had totally depleted itself. What men were still in the line were all they possessed.

Opposite Gerhardt, General Kraiss pondered his own limited tactical options. The city now could be hit from either flank, perhaps both simultaneously. The northern front was still held securely. Kraiss was under direct orders from his superiors to withdraw no fur-ther despite his exposed flanks. Then troubling reports came in from the front. Troops had begun disobeying orders, leaving their positions, just blindly heading for the rear. The sergeants who were still alive had to physically restrain their own men. Was this the final nail in the coffin for his whole division, or was it just a few exhausted, hungry individuals? The General felt it was the latter, and was proven correct as calm returned with the arrival of rations. All that was left in the divisional stores had been sent up to feed them – perhaps this was the 352nd's last supper.

It was discovered that those Volksdeutsche who remained behind fought better, in some cases, than homeland Germans, and ironically, those who deserted and surrendered in a way were tactically even more effective. When these men gave themselves up in any sort of a group, it tended to hold up the Americans while they were disarmed, searched and sent to the rear. Leutnant Heinze was philosophical as to their actions: 'Our star was setting, so who could really blame them?'

General Kraiss was still perplexed by the US commanders constantly stopping just short of victory, as they did once again on the evening of 16 July. Several times the city of St Lô could have been taken with few casualties but Allied inaction allowed the 352nd to regroup and reinforce the front. Perhaps this latest pause would allow the three promised divisions to arrive.

This was not to be. A communiqué to Kraiss from Meindl would seal the fate of his beleaguered division. Meindl informed him that all of the bridges south of the city, save one, had been destroyed. The lone surviving bridge was heavily damaged. Thus, all supplies and reinforcements would have to cross the remnants of a bridge at Baudre, then travel down a road under constant air attack into the impassable rubble that was once a city. No relief would come in time. Kraiss had already sent most of his staff out of the city to start work on defences to the south along the Vire river. He felt that from there he could hold up the Americans until the new divisions arrived. With this in mind he formally asked permission to withdraw his men to a more tenable position. The answer was no. St Lô must be held. Disregarding the order, the General pulled his men back to the northern part of the city; this would give them a better chance. When would the Americans finally grasp the opportunity to take the city that author Samuel Beckett christened 'the Capital of the Ruins'?

fourteen

DEATH IN THE RUBBLE

THE shell landed close. The concussion ripped the air from his lungs while he fell to the bottom of his foxhole. Amidst a shower of dirt and debris, his tangled equipment came down upon his back. Obergrenadier Wegner, 17 July 1944:

> I was still in a fog laying in the dirt. Moments before I had just dozed off after completing my watch. There would be no rest today for me, just my luck. I grabbed my helmet, which had fallen off, and crammed it onto my head. I looked around to make sure that everyone in our group was still present. It was still somewhat dark but the flashes illuminated the sky enough for me to make out their faces. We faintly smiled at each other, sort of saying that all would be OK. Then the Arifeuer moved off to our rear. We knew what this meant.

Gefreiter Simeth was crouching under cover with his friend Karl Wiesmüller; both were the last surviving men of their respective platoons. At the other end of the military spectrum, General Kraiss was doing the same with his staff officers.

The US 29th Division was mounting a new effort to relieve Major Bingham. This task was given to Major Howie and his 3/116th Infantry. Even though his battalion was under strength, Howie was ordered to link up with Bingham and then push into St Lô from there; his flanks would be protected by the remainder of the division.

The Major issued strict orders for his men just to use the bayonet and hand grenades, so that the Germans in the area could not gauge their strength or positions to bring artillery fire on them. At 0430 hrs he personally led his men out into the early morning mist. With minimal resistance encountered, the GIs made it through the lines of the decimated German paratroopers and reached La Madelaine, less than a kilometre from St Lô. But he had missed Bingham altogether and Howie had to backtrack to find Bingham and relieve him. Both officers conferred on the best way to get into the city considering both units were lacking men and supplies. It was decided that Major Howie would lead the drive towards the elusive prize.

Collar tabs removed from German paratroopers killed in action on Martinville ridge by then Staff Sergeant Don Van Roosen. *Top left*: Obergefreiter collar tab on mid war pattern Luftwaffe tunic. *Top right*: same rank on an early or pre war piped Luftwaffe tunic. *Bottom*: officer rank of Leutnant collar tab on wartime enlisted Luftwaffe collar.

These actions did not go unnoticed, since General Kraiss had been keeping an eye on what was left of 3. Falschirmjäger-Division. He had no troops to throw against the GIs, and it was unlikely that the few survivors of Falschirmjäger Regiment 9 could stop them. He could shift some artillery and mortar barrages against the units of the US 29th Division. This, Kraiss hoped, would bolster the paratroopers enough to hem in the Americans.

These barrages had a devastating effect. One of the first casualties was Major Howie, killed just after briefing his officers about the impending attack on the city. The Germans were able to increase the fire to such a level that it caused the 116th Infantry to go to ground. They could not afford to lose many more men before the actual advance started. While they waited for the German artillery to wane, companies from the 115th Infantry pushed up behind them. These men encountered the sombre evidence of the intense struggle that had raged on Martinville Ridge. Sergeant Van Roosen explored the aftermath of one specific action:

> We came across some dead of the 116th. From where we encountered them we could deter-
> mine where the German gun position had been. It was a good one. We went up to take a look.
> We found several dead German paratroopers and one dead GI. You could see the way that he
> worked himself up and around them. He hit them from behind before they got him. That guy
> deserved a medal.

Before he left the scene of carnage, Sergeant Van Roosen took out his knife and bent over the dead Germans, all members of Falschirmjäger Regiment 9, and cut off several of their collar insignia, reminders of a hard-fought action that most would never knew occurred, save the families of the men who would never come home.

General Kraiss received orders from General der Falschirmtruppe Meindl to bring his men back along a front that would run from Martinville through St Georges Montcocq and end at Rampan. This would skirt the northern edge of St Lô where he had already placed his men. His left flank would still have to pull back farther to Rampan. However, Kraiss had to question the move to Martinville, reminding his commander that the village was already in American hands. Meindl countered that he was aware of this, but had full confidence that his paratroopers would take back the area by nightfall. Kraiss was ordered to leave rearguards as he withdrew. In following these latest orders, some that he had already given, he decided to bring back his men as close to St Lô as possible, in order to give them more protection and afford them the opportunity to withdraw southwards across the Vire when the time came. He did decide to hold onto the high ground outside Emelie, a tactical decision that he reasoned would keep the Americans in the area away from the city.

This impending withdrawal brought Leutnant Heinze some small satisfaction. Hauptmann Loges would have to leave his safe hiding place, the command bunker. Loges was visibly upset at having to venture from his refuge into the daylight, a sight relished by many members of GR 916.

Obergrenadier Wegner was only concerned with getting out of his predicament in one piece. The fighting on Hill 122 was tenacious at all levels:

> I know that when we were fighting on that hill, it wasn't just a matter of holding the high
> ground. It was staying alive first and tactical stuff second, a distant second. We kept the Amis
> far enough away so that they could not use grenades. When the Arifeuer or mortars found our
> range we simply fell back a little bit. In some instances we left just as the shells were landing
> upon us. In fact, the second time we moved, a shell landed very close, which made me take
> the gun off the tripod and roll away. Another shell hit, the ground gave way beneath us and
> shrapnel flew everywhere. We survived, despite some scratches, but the tripod was just obliter-
> ated. A few small twisted pieces of junk were all that was left. Kalb said that was just fine with
> him since we didn't have to carry it any more. As time advanced so did the Amis; eventually
> we only had a small part of the hill.

The stalled battalions of the 116th Infantry soon discovered why Meindl was so confident about his paratroopers. The Germans had once again pressed forward and encircled both units. The GIs were in desperate need of supplies and many needed immediate medical attention. Then they had a stroke of good luck; a German medical officer was captured. He treated – with the aid of the US medical corpsmen – all the wounded, both American and German. He saved many lives but like so many good men in bad times, his name is unknown.

The 115th Infantry was still much too far away to mount any sort of an effort to relieve these battalions. Attempts to reach the area with the use of halftracks were turned back by heavy debris on the roads and German paratroopers in the woods armed with pan-zerfausts. The stalled columns were pulled back so they would not end up as ripe targets for German artillery. Many men from 1/116th volunteered to try and get through to the pocket on foot but failed as well.

Rumours spread of mass attacks against the encircled battalions and the units of the 29th Division redoubled their efforts to reach them. In reality, the situation was more of a 'Mexican stand off'. 3. Falschirmjäger-Division was not strong enough to destroy the pocket *and* hold off the efforts to relieve it. It could do one or the other, but not both. The Germans chose the latter. For General Gerhardt this simply would not do, he wanted his men back on track and pushing into the city. He had the entire 175th Infantry Regiment attack through the rest of the division to link up with the 116th and end the stalemate once and for all.

While plans for this were being made another group was being assembled, to be titled Task Force C. The mission for this group was to seize St Lô in a lightning strike through the German lines once the highway was opened. The commander of these men would be General Norman Cota, the Assistant Divisional Commander of the 29th.

The 175th drove forward, just shy of 1430 hrs, running into fierce resistance from the German paratroopers. The advances were extremely limited and casualties very high. Some companies reported that they had only 50 or fewer effective troops in the line.

The 115th Infantry finally made headway. Its 2nd Battalion broke the enemy line, and pushed through to Martinville Ridge, placing them in an excellent spot to relieve Bingham. Although they had to stop for rest and supplies, they could finish the job the next day. As it turned out it was this success that drew enough Germans away from the 1/116th Infantry to enable them to reach their own men. Two separate patrols of twenty men succeeded in getting through, suffering only minor casualties. This allowed the rest of 1st Battalion to form a corridor through which the wounded could be brought out and replacements carrying supplies could go in. The German paratroopers had nothing left to throw in front of the 29th Division. The Americans knew that night that St Lô was, quite literally, just over the next hill.

As the darkness encroached, weary Grenadiers were heading back towards St Lô in sombre columns. A few men stayed behind as rearguards, while others stayed hidden as their companies pulled out. These were mostly Volksdeutsche hoping to surrender to the Americans. Discarded equipment filled the ditches along the roadsides. No one knew when the war would end but now a general mood of defeat permeated the air, deepened by the knowledge they faced another night without sleep. In hushed tones Obergefreiter Kalb talked to Wegner:

On that last night he said to me 'Karl, any fool can see that we're beaten. There is no hope of holding this lousy French ruin. If those fools with the oak leaves and crimson on their collars had any sense they would let us keep going until we got to the other side of the river, or even better they'd end the war before we're all dead.'

I felt very much the same but did not have the courage to speak out like him. Any more losses and no one would be left at all from our company, a sobering fact. We ended up in a village that was just north of St Lô itself [St Georges Montcocq] and here we began to dig once more. Work was very slow; everyone was very dispirited. One could see that most just didn't give a damn anymore.

General Kraiss opted to stay in the city and personally direct the deployment of the remains of his division. So far, it seemed that the Amis had not detected the movement of his units to within the city limits. Messages from the remaining outposts stated clearly that US troops still held their positions from the previous afternoon's fighting. With this news, he decided to shift some men to shore up the faltering 3. Falschirmjäger-Division. None of the promised reinforcements had appeared, so all that could be done was round up any stragglers and comb out the rear echelons once again. Kanonier Förster and his friend from Hamburg were amongst those pressed into this last line of defence:

We had walked around, avoiding the sounds of battle in hopes of finding our way to some other artillery battery. Without anyone actually stopping us we just headed towards St Lô. We made it there but it was in such a state of confusion we just found a place with many other dislocated men and waited, perhaps in hopes of being evacuated. The next day infantry officers appear and order all of us to follow them. In short time all our papers are checked and names listed. We were told that we were in the infantry now, regardless of uniform. That night we walked back much of the way we had on our trip into St Lô. I was not very happy at the prospects of fighting from a little hole in the ground.

On 18 July, runners and telephone lines brought Kraiss the news he wanted to hear. The inevitable morning barrages were hitting the old front line. This would spare many of his men and give them more time to prepare. The General also knew that once the Americans discovered the move that they would push forward hard and fast. Once more he telephoned Meindl, and asked about the arrival of the three new divisions and once again the answer was the same: they were on their way.

General Gerhardt's 29th Division was making good gains this morning, far better than it had over the past several days. The 115th Infantry succeeded in linking up with the 116th at La Madelaine and the 1/115th was beginning to push against the weak elements on the 352nd's flank. This was Kanonier Förster's first and last action as an infantryman:

> After a night of trying to dig in the hard earth the Amis came at us in large numbers. I fired several wild and un-aimed shots at them; it did no good. Within minutes our ad hoc company was broken. Men ran back past me. I was scared and afraid to move. The kid from Hamburg took off with the others. A wounded man tumbled into my rather poor excuse for a foxhole. He was a truck driver but he was also a Gefreiter, so I asked him what to do. He asked for something white; I gave him a handkerchief. He tied it to his rifle and stuck it up side down in the dirt in front of us. Then we just waited for the Amis to get to us. I felt like 100 rifles were pointed at me when we peered over the mound of dirt. With my arms straight up in the air as far as I could get them, I climbed out. I was shaking from fear. They pulled the wounded man out. They searched us quickly then pushed us towards the rear of their lines. My war had lasted three days. I was one of the lucky ones.

After brushing aside the stragglers that General Kraiss had placed in their way, the 1/115th Infantry reached the area just west of St Georges Montcocq. Here, the 35th Division had just crossed the old German front and were beginning to press towards the Grenadiers in the village itself. Now both divisions would catch this village in a deadly crossfire. The rest of the 29th was sweeping whatever was left of 3. Falschirmjäger-Division south of the D-972. This is just what Lieutenant McNutt and the rest of Task Force C were waiting for.

Task Force C was coiled up at a farm near Couvains awaiting orders to strike into St Lô. The force was made up of the 29th Cavalry Reconnaissance Troop, less one platoon; a platoon of medium tanks of the 747th Tank Battalion; a platoon from Cannon Company, 175th Infantry; a platoon of Anti-tank Company, 175th Infantry; a detachment of the 29th Divisional MP Platoon; a Civil Affairs Section; a platoon from the 121st Engineer Battalion; the Reconnaissance Platoon of the 821st Tank Destroyer Battalion; Company B 821st Tank Destroyer Battalion; and two artillery observer parties, one from the 227th, the other from 29th Division Artillery Headquarters.

There was a feeling of exhilaration in the command group and among the attached war correspondents. After so many days of hard fighting from Omaha Beach, the capture of St Lô would be a major victory and a breakout from the Normandy pocket – the Battle of the Hedgerows.

Gefreiter Josef Brass and his 'Kumpel' (best friend), Pionier Paul Hundiers. They spent three years together. Hundiers was killed south of St Lô at the Vire river. He is buried in Martigny. Photograph taken during a happier time in Dusseldorf, 1942.

Upon hearing of the gains made by the 29th and the plight of the paratroopers on his right flank, General Kraiss realised that it was only a matter of hours before the city fell. His staff urged him to leave at once, especially as with practically no forces on the right he would almost certainly be captured. He refused.

In the ruins, several hundred metres away from his General, Obergrenadier Wegner prepared to meet the onrushing US forces from the last hole he would ever have to dig. He just didn't know it yet.

During the morning we were quite happy to see the fireworks show as the Amis rained shells down upon the places we had been the night before. A few stray shells landed around us but it was nothing to worry about. By mid morning some survivors of the rearguard detachments had crossed the front. They said the Amis were on their way with everything one could think of, and hundreds of men too. The terror in their eyes said more to us than the words. When we were finally attacked it was the usual story, lots of tanks and artillery. Our group was in an orchard that rested in somewhat of a depression. From here we could shoot at the Amis when they crested the hill to our front. This was especially good with regard to tanks. Though it did have its bad points. The Amis were gaining all the high ground and then could rain artillery down upon us with accuracy. But for quite a while we held our own.

With support from the 35th Division, the 1/115th Infantry pushed close to St Georges Montcocq taking the heights overlooking St Lô. When this news reached Gerhardt, who had been ordered by General Corlett to take the city this day, he sent a message to General Cota. At 1500 hrs Task Force C and Lieutenant McNutt thundered down the road; it was the long awaited express to St Lô.

When word came that leading elements of the 115th Infantry had reached the high ground overlooking St Lô the order was given for the battlegroup to move out. As the column struck out along the St Lô–Isigny Road, General Cota was about two-thirds back in the column in 'Fire and Movement' [the name of General Cota's jeep] with me and Williamson, the driver. From time to time the column was halted by intermittent artillery fire and once by an enemy roadblock that was soon eliminated. Each time the column halted the General would urge Williamson forward to find out the cause of the delay and get the column moving forward again. Due to this leap frogging we came along side the lead tank called a 'flail'. This tank had a rotating drum installed at the front with long logging chains attached to beat the ground before it, to detonate any mine planted there. It looked like a terrified monster beating out in panic against unseen attackers. The noise of the motor, the crashing of the chains and a great cloud of dust must have let the enemy know we were on the way. If St Lô was taken by surprise it was due to rapid movement, certainly not stealth.

General Kraiss got more grave news. Panzer-Lehr-Division had retreated and exposed his left flank. Most of his artillery, about 46 guns, were out of munitions. This meant that the entire division, save the staff units south of St Lô, would be cut off and destroyed. Bypassing Meindl he requested permission of 7. Armee to withdraw his men. To his astonishment he was told that this withdrawal would only be back to the position he was already defending. It was clear that Meindl had not notified 7. Armee of the moves on 17 July. In disgust he used his own initiative and ordered his artillery to move to the high ground south of the city. From there, those guns with munitions could support the infantry fighting in St Lô by firing on pre-plotted targets. This would leave the infantry with only the support of mortars for the time being. The artillerymen were well versed in this kind of work, and first moved all the guns for use in support fire, completing the task within two hours.

When Task Force C reached the 115th at St Georges Montcocq it was decided to leave enough men to keep the Germans pinned down in the orchard, with the rest of 1/115th joining the battlegroup. With this done, Cota broke through the 352nd's lines and made for the cemetery in the eastern part of the city.

Leutnant Heinze had been summoned to the Divisional Command Post, near the cathedral in the centre of town. He had been coordinating defences with Leutnant Heller, and was ordered to bring his company with him. He entered the building and was briefed on the situation. He was being sent out to confirm and contain a reported breakthrough of American tanks, and to destroy the bunker that Loges had evacuated. Loges was also there, hovering in the background:

> I was outraged at this and demanded that Hauptmann Loges go back with us to destroy his bunker. It was his responsibility to do this when he left it. Loges adamantly refused. I started towards him and he shrunk away. My commander stopped me and said that he would deal with him.

Heinze left the headquarters building enraged. He gathered the few remaining men of his Nr. 5 Kompanie Grenadier Regiment 916, then led them down the rubble-clogged streets towards the cemetery.

Task Force C, taking scattered small arms and mortar fire, officially entered St Lô at 1800 hrs. Leutnant Heinze at the head of his column suddenly realised that a large force of US troops and armour was bearing down on his men. They were caught in the open with no time to manoeuvre. His only option was to gain them some time to fall back and defend

Member of 352. Infanterie-Division who did not make it out of St Lô, near St Lô Cathedral. (US Army Archives)

the command post. While ordering them to do this, he grabbed a panzerfaust. Running out into the middle of the debris-strewn street, he knelt down and took aim at the first tank. It was already well within range:

> The next thing I knew I was lying on the ground. I tried to move and discovered that my right arm and side were hit. In the momentary lapse between consciousness and blacking out, my first thought was that I would never play tennis again. Then the fog in my mind cleared and I realised that if I did not move the oncoming tanks would crush me. I reached into my pocket and pulled out a handkerchief, with my left hand, and waved it frantically in hopes that the Amis would see it and drive around me. To my surprise the lead tank halted. The hatch popped open and the commander came out and asked what I wanted. I yelled back that I just was trying to get out of the way. He said it was OK and for me to get out of there. I tried to move but after some struggling the pain and loss of blood took their toll, I faded into blackness.

His men did not forget Leutnant Heinze. The kindness and chivalrous behaviour of the American tank commander gave them the chance they were waiting for. Two men had stayed behind to support him and, as the wounded Heinze would later learn, ran out in front of the stopped column to retrieve their officer. He was brought back to the command post. The breakthrough was confirmed. For the second time Hans Heinze was severely wounded whilst fighting amidst the rubble-strewn streets of a city; the first time had been at Stalingrad. This time, with his blood this officer gave his men enough time to withdraw in good order.

As a result of hopscotching along the column, General Cota along with Lieutenant McNutt arrived in St Lô with elements of the Reconnaissance Troop. Alighting from his jeep, Cota set about coordinating the activities of Task Force C and the 1st Battalion of the 115th Infantry, whose commanding officer had set up his command post. He then moved about the streets checking the disposition of troops. Task Force C began to fan out into the debris in the hope of seizing the city as fast as they could, however they came under fire from the guns that Kraiss sent out of the city.

General Kraiss now felt it was time to order his men to retreat from St Lô. His last message reported the breakthrough of Task Force C to Headquarters 7. Armee; their reply was an order to take out this 'weak' battlegroup and regain control of the city. Kraiss simply ignored this command. His division was being split in two, and thus only had one course of action. He ordered his men to hold open the routes to the south through the city as long as possible while they withdrew out of the rubble.

For some of the lucky ones, the retreat was easy. Peter Simeth, Karl Wiesmüller, Georg Seidl, and Alois Meyer all made the trek out when parts of GR 916 were withdrawn with some of the divisional command post staff. The Grenadiers in the northern part of the city were amongst those who would have the most difficulties in getting through. Karl Wegner and his comrades were there:

Somehow word got through to us that the Amis were in the city, behind us. We now were in a very real danger of being surrounded. The order then came down to fall back and regroup outside St Lô to the south. Under fire we left our holes and headed into the debris-strewn city. Some men did not come; whether they were dead or just decided it was over and were waiting for the Amis is something I'll never know.

Out of sight of the enemy, just for the moment, we found that we only had about 30 men left. No officer at all, most were dead or captured. The senior man was a wounded Feldwebel. He decided that the best thing to do was to break up in small groups and make our way south through the city, avoiding all fighting with the Amis. We broke down mostly along the lines of friends or men from the same companies. The four of us would go it alone. The Amis were getting closer and these groups disappeared into the smoke and dust. The wounded Feldwebel just sat down behind a wall. Kalb went over to him, spoke a few words then came back to us. The man was going to wait for the Amis; he had a family and his days of running were over. We moved out fast, running through the destroyed streets. We kept close to the walls and remnants of buildings for the best cover. St Lô was not as I remembered when I first marched through it.

While the Grenadiers scrambled to extricate themselves, the GIs seized many of the major points in the city. By 1900 hrs most of the important road junctions and strategic points were in their hands, although some were held at the moment by a mere handful of GIs. Artillerie Regiment 352 and its attached batteries were still pouring accurate fire onto these points. Snipers and pockets of resistance still had to be dealt with, though these tended to be Germans trying to get out and they were not looking for a fight. At 1930 hrs, General Cota radioed that St Lô was secure, 43 days late and after much hard fighting.

The other General in the city, Kraiss, was preparing to make his way towards the parts of his division in the hills. He would have to avoid capture or death. One final message crackled through on the radio, announcing that 272. Infanterie-Division had arrived and that one battalion was being subordinated to Kraiss. This was laughable, much too little, much too late. The General and the last of his staff bolted out of the church just as an American armoured car pulled up in front. Shots rang out but no one was hit.

Lieutenant McNutt then watched as his General was forced out of his hard-won city:

I was walking along the street with the General going before me when a flurry of enemy shells landed. As I was to his left rear, I noticed an L-shaped tear in his jacket about three inches above his left elbow. I recognised it as typical of a shell fragment entry and wondered how he could have been hit without it passing through me. (I even checked.) I said, 'General, you've been hit.' He ignored me and we continued down the street until we came to the cemetery. Shells were falling all about by this time and I took his arm and steered him into the cemetery thinking to take shelter behind one of the tombs. A tall sergeant who had set up his mortar crew there said, 'Don't bring him here, we're catching hell!'

We returned to the command post where someone broke out a first aid pack and sprinkled sulfa on the General's wound while he directed his next in command how the occupation of the town was to be continued. He was then evacuated through medical channels and Williamson and I returned to check at the medical battalion on his condition. When they brought him out of the operating tent, still groggy from the anaesthetic he murmured, dreamily, 'Everyone is so nice to me.'

While General Cota was out of commission, Lieutenant McNutt was detailed as Liaison Officer between the divisions in XIX Corps.

Of course some of the German artillery fire was was landing on their own men, who were trying to get to safety. Wegner:

Many times our little group had to dive for cover. Kalb was very mad about this and I knew why. The artillery was ours. We skirted through the city, peering cautiously around every corner or pile of rubble. Often Kalb would look around a corner then pull back quickly, telling us quietly to go the back the other way. It was like a game of cat and mouse and we were the mice.

Then it happened, I suppose it was inevitable. Kalb looked around a corner and was shot at. The bullet hit him in the right hand, but it was only a scratch. I sent off a burst from the machine gun and we bolted down another alley. Kalb was in the lead followed by Willi, Gunther, then myself. We went from the frying pan into the fire. When Kalb rounded the next corner he ran right into a group of Amis and armoured vehicles. He turned and yelled for us to go back down the alley we just passed. Gunther and I were able to make the turn on the run. The Amis were reacting by now. Willi was not able to stop quickly enough, he slid forward on the cobblestones because of those damn hobnailed boots. He bumped into Kalb, knocking him down, then tripped over him falling around the corner into the open. Gunfire pierced the air, screams and shouts followed. Gunther and I got down behind this destroyed wall in a hole made by a shell, we then sprayed mad gunfire over our friends' heads to keep anyone from coming around the corner. I watched Kalb drag Willi by his boots back around the corner. Then by the belt with his good hand he dragged Willi towards us, both toppled over the wall. Willi's cries of pain sent shivers down my spine. I gave the machine gun to Gunther and told him to fire at anything that came around that corner.

I went to Willi and Kalb, whose bloody hands were placing a second bandage on Willi's chest. The wounds were bad, through the lung and stomach. My God how Kalb tried to save him, as if he were his own brother, the look on his face told me that. I held Willi's hand and cradled his head in an attempt to calm him. Kalb looked at me and shook his head, Willi was going to die. His face became sunken and lost its colour. He knew he was finished. He stopped shrieking in pain and began to cry, softly. He looked at me with eyes one cannot describe and said his last; I never forgot it. Willi said to me 'Karl, through all this just to die in the rubble, it makes no sense.'

Willi Schuster's grave marker in the German Military cemetery at La Cambe. He died without knowing that he had been promoted to Gefreiter. (P. Botting)

Willi Schuster's bloodstained German/French dictionary. This was taken from the lifeless body of his best friend by Obergrenadier Karl Wegner to remember him by.

Question or statement I didn't know, either way it struck us both. I held him until he died. The whole event only took a few moments. Willi's last words may have been the trigger for Kalb's next action. He took off his helmet and placed it over Willi's face, then broke off the bottom of Willi's identity disc. He took this, his watch, medals, wedding ring and the pictures of his family and wrapped it all in his handkerchief, which he thrust down the front of his trousers. No one would look here. He placed his battered cap on his head and told us to do the same. He took Gunther's rifle, tied a dirty undershirt to it and waved it above the wall. He told us that he would go first, if everything was OK, we should follow. He stepped over the wall with his arms held high. I looked one more time at Willi's lifeless body lying there in the rubble, then scrambled out into captivity. Thank God it was finally over.

The three men were quickly searched and sent off to the rear. Karl Wegner, although a prisoner of war, recalled later that at this moment he felt truly free for the first time in his life.

In another part of the broken city one more body lay on a mound of rubble. It was that of Major Howie, brought in with Task Force C under the direct order of General Gerhardt. He was placed in front of the cathedral of Notre Dame with an American flag draped over him, a sign of respect and honour to him and all the GIs that had been lost on the drive from the beaches to St Lô; a brave man who was the symbol of the price of victory.

Grenadier Willi Schuster was the symbol of defeat. A shattered body, forgotten by all except by those who were close to him, and in time as these people passed, remembered by none. No monument would mark his death as it would for Major Howie. But both shared a common bond. They each had fought for their country and gave the last full measure of devotion.

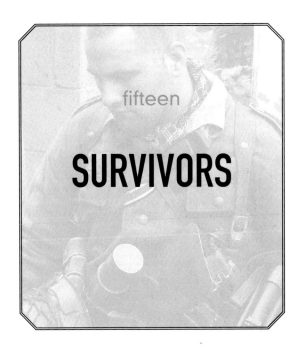

fifteen

SURVIVORS

THE battle for St Lô was over, but not the war. The few remaining men from the 352nd now waited for an American push south from the city. They numbered 1800 men, all services, from a division and attached units that had numbered over 10,000. Few remained who had begun the fighting on that dismal morning in June, 43 days earlier. One was Gefreiter Peter Simeth, who gave thanks to his guardian angel. This is the rest of his war:

We left the city and came to the banks of the Vire. We crossed on pontoons because the bridges were all destroyed. About 500 metres away from the bank we began to dig our holes in the tree line. Well in front of this we built a two-man machine-gun position that was also an observation post, to be manned at all times. At night we would sneak down to the river for water and to see if the Amis were up to anything. It went on like this for several days and, save for an odd artillery shot, all was quiet. Then came 24 July 1944.

It was a lovely summer morning. Around 1000 hrs we heard a loud humming, then the bombers appeared and headed right at us. We could see the bombs fall from their bellies. We jumped into our holes as quick as we had ever done. There was terrific noise, booming and thundering. Branches and trees flew everywhere. One fell right over my hole, which stopped some of the stones and flying debris from hitting me. For about four hours this went on. One wave of planes after another. When it was over, the whole forest was gone. Before this bombardment we couldn't see the Vire but now it was clear right up to the water. The rest of the day was peaceful. On the 25th the bombers came once again and dropped tons of bombs on the remains of the forest.

Early in the morning on the 26th I was put in the forward machine-gun position with three other men. All were Marines [men from coastal artillery units]. We had heard that the Amis had attacked all along a wide front. I left the position to go and relieve myself that morning. I had just got my trousers down and was preparing to squat when a shot went by my head. I let out a shout and got down. More shots rang out and I crawled away. When I felt I was safe, I pulled my trousers on and straightened out my uniform. Then I went back to the position. The Marine Feldwebel told me to go back and get my rifle and equipment, which I had forgotten in my haste. I went forward and retrieved them but heard much more gunfire from all around. I came back to find all the Marines dead, lying in pools of their own blood. I made straight for our camp. Almost everyone was gone but I did find Wiesmüller, the only other survivor from my platoon. He was wounded so I decided to stay and help him. Then a group of men appeared led by Leutnant Ambrost. He found us and another older man from the Organisation Todt in the camp. He threatened to shoot us for desertion. I explained that my Kamerad was wounded and I was aiding him. He did not care and said we had to go and fight but that afterwards we might be shot. He passed out grenades to us and led the group out. Wiesmüller and I took our chance when it came. We got away and crawled on our stomachs. We came across another man from our regiment; he was shot in the belly and was bleeding to death, nothing we could do. We found a dugout and went in; it was occupied already by another Kamerad. He said to be quiet and lie still. The Amis were still fighting around us. We lay still until the evening. It was then we heard voices and movement. We looked out and saw so many soldiers it astonished us. Each of the Amis had a tommy gun and grenades. There were so many we couldn't count them. It was foolish to even try and fight. A few minutes later we were taken prisoner.

Later in the evening we were rounded up with another group of prisoners and three Amis lead us back, always with our hands over our heads. We walked about two hours and came to this house. Here we were all questioned, photographed and had everything taken from us. It was quite dark when we were led into a stable. We lay on the stone floor but slept as peacefully as if it were a feather bed. One man guarded us. We awoke late the next morning; the sun was already high in the sky. In the distance was the thunder of the guns at the front.

PoW photo of Gefreiter Peter Simeth.

Despite Red Cross markings, medical convoys still needed to take cover from Allied air activity. This field surgeon carries supplies back to his vehicle.

Another shot of the same field surgeons unit and their vehicle standing outside a bank somewhere in Normandy.

Members of the unit carrying out some vehicle maintenance. Note the Red Cross marking on the bonnet for identification from the air. Sometimes food and other non-medical supplies were carried to the front in these vehicles.

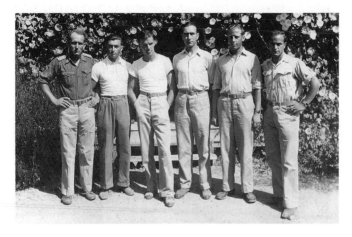

Leutnant Heinz Fuehr
pictured on extreme right,
whilst a PoW at Camp Como,
Mississippi.

In the course of the day more prisoners were brought in. One was the older man from the
Organisation Todt. I asked him about Leutnant Ambrost. He said that most had been captured
from the group, and he was glad because he had many children at home. Ambrost was also
taken but just cracked up and went after one of the guards, yelling and screaming. He just
wouldn't stop and they finally had to shoot him.

That afternoon we went further back towards the coast. On the way we saw all the supplies,
tanks, guns and infantry that were on the way to the fighting. The line never seemed to end.
As darkness approached we assembled on a large camp on the seaside. After spending the night
in a meadow we walked down to the water and were loaded onto ships. The next morning, 29
July 1944, I was in England.

Leutnant Heinze had been evacuated with many other wounded from St Lô. His wounds
were severe and so would be sent back to Germany. On the road in the ambulance he
noticed something that worried him when he saw the roof of the vehicle:

To my amazement I saw that the roof of the ambulance was full of bullet holes. I asked the
driver how many times he had been shot at, and he replied that almost every time they drove
they were strafed. He added that if an ambulance stopped it was always shot up, so they
had orders to keep going no matter what happened. This surprised me because the Amis I
had encountered had always fought with chivalry, evidenced by their treatment of me. The
rumour was, as the driver said, that the Amis felt the ambulances were bringing up munitions
to the front. He did say that they did bring up medical supplies, food, and sometimes the mail.
During our ride we were strafed several times but the drivers stayed cool and kept going.
These men are owed much credit.

Leutnant Heinz Fuehr had also been wounded and survived but fate had dealt him a better
hand:

I was sent to England were I spent three months in the hospital. I was then sent with 100 other
prisoners aboard HMS *Mauretania II* to the United States. I was in a place called Camp Como
[Mississippi] where my treatment was excellent. I learned at the end of 1944 that I was promoted to Oberleutnant. In March 1946 I was released and went home to Duisberg in Germany.

PoW Georg Seidl, on left, in British uniform. Photograph taken in August 1947 in Lourdes, France.

Gefreiter Georg Seidl and Grenadier Alois Meyer were the sole survivors of their platoon. After the fight along the Vire, they fought in the line without respite. The offensive that brought Gefreiter Simeth into captivity had taken the life of Generalleutnant Dietrich Kraiss, killed in action as he had wished to be. Oberstleutnant Heyna, commander of the handful of men once known as GR 914, was the senior officer of those that had survived. He assumed command of 352. Infanterie-Division, which did not even equal the pre-invasion strength of his old regiment. His first orders subordinated him to 2. Panzer-Division; it appeared as though no one from the 352nd was destined to get out of Normandy alive. For two more weeks they fought on, and the numbers dwindled. Then, during the second week of September, the division was withdrawn, to be sent back to Germany for rest and refitting. Those still standing gladly left the bloody fields of France behind them.

A feeling of ease flowed through them as they crossed the border into Holland, a sense of being much closer to home. Leave was beginning to seem plausible. Then one morning, the sound of large formations of aircraft filled the skies overhead. Everyone, including Seidl and Meyer, looked up expecting to see bombers heading for the Ruhr. Instead it was wave upon wave of transport planes pulling gliders behind them. It was 17 September 1944 and they were just outside a Dutch city named Arnhem. Another invasion was catching the 352nd in its sweeping arms, yet hope persisted that they could avoid the coming battle and get back to Germany. A messenger brought Oberstleutnant Heyna orders to send all available combat troops to support 10. SS Panzer-Division 'Frundsberg', then proceed to Germany with the remainder of the 352nd. Heyna followed the order, but the result was pitiful. Of three Grenadier regiments, a fusilier battalion, a pioneer battalion, Schnellebrigade 30 and all the other infantry units added to the 352nd, only 200 men were fit for combat. Gefreiter Seidl and Grenadier Meyer were amongst these 'lucky' few. This time the battle was different, and these men helped the German troops in the area gain a victory for the floundering Reich. Those that went unscathed during this campaign hoped that now they too could return to Germany and the 352nd, but these men were permanently transferred to 363. Infanterie-Division, also operating in the Arnhem sector.

Five more weeks of combat followed with this new division, and the numbers reduced, yet Seidl and Meyer still hung on. Perhaps they were also blessed by guardian angels. Their war came to an end on 6 December 1944, with a reunion of sorts. These men were amongst

Save this sweetheart - Jim

THE STARS AND STRIPES

New York—London
Paris—Rennes
Monday, Sept. 18, 1944
Vol. 1. No. 65

Daily Newspaper of U.S. Armed Forces

In the European Theater of Operations

Ici On Parle Français
Où est votre mère?
Oo ay vohtruh mair?
Where is your mother?

Holland Invaded by Air; Siegfried Line Is Burst

20,000 Nazis in Mass Surrender to Yanks

By Bud Kane
Stars and Stripes Staff Writer.

BEAUGENCY, France, Sept. 17. — More than 20,000 German troops, including members of the Luftwaffe, Wehrmacht and Nazi marine units, were marched into U.S. Army prisoner of war camps today after their mass surrender had been effected principally by the reconnaissance work of one officer and 24 enlisted men of an 83rd Infantry Division platoon.

In a ceremony marking one of the strangest mass surrenders in this war, Maj. Gen. Erich Elster formally turned over his pistol to Maj. Gen. Robert C. Macon, 83rd Division commander, and then directed his troops as they, too, turned over their weapons and other tools of war—including 1,900 vehicles of all kinds—before crossing the Loire River to become prisoners.

The story behind the surrender goes back to September 8, when Lt. Samuel W. Magill, of Ashtabula, Ohio, leader of an intelligence

and reconnaissance patrol reaching across the Loire, learned that a large body of Germans coming up from the Spanish border was attempting to slip through the gap at Belfort, a gap already being closed by the Seventh Army from the south and the Third Army from the west and north.

Magill and his men, knowing that the Ninth Air Force and the Maquis were raising havoc with this army of men, slid into this open territory on September 8 and established patrols up and down the Loire. Pfc James Reilly, of Thomaston, Conn., and Pvt. James E. Townsend, of Petoskey, Mich., slipped over to the other side of the river to constitute the entire force of Americans on that side. The outfit ran patrols north and south for 40 miles and east and west for nearly 30 miles—all with 24 men.

Late in the day, Magill was approached by two members of the Maquis who stated there

(Continued on Page 4)

Yanks Through Gap; Giant Fleet Lands 'Chutists

Strong forces of the First Allied Airborne Army were landed in Holland yesterday by a huge fleet of gliders and transports, and last night were reported to have captured several cities behind the German lines.

Inside Germany, the First U.S. Army poured reinforcements through a gap torn in the Siegfried Line south of surrounded Aachen in preparation for a drive toward the Rhine. U.S. troops were less than 30 miles from Cologne.

U.S. Troops Mass For Rhine Drive

American troops are through the Siegfried Line having

Airborne Army Behind Nazi Lines

Transported in broad daylight by a gigantic fleet of more than 1,000

---

the German troops defending the village of Hasenfeld Gut, facing familiar Amis in the form of the US 29th Division. The combat was tough and casualties mounted on both sides. Finally the Germans had had enough and made overtures to surrender. Gefreiter Seidl and Grenadier Meyer were in the vicinity of a drained pool, which was being used as a shelter. A detachment of Americans appeared to collect them. The officer in charge spoke German, one of the reasons he was chosen for the detail. He ordered everyone out of the pool, to disarm. Both German survivors of D-Day were marched off by another survivor of that same day, a newly commissioned Lieutenant Don Van Roosen.

Very few officers from GR 916 survived the campaign unscathed. Almost all were killed, wounded or missing. The admirable Leutnant Willi Heller had made it through. This officer was well liked and respected by his men and superiors. Like Heinze, he had worked his way up from the ranks, demonstrating courage and natural leadership abilities. He visited a recovering Leutnant Heinze while the 352nd was refitting in Germany. In December 1944 he led a new 6th Kompanie/GR 916 during the Ardennes Offensive. Sadly, Heller was reported missing during the fighting in the town of Diekirch, Luxemburg. He was never found.

sixteen

A TIME FOR REFLECTION

THE battle for St Lô was over, and the US forces were now in possession of the city. With hindsight, this outcome is seen as inevitable, but things could have been different. Could the Allies have been stopped at the beaches or beyond? Was every opportunity exploited and advantage taken on either side?

The Atlantik Wall was an impressive piece of fortification, with staggering amounts of manpower and materiel put into its construction. There have been many critics of this defensive structure and the theory behind it. History has since shown that fixed fortifications simply do not work in an era of mobile warfare. In the words of General Patton. 'Fixed fortifications are monuments to Man's stupidity.' Rommel got the unenviable task of making it work, regardless. One of his many ideas was to send the 352nd to the area to bolster the rather average troops stationed there.

Consider the 352nd's contribution to the battle at the beach as a microcosm of the overall battle situation at the moment of landing. They were on alert for imminent invasion, although under the guise of war games. The Grenadier in the field had no doubt that the threat was real and acted accordingly. The result was a far more effective defence in the 352nd's sector. Had this level of readiness been common along all the beaches in the area, the Allied landing would have been far harder.

What would a delay have meant? Don't forget that the landings were timed for a narrow window in the weather. Already delayed a day by bad sea conditions, had establishing a successful beachhead been in doubt, would the Allies have pulled back their forces in the hope of trying again? It didn't happen that way of course, nor was it ever likely that the Atlantik Wall would ever have been brought up to the planned levels of readiness. On the other hand, the 352nd might not have been brought to Normandy. That was up to Rommel. What might have happened if he had not added them to the defence?

Caen was a vital objective for the Allies. It was an important nexus of railways and roadways, with much of the rail traffic passing through the area. Control of the railheads there would give the Allies the ability to move men and materiel inland at an even more

Veterans at the US cemetery St Laurent 1988. Left to right: Franz Gockel, Heinz Severloh, Josef Brass, F. Deville (French historian) and Georg Seidl.

A meeting of the veterans in Neukirken, Germany, 1989. Left to right: Eduard Schötz, Martin Eichenseer, Alois Meyer, Elizabeth Milano (author's wife), Josef Fuchs, Georg Seidl and Peter Simeth.

Veterans in LeMesnil Rouxelin, north of St Lô, summer 1989. Left to right: Chris Coxon (friend of author Vince Milano), Georg Seidl, Dan (friend of author), Hans Heinze, Frau Heinze, Elizabeth Milano and Frau Seidl.

Hans Heinze, on the left, and Georg Seidl with their wives in Vierville, 6 June 1989. Behind them to the left is the D-Day Museum.

rapid rate than was possible with the Mulberry harbours and amphibious vehicles. It gave the Germans less of an advantage while they held it, because they did not control the skies. The Jabos could, and did, interdict rail and road traffic to a great extent. Movement and track repair could only take place safely at night, so there was far less that the Germans could do with this asset.

Caen was also the location of various unit headquarters and a communications centre for the Germans. Coordination of troop movements and dissemination of intelligence being so fundamental, it is easy to see why the city was so hotly contested. Keeping the Allies out was crucial to keeping communications functioning, as well as keeping the rail system and canal port facilities out of the hands of an enemy who could make better use of those assets. Furthermore, the southern area beyond Caen was open country and contained strategic high ground. This was the real prize, as it was the sort of environment where tanks could be best employed, and the momentum for breakout achieved. Without this mobility for armour, the hedgerow country would prove to be a difficult place to fight, as history has subsequently shown.

Montgomery was stopped in his move toward Caen by the unexpected resistance of the 352nd, with reports of armour in support of them. On his other side, 21. Panzer-Division actually pushed to the beach, and these reports also caused Monty to be cautious, as he assumed it must be a potent force in order to have accomplished this. The simultaneous attack on his right flank by the 352nd gave the impression that there was a much stronger German force than he had been given to believe. His perception was that he had armoured forces on either side. Expecting the usual German battle doctrine of massive counter-thrust, Monty dug in instead of pushing forward immediately. This stalled the thrust to Caen.

Was Montgomery wrong to dig in? Historians have gone over this metaphorical and real ground many times, some cursing his caution and some even going so far as to claim that his real objective was not, in fact, Caen. Montgomery was, as were many of the leading figures in the Second World War, heavily influenced by the experience of the First World War. There was no love for a commander who threw lives away and gained no ground for it. He was also very much a man who liked to have things his own way – which meant a force that outnumbered the enemy, and a well planned schedule of attack. Though no one can doubt that he was a popular leader and a skilled General, the highly volatile atmosphere in Normandy was not a place where he would shine. He expected the Germans to behave in certain ways according to his past encounters with them, which coloured his vision of the battlefield. When he suddenly saw armour from 21. Panzer-Division to one side, and met with fierce resistance and unexpected tactics from the 352nd, combined with the reports from his own units that there was armour to his right (mistaken reports as it turns out, these were a dozen low turret assault artillery pieces, not armour), he naturally assumed his position was not what he had originally envisioned. He did not feel that he had overwhelming force to bring to bear against the German lines in his sector, so he consolidated and went on the defensive until such time as he could get the men and resources to do the job his way.

His actions were not imprudent when taken in context. He had little knowledge of the actual numbers and disposition of the enemy forces he faced. The 352nd's presence was a great surprise, and the timing of their push gave the appearance of a well disciplined and coordinated attack. Had Montgomery known exactly what he was facing, he certainly would have bashed through and taken Caen within the expected timetable. What is less clear is why Montgomery did not go on the offensive when it was made clear the next day that his situation was not as bad as he had assumed. Faint heart never won fair maid, nor did it win Caen during the critical early phases of the invasion of Normandy.

Was this such a disaster? Didn't the Allies win the war anyway? They did, but at a great cost in lives on both sides. Had Caen fallen quickly, the Normandy campaign would have ended far sooner, triggering a cascade of events that would very possibly have shortened the war in Europe by perhaps six months.

Consider that Caen was a combination of desirable assets to the Allies: a railhead, a port facility and a major crossroads. Any one of these is usually worth fighting for. The port facility, whilst only served by a canal and not a deep water port, would have given the Allies a superb point of distribution to the railhead and roads and would have reduced the load on the Mulberry harbours. There is a strong probability that Mulberry 'A' – the American harbour – would have been better anchored had it not been under such pressure to get supplies ashore. The Americans were more concerned with getting things moved and had taken shortcuts in the setup. The great storm of 19–22 June might not have destroyed Mulberry 'A' had it been properly estabished, as was demonstrated by the survival of Mulberry 'B', which was well anchored by the more meticulous British. The additional offloading capacity of the second Mulberry harbour would have been even more important had the breakout occurred sooner.

Would the breakout have happened earlier if Caen had fallen swiftly? Almost certainly. If the British had pushed through to that extent, the flank of the 352nd and others would have been open and they would have had to give up, retreat quickly, or get bottled up by a sweep around them. The fighting through the bocage area would have been unnecessary. The Allies would also have been able to establish fully functioning airfields during the very first days of the invasion. Having airfields that close to the fighting would have given the Allies a mighty hammer with which to pound the German positions and prevent movement. With all these factors in place, the breakout would have taken place within days, and the Germans would likely have fallen back to create a defensive line behind the Seine; the coast would have been open to the Allies.

This is, of course, speculation. Rommel did bring the 352nd into Normandy. They achieved much and fought hard. Sometimes the victories were apparent to the commanders and men involved, other times their accomplishments could only be seen in retrospect.

In other historical accounts, little mention, most in passing comments or footnotes, is given to 352. Infanterie-Division, yet it played one of the most significant roles in the entire campaign. These men did not break when the other divisions around them did. Contrast this with 3. Falschirmjäger-Division at Martinville Ridge, who left the 352nd's flank open when they crumbled. The result was Task Force C punching through and getting an opening to the D-972 highway. The elite troops fled, while the common infantry solder of the 352nd stood his ground until the situation was hopeless.

Within 24 hours, the 352nd had in its possession both US Corps' operational orders. The commanders on the scene made good use of these captured orders, especially when it was recognised that these were authentic and that the Allies were following the timetable set out in them. This same information, once filtered up to higher command, did not produce the same reaction at that level. They thought the orders were a ruse and delayed making a bold move to capitalise on their extraordinary luck. They had this information

Breast eagle still on uniform cloth, presented to author by Hein Severloh. Severloh said that this was all that remained of the uniform he wore on D-Day.

Hein Severloh on 6 June 1989 standing where his MG position was in WN62.

Peter Simeth and his wife at their home in Atzlern, Germany, June 1989.

Heinz Fuehr (born 1918 in Duisberg, Germany) pictured at home in Kassel, Germany, in 2008.

in their hands with sufficient time to act on it, but did nothing. Also the capture of the 29th Division's communications truck, with frequencies and codes intact, was a boon to the local commanders. And again, higher command did not seize the moment. It was left to the 352nd to make the most of these prizes. They did so because of their greater experience and training. Their officers had learned to be flexible and act quickly, on their own, recognising the shortcomings of 7. Armee Command.

Behind overstretched lines, outgunned, outnumbered and fighting the higher command's impossible orders, these Grenadiers almost changed the course of history on Omaha Beach. If their ammunition reserves were at the normal level for a stationary division, the assault by the US landing forces between Vierville and Colleville would most likely have been forced to withdraw. No major US thrust inland took place until the 352nd exhausted nearly all munitions on hand. This would not have won the war, but it would have isolated the US troops on Utah Beach from the British beaches. This delay in consolidation may have given the German divisions the time they needed to arrive in the battle zone, making the campaign a fight for a beachhead, rather than of expanding one in the hedgerow country. In any event, the 352nd was a cornerstone in the German defence, delaying the capture of St Lô for 43 days.

In accounts of the campaign fought in Normandy during that fateful summer, the German side is nearly always told through the filter of the deeds and actions of elite units. These men were good, and deserve their place in history, but lost in their shining glories are the stalwartness, endurance, bravery and sacrifice of the common soldier who shouldered most of the burden.

Leutnant Hans Heinze called his own division a 'thrown-together mob'; some US generals at the time felt that it was one of the best divisions in the German Army. Perhaps the truth is somewhere in the middle. Regardless, these Grenadiers have earned their place in history next to the victors, the stalwart Tommy and the tough and determined GI.

UNIFORMS AND EQUIPMENT

EVERYDAY survival is the most important thing to the common soldier. The fighting in Normandy was no different in this than any other war waged before or since. In order to better understand the battles and their outcomes, a historian must be familiar with the everyday life the soldier led, because this could, and did, have an effect on the course of battles as much as the tactics and strategies used by the commanders.

Since the latter part of the seventeenth century soldiers have spent their time in service wearing the uniforms and equipment issued to them by the governments that they served. Each country maintains its own distinctions of colour, badges and evolution of certain individual items, some better or worse than that of the enemy. A quick comparison of the uniform and personal equipment of the Grenadier and GI should give the reader a clearer insight into each soldier.

Starting literally at the top, the steel helmet. The German helmet was one of the most advanced and admired designs of the war. The rounded dome with its visor and flared side skirt gave excellent protection from shrapnel or the elements. It was produced from high grade steel and painted field grey. The leather liner was kept in by an aluminium band and ring system. Both the liner and shell came in metric sizes, ranging from 54 to 61 centimetres, to offer the wearer a close and comfortable fit. The shell possessed two air vents. A leather chinstrap and metal buckle kept the helmet in place and secure on the soldier's head when running or fighting. The one drawback was that it tended to muffle some of the soldier's hearing. Sounds not heard could mean the difference between living and dying.

The American helmet was of a different and, at the time, totally new design. True, US forces started the war wearing an updated version of the First World War 'Tommy'-style helmet. The 'improvements' were limited to a new liner and chinstrap; this version was considered totally inadequate for modern warfare long before the US entered the war. After much design and experimentation, the US Army adopted the Mk II helmet, known as the M1 Helmet Assembly. This headgear consisted of two main parts. First was the outer steel shell, rounded dome with small visor and side flares, to which a webbed canvas

A recreation of a German signal post in operation. The offizier carries an MP40 machine pistol.

chinstrap was permanently attached. The second part was a liner, in the same shape as the shell, just a little smaller. The liner was made of various materials over the years, including cork and paper/canvas in the early years, and later fibreglass, linen or cotton. The later materials were made as a composite using phenolic as a binder, resulting in a stiff, plastic-type shell. Inside the liner dome was a webbed suspension to which was fixed an adjustable leather headband. This enabled the wearer to set the helmet to his size, with or without caps and so on. The one-size-fits-all approach allowed for easy production and issue. However, if not adjusted properly, and sometimes even with a good fit, it would bounce on the soldier's head when he ran, hence the familiar image of the GI charging along with one hand holding down the helmet on his head. GIs frequently used toilet paper packs and the like in order to make the fit better and the bounce more comfortable. On one occasion, witnessed by Don Van Roosen when he was a squad leader, this caused a unique complication:

> Once while my squad was attacking across an open field we had to move fast during the assault. But I noticed this one guy who would run a few feet, take off his helmet, pat the inside of it a few times and put it back on. He repeated this several times during the assault. I finally went over to yell at him for playing with the liner of his helmet. Then I discovered that a bullet had passed through the top of his helmet, possibly an incendiary or tracer, and ignited the toilet paper packet that he had padded his helmet liner with and he kept taking the helmet off to try and pat out the fire.

A small overseas edition of the *Boston Herald* printed for US troops abroad. This one was folded and used as extra padding in the helmet liner of PFC Merle Hescock when he landed on Utah Beach on D Day.

The US M1 Helmet, or Steel Pot as it was called, was by far the most useful of all to the combatants engaged in the war. Without its liner, it became a pail with which the soldier could carry almost anything. Washing, shaving and cooking out of it were commonplace. It was even useful as a shovel to dig a hasty foxhole. A design with slight variations, it stayed in the US military for over 50 years. Oddly enough, its eventual replacement was a design quite similar to the German type.

The uniform issued to enlisted men of the German Army during this period consisted of tunic, shirt, trousers, boots and field cap. The tunic was of the basic thigh-length coat style common to most European armies at that time. The German design was a four-pocket, single-breasted, tapered coat made of wool. Many variations exist, as do books solely on the subject, but here we are dealing only in generalities. Those uniforms made before and in the early days of the war were of finer quality and lasted a long time as well as being more comfortable than their successors. The initial colour was field grey, varying in shades based on the quality of the dye used in producing the base cloth. Several of the men within 352. Infanterie-Division who were inducted during earlier periods in the war still wore these uniforms during the Normandy campaign. The length of the war put a strain on the German uniform manufaturers leading to economy-driven changes: chiefly, simplicity in construction and the use of reprocessed wool combined with early synthetics, mainly Rayon. These later issues tended to be rough and scratchy. The material was shoddy and lacked warmth and durability. Soldiers issued these lower

Certificate issued to a Gefreiter to give permission to acquire cloth for a privately purchased uniform. Enlisted men required permission to buy uniform cloth due to the war time shortages.

quality uniforms encountered problems, particularly after heavy rain, or during exercises where they became wet. Wegner:

> When I was inducted I was issued the new pattern of uniform. It was quite different from that of my older brother. I was not allergic to wool but this stuff really made me itch. I thought of how proud my brother looked in his smartly cut uniform; mine was quite dull looking. All of my insignia were indistinguishable from the tunic itself unless you were right up close to the person. I felt very inferior to my brother. Then one day while we were out on a long march of several kilometres the sky just opened up and the rain fell without mercy. Wet to the bone, we sloshed back to the Kaserne and up to our rooms to change for evening mess. To my complete astonishment as I unfastened the buttons they came right off the tunic still attached to the patches of wool to which they were sewn. I was not the only one; all of us had the same happen or worse. We were marched to the Quartermaster the very next day to get new uniforms issued to all of us, better ones. Subsequently we were told that the cloth had been defective. Despite this I still wondered how we could win the war if our uniforms melted in the rain.

The style of trousers improved during the war. The first were cut very high and required braces. These, produced in the same high quality wool as the earlier tunics, had the same durability. As a result they were still very commonly worn right up to the end of the war. Wartime experience resulted in later issue trousers that were baggy and heavily reinforced, especially in the seams. These later war versions could be worn with or without braces because they had belt loops.

German uniforms were also produced in cotton herringbone twill (HBT) material, intended for use in hot weather and fatigue duties. Their colour was a dark green that tended to fade after use and washing. The same insignia worn on the wool uniforms was present on the HBT version.

The German shirt was of a pullover design of several different versions, with or without pockets, with or without collars and so on. Its colour also varied. Early in the war the shirts were white or natural colour, later replaced by grey or field grey and even olive. Grey and field grey were the most common in 1944 but all types were in use. The shirt itself was full cut and very comfortable. In the hot weather, shirtsleeve order, the wearing of the shirt instead of the tunic was permissible.

American soldiers were issued uniforms similar in many ways to their counterparts, designed for hard use in combat. The field jacket, officially the M41, was made of a heavy tan or olive cloth with an inner liner of olive drab blanket material. It was waist length and closed by both button and zipper, having two 'slash' pockets, one on each side of the stomach area of the jacket. These were kept closed by the use of a single centre button. The jacket had shoulder straps held by a single button and its cuffs and rear waist were adjustable by means of pull tabs and buttons. This jacket was comfortable and well liked, although it lacked warmth in extremely cold weather.

The US shirt was of olive drab wool in a button-down style with top pockets. The wool varied in shade and roughness depending on the manufacturer. Earlier model shirts had a secondary flap of wool that went across the soldier's chest before buttoning the shirt. The shirt's cuffs also had smaller flaps. These were called 'gas flaps' and their intent was to protect the wearer from burns caused by gases that could get through the openings in the shirt during gas attacks. These flaps caused the wearer to get very hot in warm weather, and as the chemical warfare threat receded, the soldiers frequently cut these out.

The trousers were of the same colour but of heavier wool. They were intended to be worn without braces, held up by a khaki web waist belt, in the same style as period civilian workmen's trousers in the US. This combination of shirt and trousers was commonly known as the soldier's 'Woolies'.

A shirt and trouser set made of olive drab HBT was issued to the GI for fatigue and hot weather duties. This uniform was comfortable in the hot weather and worn in combination with the Woolies in combat. The HBT shirt was cut more like a jacket and was worn this way instead of the M41 in hot weather. The HBT was cut larger, for better ease of movement. Several men, especially in the 29th Division, found out how cold the southern parts of England could get while training in Devon and Cornwall. Some men sleeping on the cold ground at night in their HBTs became casualties.

A third model of uniform began to appear in Europe after the invasion, worn primarily by new replacements. A new jacket and trouser set, intended to replace the M41, made of a heavy duty olive drab cotton poplin was introduced. This was officially the M43 field jacket and trousers. Although a big improvement over the M41, this new uniform would not be seen in great numbers until later in the campaign. For most men in Normandy it would be Woolies and HBTs or a combination thereof.

Poor boots most likely make a poor soldier. The Germans made exceptional boots for their servicemen. The most famous was the Marching Boot, more commonly known as the 'Jackboot'. These were produced in good quality leather with thick soles and heels. The heel was 'iron-shod', similar to a horseshoe, and the sole was hobnailed for traction. The boot was high, reaching mid calf, and pulled on or off easily. When well maintained, they stayed soft and waterproof for lengthy marches. The German soldier affectionately called them his 'Dice Shakers'.

Wartime shortages and the time it took to produce marching boots resulted in another boot, made to the same standards, but a lace up, ankle high style. It was still iron-heeled and hobnailed, but required less time and less leather to produce. To keep the trousers gathered at the ankle with this boot, a canvas legging held by two leather straps was issued. They were called 'retreat leggings' since as they began to appear at the front, things were going badly. The older veterans held these boots in contempt, going to great lengths to repair or replace their Dice Shakers.

The US soldier began the war in a short ankle boot of a lace up pattern. The boot was manufactured in brown leather with rubber heels and soles. The leather uppers were produced with the rough side of the leather exposed, hence these boots were generally referred to as 'roughouts'. Some are known to have been issued with nails and heel irons like German boots, but the rubber sole construction was the most common by far. A version of this boot existed with the smooth side out as well. Calf-length canvas leggings were issued to be worn with them. The leggings were khaki in colour and laced into the calf by a series of metal eyelets and hooks. The legging covered the top part of the boot, the laces in particular. A buckled strap of webbed material went under the boot to keep the legging secure and in place. The legging was functional and did its job of keeping water out of the boot as well as mud and brambles. They were highly disliked, primarily because they were tough to get on in a hurry. A new version of the roughout was developed for use in the field. This version had a leather gaiter with two buckles sewn directly to the top of the boot. They were very successful and much sought after by frontline troops. Called 'combat boots' or 'buckle boots' they began to appear in large numbers after the beginning of the Normandy fighting. Most GIs fought the campaign in leggings.

Other than his helmet the GI wore his HBT cap, the now famous 'Jeep' cap, or his overseas hat. The HBT was of a short-visored baseball cap design. The olive drab knit Jeep cap was intended for winter wear underneath the helmet but was worn on its own in all seasons. The overseas cap was intended for general duties, except fatigue, and Class B dress (field jacket, woolies, tie and OS cap). It came in both piped – blue for infantry, red for artillery etc – and unpiped versions. It was not intended for combat but was frequently worn at the front.

The Germans had two major types of caps for the field. The first was their version of the overseas cap. It was made from the same wool as the uniforms, with the national insignia on the front. These were of earlier war vintage but were still possessed by a good portion of the troops. The second was the most famous, the M43 *Einheitsmutze*, general service cap. This cap was also of wool and was a copy of the German mountain trooper cap. It was visored, with fold down earflaps for the winter, which were held in place by two small buttons on the front of the cap. Above this was the national emblem, the army eagle and rosette of the national colours (red, white and black). This cap was very popular and worn slightly cocked to the right to give a jaunty look to the wearer.

The German soldier's personal gear was usually leather, but web appeared in large amounts in the 352nd Division because of the large surplus stocks left over from the African campaign. The belt was black, as was all army leather, and issued with a steel or aluminium buckle with a pin with two prongs on it that fitted into holes punched into an inner tongue stitched into the strap. The buckle clipped to a hook permanently attached to the other end of the belt.

Onto the belt the soldier would place his ammunition pouches. These were worn on the front; left and right of the buckle. For the K98 rifle the pouches were of leather, divided into three separate sections, each holding ten rounds of 7.92mm ammunition. This gave him 30 rounds per pouch, 60 rounds total. Other weapons, which were magazine fed, had pouches made of canvas, with either web or leather fittings. All of these, except that of the G43, also had three sections. The pouch for the G43 only held two magazines because the width of the magazines would have made three uncomfortable and impractical to wear. On the back of each type of pouch were two loops, through which the waist belt passed, and a D-ring. This ring, sewn into place by means of a leather tab, allowed the front

US GI as he would have been attired in June 1944. M41 field jacket, M37 trousers, M1938 leggings (dismounted), low quarter boots, M1923 Garand cartridge belt with medical pouch attached. He wears a M1 helmet and carries a standard issue M1 Garand rifle fitted with M1907 leather sling.

Rear view of US GI infantryman. He wears a M1928 haversack with T handle entrenching tool. Also shown on left of haversack is M1 bayonet. Hanging from the right side of the belt is a M1910 canteen.

Ostbatallion Feldwebel. These battalions were comprised of ex-Red Army PoWs and other volunteers to fight against communism. There were many ethnic groups including Asians amongst them. US PoW records indicate many Asiatics were captured in Normandy. This soldier's sleeve badge is in the imperial Russian colours of red, white and blue with the Cyrillic letters 'POA' that represented 'Russian Army of Liberation'. This was translated by the Allies as 'Pals of Adolf'.

German Grenadier in light combat kit. The Y-straps are worn over shoulders and attached to middle rear of the belt. He carries standard gas mask canister, bread bag and canteen on his belt. On left a straight handled entrenching tool and bayonet are also slung from the belt. A grenade launcher pouch is clearly shown on the left side.

German Grenadier wearing full marching kit. He wears an M43 tunic, M43 trousers and standard leather marching boots. On his back, mounted to an A-frame are a zeltbahn shelter quarter (pegs, rope and pole sections are rolled inside). Above the zeltbahn is the mess kit with standard issue blanket rolled around outside. Gas mask canister (with gas cape bag attached by strap), bread bag and M31 canteen are mounted below the A-frame attached to leather belt supported by Y-straps. Bayonet hangs from left side of belt. He is equipped with a K-98 Mauser rifle.

hooks of the equipment braces to attach to the pouches and help support the belt and distribute the weight of the load. The equipment braces were known as Y-straps because of their shape. The two heavy front straps went over the shoulder and joined at the upper centre of the back at an O-ring. From there a separate back strap joined and went down to the belt where it had a metal hook that went under the belt. This strap was adjustable to accommodate the height of the wearer. Each of the front straps had a D-ring sewn to its rear that would sit at the back of the soldier's shoulders. To these, many types of packs and equipment could be attached, mainly the Tornister, rucksack or assault frame. Two smaller adjustable straps were riveted to the front upper of the straps. This smaller one passed under each arm and had another D-ring on the end, to which the bottoms of the packs attached. The first basic pack was the tornister, a horsehide-covered canvas pack. It was not big enough to carry the basics and was disliked; the rucksack was introduced to replace it. The 'ruck' was very large canvas sack with two outside and two inside pockets. It closed via a drawstring, over which a flap could be attached, to D-rings, so that the A-frame could be attached to it when both were worn, giving a comfortable and well liked pack still in use today by civilians.

The assault frame, known as the A-frame because of its shape, was a wartime innovation based on the combat needs of the infantryman. The A shape had a D-clip in each corner to allow it to be worn on the Y-straps as a pack would have been, and to which a zeltbahn and a small pack specifically designed for the frame were also attached, both of these held in place by the two straps at the bottom of the frame. The pack contained a special pouch in the flap for the soldier's rifle cleaning kit. The size of the bag allowed him to carry the basic personal equipment into combat. The assault frame was easily removable from the Y-straps for close-in assaults and one man could carry the frames of the entire squad while in reserve, something that could not be done with tornisters or rucksacks. On the left rear of the soldier's belt he wore his bayonet, hung in a leather carrier called a frog. The bayonet was well made, suited for combat both on and off the rifle. It was a prized trophy for many GIs.

Next to the bayonet hung the 'breadbag'. This was a haversack made of heavy linen or canvas. Three loops, two of which buttoned on each corner, and one in the centre, attached to a hook that clipped over the belt. The flap of the bag had one D-ring with a leather loop stitched below it on each side of the bag, directly below the belt loops. To these the canteen was secured, and sometimes the mess kit. This flap was secured to the bag part by two straps that buttoned to it. The bag was used to hold the soldier's personal items and field rations. On the rear upper corners of the bag were two smaller D-rings, to which was clipped an adjustable shoulder strap of the same material. This allowed for the breadbag to be worn separately or help carry all the weight. The strap for the breadbag had a multitude of uses, only limited by the imagination of the soldier. It could be strapped around the helmet in order to hold foliage for camouflage purposes or around the neck and clipped to the ammunition pouches for support in lieu of the Y-straps. These straps saw service as trouser braces, slings and tourniquets, amongst much else.

Slung over the soldier's other shoulder was his gas mask can. By this time in the war the gas mask itself was discarded by combat troops but the can was a different matter. First, it was a required piece of equipment. If the soldier was not carrying it, the Field Police could place him under arrest. Luckily they rarely, if ever, checked in the can. It opened at the top with a hinged cap secured by a spring-loaded catch. This cap was watertight and made it useful for crossing rivers or in the rain or snow. It carried food, bottles of beer and personal effects; experienced soldiers would never throw away an item that would keep his socks dry and his beer bottles from breaking.

The last two articles he carried were a zeltbahn, discussed in Chapter 2, and his mess kit. The German mess kit was kidney shaped with a short top piece and long bottom one. To the top was attached a hinge handle which allowed it to be used as a frying pan. The bottom, or pail, had a wire handle, and was used for soups and stews. A folding spoon/fork utensil was the general issue for the enlisted man.

German field gear, when worn correctly, was comfortable and practical, but did have some drawbacks. When taken off, the system of clips and hooks that held the Y-straps to the belts was disconnected or pouches slid out of place, taking time to put back in order. When worn the regulation way, it made distinct noises when the soldier was on the move. For example, the canteen, clipped to the breadbag, would bounce off the soldier's hip and strike against the mess kit. Men learned to wear this array of equipment contrary to regulations in order to prevent these noises and distribute the load better.

Obergrenadier Martin Eicheneseer recalled that the sound could identify you immediately to friend or foe, something you noticed the first time anyone ran in all the gear:

When issued all my personal field gear I was instructed on how to wear it. At first I thought that it wasn't so bad, but when I first ran in full gear I noticed that sound right away. The sound went like this, 'klunk-bang, klunk-bang, klunk-bang'. It had a metallic ring and happened with every step. And when the entire company ran it was a veritable symphony.

In the field a lot of the noises were eradicated by different methods of wear or discarding equipment altogether. Obergrenadier Wegner was instructed on this:

Before the invasion, the first time I went on a night patrol, Thiessen told each one of us to jump up and down in turn. If we made noise he showed us how to correct it since noise could cost us our lives. He showed us how to hook our canteens to our right pack strap on the Y-straps and loop it around to our back. This was much more comfortable and kept a lot of the noise down but on parade we would not be allowed to wear our equipment in such a fashion.

The US Army had a totally different style of personal field gear. This was produced entirely of webbed material except for a few small items. Webbing was canvas strands woven tightly together to produce a very durable and flexible material. The belt came in two general issue patterns. The first was the cartridge belt, commonly known as the Garand belt after the rifle for which it held ammunition. Each side had five flapped pockets, each of which held an 8-round clip for the M1 Garand. On the bottom of the belt were eyelets for the attachment of the canteen, first aid pouch and bayonet. The top also had eyelets for the attachment of the support straps.

The second style of belt was called a pistol belt. At first it was solely intended for troops who carried only pistols. The belt itself was produced with a row of eyelets, top and bottom, in order to carry the same equipment as the Garand belt. One side was looped back with sliders and a hook end; this was the side that was adjustable to the waist. The holster, canteen, knife or bayonet and all other individual items intended for use with these belts had a double hook on the rear which went through the eyelet on each type of belt.

German Grenadier's personal effects carried in an A-frame combat pack. Clockwise from top left, Esbit field stove, K-98 rifle cleaning kit, pack of cigarettes, sugar cube tin (*zucker*), can opener, razor blades, solid toothpaste, ID disk in leather pouch, folding spoon/fork utensil, novelty wallet in shape of a military cap, sewing kit and butter dish.

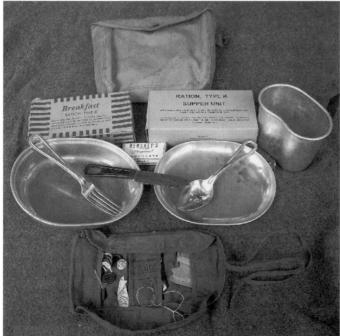

US GI mess kit set. Shown is the M1910 mess kit with carrier. Fork, spoon and knife, M1910 canteen cup and two boxes of K rations. The GI had the benefit of plenty of pre-packaged food available. Also shown is an issue personal sewing kit.

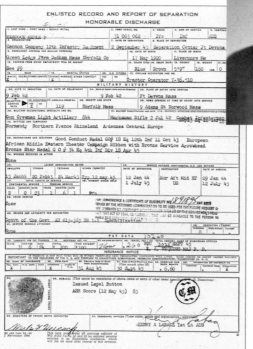

PFC Merle Hescock's discharge papers (front).

PFC Merle Hescock, Cannon Company, 12th Infantry Regiment, 4th Infantry Division.

PFC Merle Hescock's discharge papers (back).

This system was most effective, with the items staying attached to the belt under almost all adverse conditions.

The personal packs were issued in either one of two patterns. The older, and obsolete, pattern of the two was the M1928 pack. This pack had straps permanently attached to the bag. Thus if the pack was discarded in combat, so were the straps that helped support the weight of the combat belt. The bag was also too small to carry much personal equipment and required several other attachments to hold the soldier's mess kit, poncho and other gear. The M1936 haversack, also known as the Musette bag, and combat braces, were developed as a replacement for the M1928 pack. The braces were in an X shape and of webbed material. The rear had single straps ending in heavy duty clips. The fronts were of the double design with primary and secondary straps, used in the same manner as when attached on the M1928 pack.

However, if the pack were discarded, the braces could remain to support the belt and the secondary now clipped to the belt. All the straps were individually adjustable by means of a slider buckle. The front top of the straps had a small D-ring riveted to them. These were for the top straps and hooks of the Mussette bag. This bag was made of heavy duty canvas; some were rubberised and waterproofed. The bag was secured by two web straps and buckles which held the flap in place. On the top were two adjustable straps with clips to attach to the braces or a separate shoulder strap. Each side held a small D-ring to which the secondary strap clipped. The interior was large and divided by a cloth partition that contained three smaller pockets for toilet articles and writing utensils. This version of pack was well liked because of its quick loading and unloading capability and versatility – it could be used as a map case, grenade bag and so on. Don Van Roosen used one to carry magazines for his Thompson sub-machine gun because it allowed him to carry more of them than the issue pouch for the weapon.

The American soldier carried, except for some minor production differences, the same canteen his father carried in 1918. A carrier/cover held the canteen and cup. The canteen itself fitted into the cup for carrying. The cup was very large and could hold over half the contents of the canteen. This allowed him to use it to cook with over fires. The German soldier had a canteen, also a modernised version of his father's, however his cup was much smaller and not suitable for cooking and certainly not the later cups made of bakelite. Both canteens were good serviceable items for a soldier, with an edge in versatility going to the GI model.

The GI was also issued his version of the gas mask, in a canvas carry bag. They littered the sides of European roads wherever US servicemen covered a long march, as they were considered useless extra weight. Within the American supply system's inventory of equipment there existed a large selection of specialised pouches and carriers allowing the GI to be very well equipped if he so desired. Both armies were matched quite evenly in equipment, each having good and bad points. However, the weapons category was an entirely different matter.

The American soldier possessed the best rifle given out in general issue during the war. This marvel was the M1 Garand. The rifle was a gas-operated semi-automatic weapon that held a clip of eight rounds of 30.06 calibre ammunition. The clip would eject when it was empty. With each man in his squad, except those carrying full automatic weapons, armed with the M1, the GI had an advantage over any of his enemies, who were usually armed with bolt action rifles of First World War design. Some of these had been updated and modernised but still could not match the rate of fire – accurate fire – that could be brought to bear by an American GI. The Garand combined firepower with dependability. It worked well under adverse weather conditions, not to mention survive what else a serviceman could do to it apart from firing it, as PFC Merle Hescock – who went ashore with the US 4th Division on Utah Beach – found out:

> The MI Rifle we had been given by Uncle Sam was a damn fine weapon. While it took some getting used to – they did have quite a kick and knocked the little guys back awfully when they fired – but when you had the rifle mastered you could hit just about anything with it, a good distance away as well. They could take quite a bit of punishment too. I saw them hit with shrapnel and keep working, I saw barrel lengths cut off and they still fired but one bullet at a time. Hell, during the war I saw just about everything happen to them and more often than not they still managed to work. The day we landed on the beach was a good point to start. First my rifle got soaking wet with seawater. Then I dropped it into the sand a few times. Off the beach I crawled around dragging it in the dirt and mud, and of course certain natural obstacles in farm fields. It was also full of concrete dust, not to mention getting banged against trees, rocks, bunkers and houses. That poor rifle took quite a lot of abuse on 6 June. And I did not once oil it or wipe it down with a rag or run a cleaning rod through it. Despite all that, in one day it never failed to fire, did not ever jam, double feed or have one single problem. For me a better rifle was never made.

Perhaps the only drawback of the weapon was the tell tale 'twang' of the empty clip ejecting from the rifle. If an enemy was close enough to hear this it would allow him to charge, move position or fire while the GI reloaded.

The American arsenal included a variety of sub-machine guns, all in .45 calibre. These weapons were potent at shorter ranges, and were handier in urban settings. The popular standard issue pistol, the Colt 1911A1, most commonly known as the '45', also used the same ammunition. The 1911A1 pistol was a superb design, highly reliable, remaining in US military service for more than a generation after the war. The M3 Grease Gun, so named due to its outward similarity to the automotive tool of that name, was an example of a change in manufacturing approach. It was simple in design and quick to build, unlike the Thompson sub-machine gun, which was made in the traditional way. The M3 had some problems with reliability, but served well.

For support fire in a US company, the three mainstays were the .30 and .50 calibre machine guns and the Browning Automatic Rifle, the BAR for short. The Browning was .30 calibre and fed by a detachable magazine holding 20 rounds. It was a dependable and sturdy weapon, but its high rate of fire caused it to expend large numbers of magazines in heavy fighting, generally more than the soldier could carry. The machine guns were tripod-mounted and although they were effective when firing in place, this was offest by their weight and awkwardness to move quickly in combat.

The German units in Normandy during the summer of 1944 were predominantly armed with a bolt action rifle, the K98. This weapon, a Mauser design, was by far the finest bolt action rifle ever designed; even the 1903 US Springfield was a copy of the Mauser system. The K98 was accurate, dependable and hardly ever broke down. But it was no match for the firepower of the MI Garand, a fact not overlooked by the Germans after their first encounter with the Americans in North Africa. Even since the beginning of

This Grenadier carries a G-43 semi automatic rifle with 10-round box magazine. The recoil system almost eliminated kick back and the weapon was extremely accurate. One of these rifles was issued per squad to enhance fire power.

This Grenadier has a grenade launcher (*Schiessbecher*) fitted to the barrel of his K-98 rifle. Standard Mauser ammunition pouches are worn on the belt. Slung across right shoulder and hanging on his left side is the leather pouch for carrying the grenade launcher and its tools. This launcher fired a 30mm rifle grenade. A special blank cartridge was supplied, attached to each grenade, as a means of launching it. This type of grenade launcher was accurate and effective. The grenades were available in many different versions including high explosive or anti-tank.

the Russian Campaign of 1941 they had been developing a semi-automatic rifle of their own. The result was the G43 rifle. This was a gas-operated piston rod system in the same calibre as the K98, 7.92mm and fed by a detachable 10-round magazine. It proved effective in combat with the vast majority produced going to units on the Eastern Front. A certain percentage went to units in the west and the 352nd was lucky enough to be issued with a sufficient number of them.

The German inventory possessed a myriad of machine pistols, both German manufacture and captured stock. The most common of these was the MP40. Called a Schmeisser by the Germans and a Burp Gun by the GIs, it was a fine weapon, in particular when fighting house-to-house or in hedgerows. It was 9mm and held a 32-round magazine, having a folding stock for accurate firing. At the time of the fighting, Germany did have new and more advanced assault weapons, chiefly the MP44. But again these weapons did not appear in the west until the final stages of the Battle for France.

For side arms, the German Army had two standard pistols that made up the majority of those in service. They were the P08, the famous Luger, and the P38 made by Walther, both very effective military pistols. There were, like the machine pistol, numerous other types used, German, captured and non-German models.

Machine-gun support was where the German squads gained the upper hand. Their machine guns, chiefly the MG34 and MG42, were some of the best ever used in combat. Manufactured to take the standard 7.92mm cartridge, they could be serviced by two men in a light support role. Even one man could wield the weapon well if the situation called for it. For use in a heavy support role, a tripod with long-range optical sights was used. Even this crew was only three men, four at the most. In either role, the gun was easy to operate, quick to move tactically, and could even fire effectively while in motion. German squads were built around the machine gun, allowing them to engage, and equal, apparently better armed opponents. This comparison points to the simple fact that the GI possessed greater firepower individually but the German Grenadier and his squad could even up the score with effective use of the machine gun. Outside the realm of direct fire weapons used in infantry actions, there exist the rest of any army's weaponry, such as mortars, grenade launchers, rockets and artillery. In these, both sides were roughly matched.

The Germans in no way possessed the number and calibres used by the Allies, especially when taking into account the heavy naval guns. They did have one of the best dual purpose guns used during the war, the 88mm anti-aircraft gun. The '88' was a superb tank killer and could outrange US armour. The only problem with them was the lack of quantity. Wherever the Allies encountered them they were trouble.

352. INFANTERIE-DIVISION ORDER OF BATTLE

Prior to 6 June 1944

Grenadier Regiment 914
Grenadier Regiment 915
Grenadier Regiment 916
Fusilier-Bataillon 352
Pionier-Bataillon 352
Nachtrichten-Bataillon 352
Versorgungs-Bataillon 352
Panzerjäger-Abteilung 352
Ersatz-Bataillon 352
Marsch-Bataillon 352
Artillerie Regiment 352

Added May 1944

Nebelwerfer Batterie 100
I Bataillon Grenadier Regiment 726
Ostbatallion 621

Replacements and Reinforcements after 6 June 1944

Schnellebrigade 30
Kampfgruppe Heintz, I and II Bataillons Grenadier Regiment 984
One company Pionier-Bataillon 275

III Bataillon Artillerie Regiment 1275
Grenadier Regiment 897 (Oberst Böhm)
Grenadier Regiment 943
Flak Regiment 1
Flak Regiment 15
Flak Regiment 32
Falschirmflak Regiment 2
Artillerie Abteilung Autun (Oberst Autun)
Cadre of Artillerie NCO School of 7. Armee
one Eisenbahn Artillerie Abteilung
Landesbau Pionier-Bataillon 17
elements from 17. SS Panzer-Grenadier-Division

Men Absorbed from the Following

Kriegsmarine detachments on the coast
RAD units in the area
labour detachments
Artillerie Regiment 1716
soldiers of all services on leave or in 352's divisional sector

UNIT ORGANISATION AND SMALL ARMS

Gruppe (squad)

Strength in 352 on 6 June 1944
9 men
1 MP
1 MG
2 pistols
1 semi-auto rifle
1 grenade launcher
6 Kar.98K bolt action rifles

Gruppeführer	Unteroffizier or Obergefreiter armed with a machine pistol
MG 1	Obergrenadier or Gefreiter who fired the MG 42 or MG 34 with a pistol sidearm
MG 2	Grenadier who assisted the above and carried ammunition and weapon equipment
Assistant Gruppführer	Obergefreiter or Gefreiter armed with semi-automatic rifle (G or K-43) who commanded the movement and fire of the rear of the Gruppe, taking over if the Gruppführer became incapacitated
Grenadier Nr 1	Senior most experienced man who carried and used the Gruppe's grenade launcher. He would command in the event the assistant Gruppführer was taken out of action
Grenadiers	Four remaining men armed with Kar.98K rifles

Zug (platoon)

38–44 men
3 Gruppen
2 MGs on tripods in heavy roles
1 5cm mortar

Kompanie (company)

152–176 men (Actual strengths varied. Nr.5 Kp/G.R.916 had only 120 men in total due to personnel shortages.)
4 Zugs

INDEX

WN =
Wiederstand nest
strongpoint